Preventing Difficulties in Learning

Preventing Difficulties in Learning

Curricula for All

Edited by
Tony Booth, Patricia Potts
and Will Swann

Basil Blackwell
in association with the
Open University Press

Copyright © Open University 1987

First published 1987

Basil Blackwell Ltd
108 Cowley Road, Oxford, OX4 1JF, UK

Basil Blackwell Inc.
432 Park Avenue South, Suite 1503
New York, NY 10016, USA

British Library Cataloguing in Publication Data

Preventing difficulties in learning.
  —(Curricula for all)
  1. Learning disabilities   2. Remedial
teaching
  I. Booth, Tony   II. Potts, Patricia
  III. Swann, Will   IV. Series
  371.9   LC4704

  ISBN 0–631–15166–4
  ISBN 0–631–15167–2 pbk

Library of Congress Cataloging in Publication Data

Preventing difficulties in learning.

  (Curricula for all)
  Includes index.
  1. Curriculum planning—Great Britain—Case
studies.   2. Remedial teaching—Case studies.
  3. Learning disabilities—Great Britain—Prevention—
Case studies.   4. Minorities—Education—Great Britain—
Curricula—Case studies.   5. Mainstreaming in education—
Great Britain—Case studies.   6. Handicapped children—
Education—Great Britain—Curricula—Case studies.
  I. Booth, Tony.   II. Potts, Patricia.   III. Swann,
William.   IV. Series.
  LB1564.G7P74 1987   375'.001'0941   86–21633
  ISBN 0–631–15166–4
  ISBN 0–631–15167–2 (pbk.)

Typeset in 10 on 12 pt Erhardt by Photo·Graphics, Honiton, Devon
Printed in Great Britain by T. J. Press Ltd, Padstow, Cornwall

Contents

SECTION THREE   INTEGRATING SPECIAL EDUCATION

SECTION FOUR   TEACHING FOR DIVERSITY

Introduction to the series

'Curricula for All' is the general title of a series of three books. The first is entitled *Preventing Difficulties in Learning*; the second, *Producing and Reducing Disaffection*; and the third, *Including Pupils with Disabilities*. They reflect the approach to special needs in education of the special education group of the Open University and are the support material for the project year of our Advanced Diploma. Those familiar with our earlier course E241, *Special Needs in Education*, will be aware of its attempt to move the concerns of special education away from a marginal esoteric segment of the education system towards the enhancement of comprehensive nursery, primary and secondary schools and further-education colleges. Within that course we examined and developed a concept of integration as the foundation for a philosophy of special education. As the principle was formulated and clarified it merged with a principle of comprehensive, community education. Integration became the process of increasing the participation of pupils, families, school workers and communities in the life of mainstream schools. A focus on one group who experience limited participation, such as pupils with disabilities, naturally leads to an examination of the causes of, and possible solutions to, the lack of involvement of other groups. The absurdity of finding appropriate forms of schooling for such groups viewed in isolation is emphasized by a pupil's possible multiple membership of disadvantaged groups.

We are concerned, then, to examine the ways in which schools can respond to and reflect the diversity of their pupils. We have come to see how both an integration principle and comprehensive principle can be elucidated by being linked to a principle of equality of value. In schools which operate according to such a principle, attempts are made to reduce the devaluation of pupils according to their sex, background, colour, economic or class position, ability, disability or attainment. In fact it can be argued that special education exists as a distinct area of concern for educators because of a particular set of devaluations of pupils on the basis of their disability, ability, attainment or background. If, however, we are to see pupils who gain Oxbridge entry as of no greater value, as no more worthy of congratulation,

than pupils with severe mental handicap, then this has far-reaching consequences for what happens in schools and for how we perceive social inequalities outside them. Yet, if it is the job of educators to discover and act in the
interests of the pupils they serve, it is hard to see how those who profess a
concern for vulnerable and disadvantaged pupils should take any other view.

For us, the purpose of providing training in 'special needs in education'
is to provide support for teachers and others to move away from a system in
which large numbers of pupils are thought to be failures and from which
pupils are selected out on the grounds of low ability or disability. We argue
that the devaluation of pupils within the mainstream and selection out of it
are mutually supportive. A training in special education which concentrates
on those who fail to adapt to existing mainstream curricula or are excluded
from them inevitably helps to perpetuate existing casualty rates. Our concern
is with an approach to special needs in education which will enhance rather
than undermine the development of comprehensive nursery, primary and
secondary provision. We are as much or more concerned with the creation
of curricula which cater for diverse groups as with overcoming the difficulties
experienced by particular pupils.

The practical implementation of a principle of equality of value is a
thoroughly utopian notion; the possibility of its achievement is remote and
partial as long as society and schools continue to provide areas for competing
interests. In such circumstances the advancement of the participation of one
group must be at the expense of the reevaluation of another. We have tried
to be clear about the principles which underlie this series of books, because
it is our firm belief that clarity over principles is the best way to facilitate
decisions about practice. But the emphasis is on practice rather than principles. We have provided a wide variety of examples of practice concerned
with making curricula in schools responsive to all pupils.

The introduction to this volume, *Preventing Difficulties in Learning*, follows
this series introduction. The book also provides the support material for our
pack, EP538 *Teaching for Diversity: preventing difficulties in learning*.

The second book in the series is entitled *Producing and Reducing Disaffection*.
In that book we have explored the links between the curriculum in schools
and the way pupils can become disaffected or disenchanted with school. It
depicts classroom practice and the experiences and views of teachers and
pupils. It looks in detail at the attitudes that are fostered in pupils towards
themselves and others by the way people, their backgrounds and families are
represented and valued within the overt and hidden curriculum. We have
examined the processes whereby some pupils are moved out of the mainstream as a result of deviance in behaviour or emotional state and the nature
of the special provision in which they are schooled. We have investigated the
scope and limits for reducing disaffection through curriculum reform.

The third book in the series is entitled *Including Pupils with Disabilities*.
We worried about compiling a separately bound book which focuses on

curricula for children and young people who have physical or mental or sensory disabilities. It is essential that the pupils who become a focus of concern in this book are also seen as an integral part of the groups who are the recipients of schooling depicted in the earlier books. At the same time we do not wish to imply that a principle of equality of value means that all pupils should be treated in the same way. Rather, it involves an acceptance – or even, dare one say, a celebration – of diversity. In this third book we have looked at those aspects of curricula which are related to specific disabilities of pupils, such as sign language for deaf pupils, brailling and curriculum conversions for blind pupils. The unifying concern of the book is the participation of pupils with disabilities in ordinary life and ordinary schools. We have examined the power of people with disabilities in society, the nature of current policies and practices, the barriers to increased participation in ordinary schooling and how they can be overcome.

The great majority of the contributions to the series are published for the first time. We have tried to overcome problems of coherence created by having large numbers of contributing authors in part by providing authors with a careful list of suggestions and by negotiating chapters through a process of drafting and redrafting. Our fellow contributors have been wonderfully persevering through all this, though doubtless offices and homes have echoed from time to time with cries of 'never again!' Yet we are well aware of the necessity for allowing many voices to be represented in this enterprise, particularly those of practising teachers and others who can tell their experience at first hand. We have also provided each chapter with an introductory paragraph and have written introductory chapters for each book. We do not expect anyone to plough straight through the books. They are a resource for learning and their use should be adapted to the needs of the particular reader. The series is the result of our efforts to reground special education in a body of knowledge which will allow practitioners to begin to implement some of the changes advocated in the rhetoric of the last ten years. The abolition of distinctions between special, remedial and mainstream education requires a radical rethink of the work of special educators and, inevitably, new forms of training. The concepts and content of training are one way of assessing whether the rhetoric of change is serious in intent or if what is to be offered is more of the same. The way to avoid a simple backsliding into old ways is to articulate the underlying principles on which a non-selective, non-categorical approach to special education could be based.

To complete our Advanced Diploma, students study E241 and a broadening education or social-science course. They then produce three projects in conjunction with 'Curricula for All'. The first of these is a study of learning from the perspective of pupils, the second a piece of curriculum analysis and development, and the third a study of decision- and policy-making within a school and/or local education authority. The demands of these projects have helped to determine the shape of the books and have made us attend carefully to the range of topics we need to cover to provide an adequate basis for training. Perhaps it is in the third area that we are weakest. Partly this is because policy-making was a particular concern of our earlier course, but largely it is because discussion about decisions and developments in schools is very difficult to find in already published form and very difficult to persuade others to write. It is honest reporting and discussion about practice and the many slips between policy as rhetoric or intention and its practical implementation from which others can best learn. Perhaps our course will begin to break down the formidable barriers to sharing such information, which many find to be excessively threatening.

There are a few final things which have to be made clear. First, we do not want our ready use of the word 'curriculum' to imply that we believe that what pupils are offered in school can be written down on a bit of paper and handed out or down in staffroom and classroom. For us, 'curriculum' encompasses the experiences of pupils, teachers and others in school and the interactions between school and community, rather than merely the written intentions of departmental heads. The kind of community a school provides is as important a feature of the curriculum as the words transmitted in formal lessons. Nor do we think it is unproblematic to match curricula to the backgrounds, interests and capacities of pupils. Understanding the needs and interests of others is complex and problematic, but it becomes slightly less so if we listen to the voices of those whose interests we claim to serve.

Most importantly, we do not argue that a relocation of the problem of difficulties in learning from inside the child, or the child's background or culture or family, to the curriculum in school can cause problems within schools to evaporate, or that teachers can be held personally responsible for the difficulties which do arise. Teachers are under massive pressures within a shrinking education system which is in turn adapting to shrinking employment opportunities for school-leavers. There is a definite danger that a new focus on the curriculum within schools will deflect attention from the handicapping social conditions outside them or even hold schools responsible for such conditions. This is a clear strand in attempts to vocationalize the curriculum in secondary schools: all too readily, high unemployment is blamed, in part, on the inappropriateness of the training given to the workforce, which is offered vocational training after school and pre-vocational training within it. Schooling is not created anew by each generation of teachers; they operate within institutional constraints not of their choosing. But, having said this, we would argue that viewing difficulties in learning as arising from the relationship between pupils and curricula can enhance the contribution of teachers to their own working lives, as well as to the lives of their pupils.

Tony Booth

Acknowledgements

The editors would like to thank all who have helped to make this book a reflection of practice in schools, particularly William Fordyce, Margaret Taylor, Eileen Lorimer and Hellen Matthews in Aberdeen.

The editors and publishers are grateful to the following for permission to reprint material which has appeared in other forms: BBC Publications for figure 1.1, taken from S.N. Ghose: *The Hallowed Horse*, 1977; Methuen & Co. for chapter 3, an extract from Robert Hull: *The Language Gap*, 1985; Helen Savva for chapter 6, taken from 'Reading development in a fifth-year girl', *Talk Workshop Group: Becoming Our Own Experts*, 1982; Carfax Publishing Company for chapter 22, an extract from Tony Booth: 'Policies towards the integration of mentally handicapped children in education', *Oxford Review of Education*, 1983; Oral History Society, Department of Sociology, University of Essex, for chapter 29, from Sallie Purkis (ed.): *Oral History*, 1980 and 1983; the ALTARF collective for chapter 30, from Martin Francis: 'Anti-racist teaching – curricular practices', *Challenging Racism*, 1984; Elyse Dodgson and *London Drama* for chapter 37, from 'The making of *Motherland*', 1982; *Clio: ILEA History and Social Sciences Teachers' Review* and Jane Woodall, Terri Carey and Elyse Dodgson for chapter 38, from 'Teaching history through drama', 1983; University of London Centre for Multicultural Education for chapter 39, from Dawn Gill: 'Geography for the Young School Leaver: a critique of secondary school geography', Working Paper 2, 1982; Open University Press for chapter 44, from Frankie Ord and Jane Quigley: 'Anti-sexism as good educational practice: what can feminists realistically achieve?', from G. Weiner (ed.): *Just a Bunch of Girls*, 1985.

Introduction

Tony Booth

OUR APPROACH

This book forms the foundation of the series 'Curricula for All'. It is based on a definition of difficulties in learning as a mismatch between pupils and curricula. Learning difficulties occur in a relationship between people and tasks. Consequently, to prevent pupils' difficulties in learning we have to ensure that their experiences in school closely reflect their capacities and interests. The book looks at the way curricula can be made more generally accessible to pupils and at the kinds of organization and support required to initiate and sustain such changes. It offers an approach which neither concentrates exclusively on the faults or defects of pupils nor consigns them to climbing the interminable small steps of a basic-skills curriculum divorced from their interests and the common curriculum of their school.

There has been a vast amount of discussion of learning difficulties and 'special needs' over the last few years. It is often presumed that we are all now busy implementing a new approach associated with the Warnock Report (Department of Education and Science, 1978) and the 1981 Education Act and characterized by such phrases as 'Every teacher is a teacher of special needs', 'A whole school approach to learning difficulties', 'an expanded notion of special needs'. In order to discover whether or not a new approach is in operation, we need to look closely at current practice and to compare it carefully with the past. The reality of some of the assumed changes has been questioned in detail elsewhere (Booth, 1985). For example, the Wood Committee (1929), which was set up to look at the 'problem' of mental deficiency, expanded its remit in the course of its deliberations:

The scheme we propose involves to some extent a fresh orientation in our conceptions and a fresh terminology. We are no longer concerned only with children who have been actually certified ... indeed we contemplate the abolition of such certification ... we have in mind all those other children of similar grade and educational capacity ... and further the still larger group of dull or backward children. (Board of Education and Board of Control, 1929, p. 126)

To what extent have current conceptions of the expanded notion of special needs moved away from ideas about the dull and the backward? There are a number of areas of the 1981 Education Act (in England and Wales) which display the traditional selective view of special education which underlies it. But most revealing is the specific exclusion, from the category of pupils with a learning difficulty, of those whose have such difficulties 'solely because the language or form of the language' at any time spoken at home is different from that used in school. The exclusion of such children from the scope of the Act is presumably because there was a wish to avoid the stigmatizing label of 'special needs' for them. There seems to be a clear indication that the writers of the Act interpreted learning difficulty to apply only to the 'dull', the 'backward' and those with disabilities. Yet, if we should avoid stigma for some children, why not avoid it for all?

The approach we advocate does not depend on the mainstream application of educational ideas developed in connection with children categorized according to their disabilities or deficiencies. For example, the behavioural techniques advocated for dealing with learning difficulties in the Special Needs Action Programme (Muncey and Ainscow, 1982) depend on a definition of special needs as defects in pupils: 'A child's special needs may result from difficulties in physical, sensory, social, intellectual and emotional development or, indeed, from some combination of these' (Coventry Education Department, 1982, p. 4).

For us, special needs are simply unmet needs. Rather than looking for an ever-wider group of *special children*, we wish to create an expanded mainstream and look there for flexible teaching approaches which can be supported and extended to resolve difficulties in learning. We have looked for ideas from the experience of mixed-ability teaching and learning, co-operative teaching and learning, integrated days and integrated studies, pupil-defined curricula and alternative approaches to assessment. We are trying to do our part in assisting the development of ways of teaching and learning which are fit for *truly* comprehensive primary and secondary schools.

In discussing our view it is sometimes objected that we underplay the difficulties faced by some pupils; that, in an often-repeated phrase, we are in danger of 'throwing out the baby with the bath water'. We would like therefore to give special mention to two cherished children. It is no part of our aim to suggest that pupils do not differ in their capacities relative to the same task. If pupils are given the same task, then they can be arranged in accordance with their capabilities. However, one's motives for doing this could rarely be called educational, except in the obvious sense that such an exercise instructs pupils and teachers about orders of merit. Nor do we wish to play down the fact that some activities in our culture, which are a proper concern of schools, can be a considerable source of pleasure and a genuine means of access to power over one's own life. We would agree that it is the duty of schools, for example, to foster, wherever possible, language skills and literacy. But we are not the first to wish to avoid the detachment of language (or education more generally) from its use as a means of power and personal fulfilment; or to argue that the teaching of literacy is best considered in the context of learning about something of interest.

It follows from our definition of learning difficulties as arising in a relationship between people and tasks that they can occur for any pupil at any age in any part of the formal curriculum. It has been suggested that many difficulties in learning could be redefined as difficulties in teaching. Yet profound difficulties can occur in pupils or groups who present no teaching difficulties. They may even 'do well' in the eyes of their teachers, yet gain little in their own understanding of the subject matter. Robert Hull's observations of the barriers to understanding imposed during 'O'-level science lessons (chapter 3) make this point well, as, we suspect, do the personal recollections of us all. For example, one of us remembers having an ability to answer advanced questions on electromagnetic radiation, cathode-ray tubes and the use of valves, yet having no idea of the workings of radios and televisions.

This book is intended to serve three purposes. Generally, it is a resource for learning about teaching diverse groups. It is also, specifically, a support for the project year of the Open University Diploma in Special Needs in Education and for a short course published by the Open University – EP538, *Teaching for Diversity: preventing difficulties in learning.* This course consists of nineteen sessions which contain a large number of practical activities to be worked on co-operatively by groups of teachers in their own areas. It has been developed in conjunction with the Grampian Region in Scotland, and the Scottish influence will be clear in many chapters of this book.

At the same time as the Warnock Report was prepared and published, HM Inspectors of Schools (HMI) in Scotland produced a slim document entitled *The Education of Pupils with Learning Difficulties: a progress report by Her Majesty's Inspectorate* (Scottish Education Department, 1978). It has been suggested that the respective impact of these two reports on practice has been in inverse proportion to their size. The Scottish report placed the major responsibility for the creation of difficulties in learning on the narrow focus and method of presentation of the curriculum in schools. It gave remedial education an extremely broad definition, arguing that up to 50 per cent of the school population could experience difficulties in learning. It suggested that, rather than provide a casualty service for school failures, who were often taught in withdrawal groups or remedial classes, remedial specialists should have a direct and officially sanctioned role for supporting class- and subject-teachers to develop differentiated curricula through planning, consultation and co-operative teaching. The report stressed this shift in approach by advocating 'appropriate' rather than 'remedial' education.

It argued for an extension of mixed-ability learning and teaching and the minimum withdrawal of pupils. Special attention was to be paid to the transfer between primary and secondary school. A principal remedial-education teacher with the same status as heads of subject departments was to have special responsibility for tackling learning difficulties in secondary schools and an assistant head teacher was to have this role in primary schools. Whilst the remedial specialists were to have a special role in fostering co-operative teaching and curriculum development, the head teacher was to ensure that all staff took responsibility for dealing with the learning difficulties experienced by pupils in their classes. All advisory staff were to recognize remedial education as an essential part of their work. Finally, each local education authority was to designate a senior co-ordinator to foster these policies and ensure that remedial staff were distributed according to need.

The Scottish HMI report recommended training in remedial education for all teachers as well as specialist training-courses. National guidelines for new training-courses were devised, and the colleges of education have produced a new Diploma in Learning Difficulties, now referred to as the Diploma in Special Educational Needs (Non-Recorded Pupils), with separate diplomas for primary and secondary teachers. The purpose of this diploma was to inculcate the 'four roles' of Scottish remedial specialists: consultancy, co-operative teaching, direct tuition and temporary support. Separate diplomas were retained too for teachers of pupils who were the subject of official 'Records' (the Scottish equivalent of 'Statements' in England and Wales).

The report, then, attempted to redefine the boundaries between remedial and mainstream education and advocated the development of regional policies to implement changes that were occurring in isolation in many schools in Scotland and elsewhere. Whilst following the drift of these proposals, this book attempts to provide a single framework for all pupils, including those currently in special schools. It offers a basis for shared training between primary and secondary teachers and people who think of themselves as mainstream, remedial or special educators.

The job of reducing learning difficulties is a responsibility of all teachers. Equally those who think of themselves as support teachers share a responsibility for ensuring that curricula reflect the interests and backgrounds of all pupils. They should not be solely concerned with difficulties which arise because of the nature or level of language or concepts. There is a current vogue for seeing initiatives about learning difficulties, and others concerned with the removal of racism and sexism from the curriculum, as separate from one another. Yet a support teacher who encounters a black girl having difficulty swallowing a dose of white male history needs to make a single curriculum adaptation; the curriculum should be made appropriate for that pupil.

If the removal of difficulties in learning is the responsibility of everyone, perhaps there is no need for anyone to be specifically responsible for that task. Such an argument confuses a desirable aim with its achievement. We might wish schools to take an equal interest in the learning of all pupils, but, as things are, many pupils find the curriculum they receive inaccessible and there are limitations on resources and social priorities which perpetuate inequalities. At the same time we would not wish to give the impression that the developments in this book can be fostered only by support teachers. Many schools do not have additional members of staff or may wish to use their adult resources to create teams with shared responsibilities.

Whilst we think that this volume contains many interesting and instructive examples of practice, neither we nor the individual contributors would wish them to be held up as examples of perfection. They are there to help others to think about their own ideas and practice.

THE CONTENT OF THIS BOOK

The book is divided into five sections.

Section One: The Experience of Learning. In order to understand the difficulties pupils encounter, it is essential to attempt to see the experience of schooling from their vantage point. Each of the chapters in this section offers ways of closing the gap between the understanding of pupils and the curriculum they may follow in school. In chapter 1 Gervase Phinn stresses the benefits of valuing and building on the work pupils produce rather than measuring them against some artificial standard of excellence. Patrick Easen (chapter 2) analyses the mistakes pupils make in arithmetic and sees the struggle for sense which underlies them. In chapter 3 Robert Hull reports on his detailed observation of the language of instruction and the distance this can represent from the experience of pupils or even the intentions of the teacher. Valerie Antopolski (chapter 4) looks at the way one primary teacher incorporates an approach to learning difficulties into her day-to-day practice. Stephen Rowland (chapter 5) provides a lesson on the benefits of gearing the pace and content of the curriculum to an interest expressed by a pupil. The final chapter in the section, by Helen Savva (chapter 6), emphasizes the importance of the relationship between a secondary pupil and her teacher as the foundation for her learning.

Section Two: Reconnecting Remedial Education. The title of this section signifies the efforts of the contributors to develop an approach to difficulties in learning based on providing support within mainstream classes. The chapters fall into three groups, which emphasize policy, school and classroom issues respectively. The opening chapter (chapter 7) is written by William Fordyce, Depute Director of the Grampian Education Authority, and describes the way his area produced a region-wide effort to develop remedial education based on co-operative teaching and curriculum development. Chapter 8, by Glenys Andrews, describes the implementation of the Scottish approach within primary schools in the Fife region.

The first chapter in the schools group (chapter 9) is about a sector of schools within the Grampian Region consisting of Linksfield Academy and its feeder primaries. It describes the 'special needs support' of the area team assigned to these schools, headed by Eileen Lorimer, who co-authored the chapter with Patricia Potts and Will Swann. In chapter 10 Charles Weedon gives an account of a Fife secondary school which has borrowed ideas from the primaries to make its organization fit the learning needs of its pupils. In chapter 11 Gerry Bailey and Karen Skoro depict an approach to learning in a multilingual community. Christine Gilbert (chapter 12) shows how her staff have welded the disparate resources available for supporting pupils into a single system in her school, Whitmore High, in Harrow. Chapter 13 is by Mike Cowie, an assistant head in Aberdeen, who supports the adaptations to the curriculum implied by the policies in his region but who also points out the obstacles to reform within existing structures.

The third group of chapters consists largely of cases of co-operative teaching between class- or subject-teachers and 'remedial' or 'support' teachers. It starts with Annabel Mercer's detailed examples of the curriculum adaptations she supported to help pupils in a primary school in Lothian (chapter 14). Chapter 15, by Susan Hart, describes innovations at the other end of the curriculum and country, in a secondary school in London. The 'Kent face' in the title of chapter 16 is the 'familiar face' of the remedial teacher, who in the Grampian Region may work in both primary and secondary schools. Here it refers too to the Kent Maths Scheme used in a Fife junior high school as the basis for a differentiated curriculum, supported by Peter Kyne, the remedial teacher. Chapter 17, by Hellen Matthews and Jim Presley, is about using remedial support to create accessible science lessons. Muriel Adams, in chapter 18, gives an open account of the way one teacher cast off her old role as a withdrawal teacher and came to see how working co-operatively gave her full scope to use her own experience in overcoming difficulties in learning. Chapter 19, by Will Swann, reports on the analysis by two teachers of their co-operative teaching relationship. It looks at the skills the teachers offer in terms of their current job descriptions, personal qualities and teaching histories. In chapter 20 Tony Booth provides an edited version of a teacher discussion about the contribution of remedial and support teachers to curriculum development, to school policies and to what is known in Scotland as 'consultancy'. Chapter 21, by Hellen Matthews, is a reassessment of the role of withdrawal or tutorial work within policies based largely on in-class support.

Section Three: Integrating Special Education. This section is concerned with extending the idea of supporting pupils within the mainstream to include all children and young people. As may be clear from the series introduction, we adopt a view of integration which is identified with a comprehensive principle. The responsive schools described in the other sections are the very places where an integration policy could be put into operation within a local authority. In fact Linksfield School in chapter 9 includes pupils with hearing difficulties, and William Fordyce makes it clear in chapter 7 how a policy for supporting learning difficulties in the mainstream in Grampian schools could be widened to bring in those from special schools. The section contains a few chapters to serve as an introduction to the theory and practice of including pupils from special schools into the mainstream. More extensive coverage of these issues can be found in the third book of this series, *Including Pupils with Disabilities*.

Chapter 22, by Tony Booth, is an introduction to the policy and practice of integration and discusses the links between segregation and selection in education. Chapter 23 is written by two teachers, Jan Moore from a comprehensive and Carmen Renwick from its neighbouring special school, who decided to put their groups together. They describe how, after the initial step, their class became unremarkable – one ordinary mixed group. Will Swann in chapter 24 describes the education at a first school of Mark, a pupil with a visual impairment. Chapter 25 is an account by Tony Booth of the efforts in one primary school to create a single entity from what were three separate parts: mainstream, and units for pupils categorized as having 'moderate' and 'severe' learning difficulties. Jenny Cobbett (chapter 26) reveals the process of integration in a further-education college with a story of the education of students with physical disabilities supported by her in the college.

Section Four: Teaching for Diversity. This section looks in detail at examples of curricula which can be adapted for pupils of differing attainments, capacities, backgrounds and interests. Chapters 27–32 are concerned with primary curricula, and chapters 33–7 with secondary. Alan Ward in chapter 27 argues for accessible science based on pupils' real questions and the stimulation of their interest in their world. Gill Blake in chapter 28 takes up the story of mathematics-teaching from where it was left by Patrick Easen in chapter 2. She is concerned with bringing pupils' skills and experience into mathematics and in looking at how maths can be used to solve real problems. Sally Purkis is a historian who in chapter 29 looks at the scope of oral history as a way of involving a wide group of pupils and also showing how they and their communities can become a valued part of the school. Oral history can be used as part of an attempt to combat classism in schools. In chapter 30 Martin Francis displays his attempts to deal with the racism expressed and experienced by his own pupils and in school books. This chapter re-emphasizes the points in the introduction to this book about the need to make the curriculum appropriate to all pupils. The stress in chapters 31 and 32, by David Boalch and Mary Caven respectively, is on the way resources outside their schools can be used to provide experiences for all pupils which can be built on within classroom lessons. The first is concerned with an ecological park and the second a street market and a local-history museum.

In chapter 33, the first of the pieces on secondary curricula, Susan Hart and Stuart Scott describe how they worked together to produce material that facilitated the co-operative learning of pupils. Ross Phillips and Stephen Jones in chapter 34 describe a mixed-ability integrated design and humanities course which is based on project work and is largely teacher-assessed. Andrew Meredith's view of music in chapter 35 builds on a respect for pupils' choices in music as a way of sharing his own in lessons. Modern languages is one area of the curriculum which can bring out the selective instincts of some teachers. Stewart Reid (chapter 36) describes how he uses computers to assist the differentiation of a largely orally based French course. Chapters 37 and 38 are both concerned with drama and the way it can be used to enable students to reflect on their backgrounds and develop a sense of the value of their experience and history. In the first of these, Elyse Dodgson describes 'Motherland', an oral-history-based drama built up over a school year. In it the girls of Vauxhall Manor School use their mothers' experience of immigration to build up a musical. In the second, Elyse, Terri Carey and Jane Woodall show how drama can be used to bring history within the immediate world of pupils. Chapter 39 is an analysis by Dawn Gill of a geography syllabus in which she reveals the racist assumptions which underlie it.

Section Five: Organizing for Responsive Schools.   Some of the chapters in this section involve critiques of school organization and practices which can subvert attempts to create schools in which all pupils have an equal place. Others provide positive examples of schools which are flexible and responsive to pupils and communities or offer suggestions for increasing the accessibility of school curricula. Chapter 40, by Patricia Potts, is the only contribution on pre-school education. She argues for nursery education to serve all children in a community and describes the philosophy and practice of Blackshaw, a nursery set up to serve the workers in a hospital. Chapter 41, by Annabelle Dixon, tells the story of the hidden categorization-by-ability of pupils in many primary schools with avowedly mixed-ability classes. Certainly the authors of chapters in this book differ in the extent to which they would oppose such groupings. Cilla Biles (chapter 42) describes her infant school and the way she and her staff use the community as a resource to help meet the needs of all the pupils. The last four chapters of the book are all about secondary schools. Chapter 43, by John Sayer, indicates the changes to the organization and curricula of secondary schools which could begin to overcome the barriers to learning which many present to their students. Frankie Ord and Jane Quigley (chapter 44) provide a reminder that good practice also involves moves to combat sexism. The book ends with Alan McMurray's survey in chapter 45 of the impact of the Manpower Services Commission on the secondary curriculum. Does the Technical and Vocational Education Initiative extend or constrict educational opportunities for pupils?

REFERENCES

Board of Education and Board of Control 1929: *Report of the Joint Departmental Committee on Mental Deficiency* (Wood Report). London: HMSO.

Booth, T. 1985: Training and progress in special education. In J. Sayer and N. Jones (eds), *Teacher Training and Special Educational Needs*, London: Croom Helm.

Coventry Education Department 1982: *Pupils with Special Educational Needs: handbook*.

Department of Education and Science 1978: *Special Educational Needs* (The Warnock Report). London: HMSO.

Muncey, J. and Ainscow, M. 1982: Launching SNAP in Coventry. *Special Education: Forward Trends*, 10 (3), 8–12.

Scottish Education Department 1978: *The Education of Pupils with Learning Difficulties in Primary and Secondary Schools in Scotland: a progress report by Her Majesty's Inspectorate*, Edinburgh: HMSO.

The Experience of Learning

1

No language to speak of? Children talking and writing

Gervase Phinn

'No language to speak of' is the phrase used by one head teacher about the language possessed by pupils when they started school. In this chapter, Gervase Phinn provides a series of examples of pupils' oral and written work, and charts the development of their confidence when their experiences and contributions are valued by their teachers and each other. He demonstrates the maturity and curiosity that pupils display in group discussion when their talk is not under teacher control, and the creativity in written work that can be discovered behind the punctuation- and spelling-errors of pupils discarded from the mainstream of school life as 'remedial'.

TALKING AND LISTENING

An Inspector colleague of mine tells how he visited an infant school in a South Yorkshire mining village. It was a rather shabby, red-brick building with little displayed on the walls. 'Most of the children come from deprived homes', explained the head teacher. 'Their parents never really talk to them about things. I'm afraid we have to start from scratch. Most of the children come here with no language to speak of.' The Inspector joined class 3, the seven-year-olds. In a corner of the classroom was a grubby little boy splashing paint onto a large piece of paper.

'What are you painting?' asked the Inspector.

'It's a jungle,' came the reply. 'Prehistoric.'

'What's that creature?'

'Brontosaurus.'

'And that?'

'Triceratops. They 'ad three 'orns on their 'eads tha knows.'

'Really?'

'This one's a pterodactyl and over here's a stegosaurus. They 'ad three brains tha knows.'

'Really?'

'One on their 'ead, one in their tail and one in their bum. It dint do 'em any good though. He ate 'em all — Tyrannosaurus Rex. He were reyt nasty he was.'

'You know a lot about these creatures,' said the Inspector.

'I know,' said the little lad. 'I luv 'em. They're great. I draw 'em all time.'

'Are there any around today?'

'Course not! They're all dead. They're all hextinct.'

'What does that mean?'

'Dead. Wiped aaht.'

'And why do you think that is?' asked the Inspector.

The little boy thought for a moment.

'Well mister,' he said, 'that's one o' life's gret mysteries int it?'

There are teachers in our schools convinced working-class children never discuss things with their parents, that they never go anywhere or see anything and that the language they do possess is lacking in many essential features. Although most teachers would not deny the vital place of talk in learning and aim to encourage children to become clear, confident and enthusiastic users of the spoken language, the reality is, in many schools, that pupils are given too few opportunities to talk. Inspections of schools have revealed that many children lack confidence in themselves as speakers and that a great many teachers monopolize talk in the classroom.

Here is part of a transcript of a lesson with a fourth-year junior class which had read with their teacher *The Highwayman* by Alfred Noyes.

Teacher Now, hands up. Who enjoyed the poem?
  (*Show of hands.*)
  Good. Hands down. Why did you like it, Neil?
Neil It was exciting, miss.
Teacher Yes, it was exciting, wasn't it? The soldiers waiting to capture him, the landlord's daughter ... Can you remember her name? Tracey?
Tracey Bess.
Teacher Yes, and she tried to warn him, didn't she? Anything else? Yes, Brian?
Brian Miss, at the end, when they shot him.
Terry Some of the descriptions were good ... er ... the man in the inn, who looked after the horses ...
Teacher What was his name?
Amy Tim.
Teacher Yes – Tim. Go on, Terry.
Terry Well he was ... he had hollow eyes and er ... hair like ... manure.
  (*Laughter.*)
Teacher Well, not really like manure – mouldy hay. Tim looked after the horses, didn't he? Can anyone remember the name of the person who does that ... who looks after horses?
Donald Stable boy.
Teacher In the poem, Donald. (*pause.*) No? Well Tim was an ostler. I'll write it on the board. It's an old-fashioned word. Tim was an ostler and he wasn't very nice at all, was he? Now what about the Highwayman? What was he like?

The teacher who conducted this lesson felt gratified by the response of her eleven-year-olds. She felt they had listened attentively to the poem, found it interesting and thought-provoking, and had willingly discussed what she considered to be the important aspects and implications of the verse. The children, she said, had appeared lively, talking with vitality and involvement and there was a general atmosphere of enthusiasm and tolerance.

A study of the transcript, however, gives a different impression: that the teacher dominates the discussion and controls quite rigidly the course of the lesson. She makes more contributions than all the pupils put together. A great many of her contributions are involved with directing and, in consequence, are restricting. Many of the questions asked of the children are not designed to elicit wide and thoughtful responses:

Who enjoyed the poem?
Can you remember her name?
Yes, and she tried to warn him, didn't she?
What was his name?
Tim was an ostler and he wasn't very nice at all, was he?

The teacher constantly interprets and clarifies, guides the pupils' thinking by leading the discussion, and requires them to provide evidence in support of her own observations. She asks questions that demand a particular answer, which must be exact to be accepted. In answer to the question, 'What is the name of the person who looks after horses?', Donald replies, 'Stable boy.' But this is not the answer she wanted him to give: 'In the poem, Donald. No?' At no point do the pupils genuinely expound their points of view, bring in illustration and anecdote from their own experiences, cross-question, criticize or comment on each others' ideas. Their contribution in this discussion is minimal.

I want to contrast this whole class approach with an analysis of a transcript of some small-group work by four eleven-year-olds, described as 'less able', who were asked to give their views on *The Highwayman*.

Barry   If he was ... if he was a highwayman then he deserved to be shot ... I mean he ... I mean he killed and robbed people didn't he ... and ...

John   You don't know that. It never says he killed anybody ... anyway highwaymen just robbed rich people ... they held them up ... just took their money and jewels.

Simon   They did kill people, John! Dick Turpin killed people. When we went to the Castle Museum at York it showed ... there was all this information ... posters and that ... he killed people.

John   Yeah, but it never says this highwayman killed anyone, did it?

Barry   Probably did though ... they all ...

Simon   Yeah, the soldiers were only doing their duty ... It was their job to ...

John   Not to kill the landlord's daughter ...

Simon   She did that herself. She committed suicide.

John   She didn't – she tried to escape.

Barry   She didn't. She ... They tied her up with a gun ... the barrel pointing at her. She fired it to warn the highwayman. Didn't she, Chris?

Christopher   I thought she killed herself to warn him and he escaped, but when he heard she was dead came back to get the soldiers and that's when he was shot.

Barry   Should have got Tim with the tatty hair ...

Compared with the earlier class discussion of the poem, this is a great deal more lively. The children talk with enthusiasm and spontaneity. There is less competition to speak, and even Christopher, the quietest pupil, is encouraged to participate. In this free and flexible atmosphere the pupils share their ideas, offer anecdotes, explain and extend each others' statements, comment, question, criticize; they struggle to reveal the complexities of thought in their heads.

The reason why these pupils are such articulate, lively and interesting speakers is due in no small part to their teacher, who from a very early stage valued talk and actively encouraged it. She had taught these pupils for three years, and had always encouraged them to ask questions, relate anecdotes and discuss topics which were important to them. She encouraged all the pupils in her class to take part, making no attempt to criticize, but rather, by asking questions, stimulated pupils to find more exact ways of expressing themselves. While encouraging individual pupils to contribute to the discussion, she did not insist on a child speaking when he or she did not wish to. Quite often, however, the quieter, more reserved pupils did speak their minds, because their teacher showed a genuine interest in what they had to say.

As pupils gain confidence in themselves as speakers, they come to realize that, in order to make useful and relevant contributions, they must listen carefully, themselves, to what other speakers have to say. In the following transcript of the taped discussion of another small group, we see how four ten-year-olds draw on each other for language and ideas, how they are concerned to establish meaning and to clarify their own and others' understanding, and how they are able to sustain the topic under discussion to a remarkable extent. The teacher provided each of the various small friendship groups making up the class with some material to discuss. This group were given the line drawing reproduced in figure 1.1.

Rachel It's quite old.
Helen Yes, it's ... well I think it's foreign, another country.
Rachel It is foreign ... it's ... the woman ... she's dressed ... she dressed like a princess ... like on the panto ... she looks ... well rich ... she looks rich ... she's got ...
Alison She's covered in jewels, her clothes are rich.
Helen It must be hot as well ... I mean it's not winter ... she'd be wrapped up ... it's a palace I think ... it looks cool ... and it's big. What's that kind of floor called? ... It's all bits of er ... marble ... stone, coloured stone.
Jane You mean a mosaic ... a mosaic?
Helen That's it. It's got a mosaic on the floor ... palaces have that, they have floors like that ... it looks lovely doesn't it?
Alison All the plants ...
Helen There's palm trees and things ... bushes ... there's that sort of bendy tree at the front ...

Figure 1.1 Cover illustration to S. N. Ghose, *The Hallowed Horse* (1977)

Rachel I think she looks a bit like Rahila ... the woman.
     (*Laughter.*)
Rahila She doesn't — not a bit like me ... she doesn't ...
Rachel She's ... you know what I mean ... she's got a long dress with ... it's coloured
     as well and she wears ... what do you call that?
Rahila Salwar, but she's not Pakistani ... she might be Indian ...
Helen The horse looks funny though ... it's too big ... it's like a giant horse. I've
     never seen horses as big as that one.
Rachel Do you remember them big horses at the Yorkshire Show ... do you remember
     when ...?
Helen They were shire horses though ... not like this one ... shire horses have right
     thick necks and ... I mean look at this one's feet ... hoofs ... it's, well, their
     ... shire horses ... they have really heavy hoofs ... really big. This one looks
     ... it's like a racehorse, isn't it?
Alison Could be a magic horse ...
Rachel I think she feels sorry for it ... it looks ... might be starving ... it looks
     frightened, it looks shy, doesn't it? ... It's like on tip-toe ... scared ... she's
     giving it ... are they peaches?
Jane They're figs, I think ...

In this transcript the children offer ideas and conjectures; they speculate,
interpret and deduce. They share feelings, reminiscences and anecdotes and
ask each other questions which they generate themselves. The talk is rich,
exploratory, good-humoured and co-operative. Rachel and Helen take the
lead; they introduce certain aspects to the discussion, focus on particular
ideas and prompt responses from their friends. In this kind of environment,
the quieter pupils can gain the confidence to enter into the discussion, and
teach the initially more vocal pupils from their own experience. By the end
of the excited and absorbed discussion, which continued for a further ten

minutes, Rachel and Helen had learnt from Rahila about the Muslim festival of Eid, about *sharam* (shyness) and about life in Pakistan. Jane told them about her visit to the Liverpool Flower Festival, where she saw some strange trees and plants like the ones in the picture.

Whether one works in small groups or with a full class in discussion, the most important consideration is the teacher and his or her skill in initiating and developing children's talk in an encouraging and tolerant setting. Perhaps if more teachers were prepared to be listening participants and to trust the ideas of their pupils, then more pupils would be given the opportunity to talk and thereby contribute more actively in their own learning.

NOTHING TO WRITE HOME ABOUT?

If the central place of talk is still widely unrecognized by many teachers, the opposite is true for writing. The survey *Aspects of Secondary Education* (Department of Education and Science, 1979) revealed that over a quarter of the time spent by pupils in the classroom at secondary school was devoted to writing, much of which was a reproduction of the teachers' or textbook language. In primary schools too, there is much written work. Simon (aged eight) had filled an exercise book by the end of one term. Described by his teacher as 'rather slow', he receives 'extra help' with his reading and writing. Having heard the story 'The ugsome thing' by Ruth Ainsworth (1963) read aloud by his teacher to the class, Simon wrote 'The creature' (figure 1.2). The teacher's only comment was that 'farmyard smell' was perhaps more appropriate than 'smelt of mountins of dog poo'. In all his stories Simon writes with zest and confidence. They all show the strong influence of stories he has heard and television programmes he has seen, and, although inaccurate and at times barely readable, they have a remarkable freshness and variety.

Compare 'The creature' to this technically correct but bare description written by a fifteen-year-old:

It was a cold day as I walked along the road. The trees without leaves and the sky as clear as crystal. There were no clouds and the strong wind blew the coloured leaves into the gutter. I looked forward to getting home where a blazing fire and a hot drink awaited me.

As children get older, many become very self-conscious about their writing, less inclined to experiment with language.

John, at eleven and described as 'in need of remedial help', was prepared to risk using 'difficult' words and imaginative phrases in his story 'The incredible man' (figure 1.3), based on the cartoon comic story *The Incredible Hulk*. His teacher wrote at the end of this story, 'Difficult to mark. Care with writing. There are a lot of mistakes, D.' The great proportion of comments on the other pieces of work in John's book were similarly negative: 'Don't just end your story in mid-air', 'Take greater care with your writing', 'Re-write!', 'I

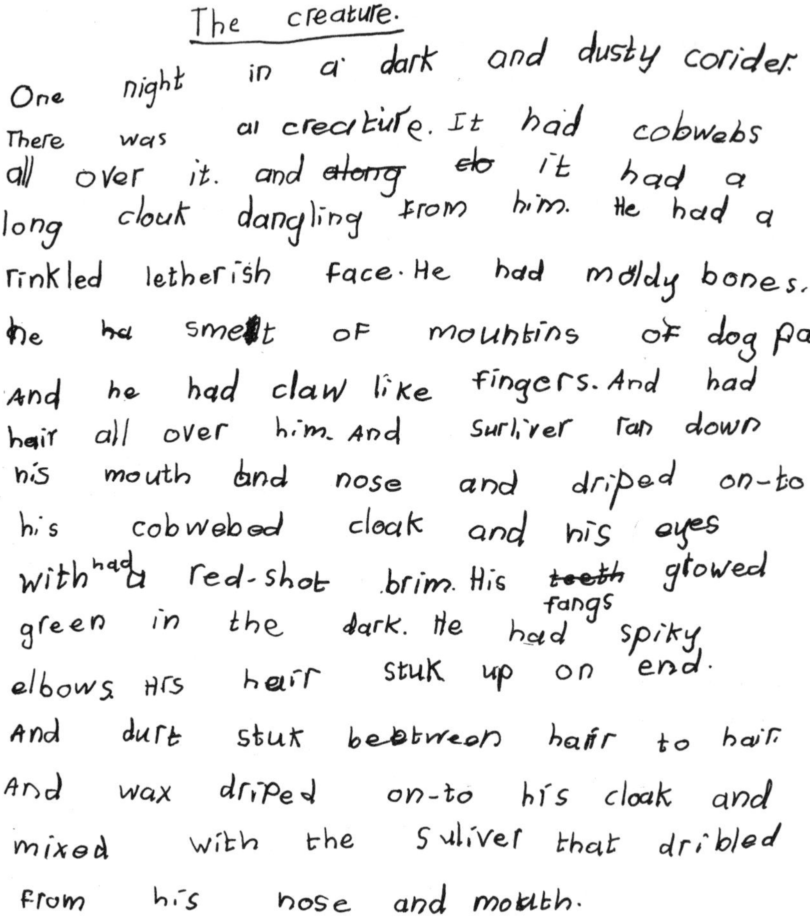

The creature.

One night in a dark and dusty corider. There was a creature. It had cobwebs all over it. and along eto it had a long clouk dangling from him. He had a rinkled letherish face. He had moldy bones. he had smelt of mouhtins of dog poo And he had claw like fingers. And had hair all over him. And surliver ran down his mouth and nose and driped on-to his cobwebed cloak and his eyes with had red-shot brim. His teeth fangs glowed green in the dark. He had spiky elbows His hair stuk up on end. And durt stuk bebtweon hair to hair. And wax driped on-to his cloak and mixed with the suliver that dribled from his nose and mobth.

Figure 1.2 'The creature'

cannot understand a lot of what you say', 'Remember paragraphs and check spellings', 'This is rushed and careless', 'What happened to Mr Walters?'

John will, no doubt, move up into secondary school convinced that he is very poor as a writer. And yet is he? With regard to spelling, John gets many more words right than he gets wrong and he is able to spell some comparatively difficult words: 'incredible', 'situation', 'because', 'walked'. He writes at some length and, on the whole, in sentences, aware when to use full stops and capital letters. Although he spells them incorrectly, he does attempt to use some adventurous and appropriate words – 'obzirvatry', 'efected', 'poshion', 'massive' – and the piece has some vivid touches: 'it was a sticky purplish green the poshoin was', 'the mixture fomed a little drible down the front of his lips', 'He shaked the place with his loud voice'. There is, then, much which is commendable in this story which receives no comment. If John moves up through secondary school receiving continuous criticism and rebuff, his facility with language is hardly likely to improve a great deal. He will underestimate the value and the quality of his writing; he will write less, abandon using words he is uncertain of spelling correctly, and become increasingly unwilling to share his experiences and ideas in writing.

How should pupils such as John be taught? It is axiomatic, but needs stating: the vital prerequisite for effective work with any children, and particularly with those who experience difficulties in learning, is a teacher–pupil relationship which is based on encouragement, understanding and respect. Too frequently we hear youngsters described in terms of their limitations: 'little ability in language', 'has difficulty with reading', 'cannot write in sentences', 'poverty of ideas', 'inability to concentrate for long periods', 'limited capacity for abstract thinking', 'moody', 'misbehaved', 'listless', and so on. Sensitive teachers very quickly recognize that less able pupils, just as much as their more able peers, have something positive to offer. They discover that so-called 'remedial' children are often capable of long periods of concentration, do have keen insights into human nature, and may talk and write with humour, directness and imagination.

Sean is a second-year pupil in a comprehensive school and is said to have severe problems with writing. His teacher set out with the clear intentions of building up his confidence and self-esteem and creating an atmosphere in the classroom of warmth and trust in which Sean could share personal experiences. His account, reproduced below, was narrated to his teacher, who typed it out at his dictation:

The time I was most afraid was when I was about eleven. I went with my mates to this leisure centre where there was this massive pool with slides and diving boards. All my mates were really good at swimming but I had only learnt a couple of years before and was a bit unsure in the water. I was a bit frightened I suppose – deep down. Anyway we got changed and they all dived in at the deep end. I jumped in at the shallow end. They all started going on this kind of long, plastic slide with big bumps in. They kept saying, 'It's great!' They kept egging me on to go on it. One of my mates called Owen kept calling me 'chicken' and making clucking noises. I thought I'd go on this slide. When I was half way up the ladder I got really scared. I don't like heights as well as water; I thought I must be mad. Anyway, I decided I'd not do it and go down the ladder. But Owen and my other mates were below me on the ladder blocking my way. I had to go on. I sat on the edge of the slide at the top. I was shaking that much, I just closed my eyes and down I went. I was really scared and bumped all the way to the bottom. I splashed a right lot. I must have looked an idiot, because my legs were in the air and my arms waved about. I must have swallowed half the pool. When I got to the side Owen said, 'It's great, isn't it, Sean. Now try going down backwards'. I'm not going to tell you what I said.

On another occasion Sean and his teacher looked together at the illustrated poetry anthology *Nightmares: poems to trouble your sleep* (Prelutsky, 1976). He dictated this lively and entertaining piece.

The incredible man.

One day there was a Docter. He was trying his new poshtoin on a man. It was sticky purplish green the poshoin was. The man was very poly. He was groning terebly. So Docter dearion Just had to hope that the sticky Poshtoin would work. It was a hard situation for Docter Dearion. Because if it didn°t work he would looze his Job. Anyway he put up his corije and did it. The mixture fomed a little drible down the front of his lips. Then a tereble thing hapend. The man went pale and stared at the Docter. He grew into a masive size and then his muslelses grow terebly big. He grouled. Docter Bairion fled out of his obzirvatry and locked the door so after him. and when he had done the the door flung open. And in its place Staod the incredible man. He Said what have You done to me. He shaked the place with his loud voice. And he shaked Gocter Dearion aswell. I have gave You some of my poshoin and it must of efected You a lot I know it has said the incredible man then there was Silance Gocter Dearion thoarght it carn't be. Then the incredible man said You Stupid Fooll and walked slowly towards Gocter Dearion and gave punch and amed at Docter Deaion and mrsed he made a masive hole in the wall. Then Docter Dearion fled in to his room and he drank some of the poshion it was the only Way to keep a lot of people alive maybe even hirself and an the Same thing hapend to himself.

They Fort the day though the incredible men did. untill they killed eachother.

Figure 1.3 'The incredible man'

It's not much fun being a Vampire. I mean, I spend all day in this dirty old coffin all cramped up. I have to stop there all day while everybody else is having fun in the sun. When I go out at night everybody runs off. It's not much fun. Then there's the blood. I don't drink anything else. It gets boring after a bit. I don't know what I'll do when I get old and my teeth drop out. I only have one lot of clothes as well – this big black cloak and this black coat and these black shoes. I hate black. It's not much fun being a Vampire.

Both accounts demonstrate how a pupil may well have hidden linguistic resources which his difficulty with writing is concealing. Giving Sean the opportunity to dictate his stories, his teacher is stimulating him to continue his efforts towards literacy and at the same time giving him an outlet for his oral creativity. A page from Sean's music exercise book shows the extent of his problem with writing (figure 1.4).

The three fourth-year secondary-school pupils who produced the work quoted below were withdrawn from mainstream English classes for remedial help. They were not given exercises in basic skills, childish comprehensions, fill-in-the-gap work or that kind of precision teaching that is so prevalent at the moment. They were asked to explore a whole range of family and neighbourhood experiences. During the miners' strike of 1984 the teacher discussed with this group, at length and in some detail, what the strike must

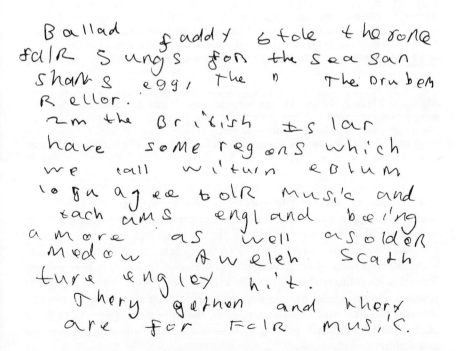

Figure 1.4 A page from Sean's music exercise book

mean for the men and their families. The pupils studied newspaper reports and watched videos and were asked to consider what the miners must be feeling and enduring. Before writing took place, relevant words and phrases suggested by the pupils were written on the blackboard. The following three pieces of work are fairly representative.

> Picket duty again. I hate it!
> Standing there in the cold,
> Rain making you sopping wet,
> Freezing cold feet.
> Hands like ice. I hate it.
> Outside the pit gates
> Holding your sign –
> 'Coal Not Dole.'
> 'I'm Backing Arthur.'
> At first we used to talk,
> Have a joke, have a laugh,
> But now we just stand.
> I hate it!
>
> (Robert)

My name is Jeff Johnson. I'm on strike for more money. It's horrible down the pit – all dirty and dark and it's dangerous as well. We deserve a lot of money for the job we do. My mate was killed last week. He was crushed by a load of coal falling on him. He was trying to get some off the slag heap. It all collapsed on top of him. I helped to pull him out. He was all black and broken up. I've got five kids to feed and I don't know where the money's coming from.   (Michael)

I think the miners should get more money and they should work for shorter hours. My uncle works at the pit. He operates the cage. That's the lift which takes the miners down the shaft. He lost three fingers when he was about eighteen. He says it's a very hard job. He says you never really get the muck off however much you wash and you get dust on your lungs. He says there's better jobs than being a miner.   (Judith)

If we are to encourage pupils who experience difficulties to write at length, with confidence and for enjoyment, then we must forgo for a time any attempt to impose formal grammatical or manipulative constraints on them. Initially we should be concerned with the thoughts and feelings which they are endeavouring to express. Very often youngsters are embarrassed by and worried about their poor spelling and punctuation and untidy handwriting. Teachers are influential people in the lives of their pupils. If they repeatedly respond to their pupils' work in negative ways, spotlighting all the errors and covering the page with critical comments, then the writing-activity of those pupils will be inhibited, leading to insecurity, poor motivation, frustration and failure.

For many pupils, the experience of school is boring and difficult; it is alien to their real interests, an imposed task which gives neither pleasure nor reward; and it does little more than make them aware of their many deficiencies. Philip, in his first week at a new comprehensive, handed in his first piece of work, 'Myself' (figure 1.5). As this sad little essay shows, Philip, more than any of his peers, needs to see the drama groups when they are in school, join the poetry workshops with visiting writers, go on the theatre trips and visit the school library. He needs to be surrounded by bright, glossy-backed paperbacks by good modern writers, to hear poems and stories well read and be encouraged to discuss them and read them for himself. He needs sympathetic, sensitive and enthusiastic teachers with wide intellectual interests, helping, stimulating, discussing, challenging, observing, reading, recommending – teachers who refuse to work from an assumption about his limitations. And, for those teachers who provide the kind of reassurance and respect which gives children such as Philip the confidence to be adventurous in their talk and in their writing, the rewards are great.

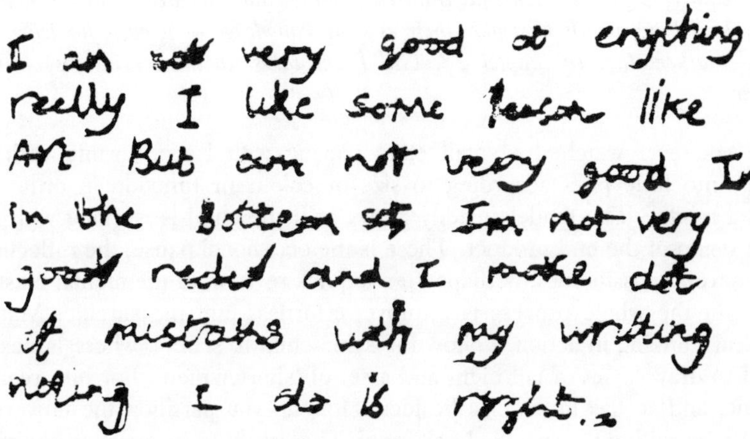
I an not very good at enything
really I like some lesson like
Art But am not very good Im
in the Bottem set Im not very
good reder and I make lot
of mistaks with my writing
noting I do is right.

Figure 1.5 'Myself'

REFERENCES

Ainsworth, R. 1963: The ugsome thing. In *Ten Tales from Shellover*, London: André Deutsch.

Department of Education and Science 1979: *Aspects of Secondary Education in England and Wales: a survey by HM Inspectors of Schools*. London: HMSO.

Ghose, S. N. 1977: *The Hallowed Horse*. London: BBC Publications, Listening and Reading series.

Noyes, A. 1981: *The Highwayman*, illustrated by Charles Keeping. Oxford: Oxford University Press.

Prelutsky, J. 1976: *Nightmares: poems to trouble your sleep*, illustrated by Arnold Lobel. New York: Greenwillow Books.

2

All at sixes and sevens: the difficulties of learning mathematics

Patrick Easen

Patrick Easen describes the experience of most pupils with mathematics as 'a process of organized alienation'. He argues that this process begins when children find they are unable to bring their existing knowledge to bear on their classroom work, and when their attempts to make their own sense of classroom tasks go unrecognized. In consequence, for many children, doing mathematics entails responding to meaningless tasks with half-remembered meaningless strategies. To break out of this self-defeating spiral requires a presumption that children's actions and talk are meaningful, and a way of helping pupils to deploy their existing knowledge as a basis for learning formal mathematics. In chapter 28, Gill Blake takes up the conclusions of this chapter.

Have you ever watched a small child playing with Lego, sorting various pieces into little piles according to size or colour or function in order to build a model? The model steadily grows as if the child is working with an inner vision of the end product. There is the occasional pause, the reflection upon several possibilities, perhaps even a quick revision of the mental master plan, but the whole process is intuitive, effortless and pleasurable. Mathematical thinking in action. Follow the same child to school, where James is asked to draw 'a set of tall men' and a set of 'shorter men'. For him reality is gone, and so has much else besides. How do you partition the universal set of men without a specified criterion? The attribute in question, height, makes no sense without some reality to measure and some standard to measure against. When you are five years old, all men are tall, aren't they? Some months later we find this, copied from the board, in his book

To find the difference you take away −

~~a~~ The difference between 16 and 9 is 7

followed by four examples to be completed.[1] Each has been completed 'incorrectly'.

So the story – a true one, by the way – goes on. It is not, of course, an unfamiliar story, but it is a sad one. There are not even any 'baddies' in the story, just people who are unsure and will not, or cannot, recognize it. What are they unsure of? Probably they are unsure of 'mathematics'; possibly they are unsure of the natural capacity of children to learn; almost certainly they are unsure of themselves. With so much insecurity and uncertainty, it is no wonder that mathematics education is all at sixes and sevens. The interesting thing about uncertainty is that, when faced with it, we have a strong urge to grasp at straws which provide an illusion of certainty–and that just compounds the problems. Now, you may feel that this is a strange place from which to begin an essay about the difficulties of children learning mathematics, but I want to put forward a simple proposition. I am convinced that the problems of mathematics education are not, essentially, mathematics problems but human problems and, by the same token, require human solutions. So the only place to start is by observing the humans involved and trying to work out what messages they are trying to give us.

THE EMOTIONAL IMPACT OF LEARNING MATHEMATICS

Let's begin with Mandy. She's thirteen and having difficulties at her comprehensive school. She is trying to take 70 away from 109, so she sets it down like this:

$$\begin{array}{r} 109 \\ -\ \ 70 \\ \hline \\ \hline \end{array}$$

She begins:

Mandy 0 from 9 you can't do ... go over to the 1 and cross it off ...

writes
$$\begin{array}{r} ^0\cancel{1}09 \\ -\ \ 70 \end{array}$$

that's a 0 ... that's a 1 ...

writes
$$\begin{array}{r} ^0\cancel{1}^109 \\ -\ \ 70 \end{array}$$

cross that off ... 10 off ... that's a 9 and a 1 ...

writes
$$\begin{array}{r} ^0\cancel{1}^10^19 \\ -\ \ 7\ 0 \end{array}$$

At this point she pauses, frowns, screws up her nose and sucks her lip. Then she slumps back with a puzzled look, bites her lip and screws up her face.

Mandy Gone wrong
Teacher Would you like to start again?

Mandy writes out the sum again and then sits there looking puzzled. She bites her lip.

Teacher What are you looking at now?
Mandy The 0
Teacher What are you trying to decide?

Mandy pauses and then, with a sheepish grin, whispers, 'How to start'.

Her classmate Nicola is in even worse trouble. She sits looking at the sum, sucks her lip, blinks, looks up and then, hesitantly, begins and, as she does so, explains what she is doing:

Nicola You can't do 9 from 0 ... so you cross out the 0 and put a 9, put a 1 at the top ...

writes.
$$10^19-$$
$$7^9\cancel{0}$$

... 19 from 9 is ...

She closes her eyes and her lips move silently as she counts in her head, '10?' She looks up in the hope of some confirmation and then continues:

Nicola Then put the 0 in there and the 1 under here. 0 from 7 you can't do, so cross out the 7 and put a 9. Put a 1 at the top ...

writes
$$1^10^19$$
$$9\cancel{7}\cancel{0}$$
$$\overline{0}$$
$$\overline{1}$$

10 from 9 leaves 1, 2

writes
$$1^10^19$$
$$9\cancel{7}\cancel{0}$$
$$\overline{2\,0}$$
$$\overline{1}$$

Now, there are many things that could be said about the mathematics asked for or, indeed, actually being used in these two cases, but the thing that really struck me when watching these two girls was the despair. When confronted by mathematics, some people (not just pupils) experience stress, and inevitably they try to develop ways of coping with it. I am inclined to agree with those who believe that unhappiness is a cause for concern, and yet, in all these cases I am going to describe, there was a sadness, a feeling of depression, pain. How can you learn mathematics if it makes you feel like that? And how can we know what someone else thinks or feels without focusing upon the individual involved? Even then it is difficult enough, but it is the most promising starting-point.[2]

Children do not walk into the mathematics classroom as a textbook example of this or that particular learning difficulty; they walk in as children. We, as teachers, do not therefore begin by solving a technical problem; we begin by observing the child and we are dependent on innumerable tacit recognitions, judgements and skilful performances on our part if we are to map our categories of existing theory onto features of the living classroom. We need to look for what is there, what gaps exist and how the individual bridges them.

THE GAPS BEHIND SCHOOL MATHEMATICS

Back to the children. This time meet Charlie, a classmate of Mandy and Nicola, and, like them, struggling with 109–70:

Charlie In this one ... 0 from 9 ... you can't do that so you put 0 down.

writes
$$109$$
$$-\ 70$$
$$\overline{0}$$

It's 7 take 0 ... you can't do that so put 0 down again.

writes
$$109$$
$$-\ 70$$
$$\overline{00}$$

There's nothing to take from 1 so I think you should put 1 down.

writes
$$109$$
$$-\ 70$$
$$\overline{100}$$

So far, then, each of the three has written the sum down using the standard algorithm, as you would expect with 'school mathematics'. Now the standard written algorithms may be very efficient mathematically–and much of this is because of their analytic nature–but that very quality makes them inaccessible to some people. Breaking numbers up into, say, hundreds, tens and units dealing with these as digits flies in the face of what we intuitively know about numbers. When asked, for example, how much he would have left if he had £109 and spent £70, Charlie replied, '£39'. How did he work that out? Here is his explanation:

Charlie Its £70 ... 70, 80, 90, 100 that leaves £30 and there's 9 so £39.

Compare that confident response with his earlier remarks where he was scratching around for half-remembered rules which were totally arbitrary and unrelated to his own experience.[3] So, if this sort of thing is going on, perhaps it is worth probing more deeply not *what* the children are doing but *why*, and whether there is some sort of logic behind it.

WRONG BUT SYSTEMATIC

Both Mandy and Nicola were using 'incorrect procedures', but their mistakes were not random. Each of them was trying to work with a rule concerning zero and subtraction; the trouble was that they only remembered certain aspects of how to achieve the desired surface features for their calculation. Thus for example:

Mandy 0 from 9 you can't do ... go over to the 1 and cross it off ...

As a recitation of a sequence of moves in this type of sum it is almost perfect; what a pity she got the 0 and the 9 the wrong way round! Nicola, on the other hand, got the recitation 'right'–'You can't do 9 from 0 ...'–but she had a penchant for subtracting digits in the top line from those in the bottom line.

Dean, aged twelve, had evolved an equally systematic procedure. On his paper he had written

$$
\begin{array}{r}
6591 \\
-\ 2697 \\
\hline
4106 \\
\hline
\end{array}
$$

Wrong yes, but a freak answer no. Here is his explanation:

Take 1 away from 7, leaves 6 ... take 9 away from 9, leaves 0 ... take 5 away from 6, leaves 1 ... take 2 away from 6, leaves 4.

Dean, it would appear, always subtracts the smaller number from the larger number. He has an intuitive sense that this is what subtraction is all about. Here is what he said when asked to take 598 from 716:

I'm trying to figure out ... well 5 from 7 leaves 200 ... as it's 98 its 118 the answer.

I think you will agree that, in this instance, he had a clear idea of what was going on. More than that, he was in control of his own calculations.

The third point, then, about observing children learning mathematics is that each evolves his or her own strategies, and that, incomplete as these may be, they are systematic.

THE POWER OF METAPHOR AND ANALOGY FOR UNDERSTANDING AND MISUNDERSTANDING

When grappling with uncertain knowledge we tend to think in metaphors. It is an intuitive way of drawing upon our store of experiences in order to move from the known to the unknown. Our striving to make sense of our world causes us to try a range of different possibilities in a search for a 'best fit' which puts meaning upon our confusion. In doing so, a metaphor will indicate an important analogy between two things–that which is known and that which is uncertain–usually without saying explicitly in what the analogy consists. So our existing experience becomes a screen through which we see the new experience; it filters some part of the latter and allows us to perceive other parts.

This very process, whilst helping us to learn, can, by the same token, prevent us from learning. Every metaphor is limited and gives only a certain perspective. Instead of illuminating the essence of the new experience, it may mask or disguise it. The apparently obvious analogy might, in fact, break down with reflective criticism and deliberative experimentation; but, since metaphoric thinking is largely intuitive, our blind spots may remain unless explicitly subjected to such processes. This misunderstanding, of course, is compounded by our own feeling that we may have learned what, in fact, we have not learned.

All this, I suspect, is much underrated in the mathematics classroom. It is, of course a truism to say that no one else can learn for us; each individual has to learn for himself/herself. Nevertheless, the implications of that seldom seem to be thought through in relation to the learning of mathematics. Each pupil constructs his or her own meaning of a new mathematical idea by trying to make sense of what confronts him or her through making connections with existing knowledge (both within and beyond mathematics). Hence the apocryphal story of the young boy who in reply to the question 'What is an average?' informed HM Inspector that it is 'something which a hen lays eggs on' (because his textbook said, 'a hen lays on average one egg a day'!).

The trouble, then, with metaphoric thinking, powerful as it may be, is that the context of use usually determines which features of the metaphor are carried over into the new experience and which are not. This becomes very important for the learning of mathematics.[4] Language, for example is learned within social contexts and the types of contexts in which words are used will affect how those words are understood. This tends not to happen with mathematics. It is not unusual, for example, to find this sort of thing presented to children:

$$16 - 7 =$$
$$23 - 18 =$$
$$15 - 6 =$$

I am not denying the value of subtraction as an operation to be learned but I am questioning the context within which it–and other mathematical concepts, techniques and processes–are presented. Convenience becomes a wedge between the child and his or her experience. Mathematics is fenced into the abstract world. Trapped in a world of textbooks, workcards and schemes, there it stays–contained, safe, irrelevant. When that happens, both the child and mathematics are the losers. A few more examples of that ilk (well, a lot, actually, because that is how schools often work) and our learner begins to construct his or her own rules for what is happening.

$$16 - 7 = \square$$
$$14 - 6 = \square$$
From 17 take 9
What is left if 3 is taken from 21?
Subtract 16 from 30 → $\square$
Subtract 24 from 25 → $\square$[5]

From such examples, children might surmise that the rules of subtraction mean that for the operation $a - b = c$ to be carried out, b must be less than a, and if b is greater than a then it is not possible (as in '9 from 6 you can't').

Lacking any real context for the learning of mathematics, but engaging in metaphoric thinking, the child constructs a host of 'local algorithms' such as this around the various isolated techniques, processes or concepts. These are brought to new situations and new learning until disaster strikes in the form of an electronic calculator (which insists on replying '−3' rather than 'can't' to '6−9') or a teacher who introduces negative numbers. Restrict children's mathematical environment and you deny them the opportunity to construct a global view of mathematics. In effect, you leave them to their local algorithms and prey to situations that fall outside them. I am sceptical of the received wisdom that the main problems in mathematics teaching are 'application' and 'retention'. I think they are mere symptoms of a deeper problem–a process of organized alienation which is enshrined in mathematics education as experienced by most pupils. Indeed, the cameo provided by an extract from the mathematics book of Abigail, aged seven (figure 2.1), says it all.

WHY CAN'T PAUL DO MULTIPLICATION?[6]

At this point, it may be worth following through the case of Paul (aged nine) in some detail. He had been having considerable trouble with multiplication.

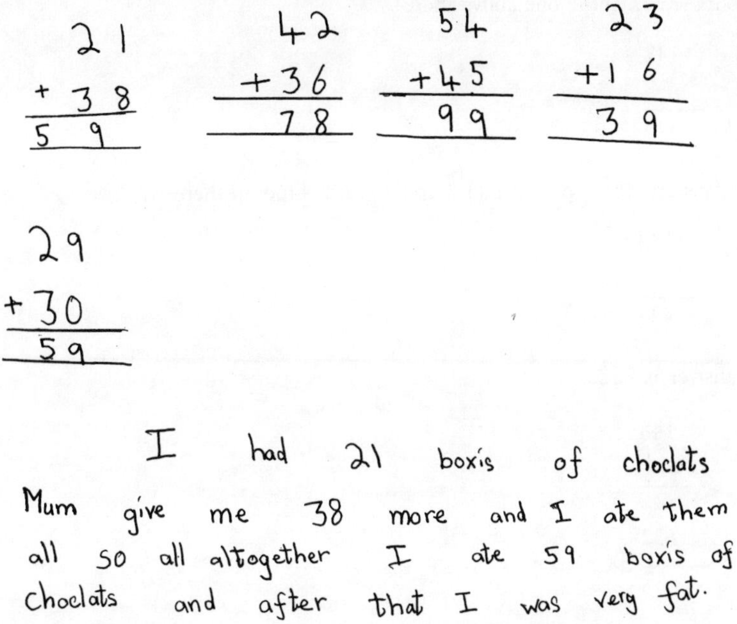

$$\begin{array}{r} 21 \\ + 38 \\ \hline 59 \end{array} \qquad \begin{array}{r} 42 \\ + 36 \\ \hline 78 \end{array} \qquad \begin{array}{r} 54 \\ + 45 \\ \hline 99 \end{array} \qquad \begin{array}{r} 23 \\ + 16 \\ \hline 39 \end{array}$$

$$\begin{array}{r} 29 \\ + 30 \\ \hline 59 \end{array}$$

I had 21 boxis of choclats Mum give me 38 more and I ate them all so all altogether I ate 59 boxis of Choclats and after that I was very fat.

Figure 2.1 An extract from Abigail's mathematics book

I find him interesting because his case illustrates so well that the only way to know why something is wrong is to observe the child's failure and try to understand it. Let's start with a typical example of his work:

$$\begin{array}{r} 148 \\ \times \ 66 \\ \hline 624 \\ 632 \\ \hline \end{array}$$

How did he work that out? Start again:

$$\begin{array}{r} 148 \\ \times \quad 6 \\ \hline \end{array}$$

Paul Six ones ...6... just do a little one ...

writes
$$\begin{array}{r} 148 \\ \times \quad 6 \\ \hline 6 \end{array}$$

Six fours ...24... little one above there ...

writes   148
         ×   6
         ‾‾‾‾‾‾‾
          6 2 4

eight sixes are 48 ... put ... add 2 and 4 ...6... little up there ...

writes   148
         × ₆6
         ‾‾‾‾‾‾‾
          6 2 4

The answer is 632.

writes   148
         × ₆6
         ‾‾‾‾‾‾‾
          6 2 4
          632
         ‾‾‾‾‾‾‾

So Paul *can* multiply. Nevertheless it is no wonder he is getting confused. First, he is working from left to right (as with reading!) This is not, in itself, mathematically incorrect, but it does necessitate a real understanding of the value attributed to each digit: for example, six fours in this case are really six forties. Such an understanding can be more easily elided with the standard right-to-left algorithm. Secondly, his system for representing intermediate calculations sometimes breaks down. For example, at the final stage he adds 8 to the units column (presumably getting 12 and carrying the 1) but then adds 1 to the 2 in the tens column, forgetting that, in his calculations, this had been superseded by 6.

At this stage, then, it is worth exploring this interpretation by asking him to talk us through a different example, 1357 × 3, explaining what he is thinking as he does it:

Paul Three one thousands ... in small just the 3 ...

writes   1357
         ×   3
         ‾‾‾‾‾‾‾‾‾
                 3

Then three threes is 9 ... means 900 ... so 9 there small ...

writes   1357
         ×   3
         ‾‾‾‾‾‾‾‾‾
                3 9

Three fives is 15 ... means 150 ... this is the hard part ... put 4 there (*indicates the thousands column*) then 5 small there (*indicates the hundreds column*) ... add on later ...

writes   1357
       × ₅ 3
      ―――
      ₄9

Three sevens are 21 ... add 21 ...

writes   1357
      ×₅ 3
      ―――
      ₄9
        21

Now this part (*indicates hundreds column*): 9 add 5 is 14, so 5 there, 4 there ...

writes   1357
       × ₅ 3
      ―――
      ₄9
      5421

So it seems that his understanding of both multiplication as an operation and of place value are basically sound (despite his slip with 150 above). It is the complication of the recording, and in particular knowing which stage he is at in the calculations, which seems to cause the difficulties. If this is so, then his system should work with smaller numbers. Paul tries 14 × 6:

Paul Six ones ...6... goes there

writes   14
      × 6
      ――
      6

Next six fours ...24... add 6 onto that makes 8...

writes   14
      × 6
      ――
      6
      8
      ――

and I put 4 there

writes   14
            × 6
            ───
              6
             84
            ───

He tries a few more like this. Each time his system works. Presumably he built up his own strategy when working with numbers such as these. So when does his system break down? He tries 267 × 5:

Paul Five twos are 10 ... that means 1000 ... put a 1 ...

writes   267
           ×   5
           ───────
                 1

Five sixties ... that's 5 × 6 ... 30 ... that means 300 ... so 3 there

writes   267
           ×   5
           ───────
                13

Five sevens ... 35 ... 3 there, 5 there

writes   267
           ×   5
           ───────
              1335

The problem begins to emerge. Paul operates well in the space of 'spoken' numbers (3 × 7 = 21; 9 + 5 = 14; etc.) but operates badly in the space of 'written' numbers (148 × 6 = 632; 1357 × 3 = 5421), so he evolves an idiosyncratic system to carry him over from one world into the other. However, there is only the most tenuous connection between the two, and the understandings he imports from dealing with spoken numbers do not necessarily equip him to cope with the highly contracted and refined ways of doing things which are to be found in the world of written numbers. So, as he moves into working with three-digit numbers, his performance becomes increasingly erratic.[7]

At this point it becomes clear that the amount of diagnostic teaching required is very small. Furthermore, it can build on very easily from Paul's system. With his teacher he returns to 148 × 6:

Teacher Let's start from this side – what we call units – instead of the other way round.
Paul Six eights are 48.

Teacher You could write the 8 big as you can't add anything on to it.
Paul   So 8 there ... and put 4 little ...

writes
$$
\begin{array}{r}
148 \\
\times\ \ \ 6 \\
\hline
4 \\
8
\end{array}
$$

Six fours are 24 ... that's really 240 ... so that becomes 8 ...

writes
$$
\begin{array}{r}
148 \\
\times\ \ \ 6 \\
\hline
2\,4 \\
88
\end{array}
$$

Six ones are 6 ... the answer is 888.

writes
$$
\begin{array}{r}
148 \\
\times\ \ \ 6 \\
\hline
2\,4 \\
888
\end{array}
$$

Paul carries on to do some more examples in this way with his teacher. They then discuss the advantages and disadvantages of both ways of tackling the sum. It transpires that earlier in his school career Paul had been taught the standard written algorithm, but he says 'putting numbers underneath' confused him, so he worked out his own way. Very astutely his teacher has taken him close enough to the standard procedures to utilize their efficiency and order without sacrificing the individual strengths that Paul has come to rely on.

INTUITION, INSIGHT AND TEACHING

Mathematics tends to stress a methodological approach to a problem, but we often forget that our inarticulate 'feel' for things helps influence the nature of our thinking and guides these methodological efforts. A methodological approach helps us articulate and examine our intuitive understandings of the problem; in other words, we reflect upon our intuitions. This could be so powerful for learning in the mathematics classroom, but, alas, often it remains a latent force, unrecognized and unused. If only school mathematics would build on the pupils' intuition!

Paul, of course, was an easy case and there are many more like him. What, you may ask, about the less easy cases? Well, for a start, they have grown out of the easy cases that went unnoticed. Take, for example, James (age seven and a half). In his book he has written sums such as '27 − 2 = 24' and yet they are interspersed with 'correct' sums. He seems to be heading for trouble with subtraction. What might we learn to help him before his mathematical world collapses? One of the first things I observe is that he uses his fingers to calculate, so let's examine what he does when given various calculations and ask him to explain what he is thinking as he goes.

9 − 5: 'I put my fingers up for 9 and then take away 5.'

He does several other single-digit subtractions using this strategy, so we move on.

16 − 7: 'I hold 16 on my fingers and count back 7 ... so it's 9.'

23 − 8: laboriously James counts out 23 on his fingers and then, silently, nods his way along the fingers. He forgets how many complete hands he has left and responds '20'. Clearly we are getting into the realms where a few more hands and feet would be useful. Sometimes, however, he gets the right answer, sometimes not, but watch how his strategy changes as we progress to some of the sums in his book.

35 − 11: 'I put 35 in my head and take away 11 ...' His head moves as he silently nods along the fingers. He is uncertain about his answer '14' and tries again until he has to say, 'I can't do that one because I keep forgetting the one I'm on.'

This happens with several other sums, but what particularly interests me is the way his strategy changed to cope with the number of fingers he needed. I get him to try some addition work.

24 + 7: 'I put the 24 in my head and add on 7...'

Sure enough, when tackling addition he always holds one number in his head and counts on, silently, using his fingers.

Teacher Who taught you to put a number in your head and count on with your fingers?
James I did.
Teacher You did? ... When?
James When I was five.
Teacher Tell me about it.
James I don't know how I did it but I did it at school.

Most of the time his system works. Being less confident with subtraction, he prefers to represent each part of the sum with a finger. This has obvious limitations as the numbers increase, so he tries to adapt his successful addition strategy. Unfortunately he finds this more difficult. Nevertheless there is so much existing strength that a number line is all that is needed to help him sort it out.

CONCLUSION

More difficult cases take more time, but if you look enough and dig deep enough there are often some unsuspected strengths that the child possesses.

Frequently these will involve some form of counting, will be iconic and, most importantly, will have the confidence of the child. It may sound slow and expensive in terms of time, but it is not in the long run. The combination of difficulties experienced by any individual is likely to be unique. Different pupils present different phenomena for understanding and action. Close observation is the route into realizing the full significance of what a child says and does—and that means real diagnostic teaching. As for the context within which that teaching and learning takes place, that means more than either using words from real life to dress up mathematics or using practical equipment; it means using meaningful parts of the child's experience as the basis of his or her mathematical education. But then that's a different story.

NOTES

1   The copied statement is basically confusing for two reasons.
   i   The *operation* of subtraction, although conventionally represented by the symbol '−', has two main dimensions. It may require me to work with one set and 'take away' some of the elements by *partitioning* that set. Alternatively it may require me to work with two sets and 'find the difference' by *comparing* those sets.
   ii   In this instance 'difference' is being used in 'mathematical English': i.e. it is an ordinary word which has attached to it a specialized meaning. Unless this is made explicit, however, it is likely to be interpreted by the child as ordinary, everyday English. Thus, some of the 'differences' are '16 has two digits and 7 has one', '16 is an even number and 7 is odd', '16 is a square number and 7 is not', '7 is a prime number and 16 is not'.
2   Space is too restricted to discuss this at any length here. Nevertheless, throughout the examples given it should be possible to identify a few components of mathematical attitude. The trap to avoid is thinking that it is possible to test a mathematical attitude by asking questions about an attitude towards mathematics.
3   The case studies of Mandy, Nicola and Charlie are from *Video 1: subtraction* of the Open University course EM235: *Developing Mathematical Thinking*.
4   A detailed discussion of metaphor and mathematics can be found in Pimm (1981b), or, in briefer form, in Pimm (1981a).
5   These examples are plucked straight out of standard mathematics textbooks. The first two examples are taken from Scottish Primary Mathematics Group (1975); the second two from Goddard and Grattidge (1971); and the final two from School Mathematics Project (1977).
6   I am indebted to Wendy Hawkins of Butlers Court County Combined School, Buckinghamshire for supplying this particular example.
7   It is, of course, arguable that this type of written calculation is a redundant skill anyway these days. See, for example Plunkett (1979).

REFERENCES

Goddard, T. R. and Grattidge, A. W. 1971: *Beta Mathematics 2*. Huddersfield: Schofield and Sims.

Pimm, D. 1981a: Mathematics? I speak it fluently. In A. Floyd (ed.), *Developing Mathematical Thinking*, London: Addison-Wesley.

—— 1981b: Metaphor and analogy in mathematics. *For the Learning of Mathematics*, 1, 47–50.

Plunkett, S. 1979: Decomposition and all that rot. *Mathematics in Schools*. 8, 2–7.

School Mathematics Project 1977: *SMP 7–13 Unit 1 Pupils' Pack*. Cambridge: Cambridge University Press.

Scottish Primary Mathematics Group 1975: *Primary Mathematics: a development through activity*. *Stage 1, Workbook 3*. London: Heinemann Educational.

3

The language gap

Robert Hull

This chapter consists of several extracts from Robert Hull's book The Language Gap. *Hull, an English teacher, spent a year and a half in a comprehensive school observing and taping the interactions between pupils and teachers, talking to pupils, collecting curriculum materials and observing the performance of pupils with them. He produced a detailed analysis of the gap which develops between the pupils' own understandings and the language of instruction. This was something that happened across the curriculum and at all levels.*

The first extract involves a pupil, 'B', who was said to be unable to cope with a class lesson and was given a worksheet to complete about cowboys' hats and their uses (figure 3.1).

B could not start. He could not complete 'The air inside the high crown ...'; nor did he know what 'brim' meant. An examination of the page makes clear why he found it hard.

Though they are not necessarily available to the pupil, a number of assumptions are made by the writer about how the page will be read. The words in the box are used to complete the sentences. They need to be combined to do so ('keeps ... cool'). The pictures describe sentences; so, they are clues. The order of the pictures is the order of the sentences; so, the pictures have to be read down the left then down the right. One could also quibble and say 'finish the *sentence*' refers to phrases such as 'the whole hat'. And a natural ending 'keeps the sun off' is not offered. The obscurity of the pictures' meanings is such that text is necessary to interpret them; pupils need the answer to understand the clue. Thus, the quaint picture of what looks like an old lady's hat (bottom left) needs 'in cold weather' for it to be understood. The first picture is so neutral as to make it hard to juxtapose specifically with 'high crown', just as 'the whole hat ...' could be completed with reference to any of the eight pictures.

Had B been working on a cowboy project, reading a Western, or writing a story, some of the puzzle-page language might have had a nearer history, a sharper context. He might have seen the rolled-up hat or the shaded face and shoulders in terms of knowledge drawn from that context. As it is, he

12   More Than Just a Hat

A man named Stetson made a special kind of felt hat for cowboys. That is why cowboys' hats are often called Stetsons.

The pictures show you some of the many uses of a Stetson hat. Write about them by finishing the sentences.

campfire	head
cool	horse
drinking	keeps
ears	pillow
eyes	pulled
fan	tied
water	

A cowboy's hat is often called a Stetson.

The air inside the high crown . . . .

The wide brim keeps the sun . . . .

On rainy days . . . .

In cold weather . . . .

The brim can also . . . .

The whole hat . . . .

He can use it . . . .

Rolled up it . . . .

Figure 3.1

starts, as it were *ab initio*, with the dictionary, and its meanings. This starting-afresh on a different subject with each new page or lesson is a way of ensuring that attributions of meaning made in reading or writing do not normally include those that have gathered over time, or those that are already in place because they are personal. Such a discreteness seems likely to cut off the pupil from his own language and its constitutive elements, and from the sense that what he uses is his own language. B's role seems restricted, almost, to merely reactive responses to fresh sets of instructions about what to do. In a profound sense, he cannot gather *his* thoughts, or *his* language.

*Hull also observed the same pupil floundering in a maths lesson. He was 'doing'
long division, but the whole operation seemed meaningless for B. In Hull's conversation with B it was clear how keen the pupil was to stay within a familiar
frame of reference.*

I resorted to 'ordinary language' to try to talk about division. Some of the
problems arising in this conversation show how difficult it is, it seems to me,
to find a way of talking about division that does not continually obtrude what
are formalisms for the pupil, deriving from one's own settled notions of
division.

Self How much ice-cream could you eat in one go?
B   About this much. (*Hands describing amount.*)
Self All right, suppose I gave you four times that amount, four lots of it, how much
    would you be able to eat?
B   I could eat it all.
Self I thought you said you could only eat *that* amount. What about the rest?
B   I could eat it later.

Either he is having me on, or it is a genuine intrusion of the empirical into
my formal hypothetical question; he perhaps hears it not as a maths question,
about relations between amounts, but as a practical empirical question: what
can be done with this huge amount of ice-cream?

Self All right, let's imagine you've got one empty milk bottle over here.
B   Yeah.
Self And over here you've got four full milk bottles. How many times could you get
    the milk that's in the four bottles into the empty one?
B   Once.

My silly question (meant to translate $1 \div 4$) produces what is empirically
appropriate, but not helpful with $1 \div 4$. Clearly you could fill the bottle once
only.

    Despite all this – including his temporary teacher's obtuse questions – he
can, providing the hypotheticality offered him looks enactable, and providing
the language is 'his', reason mathematically:

Self All right, supposing ... how many times could you run round the school field,
    do you think?
B   About twice.
Self Supposing there was a field that was twice as far round as the school field, how
    many times do you think you could run round that?
B   Once.
Self If there was a field that was four times as far round as the school field, how
    many times do you think you could run round that?
B   Half-way round. ...

I take it that most of my questions, apart from the running-track ones,
somehow brought him up against a way of speaking that did not elicit or
accommodate the reasoning demonstrated in his answers about the running-
track. In some way those modes of questioning became formalistic obstacles

to understanding. He tended to treat various modes of questioning 'arbitrarily'. Thus all these written questions produced the answer '6':

What is 2 into 4?
2 add 4
4 divide by 2
4 ÷ 2

Even when it seems one has found a reality and mode of speaking which does accommodate his thinking, communication is still precarious.

Self How much pocket money do you get?
B   50p.
Self Every week?
B   Yeah – once a week.
Self How many weeks in a month?
B   Two – no ten.
Self What is a month do you think?
       (*Long pause.*)
Self Could you name one?
B   Er – Saturday.
       (*A little further clarifying talk about months.*)
Self If you had your pocket money every week for four weeks and then added it up how much would you have?
B   £2. (*Very prompt – in answer to a syntactically complex sentence, moreover – though the context which has begun to be established renders it, apparently, immediately apprehendable.*)
Self How much would you have if you had 30p a week for six weeks?
B   (*After a pause of several seconds.*) About £2.
Self If you had 30p a week and not 50p, how much would there be if you put two weeks' money all together?
B   (*After about ten seconds.*) Er ... 60p.
Self If you had three weeks?
B   (*No reply ... but counting on fingers uncertainly.*)

The way that hypotheticalities might be rejected, and the empirical world become intrusive, is hinted at in the next interchange, which was meant to deal further with amounts of 30p pocket money.

Self Suppose I borrowed 90p off you last week.
B   Yeah.
Self Then I asked you to lend me another 30p.
B   I wouldn't give it yer.

The next extract presents history material given to a first-year class. It illustrates the teaching technique of 'simplification' designed to make complex material accessible and interesting to pupils but which in distorting the depicted events may actually prevent sense being made of the subject matter.

First-year history began with prehistory: 'The British Isles before man ... many thousand years ago ... when coal was formed ... and we were joined to Europe.' There followed the Bronze Age (October), the Romans (October–November), the Anglo-Saxons (December), the Vikings (January–February),

Alfred (February), the Normans (March), the Feudal System (March), the Medieval Church (April), King John (May), Henry III (June), Crécy, Agincourt and Joan of Arc (June–July). The bulk of the work written in the exercise books was dictation, short answers to questions, reference work done in single sentences, and short paragraphs. One simplifying model dealt with political relationships (figure 3.2).

The high degree of compression that marked this programme allowed only for elementary treatment. A collection of topics on Hastings, William the Conqueror, the Domesday Book and the Feudal System took up four sides only, covering three weeks (six lessons), and two and a half sides were diagrams and models. One of these was about William's achievements (figure 3.3).

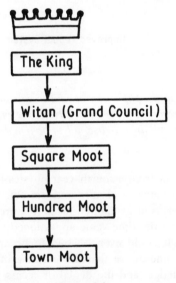

Figure 3.2

One can only speculate about the diverse meanings pupils might ascribe to the highly elliptical statements in this diagram. A sword is hardly an adequate image for 'rebellions', and 'made the Domesday Book' implicitly hides the scale of the enterprise. The usage 'William did x' is extremely common though, and it is worth pausing to examine this 'simplifying convention of written history'. Literally, all five diagram propositions are untrue. *William* couldn't 'crush rebellions', build a church, 'give' words to English, and so on.

But problems of sense are not confined to the first stages of the curriculum or to pupils categorized as in need of remedial help, as the next extract, from a lesson with an 'O'-level set, shows. The sense that pupils are to make of their lesson on radioactivity is deferred by the teacher to some future time when they will be older

William I

crushed
rebellions

made the
Domesday Book

built churches

gave English French
words-porc=pig

Improved Feudal System

Figure 3.3

and wiser. In this lesson the pupils can be said to encounter difficulties in learning as profound as others regarded as 'less able'. Here, the enemy of sense appears to be the scheduling of topics within a course, all to be completed in their allotted space of time.

In the following extract from a fourth-year physics lesson with the top 'O'-level set, the relation between closure and the objectivistic tendency to see a lesson entirely in terms of its allotted place in a predefined course – which means that topics have the time value apportioned to them by the course – seems even clearer. It could even be said to be apparent to the students themselves, who become aware that the exercise of close control over the distribution of knowledge, and the denial of access to topics raised prematurely, is here integral to 'teaching'.

The first part of the lesson, which had been devoted to reworking an equation done for homework, was quiet; the second was less so, and the teacher's discomposure when discipline wilted seemed to energize his flight to rigorous definitions of content explicitly apportioned to units of time.

Teacher We're going to start today doing radioactivity.
    (*This was announced amidst noise and talk.*)
Pupil 1 Have you got my book, sir?
Pupil 2 What's the date?
Pupil 3 Have you got my book, sir?
    (*And there were other questions as the teacher wrote on the board* 'Introduction – radioactivity'.)
Pupil 4 Is 'radioactivity' all one word?
    (*It was evidently to be a note-dictating session.*)

Teacher Now I'm going to start by talking a minute about the atom.
Pupil 5 Radioactivity's hyphenated.
Pupil 2 S'not!
Teacher Now, who knows anything about the atom?
Pupil 6 Molecule. (*Indistinct; the only reply.*)
Teacher Who knows anything about the structure of the atom?
    (*No reply.*)
Teacher No? (*Pause.*) Well, an atom is made up of a nucleus with a positive charge,
    and around it it has a field of negative charge ... the nucleus is very small
    ... you could compare it with the size of a pea on the centre spot of Wembley
    Stadium ... So an atom is mostly ...? (*Pause.*) What's in between?
Pupil 7 Air.
Teacher Air is made up of atoms ... What's in (*indistinct*)?
Pupil 5 How do you split them?
Teacher We're interested in ...
Pupil 5 How did they find out about the nucleus and (*indistinct*)?
Teacher It would take too long to tell ... it would take half a term in the sixth form.
    (*Noise.*) All right, then ... there was this chap called Rutherford ... he produced
    a sheet of atoms of (*indistinct*) ...
Pupil 5 How?
Teacher ... and bombarded it with particles.
Pupil 5 *Where* did he [bombard them]?
Teacher Well, it would take a long time.
Pupils Half a term in the sixth form!
    (*Small chorus.*)

Some of what was said in this discussion was indistinct, but the dramatic
shape of the passage, the urgency of the questions, and the continuous,
rather grudging, redefinition of content as it reflects the teacher's priorities
(in particular his need to cope), seem clear.

Pupil 2 How did he get the atoms off it?
Teacher He knocked them ...
Pupil 2 (*interrupting*) *HOW?!!* How did he get them ...
Teacher Well ...
Pupil 2 I want to KNOW! (*Voice rising in exasperation.*)
Teacher Jane!

After this small explosion his exposition went on for a short while unin-
terrupted by questions, or anything else.

Teacher They thought an atom was just solid, but because ... (*indistinct*) they found
    that 99 per cent went straight through, 0.9 per cent got deflected, but 0.1
    per cent got bounced straight back.
Pupils Cor!
Teacher They couldn't explain it ... they thought the only reason could be ... the
    mass was concentrated at one particular point ... if all the rest went through
    (*indistinct*) ... RIGHT, so we have ...
Pupil 8 (*interrupting*) Is that splitting the atom?
Teacher No, we'll get on to that later.

The teacher then rather abruptly started his dictation of notes.

Teacher ... small heavy particle, positively charged. It was found that if you shot
           particles at a nucleus, it would break up. It was found that there were two
           types of particles, neutrons and protons ...
Pupil 8 So the nucleus (*indistinct*)?
Teacher Well, yes, we'll see ...

The note-taking was completed two minutes or so later with the words
'surrounding this are electrons in constant motion'. Immediately, a pupil
spoke:

Pupil 9 Do they go round?
Teacher Yes, but it's not as simple as that, because they behave both as particles and
           as waves – it's a very complex part of chemistry.
Pupils Half a term in the sixth form?
           (*Small chorus.*)
Pupil 5 University.

The bell went, appropriately enough, at exactly this point.
   It is worth recapitulating the questions pupils asked:

1   'How do you split [atoms]?'
2   'How did they find out about the nucleus and...?'
3   'Where did he [bombard it with particles]?'
4   'How did he get the atoms off it? ... *HOW?!!*'
5   'Is [bombarding, etc.] splitting the atom?'
6   'Do [electrons] go round?'

Questions 1, 3, 4 and 5 went unanswered. The questions about splitting the
atom seemed to be met by the suggestion that the subject would be done
later, presumably in the sixth form. This deferral was not accompanied by
any provisional enlightenment, only the reminder that (at the moment) '*we*'re
interested in' the structure of the atom. Question 2 was 'answered' – almost
as a favour – with 'All right, then ....' Its appropriate slot was the sixth form,
but in the circumstances the pupils could have some of the knowledge now.
Question 6, 'Do [electrons] go round?', also met the closure of 'it's a very
complex part of chemistry', presumably implying something like 'too much
so for you at the moment'.
   It is an obvious point that these pressing questions – at least 1, 3, 4 and
5 – seem related to the lay person's everyday curiosity about atoms and how
they function. What is interesting also is that the questions seem to imply
an awareness that language such as 'splitting atoms' of itself means very little.
The pupils' questions are questions about the language of science. They
could be seen as asking, 'What does it mean to say "split the atom", "bombard
with particles", and so on?' The teacher's attempts to 'simplify', using words
such as 'knock' (presumably for 'bombard') and metaphors such as the pea
in Wembley Stadium, left untouched this particular dimension of the pupils'
curiosity.

These pupils made it clear to their teachers that they did not understand. In the final extract, from a first-year geography lesson, many pupils appeared to have grasped the main ideas, but there remained an extensive gap between their understanding and their teacher's. The lesson was about the Great Artesian Basin, Australia.

A worksheet had been given out the day before and the class (twenty-nine mixed-ability first-years) had to 'use the notes in the textbook' to describe how artesian wells work. The artesian principle was re-explained orally before they began. The teacher described the drawing on the board, which was reproduced on the worksheet, as a 'cross-section', and compared it with a cut sandwich cake. He said there were two kinds of rock: one with 'large spaces between the grains ... like a sponge', called 'porous' rock (this word was written on the board and appeared in both the worksheet and the textbook). In the other kind the grains were close together and water did not 'get into it'. He went on to describe the subterranean movement of water. All this was revision of work done in the previous lesson, and my notes refer to the teacher's 'very clear explanation' and the 'very clear worksheet'.

The teacher then described how the clouds lose their moisture before they reach the artesian basin, comparing their drying-out with clothes on a line in the wind: 'Will there be a lot of moisture or a little?' His tone was colloquial: 'What he [a farmer] does is drill a hole ... What's going to happen if there's a dry summer?' There was mention of 'artesian' and 'sub-artesian water', and of the 'Eastern and Western Highlands'.

To some extent, then, the written language of the textbook was supported by oral explanation which drew on the pupils' real world ('sponge', 'clothes drying'); this talk was colloquial in idiom and easy in tone. There were signs, in short, of an oral style that spoke directly to his audience.

Afterwards, I talked to a boy who had not been very attentive, doodling during some of the explanation and thumbing through the textbook, though he said he 'listened' for the last half. I asked him questions about the textbook and worksheet language. He thought 'the rainfall is light' meant it came down 'gently'; he was unsure about 'pastures', but thought the 'plants were poor' because 'there wasn't much water'. When I asked whom it would matter to, he said 'farmers', because they 'can't feed cattle'. When I asked if he could draw a simple sketch of the kind of reservoir that was referred to, he drew the sketch reproduced as figure 3.4, with the strata flat, and then altered it as in figure 3.5. He referred to pressure, but 'wasn't sure what caused it', and was not sure what 'porous' or 'sub-artesian' meant.

Evidently, though he gave me what my notes referred to as a 'coherent explanation' of some aspects of the artesian concept (which did not include a view of how the pressure was caused), he could not handle some of the key terms, nor the written passage in which they were embedded. I wondered how far such kinds of difficulty presented themselves for other pupils.

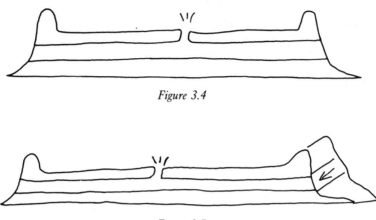

Figure 3.4

Figure 3.5

Later Hull asked pupils to draw their view of an artesian well, and he compared it to what they wrote.

One boy wrote persuasively, 'The water seeps through the porous rock and because the non-porous rock does not let water through the water collects and forms a reservoir.' As a piece of complex thinking-in-language this was coherent; the teacher presumed he understood, thinking of the reservoir as formed 'in the porous rock', yet his drawing, reproduced as figure 3.6, shows that this 'through' is 'through and beyond'. Non-porous rock allows water to enter to form a reservoir, but not to 'go through'. The language is appropriate, but the diagram shows an inappropriate empirical projection for it. There are two categories where one has been used (soft and porous), and the drilling is done from the highest point. The reservoir, in non-porous rock, collects, with an unempirical neglect of gravitation, to form a balloon – not a puddle-shaped thing.

In other diagrams, the pupils' empirical images for 'holds' are also revealed as inappropriate. One boy wrote, 'Porous means rock that holds water.' His drawing reveals (figure 3.7) this. His slip (perhaps he half-recalls the phrase 'trapped between layers of non-porous rock') is crucial, but he seems to have had no empirical awareness to draw on that would alert him to it. Three other pupils also drew this version.

For a third version, 'porous lets water through' and 'trapped between layers of non-porous rock' seems to produce an uncomfortable compromise, represented by figure 3.8.

A variant of the figure 3.9 occurred three times. One of these three was oddly labelled 'water soaking through non-porous to stop at porous rock'.

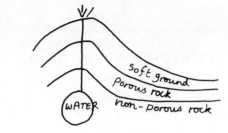

Figure 3.6

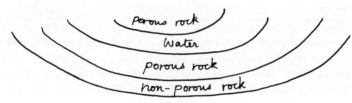

Figure 3.7

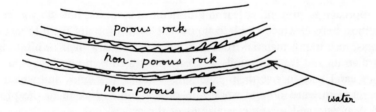

Figure 3.8

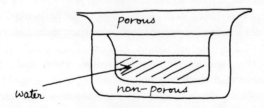

Figure 3.9

   Thus six drawings out of the twenty-seven suggested an inappropriate empirical projection for the language; a further three, envisaging a cavernous gap between strata, produced a central and gratuitous feature. As a group these drawings exhibit the consequences for language of presuming that appropriate language points to the appropriate 'facts' of the empirical world.

4

Getting children going

Valerie Antopolski

Valerie Antopolski gives an account of her approach to preventing learning difficulties, by describing the work of three nine-year-old boys. She indicates the way her personal knowledge of the pupils modifies her approach to them. Such work raises questions about attempts to analyse the learning difficulties of pupils in the absence of acquaintance with them and the curriculum they are expected to follow. This chapter takes up a theme raised by Gervase Phinn in chapter 1: the need to establish working-relationships between teacher and pupils in which both can contribute their ideas and skills.

My approach to preventing learning difficulties is to ask, how do you create an atmosphere in which children flourish? How do you get them to talk and discuss, to bring in material from their homes, to follow their own interests? I have an idea of the way pupils will learn successfully in my classroom, and if they can't I try to give them experiences which they enjoy and which will help them to learn how to work with others and to link in to the project work I initiate and the other activities of the group.

During the first term at my present school a few pupils stood out as having particular difficulties in producing written work or reading or in making a contribution to class activities. They were lost, they couldn't get involved in learning. There were three nine-year-old boys in particular, Peter, Arthur and Lennie, who I felt might begin to overcome their difficulties by developing mutual support and by sharing simple experiences. By getting them to work together I took the pressure off their individual efforts and I tried to share in and take pleasure in their learning.

I started by giving them a simple investigation to conduct around the school grounds each day. I wanted them to organize their time themselves, but they knew that they would have to develop a joint report with me when they returned. They had to decide who was going to concentrate on which part of the report. They felt they were grouped together for a special assignment, which they found very exciting.

For example, one day they had to investigate the wind, to see how they could detect it, how it affected them and their environment. They divided themselves up; one went down to the field, one to the playground and one to the pond, and they examined the effect of the wind on the water and the trees and themselves. When they returned they prompted each other to contribute. Because of their difficulty in writing and to keep it as a joint project, I recorded their experiences for them. They were free to jog each other's memories, prompting each other about the bits of their story that had been left out. We recorded the whole set of their assignments in a book and they read the reports to each other. There was a lot of talk and I was impressed by the way they began to examine things scientifically. Three of the reports are illustrated in figures 4.1–4.3.

I gave them minimal instructions. I might say, 'Find out the effects of the rain on the surroundings of the school.' I gave them ten minutes to find out all they could. I could see them out of the window staring down the cracks in the paving-stones and testing the slipperiness of the grass. They were not threatened by each other at all. They seemed able to organize an activity in a very democratic way. They looked at the way the rain made things shiny and showed up the dirt on the windows. We were doing erosion in class, so their attention had been focused on the effects of wind and rain. Another morning they took compasses out; they tried to sort out the direction of the school in relation to the gate; they started talking to me about direction and the use of the compass. It made it very easy for them to talk.

On another occasion they looked at the effects of the sun, not just on the school and its surrounding buildings and plants but also in relation to their emotions; they discussed feelings they hadn't tried to put into words before. That's something that they won't lose: they will feel the sun coming through their shirt or making a warm patch on their head.

They had had great difficulty in talking with me, in responding to questions. I noticed even in the playground when I had been on duty that their participation was very silent. I have met their mothers and one of them explained that her husband doesn't read or write and that there is very little talk at home. Her son has grown up in a household where experiences are rarely discussed at all. He hasn't fully realized that it is possible to talk about his ideas. But as I have got to know them I have found that my first impressions could be very inaccurate. I thought Peter paid least attention to what was going on around him, but I found he was really quite observant; it was simply that he didn't have a way of drawing on his experience. This is growing rapidly now. He has a much wider vocabulary than I had thought. When I wrote down the stories, he was the one who was able to express ideas in the richest language. He has begun to laugh much more; he is much more open to relationships.

Arthur was very silent in the large group. He found it difficult to answer a question with 'yes' or 'no'. He went very white and strained and couldn't seem to remember what I was asking him or to what it related. If I read him a story about a fox he wasn't able to tell me what animal was in the story. Yet he was happy to tell me about his expeditions. He felt very involved in

Tuesday
March 5th.

<u>The wind.</u>

Lennie had the wind box. The
flap was pushed by the wind.
It went up to 40°. When we
(tried) (another) direction it went up
to 30°. When we (tried) another
direction it went up to 80°. The wind
was coming from that direction
When we held up the paper it
(flapped) quite hard. It was quite
cold. Peter says, " I felt the wind
most on my jumper." Arthur says,
" I felt it on my hands and face".

Figure 4.1

Wednesday
March 6th <u>Using a compass.</u>

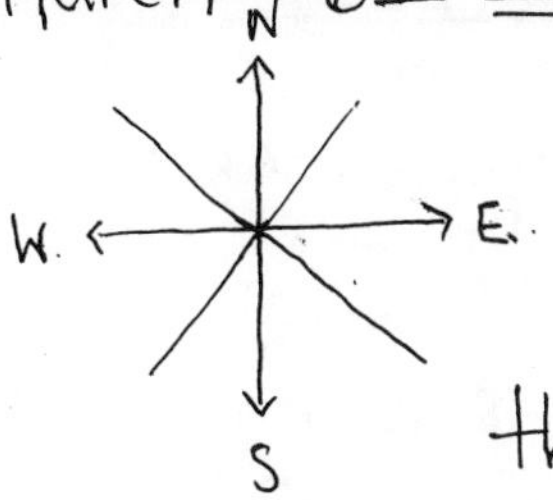

(Today) We found
out the direction of
the School gate. Peter
Lennie and I took a compass
(from) the drawer. We ran
Outside. We felt (excited.)
Peter had the biggest compass.
Arthur had the smallest compass.
I (Lennie) (found) out. Where.
North was. The school gate
is south. Our classroom is
North. Lennie says, " We have
(enough) room to do a picture."

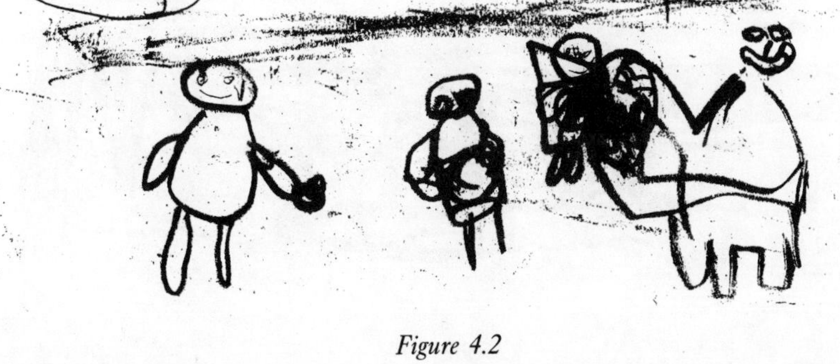

Figure 4.2

Thursday
March 7th It's raining.   all
                                     wall

The (pipes) and the pavements
were wet. They were (shining) The
door and the walls of our
classroom   were (quite) dry (because)
they were sheltered by the roof.
Part of a slab with stones in
it, was dry and part was wet
and part of it had mud on.
The grass looked (bright) green
(because) it was wet. We could see

drops of water on the wind
Arthur. I breathed deeply in the
fresh (cold) air.
          Room for another picture.

Figure 4.3

them and I'm sure that it was because he was in charge of the whole situation that he was able to talk about it. His father left the family unexpectedly last year. I don't think there had been a great deal of talk about it at home. He felt rejected and very strained and that has made it even more difficult for him to communicate. He is reading quite well now, and he is very confident in a small reading-group with two girls who are on the same level. He can offer them as much as they offer him and he likes that.

Lennie laughs a great deal. He likes to talk, he's not intimidated at all by the group. But he's another one who has found it very difficult to relate to events in a larger group. His experience in the small group has helped him to focus on a single theme, but it is a slow process. For example, we were watching a programme about brick-making. At the end I asked a question about the fumes from the chimneys and the effect on the houses and he said there had been an 'earthquake'.

SIX MONTHS LATER: A PROGRESS REPORT

Peter

Peter has become much more ordered and responsible in his approach to school. I've noticed of late that he even helps me organize myself! He reminds me to get the right materials, about things I ought to be telling the children about project work. He wanted to watch *Space Boy*, a reading programme on television. He came to me at the beginning of term and asked me if anyone would be watching that programme this term. I said another teacher probably would but that he could go and sort it out for himself and anyone else who wanted to watch it. He is much more confident with other adults too. He still doesn't read or write much on his own: I try to get him working co-operatively with others and he has learnt to link with them, so he can get as much as they from what we are doing.

I haven't made a real breakthrough with his reading. It is possible that he may never read all that well. But he has made vast strides with decision-making and organizational skills; he knows how to get what he needs.

Arthur

This year Arthur is also one of the class elders. He has spontaneously taken on certain tasks. For example, he makes sure that my register is on my desk in the morning. He has made a relationship with a very able younger boy, who has a paternalistic attitude to him. He is small and a year younger, so it can seem quite strange at first. I thought Arthur was a passive partner, but now I see that they both support each other, recognizing each other's needs. I've noticed particularly in drama how the two work closely together. They generate confidence between them and Arthur can role-play now in a way I had never thought possible. His flow of language is impressive. Arthur has an animation now; I don't know how much he has come to terms with his home, his father having suddenly walked out a year ago.

I read a poem to the class: 'Legend' by Judith Wright (in Maybury, 1972). It is about a child who sets off on a quest, though it's not clear what kind of quest until halfway through. The imagery is powerful and the poem was very stimulating for the children. Arthur had done an illustration as part of the poem. For assembly, the pupils showed their pictures and recited the part of the poem that went with it. Arthur was one of the few who had learnt his part off by heart. His was a dramatic presentation. He glanced over at me as if to say, 'See, I'm doing all right now.' He wasn't seeking my approval; he just wanted me to know that he knew.

Lennie

Lennie has kept his interest in the world around him. He is also very involved with his family, especially his grandpa and an uncle, and with friends of the family. These people take up a lot of his mental space. His brother died a year and a half ago, and at last his family seem to be recovering from that. He continues to be lively-minded and active. His reading has improved enormously and he can set out his ideas and find the help he needs from me or other members of the class. He has been very interested to contribute to projects in school with things from home, and his mother is helping too. He can be a nuisance and is not popular in the groups. The other children find him difficult. I talk with him and try to sort out the problems when they arise. He listens, but he can't respond at the moment. He doesn't take the group activities seriously, especially PE.

He is rather grubby and that puts other children off, though he is not as dirty as he was. He does take more responsibility for himself. Last year he had a lot of time off to console his grandpa, who was so upset about the brother's death. There was a lot of other time off too. But this year the attitude is different. He is as eager as he always was, but he finds it difficult to focus on activities. He is in a different world from many of the others.

REFERENCE

Maybury, B. (ed.) 1972: *Thoughtshapes*. Oxford: Oxford University Press.

5

Ian and the shoe factory

Stephen Rowland

Stephen Rowland provides an account of a sustained teaching- and learning-episode which has its origins in the interest and personal experience of one pupil with learning difficulties. The story is drawn from Rowland's year-long participation in a junior classroom, spent watching, promoting and sharing in learning, alongside the class-teacher. The full account of this work is given in The Enquiring Classroom *(London: Falmer Press, 1984), where further episodes of Ian's learning are described. By taking Ian's efforts at expression seriously, Stephen Rowland reveals Ian's capacity to bend his existing means to the service of his chosen end. This is essentially a collaborative enterprise: the teacher himself becomes part of the means by which Ian's goals are achieved.*

I am reluctant to describe any child as having special needs. The term seems to bring with it four assumptions, each of which I think is highly questionable:

1 that the needs of every child are not special;
2 that a child who is identified as having special needs requires 'treatment' based upon a different set of learning principles from those which apply to the 'normal' child;
3 that it is the child who is somehow at fault, rather than the strategies employed to teach children in general, which pay scant regard to the needs of all children;
4 that it is most appropriate to classify someone's educational state in terms of their deficiencies rather than in terms of their competencies.

That a large number of children, whether we take this to be 2 per cent or 20 per cent, abysmally fail to learn what we think they ought to at school, is without question. The concern of teachers to focus special attention on these children, to attempt to improve their experience of schools and their self-image, and perhaps positively to discriminate in their favour is a laudable intention. But, if our concern leads us to concentrate primarily upon devising a machinery for diagnosing children and preparing detailed packages for learning according to clearly defined objectives, I fear we shall be missing out on the heart of what these children, and indeed all learners, need from their teachers. The need is for teaching- and learning-relationships in which the children's interests, abilities and concerns are seen to be at the centre of their curriculum, and in which their expressions – whether in writing, painting, speech or other symbols – are taken as being serious endeavours to communicate something of significance.

The challenge with which children who experience learning difficulties present us is to listen more carefully, and take bolder steps towards understanding their world as reflected in the choices they make and the interpretations they form of their environment. Such a challenge is not easily met in the classroom.

Ian was a child who presented me with this challenge. At the time of the work which I shall describe, Ian was nearly ten years old, a third-year in a class of third- and fourth-year juniors. I taught and researched alongside Ian's own class-teacher, Chris Harris. Chris worked with his class in an open area occupied by three other teachers and their classes, which spanned the whole junior age range (from seven to eleven). Although the space was somewhat cramped, the teachers in this area made use of the open-plan arrangement in the flexibility and co-operation it offered in the use of resources, timetabling and the setting-up of occasional shared 'workshops'. Broad and integrated themes were adopted by the teachers in the area in consultation with each other. These themes provided a focus for much of the classroom activity, but the individual teachers interpreted them in their own ways with regard for the needs of their particular children. Within the open area teaching was organized on a 'co-operative' rather than 'team' basis. Thus the children would feel free to approach other teachers for assistance, but looked to their class-teacher as having responsibility for guiding and developing all the central aspects of their work. Chris organized his classroom in a way which gave all the children plenty of opportunity to make choices in both the form and the content of their work. Although I did not have the overall responsibility for the class, I worked with Ian, and with all the other children in the class, in much the same way as the class-teacher.

While Ian was not particularly unhappy at school, he was very aware of his own failure in reading, writing and numeracy. He was barely beginning to read. Although he struggled hard with his handwriting, the tension with which he held his pencil, and the way he protected his work from the sight of his neighbours, indicated that he knew this struggle would never meet with success. He could usually count up to twenty, but could not reliably add together a pair of numbers greater than three. In any teacher's terms, Ian would have been deemed a 'slow learner'. Considering these difficulties, his behaviour in the class was often amenable – and he was in many ways a gentle child – but he would at times get involved in scraps with his peers which, I suspected, were often aggravated by his own failing self-image. In a more traditionally organized classroom, I'm sure that this sense of failure would have led to greater problems for Ian.

I would quite often sit beside Ian for five minutes or so when he wanted to write, helping him with each word, if that was what he wanted, or, at other times, writing for him at his own dictation, to be read and copied by him later.

The fieldnotes which follow describe the development of a sequence of activity revolving around some investigations in the grounds surrounding his school. I offer these notes as an attempt to trace how a world began to emerge in which he and I, and a few of his friends, shared a sense of discovery. It was, I believe, this shared sense which stimulated Ian to use his intellect to its full in an activity which he could control, and which gave me a window onto the quality of his thinking.

FIELDNOTE: 12 MARCH

Last week, the work of the class centred around a series of visits to the brook which runs near the school grounds. I was returning from one of these visits with David and Ian after David had been examining the layers of clay and shingle in the stream bank, and Ian had been collecting clay, from which he was going to construct a model of part of the stream.

Ian said to me, 'I bet those layers of clay have been there a long time.' He then told me how he thought there must at one time have been buildings near the brook. He said there would have been a place where they made shoes. Surprised by this surmise, I asked Ian why he thought that. He said there were bits of leather scattered around the field beside the brook. I had not noticed this. Ian then told me how one time, when he was playing by the brook, he had found what he thought was a cobbler's tool.

I was somewhat sceptical of Ian's view that there had once been a shoe factory there, but later suggested that he might take a closer look and see if he could find any other remains. So Ian returned to the brook with a spade and started his search.

An hour later he returned to the classroom and excitedly showed me his finds. They consisted of a number of metal 'patterns' or 'forms' for cobbling shoes – at least, that is what I assumed them to be – and various unidentified pieces of rusty iron. Ian showed me how some of these iron patterns were made in the shape of the complete sole of a shoe and others were only for the heel. There was much discussion between Ian, Philip and myself as to how these metal pieces were used in the manufacture of the shoes. Philip at first thought they were actually parts of shoes whose soles were built onto a metal frame. He then realized that shoes made in this way would be too heavy and inflexible. I thought that perhaps they were used to mould the leather into the correct shape. Ian was not at all sure.

Many of the children came and examined these metal pieces. The next day Ian returned to the brook with Philip and found many more similar heel and sole patterns and also a wheel attached to a piece of iron. Philip and Ian explained how this wheel would have been part of a trolley – perhaps one they used for carrying the shoes from place to place in the shoe factory. Philip said he thought the remains were very old: 'About nine, or even fourteen years old, I should think.' Ian said he thought they were probably sixty years old. He said he didn't think that they made shoes like that these days. His observations and estimation here seem to be remarkable for a child who can barely count.

Someone else found an old leather slipper in the same area. Everyone was now convinced that there had indeed been a shoe factory or cobbler's shop down by the brook.

Ian and Philip displayed their finds and Philip did several pieces of writing about them. Ian wanted to write too, but I was not available to offer him much help and he soon found it too difficult even with Philip's help. It would be good to give Philip more encouragement to help Ian in this way.

By Friday, however, I was free to help Ian, so I suggested we went off to do some writing together in the quiet corner. Ian was enthusiastic. He said he wanted to write as in his earlier pieces: that is, dictating word by word to me and copying each word as I wrote it, rather than asking me for spellings as he wrote.

Before we started the actual writing, we collected together a selection of the items Ian had found. I asked Ian how he thought the iron patterns were used. He explained his idea that the pattern would be put into a fire until it was red hot. It would then be placed on the skin of leather and would burn out a piece of the required shape. (This sounded an ingenious idea, though I've a feeling it's not correct.)

We soon started the writing, but were not able to finish the piece on Friday, and completed it today:

Shoes

When I went down the brook (and) I found bits of shoes and I thought and I said to myself there was a cobblers and I thought there could have been a village and I said it was Syston and I found bits of clay pottery and some leather and I found a wheel. The wheel would be a trolley and I found a heel moulder. You stick it in the fire and when it is hot you bring it out of the fire and put it on the leather and I found a shoe and it was my size and the cobbler would put the shoe on my foot and he would get shoes for me. The man used it to see if it was my size.

While we were writing I also made rough notes to record all the conversation between us which seemed significant. I gave Ian no help with the style of the writing.

Immediately before Ian started to write he said he was unsure of how he should start. He asked if he should write about how we all went down to look at the brook. Anxious that Ian should avoid what seems a common trap in writing such as this of spending too long on the preliminaries, I suggested that he should not do this, but should confine himself to writing about the actual items he had found. Ian protested that he would have to 'explain about them'. His clearly stated intention here is well fulfilled in the opening sentence. Indeed, the opening lines explain not only his visit but also the thoughts it aroused in him about the historical context. These lines immediately enable one to identify with the imaginative, hypothetical nature of Ian's thinking. Writing word by word, Ian at first put in the '(and)' in line 1. Later he reread his work missing out this 'and'. I asked him if he wanted the word included or not. He asked me to read it aloud both with and without the 'and'. He said he preferred it without the 'and'. His judgement here was sound.

Before 'cobblers' Ian asked me what the name of the place was where shoes were made. I suggested it could be a shoe factory, or did he want it to be a cobbler's? He said it was a cobbler's because shoes were not made in factories 'in the olden days'. He seems to have quite a well-developed notion of change over historical time.

Instead of 'could have' (first sentence), Ian actually said 'could of', but I wrote this down for him in the grammatically correct form, repeating my version as I did so.

In the second sentence, Ian puzzled over what to call the piece of metal. Even though he had an adequate explanation of the function of the piece he was very concerned to know its proper name. I said I didn't know, but asked Ian to explain again how it worked. He did so, and then said it could be called 'an 'eel moulder'. Later he changed this to 'a heel mould' when he reread his piece.

The writing on Friday ended after 'and put it on the leather'. He said he felt very uncertain about how the various moulds were really used and it would be better if he went to visit his grandad, who used to be a cobbler, over the weekend, and ask him about it. He would then continue the writing on Monday.

However, when Ian came to school this morning it appeared that he had forgotten to take the metal pieces to show his grandad. He said his grandad had books which would explain how shoes were made, but Ian felt that this would not help him, as he could not read. All the same, without any further information on the subject, Ian wanted to finish his piece of writing. And so the last lines from 'and I found a shoe' were written. After Ian had written the penultimate sentence I asked him what the purpose of this shoe was that the cobbler put on his foot; was it the one he would buy? He said the cobbler put it on his foot 'because that was the one to see if it were the right size'. I gathered from this that it was a kind of standard against which the foot size of the customer would be measured. I said I thought Ian ought to write down this explanation. But he said he didn't know how to explain it in words. Clearly, he felt that the explanation he had just made to me orally would not do as a written explanation. (Even though I spell and even write out each word before he copies it, Ian is very conscious that written language has to be much more precise than spoken language.)

David was working beside Ian at this point and had become interested in his work, while he himself was drawing a picture of a bird. Overhearing the last bit of conversation, David said that Ian could write an explanation like this: 'The shoe the man put on me was like a tape measure to see what size my feet are.' Ian confirmed that this was just what he meant and went on to write, 'The man used it to see if it was my size.' David's intervention here was very appropriate and gave Ian the confidence to express himself in his own way.

Ian said his piece was now finished. I helped him to read it aloud to David. David remarked, 'I like it. It's got something about it that makes you feel like you're there.' Ian replied somewhat drily to this compliment, 'Yeah, that's why I wrote it.' Despite the enormous difference between David's ability and Ian's, David is able to treat Ian's work sensitively, without patronizing him, recognizing its real value. How much healthier this than the competitive attitude engendered by so much programmed work!

I think David's remark aptly sums up the piece. Ian does succeed in bringing the scene to life. He does this by first writing speculatively, then including the details of the finds and their purpose, and finally writing in the first person as if he were actually present at the cobbler's shop. This transition to the first person is made appropriately by using the conditional tense: 'and the cobbler would put the shoe on my foot'. It is interesting that David should have liked the piece for this reason, since his own concern in his writing recently has been with 'making you feel like you're there' by his use of direct speech.

This is perhaps the most problematic piece that Ian has written. He was constantly aware of the difficulty of putting into words what he wanted to explain. It was perhaps his foresight of these difficulties that led him to use the word-by-word dictating method of writing. Yet again, his decision about how to use my help seems to have been appropriate. The actual writing, however, even with my help, forced him to clarify and relate his ideas. Previously he had thought that the old shoe was just a shoe made by the cobbler, but its purpose was changed for the story. Since it was a lady's shoe (I had not initially realized the significance of this for Ian's story), Ian realized that it could not be the one that he might buy, and so he ingeniously invented a measuring-function for it. The requirements of the story itself to some extent affected his interpretation of his finds. How often, I wonder, is this the case in history? The writing is not merely a description of the pieces, but, rather, the pieces are the clues around which he reconstructs a historical scene. There is thus a two-way relationship between the objects and the writing. The writing serves as an investigation of the objects by clarifying his ideas of them, while the objects act as a focus around which he constructs a 'historical drama'.

At the end of a sequence of activity such as this it is difficult to be precise about what has been learned. Indeed, if what we mean by 'learned' is anything more than short-term recall from memory, I wonder if we can ever precisely state what has been learned. What is clear in this activity, though, is that Ian has confronted at least two important features of language: first, he has realized that writing is not a direct representation of spoken languages; and, second, that writing can have a real purpose directly related to the concerns of his curiosity and imagination. During this piece of work Ian did not confront the intricacies of writing English. He used me to solve that problem for him. But what he did do was grapple with the problems of writing at a level which was appropriate to his needs at the time. Some time later he felt confident enough to 'go it alone' with the writing, now that he was quite sure that I was genuinely interested in the content of what he had to say. For Ian, writing was not then an exercise to be practised so that it might only later be put to significant effect. It was a means by which interesting ideas were explored and shared.

Ian normally decided how I should help him with his writing, time permitting (which was not as often as we would have liked). He was able to make this decision appropriately, because he saw the point to the activity. It was in pursuance of *his* goal, in an activity over which *he* exercised control. In activities such as this, my ability to facilitate his learning – albeit at times slow learning – depended upon the extent to which I could understand and respond to his interests, rather than upon my ability to diagnose his 'problems'.

6

'Taking a real interest': learning to read at fifteen

Helen Savva

The final chapter in this section concerns a girl who went through almost her entire compulsory schooling unable to read anything but the simplest material. Helen Savva encouraged 'C' to use a tape-recorder as a means to base her learning on her own ideas and interests. The transcripts offer more than a teaching-tool. They also give us an insight into C's own perceptions of the many attempts to teach her to read. C judges her teachers in part according to their success in understanding the reasons why she can't read. Yet, in discussing her more recent success, C refers to Helen Savva's personal interest in her, rather than the use of any particular methods. This does not mean that the choice of method is irrelevant; rather, that any method may be irrelevant outside the kind of personal relationship established here.

A PORTRAIT OF C, AND AN ACCOUNT OF WORKING WITH HER

C first came to my attention in the fourth year, when I began to teach English to her class. We were well into the autumn term before I realized that C had difficulty in reading and writing. I am ashamed to admit that it was C who pointed this out to me. It was an occasion when I sat with C to look through her folder and go over her work with her. I asked her how she was getting on, anticipating a confident and positive response, because she seemed to me to be highly motivated and industrious, and because she had considerable facility with the spoken language. C said something like, 'Well, not very well, I can't read or write very well you know Miss.' I can remember feeling confused and guilty.

I think at this point that it would be useful to draw as detailed a picture of C as possible.

Although it is extremely difficult to assess the extent to which emotional problems affect reading progress, and although they are rarely the sole causative factor, emotional difficulties often feature in the lives of many children who make poor reading progress. C's tapes, on which she talks about her reading difficulties and her reading teachers, illustrate how her failure to make progress in learning to read made school a nightmare, because she was isolated, insecure and friendless.

The following are some of the observations made on C during her school life:

1966. In the first year of the infant school C is friendly and mixes well with other children. She is a good reader, and her oral and written expression is good.
1967. Friendly, helpful, interested. She loves reading. She mixes well. She can express herself well.
1968. Helpful, friendly. Tries hard but inclined to daydream. Finds work difficult and does not pick up ideas easily.
Reading. Slow.
Writing. Finds this extremely difficult and is not able to write more than a sentence.
Oral. Expresses herself fairly well but has limited language.
1969. First year of junior school. Lacks confidence, is lonely, rejected. Lacks concentration. Reading age [Schonell]: 5.1. Experiences great difficulty.
1970. Nervous, withdrawn. Tries hard, friendless. Reading age: 5.4. Stammers occasionally.
1971. Nervous, withdrawn. Nervously articulate. Never gives up.

There is a sharp contrast between the comments made on C from 1966 to 1967 and those made thereafter. C becomes withdrawn, nervous, friendless, becomes isolated and insecure, and is rejected totally by her peers. The unhappiness and misery she experienced in the infant school, where she was considered slow and stupid because she could not read, must have added a new and more complex dimension to her increasing learning difficulties.

As C's learning difficulties began to assume increasing complexity, so she began to be labelled 'stupid', 'slow', 'backward'. We appear very apt at labelling children in this way; we can make judgements about their 'personality', their 'potential', their 'intelligence', but we are often quite unable to prescribe a realistic solution for their learning difficulties.

Again, it may be useful to look at comments made about C when she was in the third year at Vauxhall Manor:

English	Usually tries hard but finds work very difficult indeed. *Must* have encouragement and help with her reading.
Science	Tries, but little progress until reading and writing difficulties are overcome.
French	Very poor. C is making no effort and her work is well below standard.
Music	Shows interest and enjoys the subject.
Maths	Works very hard when present and has made excellent progress.
Religious Education	Finds work very difficult but is always willing to try.
Environmental Studies	Excellent. C tries extremely hard and shows interest. Orally she is very alert, but her reading is non-existent. She must have more help with reading.
Needlework	Fantastic effort and attitude. Something must be done for her so that she can read and write.
General Comment	Timetabled for reading but did not attend lessons. Next year she will have Basic Education as a main subject.

I do not wish to imply that C's reading difficulties resulted entirely from her emotional insecurity, although I do believe that her feelings of isolation and insecurity hindered her progress. Certainly, from the third year at least, C was highly motivated, tried terribly hard and desperately needed to succeed. At home, C's mother had for a long time suffered periods of depression and consequent inactivity. By the time C entered the fourth year, she and her sisters were old enough to look after themselves and help their father with the housework and the younger children. The situation began to improve at home, as it did at school, where C started to gain confidence, form firm friendships and get on well with the rest of the class:

I feel able to work, I feel in this year and last year, when I was a fourth year, have been the best two years, including for my reading because I've felt secure in the classroom and I haven't been sitting there thinking who, who, who do I hate and who hates me like in the primary school.

I cannot believe that C was not capable, or willing or ready, to learn to read a long time before she began to make progress. She always worked with enthusiasm and responded and still does respond to people who are sympathetic to her learning difficulties. If we look at her third-year report we can see that in all subjects, with one exception where the teacher was unsympathetic to her learning difficulties, she tried very hard even though she could not read or write. Five out of nine teachers who commented on her progress or lack of progress insisted that C should have 'more help with her reading', 'Something must be done for her so that she can read and write,' But C was going through all the normal channels, she was 'receiving help', and she was failing. The five teachers did not see it as *their own* responsibility to help C with her reading – this was for someone else to do and was not *their* job.

If we read the transcript of C's tape 'My reading teachers', we realize that C had probably lost faith in the ability of reading-teachers to help her overcome her reading difficulties:

… she seemed to think there was something wrong with my speech or something.

That didn't do much good because all she did was show me reading cards and that didn't help.

… she didn't seem to be able to understand why it was so hard for me to read and therefore she didn't know how to help me.

She wasn't a very nice teacher, she used to shout. My reading didn't even improve one bit when I was with her.

If C wanted to read and was capable of learning to read, why did she fail for four years to make any headway? Listening to her words, her thoughts, poems and stories, we cannot fail to appreciate that she is a sensitive, articulate girl.

It has become increasingly clear to me in working with C that our attempts to help children with reading difficulties are unrealistic and uninformed. In a school which has on roll approximately 1200 pupils and a staff of seventy or more, we still have teaching-groups of 30 in many subjects, including English. 35.2 per cent of our intake this last year (1976–7) had reading-ages of 9.0 or below. We have a handful of teachers within the school, some of whom are trained reading-teachers, who are expected to cope with all these children and their various difficulties.

When C came to my attention, my immediate reaction was to refer her to someone else, to organize extra or 'outside' help for her. I didn't see C's problem as my problem, it wasn't my job to teach her to read, and I didn't believe that I had the necessary skills. I know now that I was wrong, and that we can no longer sit back and expect a handful of reading-teachers, no matter how skilled they might be, to solve the problems of the many children we teach who are experiencing difficulty in learning to read and write. This is a luxury we cannot afford.

The concept that there are special teachers who are 'reading-teachers' is misguided. We must all find time to teach children to read, just as we should all see ourselves as teachers of language. There is a mystery surrounding the teaching of reading which is negative and confusing. All teachers can and should assume responsibility for teaching children to read, because they might be the right person, in the right place at the right time, for that child. That is the kind of relationship which exists between C and myself. I was a reliable person whom she liked, who wanted to help her learn to read and write. I wasn't doing it because it was my 'job', but because I wanted to help her. We must not continue to fail children such as C. There are many others like her.

I should like to outline how C and I set about learning to read.

In September 1976 5A became my form and I was able to establish a close relationship with C. I decided to try to teach her to read. I knew that C had considerable facility with the spoken language, and that a good vocabulary and the ability to use language is extremely important to the process of learning to read. I explained as honestly as I could to C why and how we were going to set about the business of learning to read and she seemed prepared and eager to give me a chance. To begin with, the help and advice I gave her were uncertain. I thought it would be essential to listen to C read as often and as regularly as possible. It seemed imperative to give her my full attention, and to show determination and a consistent attitude in my efforts to help her. I was consciously trying to give C some of the confidence that time and circumstances had cruelly eroded. I listened to C read as often as possible during English lessons and after school. We read books together and C began to make tapes of her own thoughts, stories and poems. I am certain that our close and mutually trusting relationship was a crucial factor in helping C make progress and certainly mattered more than my crude attempts to diagnose and analyse reading-errors such as reversal of letters or words, mispronunciations, substitution of one letter for another, addition of letter and omission of letter, although this was useful and gave me insights into the problems which I have not as yet pursued but hope to do in the future. I inquired into C's environment, educational history, her experiences in school, both social and intellectual, and her oral language development.

My work with C revolved entirely around her thoughts, her words, her language. All children *have* language, and we should begin positively with what the child *can* do, and from where the child is, from his or her standpoint. If a child cannot read or write he or she can talk into a tape-recorder and have his or her words transcribed: 'I can put it into words but I can't put it on paper'.

I believe that the most valuable work I have done with C has been for her to talk about her experiences on tape, to recite her stories and poems onto tape, to have these transcribed and then to use them as reading-material. There is little doubt in my mind that C has gained tremendous confidence and pleasure from seeing her words typed and printed, and that C and other children find it easier and most relevant to read *their own words*.

It was as a result of confidence derived from using her own words that C began to read. We must demystify reading, not only for the teacher but also for the child, who should be consulted about her difficulties and encouraged to share her experiences. We can no longer afford to hide behind the 'mystery' surrounding the teaching of reading or pretend that we are helping when we are not. We must give children confidence to learn, not by mystifying them with language forms which are alien to them, or by reading books which are irrelevant to them, but by using the talents they have and by using their language, thus showing them what they can do rather than what they can't do.

There is no doubt that in a short time C has made remarkable progress. She has the confidence to read books on her own, and she is reading books for the first time in her life.

I make an effort to provide C with as many books as she appears interested in. These are often books which are well within her capabilities in order to improve her fluency and boost her confidence. Just before Christmas I gave C three books, and when we returned to school she informed me that she had finished reading one of them and she had done it on her own. . . .

The change in C has been delightful. She is full of new confidence, which has benefited not only her reading but also her writing. She is writing poems and stories of real quality: she presents her work beautifully and takes great pride and pleasure in it. C recites poems and stories onto tape and organizes me into having them transcribed or types her poems herself. In reality she is participating fully and constructively, and involving herself in every way possible in her own learning.

SECTION TWO

Reconnecting Remedial Education

7

A policy for Grampian

William Fordyce

Support for pupils who experience difficulties in learning, provided in mainstream classes across the curriculum, is now an established, ordinary feature of school life in Grampian Region. This policy was established in 1977. In this chapter, William Fordyce, Grampian's Depute Director of Education, describes the introduction of the policy and considers the progress that has been made despite the vicissitudes of public-expenditure cutbacks, which left some parts of the Region without effective support teams. He discusses how, in the future, the model of learning-support could be extended to accommodate all pupils with special needs in comprehensive primary and secondary schools.

Grampian Region occupies the north-east corner of Scotland, covering an area of approximately 3200 square miles, with a population of almost 500,000 people. Education is provided in 48 nursery schools and classes, 287 primary schools, 39 secondary schools; 31 special schools and units, and five colleges of further education. The nature of the schools varies widely in such a large geographical area, with primary schools varying in size from five pupils to 800 pupils; similarly, secondary schools vary in size from 34 pupils to 1800.

In 1975 the reorganization of local government in Scotland resulted in the amalgamation of five education authorities to form Grampian Education Authority. The upheaval caused by reorganization did have some advantages, as it forced the new authority to consider many different aspects of educational provision due to the need either to amalgamate policies of the previous authorities, or to create completely new policies. Once a close look had been taken at the provision already made for remedial education, it was obvious that this fell into the category of a need for a completely new policy.

The process of developing a new policy started with the then Depute Directors of Education (Primary and Secondary) instructing that a survey of existing provision be carried out. This investigation showed that provision for children with learning difficulties was at a relatively low level, with 80 remedial teachers making provision for a total primary-school population of 49,000 and 71.5 remedial teachers providing for 35,000 pupils; the teachers being spread unevenly and in an apparently random manner across Grampian Region. What was also of concern was the discovery that, in the majority of cases, provision for remedial education consisted exclusively of extraction from normal classes for additional tuition in English and mathematics alone, at the best, and in some cases general language work alone. The working-day of many remedial teachers consisted of twenty- to thirty-minute scheduled periods with either individuals or small groups of pupils in the remedial room and in splendid isolation from the normal work of the child in the classroom situation.

Discovery of these facts resulted in two courses of action. The Depute Director of Education (Primary) decided to recommend to the Education Committee that the number of remedial teachers in primary schools should be doubled to 160, with provision being made for pupils in Primary 3–7 and distributed on the approximate basis of one remedial teacher to 300 primary school pupils. The Education Committee agreed to phase in this policy over a period of four years, starting in 1977. At the same time the Depute Director of Education (Secondary) set up a working-party with the following remit.

1   To review the present provision of remedial education in secondary schools in Grampian Region.
2   To ascertain the need for remedial education in terms of:
   a   literacy and numeracy;
   b   social competence.
3   To make proposals as to how the needs of pupils might best be met.

This working-party consisted of representative staff from schools, the Advisory Service and the Child Guidance Service and met under the chairmanship of the Depute Director of Education (Secondary). Its main recommendations can be summarized as follows.

1   The needs of the individual child must be met.
2   At some time during his or her school career, any child may have learning difficulties. Hence concern should extend beyond the slow-learning child to encompass the under-functioning child, irrespective of his or her level of ability, and those who have difficulty with social competence.
3   If a child who is experiencing any kind of learning difficulty is to receive effective help, then there are critical relationships between groups of people that must be recognized and fostered:
   a   remedial teacher and subject/class-teacher;
   b   remedial teacher and parents;
   c   remedial teacher and guidance teacher;
   d   remedial teacher and educational psychologist;
   e   secondary and primary school;
   f   secondary/primary and special school or unit;
   g   secondary school and post-school.
4   In a system of comprehensive education, there is no place for the traditional remedial class. Subject/class-teacher and remedial teacher

must work closely together to ensure that appropriate methods and materials are used with the child who has learning difficulties in the normal classroom setting. This team approach must involve joint planning as well as operation.

5   If the desire to meet the needs of the individual child is to find practical expression, two fundamental principles must be applied:
    i   need occurs right across the curriculum;
    ii   the professional insight of the class/subject-teacher and the remedial teacher, together with the informed use of diagnostic tests can ensure that needs are identified, continuously monitored and updated.

6   Additional remedial teachers are required. Working on the assumption that, at any point in time, 10 per cent of the secondary-school population will require the help of a remedial teacher, the numbers of such staff should be increased to 147. These staff should be distributed amongst schools on the basis of measured need, rather than purely on the basis of numbers of pupils in schools.

7   The most effective way to ensure that there is a positive curricular interaction between primary and secondary schools, so easing the transition for those pupils with learning difficulties, is to have a group of remedial teachers who work in both a secondary school and one or more of its associated primary schools. This will enable such teachers to 'float' between schools and develop meaningful links between them.

8   It is essential that remedial teachers work as a team which cuts across all subject and class boundaries. Hence, all remedial teachers who work in a secondary school and/or its associated primary schools should be formed into an area remedial team led by a principal remedial teacher who will be responsible to the head teacher of the secondary school and the head teachers of the primary schools whilst maintaining close links with the principal educational psychologist for the division in which they work.

9   The implementation of the plan should be carried out on the basis of one area remedial team at a time, in order to ensure that the system of float remedial teachers is introduced in a logical manner.

The Education Committee agreed to phase in this policy over a four-year period starting in 1978.

Having now reached the stage of having formal development policies for remedial education in both primary and secondary schools, it now became the responsibility of the respective Depute Directors of Education for Primary and Secondary Education to ensure that the Committee's policy was implemented.

Initially a random 25 per cent sample of pupils in Secondary 1–2 sat a series of standardized tests in order to obtain some measure of how the need for remedial education was distributed across the Region. From these sets of figures, a remedial need factor was produced for each secondary school and its associated primary schools. This factor was then used to determine the size of the area remedial team needed in each case. This resulted, for example, in two school areas in Aberdeen City being staffed as shown in figure 7.1.

Having carried out the paper exercise producing possible area remedial teams for each of the comprehensive schools and their associated primary schools, the next stage was to undertake a whole series of meetings. During the first year of the development exercise, the Depute Director (Secondary), the Depute Director (Primary) and the Regional Psychologist held the following meetings in each of nine areas.

1 A meeting with the head teacher of the secondary school and the head teacher of every primary school in the area. The objectives of the development exercise were discussed, the method and rate of implementation and queries and problems dealt with. The head teachers were asked to explain the programme to their staffs.

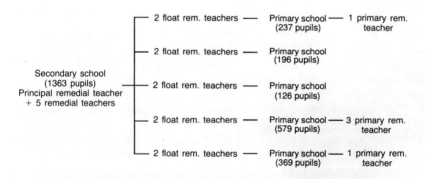

Area A   A total remedial team of 21 staff

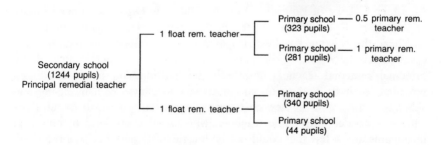

Area B   A total remedial team of 4.5 staff

Figure 7.1 Two area remedial terms

2   Immediately afterwards, a meeting was held with all the existing remedial
    teachers both to explain the development programme and to seek vol-
    unteers for the first appointments of float remedial teachers.

At the same time, similar meetings were held with the Child Guidance
Service, primary advisers and subject advisers. Appointments were made of
the first principal remedial teachers, and attempts were made to recruit forty
high-quality class/subject-teachers as the first phase of the expansion of the
remedial education service. The appointment of the principal remedial
teacher was made several months before the formal setting up of an area
remedial team, wherever this proved possible. Meetings of principal remedial
teachers were called by the two Depute Directors and the Regional Psychologist on a regular basis throughout each academic session.

During the second year of the development programme, a similar set of
meetings was held in new areas where teams were to be set up, and repeat
meetings were arranged for areas where teams had been in existence for a
year. In the latter case, this was to deal with problems that had arisen during
the year.

This kind of exercise was carried on until the remedial education development programme became a victim of government restrictions on local-
government expenditure in 1980–1. We had set out to recruit 155 extra
remedial teachers over a four-year period. By August 1980, we had obtained
100 of these additional staff. The training of these teachers was a matter of
particular concern, but fortunately, as the result of the publication of a report
by HM Inspectors, the national provision was changing with the introduction
of a one-year full-time course leading to a Diploma in Learning Difficulties.
This has now been superseded by a Diploma in Professional Studies in
Education (Non-Recorded Pupils)[1] validated by CNAA.

The policy Grampian has adopted is of recruiting experienced teachers
from both primary classrooms and secondary subject departments; getting
them to spend a year with an existing area remedial team, during which time
open assessments are made of their performance; followed by a year at
Aberdeen College of Education to obtain the new Diploma, either primary
or secondary dependent on the teacher's initial teaching-qualification.

Where the scheme has been a success, as it undoubtedly has in many
cases, it has been due to the persuasion, patience and persistence of the
principal remedial teachers and both the existing and newly appointed
remedial teachers. Persuasion was necessary to convince many class- and
subject-teachers that the new co-operative approach was worth trying. Patience was needed with some teachers, who raised every kind of objection
imaginable and a few that could not be imagined. Persistence was required,
in what was fortunately a few cases, where class- or subject-teachers wanted
nothing to do with the new policy. Some teachers objected to the finance
that was being pumped into the system to help children with learning
difficulties; others wanted children with problems removed from their classes

on a regular basis rather than retaining them and having to learn to plan and work together with a remedial teacher.

We have now reached a situation where Grampian Region should have thirty-nine area remedial teams, but in practice has twenty-one fully implemented teams. The Region is split, therefore, into the haves and the have-nots, and this cannot be allowed to continue. Grampian, like the rest of the country, has been significantly affected by an overall drop in school rolls, although this total figure masks massive oil-related expansions in some areas partially balanced by significant reductions elsewhere. Hence the initial estimated need for a total of 307 remedial teachers can now be revised to approximately 270. The aim is that area remedial teams should exist in all parts of the Region by August 1987.

It is difficult, if not impossible, for anyone in Grampian to provide a detached assessment of the effectiveness of the provision that has been made, but a number of factors can be highlighted as a result of a follow-up survey that was undertaken in all schools in 1981. The scheme itself allows head teachers and principal remedial teachers sufficient professional freedom to devise their own styles of the leadership to realize the potential of the development programme. The specific improvements that can be identified are as follows.

1 Remedial teachers and class- or subject-teachers are now learning to work together to plan and prepare meaningful material for pupils with learning difficulties.
2 Provision is now made across the curriculum rather than merely in language and number work.
3 By having remedial teachers working with class- or subject-teachers in the normal teaching-area, pupils with learning difficulties no longer feel isolated from their peers. This has produced an improvement in their self-image, concentration and work rate.
4 The policy of positive discrimination in staffing has ensured that help is given where the need is greatest.
5 The provision of float remedial teachers who work in an area comprehensive school and one or more of its associated primary schools has made a contribution to easing the transfer from primary to secondary education of children with learning difficulties. The pupils are happier and there is greater continuity of work between primary and secondary school.

Having said this, much work remains to be done in order to ensure that the development programme is as effective as it can be. Proper programmes of staff development need to be produced in order to see that specific skills in assessing and preventing difficulties in learning and developing appropriate materials are developed by all teachers. In addition the difficulty must be faced of those teachers who have an antipathy towards the development programme. It is hoped that, in time, by patient discussion and example, these attitudes can be modified.

What will happen in the future? There is little doubt that, where head teachers and the principal remedial teacher are committed to the provision for children with learning difficulties, the system works well. In a number of situations young pupils who in earlier years would have been transferred to special schools or units have remained in mainstream schools because of the support provided by the area remedial team. Perhaps we can look to the day when the area remedial team is incorporated into an area special educational needs team, comprised of a mixture of remedial teachers and special-education teachers. This team would provide the support necessary to ensure that as many pupils as possible, both those with recorded needs and those without, are retained in mainstream education, with those pupils with very special recorded needs being placed in a home base for some aspects of their education. Some progress has already been made in this direction, with one area remedial team accepting responsibility for a significant number of hearing-impaired pupils placed in mainstream education in their area and for the integration of pupils with behavioural problems. It is possible that in the next year or two the Education Committee will look at a long-term policy of integration of pupils with all kinds of special educational needs into mainstream schools. That, however, would require another major development programme.

The important question to ask is what is required to produce a successful development programme. The answer consists of a number of very important basic factors.

1 Commitment. Political commitment is essential both to identify a worthwhile policy and to obtain the necessary finance.
2 Commitment. Central administration must have a professional commitment to the idea so that its members can provide the leadership that is necessary to see the project through its birth pangs.
3 Commitment. Head teachers and principal remedial teachers must have the greatest degree of professional commitment both to lead the staff in the schools and to sustain themselves when the going gets rough.
4 Communication at all levels. In Grampian Region, members of the central administration attended over 200 meetings in a four-year period. Principal remedial teachers must continually meet with primary head teachers and heads of subject departments. The remedial teacher must meet continually with the class- and subject-teachers and discuss diagnosis, material production and implementation.

To sum up: commitment, communication and determination are required by many people, as well as persuasion, patience and persistence. The task is not easy, but the rewards are immeasurable.

NOTE

1 In Scotland, separate diploma courses are provided for teachers of pupils 'recorded' under the Education (Scotland) Act 1981 and teachers of non-recorded pupils. A 'Record of Needs' is the equivalent of the English Statement of Special Needs.

8

Putting policy into practice in primary schools in Fife

Glenys Andrews

In this chapter, Glenys Andrews, formerly a Programme Co-ordinator for the Education of Pupils with Learning Difficulties in Fife Region, describes some aspects of Fife's response to the Pupils with Learning Difficulties *report published by the Scottish Education Department in 1978. She describes how this policy has been implemented in five primary schools, and in one area in which three peripatetic remedial teachers support twenty-two primary schools.*

In 1978 the Scottish Education Department produced its report *The Education of Pupils with Learning Difficulties*. The main recommendations of this report are described in the introduction to this book (pp. 3–4). This chapter is an account of the way in which the recommendations of the report have been translated into policy in the primary sector in Fife. In order to describe what has happened, I have selected five individual schools and an area served by a team of peripatetic remedial teachers as a representative sample of the different contexts in which development has taken place. Table 8.1 sets out some background information on the schools.

Each school has a written policy on the education of pupils with learning difficulties. The policy documents differ in length, emphasis and degree of detail, some including skills checklists, sample record sheets and resource lists. They all emphasize the need for a whole-school, co-operative approach to tackling the problem of learning difficulties. Take, as an example, the policy document for Inverkeithing Primary School. The head teacher is most anxious to point out that this document does not imply a static policy; neither does it dictate what will happen. Rather, it is a description of present practice in the school. Above all, the policy is flexible and is reviewed and revised in the light of changing circumstances within the school and a growing appreciation of what is involved in, for example, co-operative teaching or in the diversity of sources of learning difficulty. The other head teachers who have co-operated in compiling this report have made similar conditional statements in submitting their policy documents.

ORGANIZATION FOR CO-OPERATION

The previous role of the remedial teacher, that of giving direct tuition on a withdrawal basis to small groups of children, could mean that there was little contact between the remedial teacher who saw the pupils for relatively short periods, and the class-teacher with whom the pupils spent most of their time at school. The programme followed by the remedial teacher could conceivably be fundamentally different from and quite irrelevant to the curriculum in class. With the introduction of the new regional guidelines, an approach to learning difficulties was advocated which demanded close co-operation between class-teacher, remedial teacher and promoted staff in the school both in preventing learning difficulties and in dealing with any which might arise. Co-operation at this level, whether it means discussing, planning, or actually teaching together, demands the organization of time to make it possible. Decisions have to be made as to how much time will be spent on the various aspects of the remedial teacher's role, and how, for example, working and discussion together can be fitted into the busy primary-school day with visiting specialist teachers, television programmes and the multitude of other demands made on the time available. Co-operative teaching, in particular, demands at times quite complex timetabling arrangements. Each of the schools involved in this small sample, however, sees it as fundamental to a collaborative approach and all have, in different ways in their individual situations, devised organizational frameworks for ensuring that it takes place in a planned and meaningful way.

Castlehill

Prior to the recent appointment of the head teacher, the school had had a tradition of class teaching and a pattern of remedial teaching based on withdrawal groups of pupils in the upper school who were having difficulties with reading. Until the appointment of the present head teacher, the school had only one remedial teacher. As part of an overall strategy of curriculum development, the head teacher, in consultation with the assistant head teachers and remedial teachers, has drawn up a language programme for the school which demands that classes be organized and taught on a group and individual basis. A similar programme exists for the mathematics curriculum. Each of the remedial teachers has been given responsibility for an area of the school (P2–4 and P5–7) and may deal with problems in mathematics or language. Children requiring direct tuition are seen regularly either in their classes or in a withdrawal situation. The rest of the remedial teachers' time is shared among all the classes in their particular areas. Negotiation takes place between the class-teacher and the remedial teacher in consultation with the assistant head teacher, on which children and which area of the

TABLE 8.1 Background information on five primary schools and Cupar area

School	Roll	Promoted staff	Remedial teacher allocation	Other relevant information
Castlehill, Cupar	737, including 84 nursery and 5 in assessment unit	Head teacher 4 assistant head teachers without full-time class responsibility	2 full-time	One of the two remedial teachers has the new qualification. The school is on a split site, P1–2 being housed in a building a considerable distance from the main building. In the P1–2 building, an assessment unit has recently been opened for 5–7 year olds.
Inverkeithing	570, including 84 nursery	Head teacher 3 assistant head teachers without full-time class responsibility	1 full-time	The remedial teacher has recently gained the new qualification
Pitreavie, Dunfermline	360, including 40 nursery	Head teacher Assistant head teacher (early years) without full-time class responsibility Assistant head teacher (P4–7) teaching a class (temporarily)	1 part-time: $2\frac{1}{2}$ days per week	The remedial teacher is appointed on a full-time basis and is shared between Pitreavie and another nearby primary school

	Roll	Staff	Remedial provision	Notes
Rimbleton, Glenrothes	316, including 42 nursery	Head teacher Assistant head teacher (early years) without full-time class responsibility Assistant head teacher (P4–7) teaching a class	1 part-time: 3 days per week	The remedial teacher, who holds the new qualification, is appointed on a full-time basis and spends two days a week working as an area senior remedial teacher in Glenrothes and north and east Fife
Valley, Kirkcaldy	304, including 40 nursery	Head teacher Assistant head teacher (early years) without full-time class responsibility	1 full-time	The remedial teacher spends two days a week working as an area senior remedial teacher in the Kirkcaldy and Cowdenbeath areas. She is replaced for these two days by a second remedial teacher in Valley
Cupar Area (excluding Castlehill), 22 schools	1,606	Head teachers	3 full-time peripatetic	Two of the three remedial teachers now hold the new qualification; the third is currently undertaking the college course and a replacement teacher is in post

P = Primary (stage of school)

curriculum will be involved in the co-operative teaching which takes place. It is unlikely that the remedial teachers will work with the same children in these classes as they work with in their direct tuition role. Since the assistant head teachers are also involved in co-operative teaching with the class-teachers, a system of substantial support for the class-teachers is being developed which will facilitate the desired changes in methodology, resources, content and organization. Thus the head teacher's overall plans for providing greater differentiation within the curriculum are being realized. Consultation between the remedial teachers and the individual class teachers takes place daily between 3.15 and 3.45 p.m. (It is regional policy that this time, after the pupils have left, be used for 'preparation and correction'.) Consultation between the remedial teachers and the head teacher or assistant head teachers is described as 'informal and regular'.

Inverkeithing

In devising a strategy which involves her with all of the classes in the school at some stage during each session, the remedial teacher has worked out a timetable with the head teacher which allows her to give direct tuition to a maximum of twenty pupils per week. (She would not expect to see the same twenty for the entire year.) Having set aside the time necessary for this role, she then allocates the rest of her time to co-operative teaching with P5–7 in terms 1 and 2, P4–5 in term 3 and P1–3 in term 4 of the school year. Her timetable (figure 8.1) shows how she works this out with individual classes.

She spends, on average, one hour per day, four days a week, with the classes where she does co-operative teaching. She may work in any area of the curriculum and with any children, depending on the needs of the classes as expressed by the class teachers or as perceived by the head teacher. She describes some of her work thus:

In term 1 my co-operative teaching with the P6–7 class involved assisting the teacher to introduce a structured writing programme. I worked with all of the children at some stage during this period of co-operative teaching. The class-teacher commented that one of the spin-offs was a 'healthier attitude from the pupils' towards me as a result of my working with more able pupils. In term 2 I worked with the class-teacher on a 'Unit Study' of a novel. My aim here was to help children with limited vocabulary and reading difficulties to understand and to enjoy the novel. I taped each chapter, provided work sheets for various aspects which helped a wide range of children, and had discussions with small groups of children in the class. In this case the class teacher said that the benefit of my intervention had been to make the topic more accessible to all of the children in the class.

She comments on her own feelings arising from this change in her way of working: 'Co-operative teaching is interesting in that it provides a variety of teaching activities. It is, however, extremely demanding in terms of time for planning, preparation and record-keeping.'

					3.15–3.45		
Monday	P3(a)	P3(b)	← P6–7* → (Room 12)		P6–7* (Room 13)	P3(a, b, c) Movement Programme	
Tuesday	P3(c)	P3(b)	P6–7* ← → (Room 21)	P5*	P6–7* (Room 13)	P6	
Wednesday	P4–5	P5	← P6–7* → (Room 12)		P6–7* (Room 13)	P7	
Thursday	P3(a)	P5	← P6–7* → (Room 12)		P6–7* (Room 13)	P4–5	
Friday	P3(a)	← P5 —	— P5* →	P7	CONSULTATION AND PREPARATION		

(Columns between sections labelled vertically: INTERVAL, LUNCH, CONSULTATION AND PREPARATION)

*Denotes co-operative teaching. (Other references to classes imply
direct tuition of individuals or small groups of pupils.)
P = Primary (stage of school)

Figure 8.1 Inverkeithing Primary School: remedial specialist's timetable,
September–December 1984

Both the remedial teacher and the head teacher have emphasized the
flexibility in the timetabling described above. 'The timetable must reflect and
respond to the needs of the children', states the head teacher. 'On no account
must a timetable preclude dealing with the spontaneous needs which arise
in a dynamic teaching-context'. The timetable and, by implication, the organization are perceived as a framework within which time can be negotiated as
needs arise.

It is crucial, then, that time be allowed for discussion, which may centre
on the needs of individual pupils or on curricular matters where the remedial
teacher may be called upon to assist. The timetable in figure 8.1 shows that
Friday afternoons in total and other afternoons from 3.15 to 3.45 p.m. are
given over to this purpose. Further time is found when necessary by one of
the three assistant head teachers (none of whom has full-time responsibility
for a class), relieving the class-teacher of his or her class to talk with the
remedial teacher.

Pitreavie

With the limited time available to the remedial teacher in a situation where
the number of enrolled pupils, after falling, has now risen again and the
school population includes a number of pupils who have difficulties of a
temporary nature due to frequent changes of school, the focus is on individual

pupils and their needs. All teaching done by the remedial teacher is planned in co-operation with the appropriate class-teacher. Programmes of work are drawn up at the beginning of each term for individuals or groups. These programmes cover all aspects of the language curriculum. The class-teacher and the remedial teacher decide how they will divide the work between them. Where possible, when the remedial teacher is involved, extra tuition for the pupils is pursued through the medium of the class theme or project. Having assessed the needs of the pupils with the class-teacher, the remedial teacher draws up a timetable in consultation with the head teacher and assistant head teacher. Areas of priority are decided upon: for example, in which classes co-operative teaching of environmental studies could be most profitably pursued, or which children would benefit most from direct tuition. At the time of writing this chapter, in her co-operative teaching the remedial teacher is concentrating on a P4 and a P5 class project, devoting two blocks of time per week to each class. As in Inverkeithing, the approach to timetabling is a flexible one which responds to needs as they arise. The head teacher express-ed her dissatisfaction with the time currently available for discussion between the remedial teacher and the class-teachers, which she feels is crucial to making progress in the school policy for co-operative teaching. She considers the half-hour at the end of the day to be inadequate and is currently exploring ways of making time for consultation during the school day. This might mean, for example, that she will take a class to allow the teacher to spend time in discussion with the remedial teacher.

Rimbleton

Co-operative teaching began in a spontaneous way with the remedial teacher co-operating with one teacher who had requested help with a wider range of pupils than were normally withdrawn by the remedial teacher. This resulted in a co-operative teaching-venture which was beneficial to both the class-teacher and the pupils. The teacher felt that having the remedial teacher in the room with the class meant that more pupils had the opportunity to have individual help from a teacher and that she herself benefited from seeing the way in which the remedial teacher dealt with children's learning difficulties. The remedial teacher felt that she was benefiting by observing the class-teacher's skills and by seeing the pupils in a range of situations where they displayed strengths as well as the difficulties on which she would normally tend to concentrate. Working together led to planning together and, initially, this tended to happen during the lunch break, or at home (the ideas being helped to flow by the occasional bottle of wine!) Later, as other teachers began to request the support of the remedial teacher in co-operative teaching and as the regional guidelines were being introduced, a more formal plan of allocating time for consultation and co-operative teaching emerged.

Now all the classes from P3 to P7 have the support of the remedial teacher in some form of co-operative teaching at some stage during the school year. The decision as to where to operate at which time of the year is taken at the beginning of each year, when the head teacher and her assistant head teachers identify priorities in the school. Decisions as to how and where the remedial teacher will teach co-operatively are taken on the basis of 'trouble spots', which may concern either individual pupils or the curriculum. The co-operative teaching may also take place to support particular aspects of curriculum development such as the use of a novel as the focus of a thematic study, which tends to take place in the P7 classes during the final term of each year.

The remedial teacher in Rimbleton feels that developments would have proceeded more quickly had there not been so many interruptions to her routine. She left the school for a whole year to undertake the college diploma course, and during that time the staff had to build new relationships with the replacement teacher. Now the remedial teacher operates as an area senior remedial teacher for two days a week, leaving only three days in the week in which to support individual pupils, spend time in discussion with the promoted staff and individual class-teachers, and become involved in the planning and implementation of curriculum development.

Valley

In this school a programme of teaching language through environmental studies is being developed, and co-operative teaching has developed principally through the remedial teacher's requested involvement in producing resources for it. The staff in the upper school (P4–7), under the leadership of the head teacher, are involved in preparing teacher-devised pupil materials for the programme, and, as an extension of her work for the Open University Reading Diploma, the remedial teacher began to prepare language materials aimed at the development of a range of skills in reading and writing at the P4 stage. Over a three-year period, she has produced a number of units of materials, and the teachers look to her for support for a wider range of pupils than they would previously have done. Through the use of a skills–resources checklist, and through extensive informal assessment of the pupils' language skills, she and the teachers have been able to identify 'gaps', which she helps to fill by producing resources and by co-operative teaching.

As she has been a remedial teacher in the school for seven years, she feels that she knows the staff and the pupils well. She makes decisions as to where and when she will concentrate her co-operative teaching on the basis of her knowledge of their needs. She tends to start each year by working in the P4 and P5 stages, concentrating on language and environmental studies. This is organized by allocating blocks of time over a continuous period to the class or classes with which she is involved. Discussion with the teachers with whom she works co-operatively and with teachers of pupils to whom she gives direct tuition takes place during the preparation period at the end of the day, either in the classrooms or in the remedial teacher's base.

In stages P1–3 (comprising the youngest pupils), where the assistant head teacher supports the class-teachers in dealing with learning difficulties, the remedial teacher's role is one of discussion on difficulties experienced by individual pupils. This takes place either in the preparation period at the end of the day or, by negotiation, at any other time during the day when all the parties concerned can be free of pupil contact. The remedial teacher also gives direct tuition to pupils in P3 who have been brought to her attention by the assistant head teacher.

The peripatetic team of remedial teachers in the Cupar area

This team faced a quite different set of circumstances in attempting to respond to the regional guidelines. The three teachers shared the twenty-two schools among them, each visiting several schools every week. The time spent at each school varied from as much as two days a week at some of the larger schools to sometimes as little as one hour per week at the small schools. With no time for meaningful consultation on planning, the teachers tended to operate mainly in their direct tuition role. Feedback from them and the schools they visited indicated that this was not a satisfactory arrangement, and so discussion took place between the head teachers, the team-members and myself with a view to finding a more appropriate role for the team in the schools and designing a system of visits which would allow them to operate more effectively. The schools and the team-members said that they would welcome a much greater emphasis on a consultancy role, with the team teachers working alongside the class-teachers in planning pro-grammes for individual pupils and in providing resource support for the class-teachers. Time for this level of consultation and follow-up had to be found by a major restructuring of the team's timetables. It was decided then that, for a trial two-term period, the team would allocate blocks of continuous time to their schools and would visit them less frequently. This might mean that a school where there had been regular one-hour weekly visits would now be allocated one and a half days every six weeks. The intention was twofold: to allow for fuller consultation, at coffee breaks, lunchtimes and preparation times, and to cut down the unproductive time spent on daily travel between schools.

At the end of the trial period the following points emerged.

1   The shift of emphasis to consultancy was widely accepted by the team teachers themselves and by schools, where the staff as a whole were clear as to their own and the team teachers' roles in preventing and

dealing with learning difficulties. There was, however, some dissent from teachers who still felt that pupils with learning difficulties should not be their responsibility.

2 The preparation of written programmes and the practical support of resources from the area resource centre were very much appreciated by the schools. The team teachers found this time-consuming and had to adjust their timetables to allow for more time at their resources centre.

3 Having assessed the needs of the schools and come to an agreement with all of the head teachers in their particular group of schools, the team teachers moved towards more flexible timetabling which allowed them to engage in co-operative teaching of the programmes which they and the class-teachers had drawn up together. As a result, more children experiencing learning difficulties were brought to the team's attention and their consultancy role was expanded.

CONCLUSION

Each situation presents different priorities which result in different bases for the distribution of time spent in consultation and co-operative teaching. In some cases, co-operative teaching is planned in response to needs identified in particular groups of children; in others its purpose is to support individual teachers. It may also be used as a strategy for implementing the schools' curriculum-development plans. In some instances it is a response to two or all three of these situations. None of the schools considers that it has arrived at a model which will apply for all time; all recognize the dynamic nature of the situation. Without exception, the staff involved are continually reappraising, revising, modifying and looking for more effective ways of collaborating to make the curriculum more meaningful to a wider range of pupils.

REFERENCE

Scottish Education Department 1978: *The Education of Pupils with Learning Difficulties in Primary and Secondary Schools in Scotland: a progress report by Her Majesty's Inspectorate*. Edinburgh: HMSO.

9

Support in operation: the Linksfield area special needs team

Eileen Lorimer, Patricia Potts and Will Swann

Linksfield Academy and its feeder primary schools formed one of the first areas in Grampian to establish an area remedial team. This chapter describes how the team established itself as an integral part of all six schools, overcoming initial scepticism and resistance. Remedial teachers are now involved, in many areas of the curriculum, at all stages of the learning process from initial planning to classroom teaching. The team has more recently extended its remit to support a wider range of pupils with special needs, including hearing-impaired pupils, and has changed its title to reflect this development.

INTRODUCTION

A major reorganization of the approach to remedial education took place in the Grampian Region of Scotland in the late 1970s. For quite some time there had been a slow drift away from separate remedial classes towards a greater emphasis on withdrawal of small groups for basic-skills training. By the mid-seventies many teachers were questioning the efficiency of withdrawal methods which removed pupils from the situation in which their difficulties arose and failed to address the nature of the curriculum which might be provoking their difficulties and might be changed to facilitate their learning. This groundswell was given a major impetus and direction by a regional policy initiative which predated the Scottish HM Inspectorate Report of 1978 (Scottish Education Department, 1978). Remedial services were reorganized into area teams serving a secondary school and its feeder primaries and new staff were appointed according to the pupil population and priority rating of the schools. Each area team was headed by a principal remedial teacher, usually based full-time in the secondary school. Grampian's policy is described in more detail in chapter 7.

The novel feature of the staffing was that many of the teams worked in both primary and secondary schools and became known as *float* teachers. Figure 9.1 is a diagram of the Linksfield special needs team, indicating the distribution of staff and the proportion of time spent at each school by float teachers and other remedial and special needs teachers. An early authority document set out the new direction of policy in the following way:

Children who have learning difficulties are likely to experience such difficulties in many if not all areas of the curriculum. Hence remedial provision must be made in all subject areas.

Subject and Remedial Teachers need to work together in planning, producing and operating programmes of work for pupils with learning difficulties.

Pupils with learning difficulties will spend their time both in working with their peers in the normal class, helped by Subject Teacher and Remedial Teacher and in extra time groups for more intensive reinforcement of classwork (for example). The proportions of integration and extraction will vary with the needs of the individual child.

In order to help bridge the gap between Primary and Secondary Teachers some Remedial Teachers would work in both an Area Comprehensive School and one or more of its associated Primary Schools. (Grampian Regional Council Education Committee, 1977)

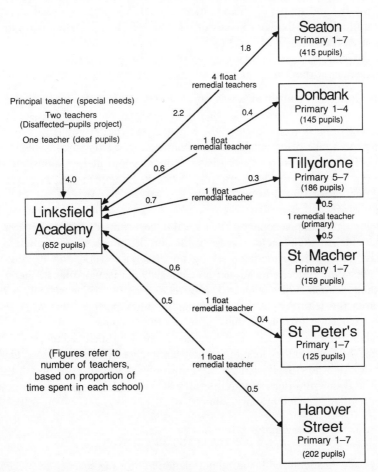

Figure 9.1 The Linksfield area special needs team

As the policies were put into practice there was an emphasis on co-operative teaching by remedial and subject-teachers and withdrawal work became frowned upon, something that was not mentioned in polite company. As chapter 21 indicates, there has gradually been a reassessment of the role and place of withdrawal or tutorial support. Teachers have begun to look at curricula with a view to assisting all pupils rather than just a group identified as having learning difficulties. The Inspectorate Report of 1978 phrased the duties of remedial teachers differently and enshrined them in what became known as the four roles. These were as follows.

1   'Consultancy': acting as a consultant for other members of staff.
2   'Direct tuition': personal tuition and support for pupils with learning difficulties in the early stages of language work and mathematics.
3   'Co-operative teaching': in co-operation with class- and subject-teachers, tutorial and supportive help in their normal classes to pupils with learning difficulties in the later stages of language work and mathematics and in any other area.
4   'Special services': providing, arranging for or contributing to special services within the school for pupils with temporary learning difficulties.

In Grampian, consultancy was underplayed and the expansion of the role of remedial teachers was seen to be an integral part of the co-operative teaching process (see chapter 20); whilst direct tuition could in some circumstances take place outside the mainstream, it was not seen to necessitate that. Pupils could be assisted in basic numeracy and literacy alongside their classmates. The main departure of practice in Grampian was, however, the introduction of the 'float'.

The principal remedial teachers play a key role in implementing and developing Grampian policy. They are the 'co-ordinator, communicator and negotiator' in their sectors, responsible for the timetabling of their team, occasional 'trouble-shooting', setting up in-service work, and liaising with the education office, educational psychologists and senior management staff of their school. They oversee the development of 'whole school' policies towards the learning difficulties of pupils. They perform this work in the same allocation of non-teaching time as other teachers.

When the new policies were introduced, the Linksfield sector was chosen as one of four sectors to pilot the developments. The rest of this chapter will describe how these changes were introduced and received in Linksfield itself and how the float system operates between Linksfield and Seaton, the largest of the feeder primary schools.

GETTING STARTED

Linksfield Academy, with a pupil population of 852 and seventy-two teachers, opened in 1975 as the result of an amalgamation of three junior secondary

schools. The head teacher of Linksfield, Ian McDonald, had been appointed
head of one of the constituent schools in 1971 and found that remedial
education was provided in a remedial class. He disapproved of such separation
and within six months had introduced a withdrawal system which continued
after amalgamation and was operated by three teachers, one from each
constituent school. This system received a massive jolt when in 1978 Eileen
Lorimer was put in charge of the new remedial team of eleven teachers in
the Linksfield area. This team consisted of five 'float' teachers, who would
work in both primary and secondary schools, two secondary teachers, three
full-time primary teachers and one part-time primary teacher. As principal
remedial teacher, her job, with the staff of her department, was to implement
the new policies and in particular introduce co-operative teaching in Linksfield to teachers totally unfamiliar with it. Initially she spent time explaining
the nature of the changes in a series of meetings with subject departments.
The response was often scepticism about the value of co-operative teaching
and at times there was open hostility. After the department had been running
for a while Ian McDonald became convinced that the changes made a very
significant improvement in the school, but at first he was not convinced that
co-operative teaching represented the best strategy. He was unsure, for
example, how a primary-trained teacher, coming in as part of the float system
and without any knowledge of science 'could come into a science room and
help someone with problems in electricity'. This kind of criticism was also
heard from the mathematics and technical-education departments of the
school. There were also negative feelings about the extra payment remedial
teachers received. Teachers grumbled that remedial staff were to be paid
more for less face-to-face teaching.

But the difficulties did not just emanate from subject departments; the
remedial department itself lacked cohesion. Secondary remedial staff were
uncertain about their new roles and about how to manage their time and
occasionally expressed a longing to return to a simple extraction system.
They doubted that they would be welcomed into subject lessons and raised
fears about role divisions and control. The float teachers, on the other hand,
were new recruits to remedial work. Some were primary-trained and they
had doubts about their ability to contribute to secondary curricula.

The English department was one of the first to welcome co-operative
teaching, but at the start remedial teachers were seen mainly as 'helpers in
the classroom', there simply to give extra assistance to children with learning
difficulties. It soon became clear that co-operative teaching could involve
much more than this. Remedial staff began to help with planning lessons,
preparing worksheets and revising existing material. In technical education,
the principal teacher began 'with an open mind, but with reservations'. He
doubted that remedial teachers could help much with teaching woodwork or
metalwork, where there is a minimum of written work and teaching is by
demonstration. But he found them useful in supporting the technical-drawing

syllabus where pupils had problems understanding the concepts and completing written work.

By the start of the second year the labours of the remedial department began to bear fruit. Most class-teachers who had experience of it acknowledged that the new approach could be made to work. They began actively to seek ways of using co-operative teaching to improve the curriculum.

PROVIDING FOR A RANGE OF SPECIAL NEEDS

Until 1984, Linksfield had a separate partial-hearing unit in addition to the remedial department. It was staffed by one teacher, who supported five children who had been transferred from the Aberdeen School for the Deaf. The teacher in charge of the unit was formally responsible to the head of that school. The children spent most of their time in mainstream lessons but were withdrawn from some English and all modern languages. However, they were not the only hearing-impaired children in the school. Another four had come to Linksfield from their primary feeder schools, supported by the peripatetic service for the deaf. One child with a moderate hearing-loss had been integrated on a part-time basis from a special school for children said to have 'behavioural problems'. These additional children were supported by the remedial staff and they too were withdrawn from modern languages. Support therefore was not co-ordinated. One class might occasionally find itself taught by a subject-teacher, remedial teacher and unit teacher. The unit teacher could not support all her five 'unit' pupils in all subjects, and increasingly the remedial department took a share in supporting them. Equally the unit teacher would often find herself in a class with time to assist pupils with learning difficulties. In mathematics, for example, two hearing-impaired pupils met with far fewer problems than some pupils said to be 'slow learners'. After extensive negotiation, the unit was merged with the remedial department so that one department is now responsible for the support of all children receiving support with their learning. This includes a small number of non-native English-speakers, children doing mainly exam courses who have specific spelling, sentence-construction or writing problems, and children with severe literacy problems who are nevertheless capable of achieving some success with alternative methods of teaching and assessment.

THE SPECIAL NEEDS DEPARTMENT 1985

The remedial department has been renamed the special needs department to reflect the extended support role of its members. It is housed in a suite of rooms in the heart of the school which are used for meetings, preparing materials, storing and displaying resources. It now comprises the principal teacher and eleven other members of the group and is one of the biggest departments in the school. Eight of these teachers 'float' between a feeder primary and Linksfield. The only members of the department based full-time at Linksfield are the principal teacher, the teacher appointed to support hearing-impaired pupils and two new staff appointed early in 1985 to a special project based at Linksfield. They offer temporary support to disaffected pupils and those experiencing emotional difficulties in the early secondary years. The project serves three schools besides Linksfield and the two teachers work intensively designing appropriate lesson material and providing support in both withdrawal and class situations. Their aim is to reintegrate the pupils in mainstream classes in their original secondary school within a six-month period.

PROGRESS IN CO-OPERATIVE TEACHING

Every subject department is now involved in co-operative teaching with special needs staff. The art department, which feels its teaching-methods are already adapted to individual needs, is only rarely involved. Styles of co-operation vary enormously. In English, Eileen Lorimer and Colin Fenn have operated lessons as a double act, sharing equal responsibilities. They plan a week ahead by finding twenty minutes free time to follow up the previous lesson and discuss the next. Within the lesson itself it may be impossible to distinguish their roles. With another first year English group, Meg Littlejohn and a subject-teacher jointly prepared material for initiating project work and then both developed and supported group work. Figure 9.2 illustrates the preparation of work around the theme 'The sea'.

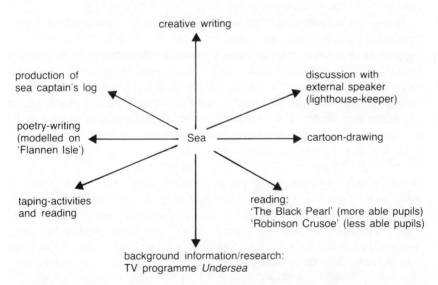

Figure 9.2 Co-operative teamwork activities in Linksfield Academy. Typical Secondary 1 project for one team: 'The sea' with group work

The special needs department has worked with subject-teachers to produce a large amount of new resource material and has extensively revised materials to allow for the realistic participation of all pupils, irrespective of ability. For example, the department has produced word searches and crosswords linked to the science syllabus in S1–3, has modified worksheets for S1 maths and has clarified and improved the design of continuous assessment tests in S3–4 social studies and science.

With the arrival of the new Standard Grade exams at 16+, which are to replace 'O'-grade and the Certificate of Secondary Education (CSE) as national exams in Scotland, the department has an additional task. Standard Grade will be awarded at three levels: Foundation, General and Credit, designed to cover the whole ability range. The remedial department has been helping subject departments to produce material for Foundation and General levels. One example of this has been the development of material in electronics, where remedial staff in close consultation with science staff have helped to design and write course material to teach children to interpret circuit diagrams and to build circuits. Two remedial staff have joined with others to plan and execute a new social and vocational studies examination course at General/Foundation level.

Another recent development has involved attempts to find alternative methods of assessment that will allow pupils with very poor reading and writing to take external exams. The department recently negotiated an agreement with the CSE board for one boy, who is effectively a non-reader, to be assessed in science and history. The exams may be recorded on tape or read to him. He may answer either onto tape, or to a scribe.

Successful collaborative working of remedial and class-teachers incorporating joint planning, joint teaching and joint review does not simply happen. Both teachers have to make a persistent effort to set aside a shared period of non-teaching time to enable them to work together at regular intervals. The flexibility afforded Eileen Lorimer to alter timetables of remedial teachers to accommodate such collaborative work can enable formal consultation to be set up at short notice. Any department may approach the principal remedial teacher for a timetable change at any time. But, even with such flexibility, pairs of teachers do sometimes have to limit their consultation to informal discussion before, during and immediately following a class lesson, which on occasion extends into school breaks and lunch hours. In general the allocation of non-class contact time to remedial staff in Linksfield is approximately in proportion to the time they spend there (it is three hours twenty minutes for ordinary full-time staff). The whole school has three weeks with more than usual non-teaching time available at the end of every school year, while the school moves to its new timetable in preparation for the next autumn term and the new S1 pupils have not yet arrived. The remedial staff use this time to collect syllabuses for the coming year, to work with class-teachers to prepare modified material to fit in with it, and to compare and discuss the progress of particular children and plan priorities.

The only timetabled withdrawal is for some hearing-impaired pupils and for spelling- and writing-tuition for examination candidates with specific difficulties, as an alternative to their leisure activities. Subject or remedial teachers can withdraw pupils when they feel it to be necessary – for example, when a pupil has been absent or for particular instruction using the computer. Withdrawal from modern languages ceased with the introduction of the oral based *Tour de France* course, based on an oral–aural approach (Scottish Central Committee on Modern Languages, 1981).

CO-ORDINATING SPECIAL NEEDS

Each June the remedial staff and unit teacher meet to revise the special needs pupils list and to discuss their timetabled support. Ideally one teacher is allocated to support an individual or group across the curriculum. But the problems of timetabling part-time float teachers can make such continuity less than perfect. Where two teachers share responsibility for a group of three hearing-impaired pupils, a weekly time is arranged for them to confer with each other, as well as consultation time with the peripatetic staff who visit about three times a week.

One teacher takes responsibility for keeping a pupil's profile up-to-date. This includes information on progress in subject classes and information about the nature and extent of any impairment, the support to be made available and any additional curriculum resources that are required. These can vary from a 'scribe' to jumbo-print books.

FUNDING AND RESOURCES

Funds are allocated to departments at Linksfield strictly according to their size, and hence the special needs department ranks with English and maths as a major recipient. It also receives a sum allocated by the local education authority to distribute to primary schools in consultation with their head teachers and remedial staff.

As the department has developed so has the nature of the resources it requires. It inherited small sets of remedial materials designed for teaching basic skills to withdrawal groups. Where appropriate, these sets have been expanded for the use of class groups, but most of the funds are now spent on the raw materials of teacher-generated curricula: spirit masters, paper, photocopying. On occasion the department's funds have been used to supplement the resources of subject departments, but it is made clear in the school that the funds of subject departments are there to support the education of the whole range of pupils.

Reconnecting remedial education

WORKING THE FLOAT: THE LINKSFIELD–SEATON CONNECTION

Staff are allocated to primary schools on the basis of one full-time equivalent per 300 children in P3–7. Seaton is one of Linksfield's five feeder schools and by far the largest, with 415 pupils. Classes are unstreamed, though children are commonly grouped according to ability within them. Parents are an integral part of the school and are becoming increasingly involved in regular school activities such as organizing the library. The school has four float teachers, whose total time in the school adds up to 1.8 teachers. It also has two assistant head teachers, one of whom is non-teaching and whose duties also involve curriculum support. Remedial support is focused on the junior years.

Seaton has gone through many of the same processes as Linksfield in response to the changed approach to remedial education. Before the regional initiative they were reducing the level of withdrawal and fostering co-ordination with the secondary school, but the new impetus to co-operative teaching and curriculum development made a considerable impact. Both remedial and class-teachers are gradually adjusting to sharing responsibility for making the curriculum appropriate for all pupils. As one class-teacher said of her remedial colleague, 'She helps me right across the board with all the children, all abilities, from my able children down to my poorer ones, and she helps in every subject. She doesn't just concentrate on reading; she helps with maths, environmental studies, anything that we're doing at the time she comes in.'

Figure 9.3 sets out the timetable for one of the remedial teachers working at Seaton, Alison Butcher. Each teacher works with about three class-teachers

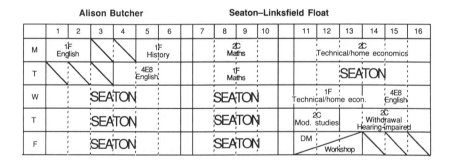

 = Non-class-contact time

DM = departmental meeting

Figure 9.3 Timetable of one float remedial teacher

for between four and five hours a week per class. At Linksfield Academy, they may work with six or occasionally even more subject-teachers. Initially, Alison Butcher was primary-trained. She completed her Diploma in Learning Difficulties, the national one-year training-course, in 1984. Meg Littlejohn, who had worked as a part-time remedial teacher in Seaton, joined the float system full-time in the same year. She holds the original primary remedial qualification.

The new diploma course is divided into primary and secondary, depending on initial training. It is far from ideal, therefore, as a training for the float system. However, a conversion course is soon to be introduced to allow teachers trained for one sector to qualify to teach in the other.

Like Meg, several teachers in the Linksfield area have transferred to a float-teacher contract. Despite the early misgivings of some of them, they have rarely experienced long-term problems in adapting to the teaching-demands of each school. The schools have begun to make use of the two-way movement of experience. Whilst group teaching and project work in Linksfield is still not commonplace, the remedial staff from the primary sector are contributing to its introduction, as in the earlier example of Meg Littlejohn's work. Alison Butcher has commented on the need for there to be more practically based work as well as a greater use of environmental resources; she finds that there is a greater expectation in secondary than in primary that she will be responsible for the pupils of limited ability. But she stresses the benefits to the pupils of working with someone familiar from their primary school with whom they can discuss any difficulties. The detailed knowledge which she brought with her obviated much of the need for testing, as she remarked: 'We know the children, and what you have to say is far more revealing than a test score.'

But primary schools have benefited from the subject expertise of experienced secondary teachers who work in the float as well as the flow of information brought by primary-trained remedial teachers. For example, Meg returned from Linksfield science department with the ingredients needed to produce an eruption in a model volcano her primary pupils had made during a project on Captain Cook's travels! Because of her particular relationships within the English department at Linksfield, her work in the two schools is quite similar. In the primary school the teachers prepare their work plans a month in advance and discuss them with the head. Meg Littlejohn is part of those discussions and plans her involvement at that stage too. She supplements the resources they discuss with new worksheets, photographs and research books, or by finding and inviting a person to come and speak to the group.

Towards the end of the school year, each float teacher identifies children transferring to Linksfield the following term who have experienced particularly marked difficulties with their primary-school work. The teacher who has been working with them in primary will then support them in their first-year mixed-ability group. Each of these pupils is the subject of a language-skills checklist, which gives basic information about reading, spelling and oral communication, and the intention is to produce a similar report for mathematics. Contact is further developed for primary pupils during their final year at primary school by four visits to Linksfield, where they spend the whole morning and join in classwork.

CONCLUSION

The new system has been running in the Linksfield area for over seven years. Particularly in the last two to three years, teachers at both Seaton and Linksfield have noticed a marked rise in the status of support teachers. Contrary to the expectation of some people, the primary schools have lagged behind the secondary schools in adopting team teaching as the main form of support for learning difficulties. Seaton is the exception in that respect. Progress is haphazard, depending as it does on the particular relationships that are struck up between staff, and hence prey to staff changes. The support staff continue, however, to attempt to tread the right side of the line between responding to expectations and working with others to change them.

REFERENCES

Grampian Regional Council Education Committee 1977: *Working Party Report on Remedial Education in Secondary Schools*. Aberdeen: Grampian Regional Council.
Scottish Central Committee on Modern Languages 1981: *Tour de France*. London: Heinemann.
Scottish Education Department 1978: *The Education of Pupils with Learning Difficulties in Primary and Secondary Schools in Scotland: a progress report by Her Majesty's Inspectorate*. Edinburgh: HMSO.

10

A room of their own: workbases at Ballingry Junior High School

Charles Weedon

In most schools, progress must be made against a background of difficult circumstances, and entrenched attitudes and practices. This account of the development of policy in one Fife secondary school is no exception. Ballingry is a school at the lower end of a selective system, in an economically depressed area. Despite this, the school has been able to innovate in ways that would be strongly resisted elsewhere. The inspiration for these innovations came from observations of primary education, although the catalyst for the developments was, as Charles Weedon explains, a concern over classroom control. He reports on the progress the school has made towards a more pupil-centred system of organization in the first two years of secondary school, though developing the teaching-methods to make the best use of such changes may be a far more difficult task.

Ballingry Junior High School serves a number of mining villages; pit closures have made these villages fairly deprived by most standards, and there is high unemployment. A low self-image is fairly common, for many pupils do not expect to succeed. In addition, the school is not fully comprehensive: a rare exception in Scottish schools. For administrative and financial reasons the building of new premises appropriate to an all-through comprehensive has been delayed again and again; increasing numbers of more able pupils leave after S4 and there is no fifth or sixth year. These factors combine to militate against optimism; they obviously do not preclude success, but they make it more difficult to achieve.

On the positive side, it is a small school, with the advantages that brings. It is very generously staffed, particularly in the learning-support service (LSS). This used to be the remedial department, but it now has a much wider role, as implied by the new title. In addition, while a low self-image in conventional terms is common and pupils do not expect material or academic success, Ballingry is a tight, supportive community, with a very strong sense of its own identity.

These circumstances combine to make it a place where the weaknesses of the conventional system are made apparent, and where circumstances favour exploration of more effective alternatives.

CONTRASTS BETWEEN PRIMARY AND SECONDARY
SCHOOLING AND TWO MODELS OF EDUCATION

Ballingry is the fourth secondary school I have worked in, either as a subject-teacher or as a remedial specialist, and a strong feeling has grown in me that the primary school works well at the upper end but that the lower secondary years are less successful. For some pupils they hardly work at all, but they should and could do so. One problem is that secondary schools are mixed-ability in composition only, and very seldom in teaching-method. Many secondary teachers doubt the effectiveness of mixed-ability work without ever having seen or tried it. Early secondary education is failing because we teach our subjects, not the children; because our whole focus, our professional centres of gravity, are determined by a tradition of subject specialism, which pays too little attention to the differences between children.

On the one hand, we have the ideal of the primary, child-centred tradition. The teacher provides, within the framework of the curriculum, what the pupils need. It's a tradition that demands close attention to the learning experience, interests and needs of individual pupils. On the other hand, we have the university model: of places where scholars specialize deeply, pursue their own studies, and gather around them groups of students, to pass on to them what they have learned within their specialism. They are specialists: the subject is all, the teaching is secondary. This model may be appropriate for a university, or for sixth-year studies; but it is not appropriate for all pupils and for all secondary years. Yet it is generally what is found.

Imagine, for a moment, a new subject being crammed into our overcrowded curriculum. Imagine that someone, somewhere, someone with clout, believes deeply and sincerely that people need to know more about – rabbits. The primary teacher shrugs, and hoists it grumblingly aboard. Hardly drops a stitch: 'If that's what they want ...'. In the secondary sector, however, there's a flurry of activity; droves of frustrated teachers apply for the rabbit course at the local college of education (the Diploma in Rabbit Studies?): there may be promotion here – *someone* will need to be Principal Teacher (Rabbits); in fact, I can think of one school that would surely run to an Assistant Rector (Rabbits). So the new specialism is born. Let's have a look in the classrooms of the two sectors, and see how they're handling it.

Primary first: perhaps the classroom looks a little empty – four are away interviewing rabbit-owners about their pets, and making notes about typical rabbit care. Another small group has gone to the library to find out what they can about the rabbits' natural habitat. In one corner, some children are sitting in front of three cages, making notes about the feeding-habits of three rather bored rabbits. On the wall are pieces of childrens' work from their Watership Down unit study. A group in another corner are working at banda worksheets, answering questions about rabbits by using the small bank of reference material provided. Another group are writing stories. Let's keep it fairly realistic: the room is not unduly quiet – one bad lad is down at a lone desk at the front, doing his work away from the others, and the group making notes by the cages are getting a bit giggly and silly; the teacher moves across the room towards them ...

Now a glimpse of the secondary classroom. It's the rabbit-studies classroom – ah, *much* better: a *proper* classroom, on the walls some rather fine posters from Heinemann's, ranging from some lovely wild-life photography of rabbits to colourful anatomical cross-sections (one or two a wee bit faded and curling, perhaps, but certainly informative). Along the back of the room, a row of cages. The rabbits in them don't seem to be listening to the lesson, but they have heard it before. The desks are in neat rows. The pupils are looking at slides of burrows and habitats. The teacher is explaining, throwing out questions as he goes to elicit from the class the next points he wishes to make. After his exposition, the class will answer questions from p. 27 of the textbook. The exercise is in two parts: section A is easier than section B, and that should keep Mrs Thingummy in the LSS off his back for a change. No one is going to accuse him of not catering for a range of needs. As he talks, he moves quietly up and down the aisles; he rather suspects that the artist who's been doing sex-change operations on the doe on p. 9 might be in this class, and he hopes the wee humorist might try again ...

What are the fundamental differences between these two classrooms, that so preoccupy me? In the primary room, there are three main points to note. First, there is a range of activities going on: it is *not* expected that everyone will be doing much the same thing at much the same time, and this simple condition is the one above all others that allows a range of needs to be met. Second, learning is self-directed and independent. In so far as pupils are accustomed to having a sequence of tasks presented to them, they can work their way through independently. Third, they are working with an adult with whom they are thoroughly familiar, and who knows each of them well. Most importantly, that tends to be reflected in the level of work, and the consistency of quality she demands from each of them.

In the secondary classroom, the rabbit specialist, who sees this class twice a week (they are thirty faces among the 300 or so he is expected to know) believes that it is an essential part of the comprehensive and mixed-ability philosophy that all pupils be exposed to the same experiences – that equality of opportunity means that grouping is wrong, ethically wrong, and that all pupils *must* have the opportunity of doing the same work. On the plus side, he is deeply interested in rabbits; he likes teaching this way; he likes kids; his enthusiasm and interest are contagious; kids *enjoy* rabbit studies.

What then are the obvious differences between the experience of the upper-primary pupils and that of the lower-secondary? First, physical stability: in the upper primary, the pupil remains in a single space, with which she can identify, and, perhaps, within which she can feel secure. Second, there is a single teacher, who knows each pupil well, and whose demands will be consistent, and based upon a thorough knowledge of the pupil's strengths and weaknesses. Third, there is an expectation in the classroom that different pupils will be doing different things at any one time – this contrasts sharply with the still widely extant secondary tradition, where, broadly speaking, a lesson is delivered, and the class responds largely as a single unit.

At Ballingry, our workbase experiment has sought to consider how and whether these three aspects of primary philosophy and approach might transfer usefully to a secondary school. There exists at present a very abrupt transition between two systems that are widely different, both in their underlying models of education and in their practice. There is evidence that this abrupt transition is harmful, most obviously so to those pupils with learning difficulties. It may be appropriate, therefore, to have an intermediate stage that reflects the best of both. This is one way of trying to find out just what 'the best of both' may be.

WORKBASES: PROVIDING STABILITY

The original decision to set up the workbases was taken early in the school year 1982–3, a few months before I joined the school. The idea had come from the principal teacher of mathematics, who was worried about a particularly difficult first-year intake and was keen to establish a stable regime and to work co-operatively with a remedial teacher. The authority agreed to provide the extra staffing but there was opposition to the scheme from some specialist teachers. Assistant head David Morgan, chair of the PLD (pupils with learning difficulties) committee said,

> Specialist teachers didn't like the idea at all, and we almost had to force the idea on them. But over a period of time I think they began to see that there was benefit from this. Some of them are still not completely sold on the idea. I think perhaps for it to work properly they had to structure their work a great deal more. It's not the case that they can go into the classroom and teach off the cuff as perhaps they were used to doing. They had to prepare, particularly when there was another teacher in with them.

When the workbases were introduced in the autumn term of 1983, there were four first-year classes and two workbase rooms. Each class therefore spent half their time in a workbase, two classes sharing one workbase. Classes were taught English, French, Maths and social subjects in their workbases. In the autumn of 1984, the roll in the first year had dropped from ninety to seventy-four, so it was decided to retain one second-year class on a workbase timetable, to compare their progress with the other three classes, and to spread the learning-support over a wider variety of class groups.

The secondary curriculum precludes the use of a single space for all learning. PE, science, technical studies and home economics, for example, all demand their own specialist spaces. But other subjects can be taught in one room with the subject-teacher coming to the pupils, instead of *vice versa*. Like some of their teachers, however, pupils do not, on the whole, like this arrangement, as it does not accord with their expectations of the 'big school'.

So what do they gain? They can identify with the room: on the walls can be work that represents their studies in several areas. Time is saved, too, with one lesson starting soon after the previous one ends. Less able and less confident pupils do not have to make an endless sequence of readjustments: new subject, new room, new deskmate. Only the subject changes, the room does not, and the pupil will probably be working in the same group. Pupils in S1 spend half their day, in a single block of time, in the workbase. They have with them a second teacher for much/all of this time, a member of the LSS.

USING THE CO-OPERATIVE TEACHER AS A PRIMARY-STYLE CLASS-TEACHER

The LSS teacher is there partly in a straightforward support role. When a pupil gets stuck, or a group needs something explained again, or in more detail, there are two teachers to help with this, instead of one. Partly, though, this co-operative teacher is carrying out some of the less explicit roles of the primary teacher: he/she knows each child, as well as the child's chameleon-like ability to be one pupil in one subject and quite another person (lazier or inclined towards disruptive behaviour) in another class. The support teacher knows that this pupil is capable of a certain standard of work, and the pupil knows that the teacher knows. Hence, perhaps there follows a more consistent output across the curriculum.

The single co-operative teacher is able to form more lasting relationships with pupils, or, if not more lasting, certainly closer. Most secondary teachers see more than a hundred pupils in the course of a day. Pupils may go to a certain teacher for only one or two periods a week. These factors combine to produce contexts that can be both impersonal and anonymous. Perhaps the pupils most at risk from this are those who have no obvious problems: the quiet, rather below average, whose names always take so long to remember, who seldom make their presence felt. The workbase teacher knows these children well. Further, he/she knows the child 'across the curriculum'; this overview of the interaction between learner and secondary curriculum is probably quite unique, and allows opportunity to know both when to help and how to help.

GROUPINGS

Many secondary teachers do not favour ability grouping within classes, arguing that this carries the stigma of streaming, made more overt by the fact that it occurs in the one room. This seems indisputable, but there are some advantages in retaining ability groups. It is not intended that pupils should always work in such groups, and in the workbases we also use alternative mixed groups. The ideal would be one of considerable flexibility. In practice, teachers have found that classes work better in one of the two ways, and have gone on to use that way most of the time. There has not been an obvious pattern to the results. One maths teacher, for example, favours mixed groups, while another favours ability groups; one French teacher teaches one of his S1 classes in mixed groups, and the other in ability groups. It has been a case of seeing which works best for which pupils and teachers together. The nature of the subject, or the teachers' general views, have not been critical.

DEVELOPMENT OF APPROPRIATE METHODS AND MATERIALS

This is the biggest job of all, the critical factor in effective mixed-ability teaching. Pupils come up from good primary schools used to working on their own, or in small groups; they are self-directed and fairly independent learners, and treated as such. There is no expectation that all the learners in the room will be studying the same thing at the same time, or doing the same work. But this expectation dominates most secondary classrooms, manifesting itself in an interpretation of the comprehensive philosophy which suggests that all pupils must do, or at least be offered, the same work; anything less discriminates against the less able. If a tradition is to be changed, then the means must be at hand to bring about the change. When a teacher accepts that different pupils might need different approaches into a topic, or different materials to work on, it is three quarters of the battle, and yet just the beginning. Differentiated materials must be available, and so far they are not, or not in any significant quantity. Further, the methods of classroom organization and control that that teacher has developed and honed down will need to be changed. Certainly the still-extant criterion of excellence for many teachers, a roomful of quiet heads bent to their jotters, will need to be changed.

The workbase context facilitates change. Where there are two teachers in the room it should be much easier to become aware of a range of needs and to respond to them. There are also two teachers instead of one to prepare more appropriate materials. It may be that the most effective use of the two, on occasions, is for one to use the lesson for preparation of course materials, while the other teaches.

This is a slow change, involving as it does a shift in attitudes. Once the will is there, methods and class organization can be experimented with. What will take time is the building-up of a bank of appropriate, differentiated materials that allow differentiated teaching. The successful practice we see in the primaries rests upon just such a foundation of appropriate resources, and it is a foundation conspicuously lacking as yet in secondary schooling.

PRIMARY–SECONDARY LIAISON

A programme of visits has taken secondary subject-teachers involved in the workbases down to visit the local P7 classes, and almost all have come away asking the question, 'What are we doing to them?' Pupils in upper primary seem to be learning more independently, more effectively, more enthusiastically and in a more self-directed way than they do in lower secondary. Certainly, the quality of work in comparable subject areas, between P7 and S1, gives cause for reflection.

We are lucky in having only two feeder primaries, both interested in developing continuity of experience between the ages of ten and fourteen, and in which there are classes and teachers well able to act as exemplars of what can be achieved with good primary methods and approaches. All teachers involved in the workbases have spent a morning working in a P7 classroom; it was hoped that this would raise in their minds the question, 'What are we doing wrong?'

Almost without fail, this has happened. Even those teachers long critical of primaries and their methods have been unable to miss the contrast between the two contexts, and this helps their receptiveness towards change. It has been interesting, though, to see how such impressions can fade, to be replaced by the earlier views. Some kind of regular contact will be necessary if the impression is to last, and this is expensive in teacher time.

There has been an open invitation to P7 staff to visit the workbases, and this has been taken up; it is hoped to develop this, and have P7 teachers regularly working in the workbases, as co-operative teachers, perhaps for a period or two a week.

There is also a routine visit to each primary, for part of one morning each week, by an LSS member. This teacher works in the P7 classroom as a co-operative teacher, thus getting to know both the pupils and the curriculum they have experienced.

Here we are getting dangerously close to the limits of what we can do without support from above: people routinely working in a sector they're not normally involved in. One may soon hear restless noises from professional associations, although I think that at this level such involvement should be acceptable. No one will be taking classes for which he/she is not qualified, but the support teacher will just occasionally be working in them alongside the normal teacher.

CONCLUSIONS AND IMPLICATIONS

At the end of the first session, the feeling seemed to be one of very limited and cautious optimism: the year's S1 did seem to be better than the previous year's on the whole, but it was too early to ascribe this to the workbases.

The subjectivities involved in the evaluation, too, are very varied: some of those considering the success or failure of the project are doing so from a standpoint of enthusiastic desire for change, while others involved retain grave doubts about the need for any change at all. In general, though, results have been promising enough for there to have been no resistance to a continuation of the project into a second year; indeed, all felt this was necessary, that it was too early to draw conclusions.

At a meeting in February, 1985, the board of studies (senior management team) and the principal teachers' group reviewed the workbases once more. They decided that the second year had not been as successful as the first, mainly because of the reduction in co-operative learning-support. For 1985–6, therefore, it was decided to revert to maximum learning-support and to place more emphasis on the physical environment and attractive resources (displays, books, and so on). Moreover, there is an agreement to discuss further such issues as differentiated material, differentiated assessment, diagnostic use of assessment, spelling policy, reading/book-use policy and pupil discussion.

THE FUTURE: A PIPE-DREAM

If it's not obvious yet that I have a most marked bias towards certain primary features, then I have certainly failed to make myself clear. I would like to see a classroom that retains the best of both worlds:

1 sometimes a range of activities occurring simultaneously;
2 pupils sometimes working independently through their programmes of tasks and assignments;
3 exposure to the enthusiasm and expertise of the specialist's perspective;
4 more exposure to an adult whom pupils know well, who knows the pupils well and who expects much of them.

Our workbases achieved objectives 3 and 4 last year, but we hoped for more movement in the achievement of the first two.

What we had in mind, and discussed, was a complete reversal of roles between subject-teacher and co-operative teacher, for one S1 class, for one year. The co-operative teacher, then, would be the class-teacher and the subject departments would set the targets to be achieved by the end of S1. The pupils in this class would do all the same tests and assessments as the rest. The subject-teachers would be at hand to do some of the direct teaching, to advise and to do all the things their subject expertise renders them qualified to do. They would almost be guest lecturers, if you like. The class-teacher, though, would organize the pupils and manage the class, set the work, arrange the groupings. In a word, do it like the primaries.

11

ਪੜ੍ਹਾਈ - ਸਿਖਾਈ ਵਿਚ ਆਉਂਦੇ ਹਾਲੀਆਂ ਮੁਸ਼ਕਿਲਾਂ ਦਾ ਤੋਰਵਾ.

Edgewick Community Primary School

Gerry Bailey and Karen Skoro

*As Section One illustrates, coming to an adequate understanding of any child's
learning is a demanding and complex task. The task may be more difficult when
teacher and child do not share a common first language. In this chapter, Gerry
Bailey and Karen Skoro chart the development of a policy on difficulties in learning
in a school where the great majority of children speak a language other than English
at home. As this policy was being developed, the school also participated in a local-
authority initiative on learning difficulties, the Special Needs Action Programme
(SNAP); this chapter also charts the school's use of this material, and the way it
was transformed as it became absorbed into the school's practice.*

EDGEWICK SCHOOL'S POLICY ON LEARNING DIFFICULTIES

Edgewick Community Primary School lies in the centre of Coventry's 'railway
triangle'. This is an area of mainly old terrace housing, rented by families
from India, Pakistan, the Caribbean and parts of Europe. The school has
180 pupils, most of whom come from families of Indian and Pakistani origin.

The children are generally bilingual – that is, able to speak both their
mother tongue and English. Fluency in each language varies from those few
children who have recently arrived in Coventry with very little English but
with a high degree of, usually, oral fluency in their mother tongue, to those
children born and brought up in Coventry of parents also born in Coventry.
These 'third-generation' children are more fluent in English than their
'mother tongue'.

The principles of the school are described in this extract from the school's
policy document:

The notion of a good learning environment in which all feel at ease, all are encouraged,
and all enjoy learning is paramount. Efforts have been made to remove the labels of
'remedial' and other self-fulfilling prophetic remarks. The roles of learner and teacher
have, at times, been reversed – children have been given a status which allows them
to actively contribute to their learning, rather than passively receive what the teacher
wants to teach. All classes are relatively small. This gives the opportunity for closer

relationships between teacher and child – for more interaction and for deeper understanding. It also allows for more opportunities for the active involvement of children in their own learning. All these fundamentals have moved us towards a more realistic understanding of children's competences, and away from presumptions and suppositions based on snippets of observable performance.

THE DEVELOPMENT OF THE POLICY

The present policy has taken time to develop. Up until January 1983, the school's response to the diversity of its pupils was to concentrate on developing children's fluency in English. Children's competence in their mother tongue was largely ignored, although it was used in school as a medium for occasional story-telling and informal oral work. Because of the emphasis on competence in English, there was a vertically grouped remedial class of fifteen seven- to eleven-year-olds, in which the language could be reinforced. The general feeling amongst the staff at this time was that children's learning difficulties were not really being identified and analysed. We felt that we needed to reappraise our approach to difficulties in learning.

The school had a generous staffing-ratio, because of two extra ESL (English as a second language) specialists seconded from the Coventry Minority Group Support Service. We were also expecting to have a bilingual language aide, funded by a Manpower Services Commission project, joining us in September 1983. She would work mainly in the role of an education assistant, particularly to help reception-class children settle into school. And, among our eleven full-time and two part-time staff, we had three bilingual teachers and two with ESL training.

We started to discuss how best to develop language work in the school. These discussions, and subsequent collection of information and planning of how to reorganize classes, carried on through the next two terms. We aimed to put our plans into practice in the autumn term 1983. We had an agreed starting-point: to make a considerable effort to meet the specific language needs of individual children. To identify those needs, we decided to gather information about the language skills which our pupils already possessed. We discovered that this was not as straightforward a task as it seemed. The only information we had in school was the list of countries of origin of each child's father, which we have to note each year for the local education authority. Broad categories such as 'Indian' told us little about our children's fathers' languages, which we knew included Panjabi and Gujerati, to say nothing of languages which might be passed on through the mothers.

Another source, which looked as if it might be more useful, was the results of the Linguistic Minorities Project Survey (1983), carried out in Edgewick and other schools. This survey included information on which languages each child in the school could read or write, and it did give us a rough idea (albeit twelve months out of date) of the breadth of language present in the school. But the survey had been administered by individual class-teachers, with varying degrees of linguistic knowledge, and it was not designed to show the total language pattern of individual children; it did not investigate their competence in English, or look into their level of fluency in the other languages.

There was a third source of information, which did give us a much fuller picture of the fluency of twelve seven-year-old pupils in both Panjabi and English. This came from the trialling of the Sandwell Test[1] in our school by a member of the Minority Group Support Service. However, even this information was open to alternative interpretations. One problem with the results of the tests was that, if a child used an English word where he didn't know the Panjabi one, then this counted as an 'error' in his Panjabi, in spite of the fact that Panjabi spoken in Coventry is often sprinkled with English words. We ended up producing two sets of results, one including and one excluding these kinds of 'errors' (children did not use Panjabi words in the place of unknown English ones). We were also unhappy about the fact that some children might have found the test very intimidating – being taken out of their class into a room with a strange adult and a tape-recorder – and that this might have affected the results.

Because of this basic lack of information we decided that we would carry out our own mother-tongue survey at the beginning of the autumn term of 1983. We had also by this time reached agreement on a number of other matters:

1 The remedial class was to be disbanded. We felt children in this class were making little progress, and there was a reluctance among staff to take the class – a feeling of 'Oh, surely it's not my turn this year.' The children themselves felt that they had been 'labelled', and tended to live up to the expectations of such labelling.
2 Each child's total language should be examined, and used as a starting-point for providing learning opportunities. The mother-tongue survey would be an important part of this work.
3 Each child's mother tongue should be used, where appropriate and practical, in addition to English, as a medium for learning. This would mean our three bilingual teachers could use their own language repertoires more extensively in their teaching.
4 As a multicultural school, Edgewick should use every available and appropriate means to ensure that each child's cultural background is recognized to be of value, and is seen as a vital part of school life.

We decided to set up a learning difficulties team of three teachers, who would work throughout the school with class-teachers and groups of children, rather than being allocated to specific classes of their own. We hoped the term 'learning difficulties' would give these teachers a very broad base on which to work – on the understanding that everyone experiences 'learning difficulties' of one sort or another.

In setting up possibilities for team teaching, flexible groupings and more collaboration generally, we hoped to break down the barrier between class-teachers and specialist teachers who had traditionally withdrawn small groups of children in order somehow to 'cure' their problems. Class-teachers sometimes felt distrustful of the remedial or ESL teacher, who had, in their eyes, the easy and enviable job of only working with a few children at a time. At the same time, the specialist teachers often felt insecure in the mainstream classroom, feeling that the class-teachers just wanted them to take some difficult children off their hands. We wanted teachers to feel more confident about working with each other, and more able to share their skills and expertise.

We worked out specific job descriptions for each of the teachers in the learning difficulties team. Briefly, one would have major responsibility for ESL stage 1 work and resources throughout the school, one for mother-tongue work and ESL stage 2[2], and one for 'remedial work' and home-school links. This third teacher, although a monolingual English speaker herself, had already done considerable work in involving parents in school life, and encouraging the local community to use the school resources. Our efforts to survey children's languages, and organize mother-tongue teaching might well have been less successful had we not been working in an atmos-phere of strong support from parents, who were themselves involved with community evening classes in Gujerati, Panjabi and Urdu on the school premises. The home–school links teacher was to set up mutual-support groups of parents, and to work especially with parents whose children were finding difficulty with the mainstream curriculum. She was responsible for initiating workshops in which parents could find out more about how maths, reading, and so on, are taught in school, and was also responsible for initiating a home reading-scheme.

It was clear that such initiatives, though valuable in themselves, did not always reach the parents whose children were experiencing difficulties in learning. The teacher had then the task of recruiting these parents into partnership. This was done slowly by carefully establishing a sound and trusting relationship. Parents were visited, and befriended. In this way involvement emerged. Parents began to come into school for all sorts of reasons.

Within school, this teacher worked mainly with small groups of children identified, through negotiations with class-teachers, as being in need of support because of learning difficulties not necessarily stemming from ESL. The work with these children had strong connections with the mainstream curriculum – maths, project/topic work, English, and so on. Beyond this, the teacher also spent considerable time in classrooms working with groups of children. For example, this teacher was a member of a team of four teachers involved in a class topic. As such, she took those children who had some learning difficulty (other than ESL) which prevented them from fully participating in this project. One other support (as opposed to class) teacher was bilingual – and so could help with those children who could understand better in their mother tongue than in English. But roles were flexible: each member of the team also took key lessons in this project.

In summary, these developments allowed the school to have a deeper insight into each child's abilities and a closer understanding of their learning difficulties. The learning difficulties team, with its individual teacher specialisms, could then be brought into action to help meet each child's needs.

THE SPECIAL NEEDS ACTION PROGRAMME (SNAP)

Coincidentally, Coventry Local Education Authority was developing the Special Needs Action Programme, which we felt might be of valuable help in meeting these needs.

SNAP is an in-service training initiative, providing information, courses, materials and support. It was devised as a response to the 1981 Education Act and the Warnock Report. It addresses itself to the special educational needs of children in ordinary schools. SNAP comprises a series of modules, the first of which concentrated on learning difficulties. Additional modules have focused on hearing, vision, problem behaviour, daily measurement and ethnic minorities. This chapter is concerned with the learning difficulties module, which was the only SNAP initiative existing at that time. It has been described as follows:

During the early part of the course, use is made of the 'Basic Skills' Checklist' (BSC) which consists of a list of skills in six areas of development, i.e. arithmetic, language, reading, social competence, spelling and writing. The items included in the BSC are based on 'market research' of those aspects of the curriculum that primary school teachers feel to be particular problems for their pupils. It is stressed, however, that the content is not seen as being comprehensive and that users are free to add further skills or, indeed, areas of concern.

Once priorities have been determined, the teachers then learn how to write these as performance objectives and, if necessary, apply simple task analysis strategies to form more finely graded teaching steps. These programmes are used to conduct a more detailed assessment of the child's existing capabilities, for planning teaching methods and materials, and for monitoring progress using a simple checklist format which can be dated as the child proceeds.(Ainscow and Muncey, 1983, pp. 120–1)

SNAP was introduced into schools in the first instance by head teachers, who at an initial meeting were asked to designate a member of staff to act as 'co-ordinator for special needs' in their school. It was to be part of the role of the co-ordinator to familiarize the staff with SNAP and assist teachers in the development of appropriate programmes of work for their pupils. In order to do this, the teacher who had been chosen to be co-ordinator participated in the course described above.

From past experience, and judging from reports from other schools, it was decided that the best way of introducing the materials into Edgewick was through a 'whole-school' approach. This meant that each member of staff would be required to attend a school-based course during the first half of the autumn term, run by the co-ordinator and the school's educational psychologist.

The initial reactions were much as expected. For example, no one was particularly happy about the prospect of giving up a series of lunch times, and having to do extra work in the process! Also, as the course progressed and teachers were beginning to undertake their own case studies, the problems that had been encountered by the co-ordinators on the initial course came to the forefront. Comments included, 'How do I find time to do this *and* teach the class?'; 'How do I know if the problems that this child is having are due to the fact that English is his second, and probably weaker, language?' (A module on ethnic minority children has since been produced to attempt to tackle this problem.)

Other reactions included a general feeling that the approach was too formal. Most teachers agreed with the principle that learning should proceed by small steps, but felt that this could be and was being achieved without the formality of filling in forms such as the basic-skills checklist, and the actual recording of the plan of work.

THE SCHOOL'S USE OF SNAP

The effects that SNAP has had in Edgewick are difficult to assess. The chief criticism that some teachers had was that it was 'artificial', especially so in the sensitive and caring atmosphere that was growing as the school was working towards being a small family–community school. This movement had given the staff a greater understanding of family backgrounds and circumstances, which made for a working-context from which more accurate judgements, rather than assumptions, could be made about each child's difficulties in learning.

SNAP's concern seemed to be only with specific, isolated skill-learning. For us, it seemed to bypass the crucial issue of the quality of the working and personal relationships between child and teacher, and to leap to an oversimplified belief that learning will follow from teaching. The fact that the first language of most of the children in Edgewick is not English had led us rapidly to realize that, unless there is a clear channel of communication, intended learning will not happen. And this is not just a matter of not understanding the teacher's English; it is also very much a matter of ensuring that those small steps that SNAP is concerned with are taken from a fully understood, not assumed, starting-point of ability. This, we were convinced, required close relationships between teacher, child, family and community.

In this context, SNAP became a tool to be used in helping children move on in their learning. The principles of SNAP, rather than its products, became the tool. The basic-skills checklist was very rarely used, but the principles provided a basic approach.

This avoided the artificiality of 'SNAP for five minutes a day'. The approach was used both within the mainstream and support curriculum to help children overcome specific learning difficulties, and also to encourage personal development. We disagreed with SNAP's emphasis on 'social competence', for this seemed too clinical in its interpretation of those skills necessary for social life. Teachers felt that it was not realistic to isolate those skills and develop them to a 'standard'. Rather, an emphasis upon personal development has been adopted which again highlights the importance of the quality of relationships between teacher and learner.

Specific programmes of work were outlined for a small number of children, but two in particular illustrate the way in which the SNAP materials and approach were used. The first example, Nasim, shows learning difficulties that were clearly defined. They were associated with a lack of English-language development, and behaviour problems followed as a result of the learning difficulties. With Nasim we came closest to using the SNAP material directly. The second example, Nadeem, shows a more complex situation where disruptive behaviour and lack of English masked a difficulty with learning. Here we found the quality of personal relationships to be a critical factor.

Nasim

Nasim is the third of seven children. Before coming into school as a four-year-old, she had attended a pre-school group. When she came to school she already had a group of friends whom she knew quite well. With the teacher, however, she was shy and sometimes very stubborn. She had little communication in English, so was withdrawn daily from the classroom with a small group for ESL help. In her first year at school she made good progress in her spoken English, quickly building up a 'survival' vocabulary. But progress was slow in her pre-reading, pre-writing and number skills. At first this was thought to be due to the fact that she was one of the youngest in the class, and that she had little communication in English. During her second year at school, she continued to join the ESL group, but it was clear that her reading, writing and number skills were not progressing at the same rate as her oral language. As the months progressed, she became more disruptive in the group, and more withdrawn in the classroom.

The class-teacher, becoming increasingly worried about Nasim's progress, consulted the SNAP co-ordinator about the possibility of using the materials to help Nasim. Before this, though, it was decided that perhaps one way forward would be for someone to talk to her in her mother tongue to see if her language acquisition was appropriate for her age. If her mother tongue was not fully developed for her age, then there was the possibility that the problem was language-based, and not limited to problems with reading, writing and number. The result of this was that she communicated well in her mother tongue, so the class-teacher and SNAP co-ordinator decided to try the SNAP materials.

Two areas of work were decided on as priorities, and the SNAP co-ordinator, in consultation with the class-teacher, outlined two programmes of work to be undertaken in the classroom: one for letter formation, and one for a basic sight vocabulary.

After a week or so it was clear that this method was not going to be successful. The class-teacher had a particularly difficult group of children and found it hard to find the time to work with Nasim on the programmes in the classroom. Nasim was enjoying the extra attention but was not experiencing a great measure of success, because there wasn't always time every day to work with the teacher on her own. So the remedial teacher took over the SNAP programmes and withdrew Nasim from the classroom to teach her on her own. This was in addition to the ESL group work she was receiving.

Reviewing the situation after a few weeks showed good results. The programmes were extended and continued. Nasim responded well to being able to see her own progress. The success of this approach was carried over into the classroom to a certain extent as Nasim grew in self-confidence. However, she is still achieving below the level of her peers.

Nadeem

Nadeem is the third of six children. He first became known to us at school when he was two years old. At family assembly times he would prove to be uncontrollable by his mother, father, aunt or anyone else who tried to take him in hand. On entering school at four years old, having spent a year attending a pre-school group, his behaviour problems were still fairly severe, although he began to settle down in the classroom.

Nadeem's first language is Mirpuri, and his communication in English was not very proficient. However, he did not receive any extra help with English in his first year. At the beginning of his second year at school, though, it was decided that he needed additional help, as his progress was slow. Because his English was poor it was decided that the ESL teacher should withdraw him from classwork for half an hour daily. She decided to work with him on his own because he was so disruptive with other children. Nadeem was delighted to be receiving all this extra attention, but was unable to concentrate on even the very short activities arranged for him. After what turned out to be a trial period of a few weeks and no obvious progress it was decided to try a different approach. The member of the learning difficulties team who gives mother-tongue support and teaches ESL, suggested that perhaps working through the medium of Nadeem's home language might help. He also thought that, being a man, he might make a difference to Nadeem's attitude.

He was right. The additional help with reading and language activities that Nadeem received proved to be much more successful. Nadeem responded positively; his behaviour and his reading improved.

After a few months the situation was reviewed, and it was decided that Nadeem had made sufficient progress to join a group to continue his additional work. The group working with the remedial teacher on a reading programme directly connected to the reading-scheme in use in Nadeem's class was identified as the appropriate way forward for Nadeem. These materials had been devised in the same way as the SNAP 'small-steps' approach, and were to be used with children who were experiencing difficulties working through the reading-scheme in the normal way. Since joining this group Nadeem has proved himself able to work less disruptively, with longer spans of concentration, and is making good progress through the scheme using this approach.

FURTHER DEVELOPMENTS

In September 1985, owing to an increase in the number of young children starting at this school, one member of the learning difficulties team transferred to become a class-teacher in school. This has meant that the ESL and mother-tongue dimensions of the work can continue, but work with children with learning difficulties not associated with ESL has fallen more on the class-teacher. All class-teachers have responded positively to this and, though it has not been in effect for long, the new arrangement seems to work well. Frequently the school's two part-time teachers are used to take classes while class-teachers work with specific groups of children in the same room. This decentralizing of work with children with some learning difficulties has meant that the essentials of the SNAP approach (though not the materials) can be seen throughout the school. It is, however, difficult to judge the exact impact of SNAP. How far the school would have been any different without the initiative is almost impossible to say. We adapted the approach and made it less formal through the quality of the relationship between teachers and children.

NOTES

1 *Diagnostic Expressive Language (Syntax): tests of L1 Panjabi and L2 English*, produced by Sandwell Local Education Authority. A screening-version of this test, *Sandwell Screening Assessment for Expressive L1 Panjabi and L2 English*, is to be published by NFER/Nelson.
2 The two stages of learning English as a second language are not always clearly defined. However, for our purposes we defined the stages as follows.

   Stage I. Children whose English is at a very elementary level, and who therefore cannot cope with the curriculum without extra help and support. Their English, because of their limited knowledge of the language, is weak at a functional level, i.e. they have insufficient English to join in with or comprehend classroom events.

Stage II. Children whose spoken English is reasonably developed, but shows signs of structural error. There may also be, behind an apparent fluency, a lack of comprehension, especially in the reading and writing of English.

REFERENCES

Linguistic Minorities Project 1983: *Linguistic Minorities in England: summary report.* London: University of London, Institute of Education.

Ainscow, M. and Muncey, J. 1983: Learning difficulties in the primary school: an in-service training initiative. *Remedial Education*, 18 (3), 116–124.

12

Pulling together: a support system for Whitmore High School

Christine Gilbert

In this chapter, Christine Gilbert, head of Whitmore, describes the progress the school has made in transforming its support services from a traditional remedial department organized on a withdrawal basis to a broadly based learning-support department. To achieve this, the school examined all its support resources, including a unit for disruptive pupils, and a 'delicate unit'. It has welded these disparate entities into one integrated support team. Development has been more than purely organizational: the school as a whole has looked critically at its teaching and assessment methods and curriculum policies. The changes have been aimed not at catering for a defined group of children, but at increasing the school's ability to respond to diversity in its pupils.

BACKGROUND

Whitmore is an eight-form entry co-educational school in the London Borough of Harrow, catering for pupils aged between twelve and sixteen. The building dates from the late 1940s, but the existing school was established as a comprehensive in 1974, when the separate boys' and girls' secondary moderns on the site were amalgamated. There are just under 900 pupils on roll, and these come from a fairly mixed catchment area. The school has the equivalent of fifty-six full-time teachers.

In January 1983, I was appointed head teacher. I believe it is important for the school to find ways of valuing all of its pupils and am committed to mixed-ability teaching as one of the key ways of doing this. From the beginning I was keen to establish an ethos in the school which ensured that children were perceived as individuals with particular strengths and with different ways of learning different things.

The school is organized in year groups and around traditional subject areas with average class sizes of twenty-five to twenty-six pupils. While in 1983 there was considerable mixed-ability grouping in the lower school, setting was the practice in the final two years. Whole-class teaching was the norm, and there was a heavy reliance on written work. Generally, examinations reflected formal teaching, involved little continuous assessment and more innovative Mode 3 exams were offered in only two or three subject areas.

The image of the school locally was not good and the school was under-subscribed. This had the very positive effect of making many of the staff receptive to the ideas for change coming from the new head. Most were keen to be involved in establishing a whole-school philosophy and policies, and the school embarked on a process of self-evaluation and planning. This has led to changes in various aspects of Whitmore's curriculum and organization. Most departments have by now, for instance, recognized the need to develop strategies which give all pupils access to the whole curriculum. The developments which have taken place in special needs provision within the school need to be set against this background.

This chapter offers a brief description of special needs provision in 1983 and this is then followed by an outline of the major phases of change: the initial discussions of classroom practice and learning within the school as a whole; the integration of 'delicate' children at Whitmore; the in-service training offered by pilot work on the Open University pack *Teaching for diversity; preventing difficulties in learning*; and, finally, the reorganization of special needs provision in 1985.

SPECIAL NEEDS PROVISION IN 1983

The remedial department consisted of a head of department (Scale 3) and two part-time teachers. It was organized on fairly traditional lines with a strong belief in regular testing and in what was referred to as 'literacy tuition'. Teaching was in withdrawal groups of differing sizes. Friendly links were established with 'feeder' schools and with parents. Fairly soon after arrival I changed the name of the department to 'learning-support'. I did so, however, with insufficient debate about what this entailed and, consequently, practice remained largely unchanged. There were a few attempts to support pupils within the classroom, but for various reasons these did not prove generally successful and withdrawal remained the pattern.

The school also had a Scale 3 'special-unit' teacher who did not belong to the normal teaching establishment. This was one of four posts in Harrow authorized by the Education Committee in 1976 as provision for on-site assistance for pupils who had become disruptive. Based in a room away from the main body of the school, he was used to contain pupils when they had misbehaved or, more rarely, to prevent major problems occurring by early counselling. His perception of his own work in relation to the school's curriculum is aptly summed up in an extract from a paper he prepared early in 1983:

There are certain pupils in the schools who experience particular problems in specific subject areas only. In some instances, it is almost impossible to reconcile the pupil's needs with what the school has to offer. In these cases, I can withdraw pupils and pursue a different and more relevant field of study or modify an existing course to suit the needs of the pupil.

A member of the local education authority's English as a Second Language (ESL) and Multicultural Support Team was also attached to the school for three and a half days a week. She taught pupils in small withdrawal groups. While there were genial and informal links between these teachers, they were located in different parts of the building and sometimes saw the same children for apparently different reasons.

THE BEGINNINGS OF CHANGE

Between January and July 1983 various staff working-parties met, and in September a formal consultative structure was set up which encouraged staff collaboration in the review and development of all aspects of the school's work. To encourage joint planning, it was agreed that the school should close early one day each week so that teachers could meet in departmental, and less frequently, year teams. After school on other days, cross-curricular committees of interested staff were also set up to examine aspects of the school's curriculum and organization. Well over half the staff participated in these groups. The structure helped the establishment of active and supportive team work.

By September 1983 the school had the basis of a common curriculum. In the lower school all students were to study the same subjects and, for the first time, both boys and girls were to study home economics and craft, design and technology. Previously, course allocation had been on the basis of sex. In the upper school, the 'cafeteria' option pattern was superseded by one which demanded that each student should study, in addition to the usual core subjects, at least one science subject, one branch of the humanities and one creative/practical subject. It was recognized, however, that there was still much to be done. In particular, there was a need to consider how teams could work on developing teaching strategies and approaches which would give all pupils access to curricula. With this in mind two key appointments were made. The first was a curriculum deputy who began work at Whitmore in September 1983, and the second a pastoral deputy who started a term later. The latter had as part of his job the task of developing and co-ordinating the special needs provision within the school. There was to be considerable overlap between the roles of the deputies. The school's pastoral system was to be developed, for instance, in a way which supported pupils' learning. Year heads were to be responsible for the organization of the new internal-assessment system, which involved regular reviews of each pupil's progress. Their image as 'fire-fighters' was also shifted to some extent by their involvement in the pastoral programme which was being introduced into tutorial time. The year staff welcomed these moves, which involved them significantly in the responsibility for pupils' learning.

Towards the end of 1983 and throughout 1984, staff had begun to talk about how children learn and were discussing ways of focusing on what children were doing in lessons. With the emphasis on processes within the classroom, departments looked at methods of observation. Teachers in the mathematics department planned a series of visits to one another's lessons over some weeks and this led to better understanding departmentally and to discussion of classroom organization and to some course-planning. This approach was taken further by the English department, which worked out a more collaborative 'pairing' programme for sharing lessons over a fairly long period. The new teacher from the borough English as a Second Language and Multicultural Support Team was interested in getting into classrooms. He worked with a member of the English department doing group work with a class in the lower school and some of these sessions were filmed on video so that they could be discussed later. He worked also with a history teacher sharing completely in the planning, implementation and marking of work for a particular class. These examples reflect the tentative beginnings of opening up classrooms in the school.

THE INTEGRATION OF 'DELICATE' PUPILS AT WHITMORE, 1984–5

Fairly soon after my appointment, I was approached by the local education authority to see whether the school would consider setting up a 'delicate unit'. In 1979 such a unit had been created in one of Harrow's first and middle schools, and provision was required at secondary level within the borough. The teaching-staff and, later, the governing body approved the establishment of a unit at Whitmore on the condition that it become a true part of the school and not merely a base on the same site or a separate class. Complete integration in mainstream for all pupils was seen by the school as the ultimate goal, although that had not been the experience of the primary unit and was also not expected to happen quickly.

The unit was to consist of twenty-four pupils who before the 1981 Education Act would have been described as 'delicate', and was to be staffed by a teacher and welfare assistant. The head participated in the procedures for the selection of these staff, but essentially these were Schools Psychological Service appointments. The unit, to be known, the school decided, as the 'support unit', was opened in September 1984.

Nine pupils were initially attached to the unit, with the number due to double in September 1985 and thereafter be brought up to the maximum of twenty-four pupils. Each pupil had to be statemented before admission. The nine pupils arriving in 1984 had all been seen by psychologists, doctors and other specialist personnel and in many cases had received considerable extra support in very varied previous schooling. Support had been in response to emotional and medical problems, together with learning difficulties. Two of the nine pupils came from the first- and middle-school delicate unit, whilst others had attended the tutorial units run by the Schools Psychological Service or received help from the Peripatetic Remedial Service. Trouble over attendance at school, severe anxiety and obsessive behaviour, speech problems, difficulties with social relationships and emotional problems requiring psychiatric help were some of the symptoms which presented themselves; other pupils had missed school in the past or had experienced medical problems over a long period leading to learning difficulties.

Initially, each of the nine pupils was placed in a mainstream form with a form tutor and, as far as possible, followed the timetable for that class. The nature of support for each pupil was dependent on each individual's needs. In certain cases pupils were withdrawn from classes, for work pitched more specifically at the rate at which they were learning. More commonly, and increasingly, the teacher in charge of the unit, or the welfare assistant, helped the pupil in the mainstream class, selecting, as appropriate, where to adjust the demands put on pupils. Occasionally, an alternative lesson was arranged – for instance, gardening instead of PE. Sometimes the unit was used as a sanctuary for a few pupils who at different stages had found the pressures of the daily routine too great. In addition the unit's base was extensively used before and after school, at break and lunch time, to deal with minor problems or worries. These periods also presented a good opportunity to allow in other pupils from the school, providing a chance to encourage social integration.

Throughout the year, the unit and its staff served as a focal point for parents, teachers and external professionals to monitor and discuss each pupil's progress. In addition, all the pupils were discussed at a formal summer review meeting. The most noteworthy feature of this meeting was the general satisfaction of all with the pupils' adaptation to the school. Although a few of the children continued to have considerable difficulties, most had advanced substantially since the previous September. Integration had come about relatively easily. By July 1985 almost all pupils were with their mainstream class for the entire week. The boy presenting greatest problems was with his form for about two thirds of the week.

Initial fears that the unit would merely be located in the school proved completely unfounded. So too did worries about Whitmore being used as a general collection point for children with behavioural problems in other schools in the local education authority. The full statements on pupils, which were sent to the school before admissions were agreed, proved to be of considerable value here, although of limited use once the pupils were actually in the school.

The considerable success of the unit stemmed in large measure from the particular skills and abilities of the teacher-in-charge. He had a broad curricular grasp and considerable personal qualities which enabled him to work effectively with a large number of very different teachers who grew in confidence as the year progressed. He was ably supported by the unit's welfare assistant. Staff were increasingly relaxed and indeed very positive about having either one of these in their classrooms and so throughout 1984–5 this pattern became a regular and very natural feature of school life.

In September 1984 a new adviser with responsibility for the area of special needs was appointed to the borough. Her support for the school and her collaboration with groups of Whitmore teachers to improve curricula have been important in ensuring this area received prominence in the school's plans for change. During the latter part of the autumn term, she approached the school about involvement in piloting some Open University materials for a forthcoming pack for teachers. A number of staff expressed interest and a fairly representative group of thirteen was set up. This included two of the special needs staff and the local-education-authority adviser.

During the spring term this group met regularly. Work focused on reading the Open University materials and working through the activities and questions suggested. Progress was slower than anticipated and by the beginning of the summer term the group had only worked its way through two of the five sections which made up the pack. While there were sometimes grumbles about what the group perceived as the vague and very general nature of some of the activities and tasks set in the pilot materials, these sessions did raise issues of importance to the school. Questions emerged, for instance about the practice of the school's mixed-ability philosophy, the organization of meetings, homework, the dissemination of information about the school's curriculum, and teaching-methods.

Several suggestions to improve current practice were made. The group felt that before moving on to the next section time would be more constructively spent in applying principles arising from the Open University units to practice within the school itself. Consequently, the group divided into three to consider the following more deeply in the context of Whitmore: teaching-methods, homework, and school and community relationships.

Throughout the summer term 1985, these sub-groups met regularly and lists of ideas to improve practice emerged for each. It was felt that it might well prove counter-productive to issue these 'cold' to staff, particularly as the most important thing was the process of debate and thought which had produced the lists. The teaching-methods group, for instance, had considered how two specific examples, 'The eye' in science and 'The pearl' in English, could be taught to third-year classes. Teachers had found it both difficult and stimulating to consider teaching approaches for a topic outside their own particular subject area. They all believed that they had gained something from this co-operative work which would be of benefit to their own teaching. The group prepared a paper which they had planned to present to a heads-of-department meeting. Following that meeting, members of the group were happy to work with departments on the suggestions emanating from the paper.

In retrospect, the most significant aspect of the group's collaboration was the gradual move towards a common understanding that it was not pupils themselves who presented learning difficulties, but the inappropriate curricula which were offered them. This was remarkable when the diversity and different starting-points of each of the group-members was considered. Increasingly, the group was considering the mismatch between learner and curriculum and looking at ways of adapting the school's curricula and organization to lessen this problem. In effect, the group was discussing ways of improving schooling for all children.

The clearest manifestation of changed perception has come from the maths department's decision to adopt mixed-ability teaching for the new intake of pupils in 1986. This brings the maths department in line with stated school policy and leaves only the modern-languages department committed to setting as a form of pupil grouping.

A more subtle indication of changed perceptions was reflected in the job description for head of learning-support, detailed below, when this post was advertised at the beginning of the summer term 1985.

SUPPORT SERVICES AT WHITMORE, 1985–6

When, in January 1985, the previous head of learning-support left to take up another appointment, her post was kept open until the school could be absolutely clear about what was wanted in such an appointment. During 1985, the experience of the support unit and discussions in the Open University group clarified considerably what was expected from the holder of this post. The only point of real debate centred on whether the person appointed should hold a Scale 3 or Scale 4 post. This was overtaken by the Burnham Triennial Review, which moved the school from Group 11 to Group 10 with the resulting loss of scale points.

The following is part of the job description sent out to applicants, together with information about the school. It made clear that some tutorial responsibilities would be expected.

The Head of Learning Support will be expected to carry out the following tasks:

i   To work with departments to meet the needs of all pupils by identifying, intervening and overcoming the learning difficulties experienced in any curricular context.
ii   To assist teachers with the development of strategies which support the learning of all pupils.
iii To develop the School's screening, monitoring and assessment procedures. This will include encouraging curriculum-based assessment and also work beginning in the School on records of achievement.

iv   To work with 'feeder' middle schools to ensure continuity at 12+.
v   To follow up those children identified as being particularly 'at risk' in terms of their specific learning difficulties.
vi   To liaise with
     – parents
     – support services
     – the wider community.
vii To teach well and demonstrate this by some mainstream teaching commitment.
viii To help shape policy and initiatives by playing a vigorous part in the decision-making processes in the School.

After national advertisement and interview, the internal candidate, who had held the support-unit post for the previous year, was appointed. He had applied for the job because he wished to broaden his role within the school. The person taking over his specific responsibility for the support unit was also to take on a wider role in the school and was, in effect, to act as second-in-command of the learning-support department. Together with the head and two of the three deputies, most of the learning-support team met for a day at the beginning of the summer break to ensure a common perspective and to devise a work schedule for 1985–6. Teamwork was considered crucial, and one period (fifty-five minutes) of the school week's twenty-five periods was to be put aside as the minimum for a regular support-services meeting. It was decided that the head of learning-support would co-ordinate support within the school, and his second-in-command would act as the link with outside agencies, particularly for statemented pupils; however, in practice the division has become blurred. Although she was only based part-time in Whitmore, it was felt important that the teacher from the borough ESL and Multicultural Support Team be part of the school team and this was agreed with the local-education-authority co-ordinator.

One of the major areas under discussion was the nature of the support that was to be given from the start of the new school year. Besides offering additional support for some pupils in some lessons, the team saw a key part of their job as helping teachers develop differentiated curricula and more varied teaching-methods. They felt that this would best be done by team teaching which involved real sharing of particular groups. It was decided that all team-members would work intensively with a particular department for a significant block of time. The English department was readily sympathetic to this sort of approach and it was agreed that each support teacher would work with one English class and teacher for one term. Other departments were to be invited to participate along similar lines in future terms. In addition to this work, other support of pupils was to be carried out in mainstream lessons rather than by withdrawal. The latter was to be used exceptionally, perhaps where there was a need to establish a particular teacher–pupil relationship or where class pressures had become too great for some reason. If withdrawal was considered essential, some form of pupil 'contract' would be drawn up. The practice adopted increasingly by many schools, of nominating a particular member of each subject team to link with the learning-support department, was discussed and rejected. The group felt strongly this would undermine the responsibility of every teacher to cope with all pupil differences.

Clearly, it is still early days, but a few weeks before the end of the autumn term 1985 the learning-support team took stock of its work since September and noted the following achievements.

1   Almost all support was now taking place in the mainstream class. Only a very few pupils were withdrawn from one or two lessons for a particular reason, and no child with a statement had been withdrawn at all. There had been no suggestion from any subject-teacher that any such pupil should be withdrawn from any lesson.
2   The team had worked in class with twenty-nine members of staff during the term. Support had been given in all the following subject areas: English, maths, geography, history, physics, chemistry, biology, general science, information technology, French, graphics, music, needlework, home economics, community work, sculpture, and craft, design and technology. Staff had become less anxious about 'unusual' pupils and more relaxed about discussing all pupils with the support staff. Even in lessons where the learning-support teacher was present to support an individual, or, more usually, a group of pupils, there was considerable informal discussion about pupils and lesson content. Some teachers had admitted that they had been made more aware of individual pupils' needs simply by the presence of another body in the room.
3   Support had been given in some degree to a far greater number of pupils than in previous years and this had been extended to the upper school.
4   Almost no formal testing had taken place and no one seemed to be missing this. Support work in classes had begun very soon after the start of the term, i.e. before problems could develop.
5   The members of the learning-support department had begun to function as a team. This was demonstrated by departmental meetings, amalgamation of capitation, regular daily discussions about pupils and lessons, and far less division of responsibility for specific 'categories' of pupils.
6   A programme of 'co-operative teaching' with the English department had been established.
7   The number of referrals to the educational psychologist had been reduced, and referral was less discussed even as a possible solution to difficulties. The role of the Schools Psychological Service in this new system is one which the school hoped to examine more fully in a pilot scheme in 1986. It was planned that the educational psychologist attached to Whitmore would allocate a number of hours each week to the school and ways would be explored of using his experience without testing pupils or referring them out of the school.
8   A pattern of middle-school liaison had begun to be developed.

In its review of the term's programme of co-operative teaching, the English department welcomed wider opportunities to concentrate on the needs of individual pupils, to develop more flexible approaches (particularly with oral work) and to share in the planning and analysis of teaching-methods and materials. The more successful partnerships shared responsibility for introducing material to classes and held equal status with the group being taught. Where the support teacher's role was less secure or identified with a particular group of pupils, the department felt such support could be under-used. It was recognized that building a secure and frank relationship between the teachers could take time, but meetings before and after shared lessons were invaluable if the support team were to offer anything lasting to the department. Joint marking and assessment, more adventurous teaching and a wider spread of support than in a 'withdrawal' system were seen as positive aspects of this term's work. The department felt that a longer period of planning, before co-operative teaching began, would have been of benefit in overcoming some problems which had arisen where the learning-support teacher felt unfamiliar with syllabus and approach. Consequently, the learning-support team had decided to adopt the following outline pattern:

Term 1	*Term 2*	*Term 3*	*Term 4*
Planning with dept X	Work with dept X Planning with dept Y	Follow up with dept X Work with dept Y	Follow up with dept Y

At the end of the autumn term the team had already begun work with the Geography department, in preparation for co-operative teaching in the spring.

CONCLUSION

Over the past three years, the extent to which curricula and school organization cater for individual difference has formed part of the wider discussion going on at Whitmore about the nature of comprehensive education. The developments in special needs provision have come out of this, but have also in their turn sharpened debate about appropriate curricula and what exactly is meant by 'learning difficulty'. It is beginning to be clear that these developments are, in practice, bringing benefits for the teaching and learning of all pupils.

The ease with which the statemented pupils intended for the delicate unit were integrated did much to allay staff fears and to demonstrate the value of an additional member of staff in the classroom. Despite the novelty for many teachers, the only comments made about the presence of the learning-support teacher in classes during the autumn term 1985 were very positive ones. Indeed, the demand for support in lessons proved far greater than the team could supply. Support teaching in mainstream classes is still in its infancy at Whitmore, but debate is concerned not at all with the principle, but only with the details of how such support should be effected. If a comprehensive school believes that the education of every one of its pupils is of equal value, efforts to 'reconnect' remedial education and special needs provision must be seen as part of the important process of ensuring that the belief is matched by practice. Developments in Whitmore over the past couple of years have encouraged teachers to work in teams, to look at their approaches and to consider the appropriateness and relevance of the materials they are using. The issue is not what the school is offering a few pupils, but what it is offering to *all* pupils, and this is something which will be a major concern for a long time.

13

A never-ending story: heads, management and reform in schools

Mike Cowie

Few changes in schools can be made successfully without the support of the head teacher, and what has come to be called in secondary schools the 'senior management'. Mike Cowie, an assistant head teacher responsible for the curriculum of a large secondary school, criticizes a great deal of secondary practice, and argues, along with many other contributors, that there is much to learn from primary practice. But improving pupils' learning experience, whether through curricular reform or through the development of learning-support, is not easy. It may meet with inertia, if not open hostility. Mike Cowie argues that heads and others with power in schools have a responsibility to ensure that progress can be made.

Let me begin with what might seem to be a contentious statement: the learning experience of most pupils in secondary schools, let alone those identified as having learning difficulties, is generally unsatisfactory. Although some may dispute this, for me it is self-evident. Pupils themselves, particularly those in S3 or S4 who are not presented for 'O'-level examinations, recognize this, and present behaviour problems or simply stay away from school.

For me the greatest conundrum in education is how, in secondary schools, we help to turn young, enthusiastic, well-motivated pupils into bored and disinterested adolescents. We are good at wringing our hands whilst blaming primary schools, parental attitudes, society and the lack of resources; seldom do we attach much blame to ourselves.

In 1978 it was argued in the report *The Education of Pupils with Learning Difficulties* (Scottish Education Department, 1978) that

It is the responsibility of the Head Teacher to ensure that a policy of help and support for pupils with learning difficulties is planned on a whole school basis. This will involve him giving a lead to his staff by making it clear to them that they all have a part to play in the identification of the full range of learning difficulties, and in the resolution of pupil problems; and, through promoted staff, ensuring that the curriculum takes account of all these pupils.

It will also be remembered that in the late 1970s secondary teachers were encouraged in the Bullock Report (Department of Education and Science, 1975) to be aware of the language processes by which pupils acquire information and understanding, and secondary schools were exhorted to develop a policy for language across the curriculum.

Both the Scottish report and the Bullock Report were widely accepted, but in 1986 how many head teachers give a positive lead to their staffs in this area? How many schools do have a policy in language? And how many secondary teachers are aware of the language processes through which pupils acquire information and understanding? An honest answer to all these questions must be: precious few.

Now, if 'whole school policy' is interpreted rigidly, then the extent to which it is feasible or desirable is uncertain, given the differences in approach, content and methodology which exist between departments. But it is surely not unreasonable to expect departments to develop approaches consistent with the philosophy of a school, assuming that a school does have a clearly stated *raison d'être*.

It is part of the problem in education that head teachers and their staffs often have no clearly thought out and articulated purposes (as opposed to pious statements of aims) which are consistently kept in mind or striven for, nor the appropriate communication and consultation procedures for formulating them.

Consideration of the learning experience in schools must inevitably involve consideration of the purpose of schools and an examination of the teacher's functions. Traditional functions are, or should be, changing: teachers in schools should be more concerned with the pupils themselves than with curriculum content; teachers should focus more on the ways of equipping young people with the knowledge, skills and attitudes which enable them to become self-directing people, able to work independently and to take control of their own lives.

Social and personal skills are best developed not through formal social-education classes, but through the curriculum, in the ways classrooms are managed and subjects taught. Self-confidence may be developed, for example, where all pupils, regardless of ability, are allowed genuine opportunities to achieve some degree of success. Youngsters are less likely to become independent or co-operative if they are not given the chance within classrooms to learn independently and to work together in groups, nor are they likely to develop positive attitudes to learning.

Secondary teachers in particular have much to learn in these respects from primary colleagues. In the interests of the children it is essential that we should give more consideration to *how* children learn and develop. In doing so we would become more aware of the language processes involved in the learning experience.

There are serious difficulties for pupils in the transfer from primary to secondary school. Some pupils are expected to repeat lessons and activities previously undergone in primary school. In secondary schools pupils may have to meet as many as ten to fifteen teachers, some for only forty minutes each week; and the more formal approaches of secondary schools, where the emphasis is still on class instruction, are very different from the methods and groupings of primary school. In most schools there are mixed-ability classes, but many are still taught from the front in the traditional manner. Where this occurs, there is little scope for learning-support teachers to work co-operatively with class-teachers; the role which they can play is very limited. Thus, the change from primary to secondary seems not to be a well-ordered progression and can become for some a disturbing experience. Where a 'float' (primary/secondary) system of support staffing operates, however, clear benefits can be seen.

In my view, perhaps the biggest single reason for our lack of success in secondary education, particularly in the early years, is that, as subject specialists, our prime concern has been with the content of the curriculum. Another is the unhealthy influence of examination-board requirements on what is on offer to all pupils in schools. Emphasis is placed on the retention of knowledge and undue importance is placed on having a full jotter with plenty of notes. Pages of facts, colouring-in and copious copying-exercises replacing learning.

Get the pupils involved through worksheets, some might say. Certainly, well-designed worksheets can stimulate, provoke and encourage. But I suspect that over-reliance on a worksheet approach leads to masses of sterile sheets which make few demands on pupils and provide little encouragement and motivation.

At the other extreme, worksheets I have seen (yes, and used) have demanded higher-order skills and been couched in language which is difficult to understand or is beyond the pupils' experience.

What is learned is 'inert' if it has no real meaning for the pupil. Where the emphasis is on passing on content, in the worst examples of a worksheet-dominated or teacher-dominated approach, the youngster is not encouraged to make the necessary links, through language, between what he or she already knows and new knowledge. Knowledge is not created by pupils; they learn to become dependent on the teacher for knowledge. What then becomes of the intention to assist young people to become autonomous, self-directing adults? One might ask if this is the result of too-detailed planning of the curriculum. On the contrary, overdependence on worksheets is the result of lack of planning and insufficient analysis of the nature of the subject and of the process of learning.

All that this entails grows in importance when we consider the role of learning-support teachers, and the relationships they may or may not develop with subject specialists. If it is accepted that the role of a teacher is to pass on acquired knowledge, then there is little scope for an effective partnership to develop between the subject specialist and the learning-support teacher.

The primary tradition on the other hand is more child-centred and more attention is paid to the needs of individual children. Secondary teachers could emulate this by considering fully the contribution their subject and their teaching of it makes to the child's development; by analysing the nature of their subject and deciding which concepts they wish to develop; by adopting alternative teaching and learning strategies incorporating group work, individualized learning, games, simulations and resource-based independent learning, from which appropriate assessment procedures would follow and learning difficulties be identified. Furthermore there would then be a clear and definite role for the learning-support teacher within the classroom and the opportunity to work in full partnership with the class-teacher.

A later stage in this development might involve a thorough evaluation of what goes on in the classroom. This may be another useful role for the learning-support teacher. This might allow for continual improvement in teaching and learning techniques, were teachers sufficiently secure and professional to adopt an honest, self-critical approach. An ideal world, perhaps!

There are obstacles in the way of progress towards this ideal. The thrust of my argument is that learning difficulties are, at least in part, a product of the system. If more teachers are to challenge the assumptions held regarding the purpose of teaching and the nature of learning, and if teachers are to work in a more productive partnership with learning-support teachers, then some changes are required. Liberation from worksheets requires more time for planning. If larger time blocks per subject were created, alternative approaches could be tried which would allow for fuller collaboration between the class- and learning-support teacher. Under these conditions, learning difficulties arising from the curriculum would be reduced. The individual child's progress would at least be more fairly monitored.

The problem goes beyond the provision of time and resources, however. Any successful development of this nature is only likely to succeed within the context of a whole-school policy. Complete agreement on policy is unlikely. In order to avoid settling on the lowest common denominator, and to decrease the degree of conservatism and resistance to change shown by teachers over the years, strong and positive leadership is required of head teachers. Senior management in schools cannot escape their main responsibility: the teaching and learning which goes on within their schools. Some of that responsibility may be delegated to departmental heads, but with that responsibility comes accountability: departmental heads should not only ensure that teaching and learning strategies employed in their departments are consistent with the overall aims and policies of the school, but should be held accountable for what goes on in their departments. As a matter of priority, head teachers and their management teams must develop management structures which encourage maximum consultation, participation and communication. Mixed-ability teaching and the role of special needs departments are often contentious issues which impinge upon people's values. They need to be discussed openly, sensitively and without prejudice. Genuine communication, with real discussion, debate and exchange of ideas, is often lacking in secondary schools; there is little opportunity to debate fully the kind of issues raised here without barriers being erected and 'straw-men' thrown up.

Lawrence Stenhouse argued that rational curriculum-planning must take account of the realities of the classroom; it is not enough to be logical. The relationships which exist between learning-support and class-teachers vary. Some work very well. There are situations, however, in which class-teachers regard learning-support teachers with open hostility. Support teachers are made to feel unwelcome in such classrooms. If effective partnerships are to develop, then much of the responsibility for overcoming misunderstandings lies with head teachers. They must establish an atmosphere which is receptive to change, through a structure which allows full, open discussion, combined with strong leadership. Consequently classroom activities may be organized in such a way that partnerships are given the maximum opportunity to develop and to prove themselves through their effectiveness.

REFERENCES

Department of Education and Science 1975: *A Language for Life: report of the Committee of Inquiry appointed by the Secretary of State for Education under the chairmanship of Sir Alan Bullock.* London: HMSO.
Scottish Education Department 1978: *The Education of Pupils with Learning Difficulties in Primary and Secondary Schools in Scotland: a progress report by Her Majesty's Inspectorate.* Edinburgh: HMSO.

14

Help where it's needed: support across the primary curriculum

Annabel Mercer

There are two hallmarks of the accounts of overcoming difficulties in learning provided by Annabel Mercer. The first is the integration of basic-skill teaching into the rest of the curriculum. The second is that the response to difficulties in learning has to be across the whole curriculum, exploiting the skills and understanding of all those involved in all areas of the pupil's school experience. Progress may as easily originate from the gym or the drama room as from the workbook. Pupils' strengths become the most important basis for further learning and continued motivation.

In common with other local education authorities in Scotland, Lothian Region has recently been restructuring its provision for meeting the needs of pupils with learning difficulty. Curriculum planning, support within the class and, where necessary, withdrawal from the class, are seen as the main channels through which needs are to be met.

One mainstream primary school in the Region demonstrates how this policy is being put into practice. The philosophy of the school reflects the view that, despite the severe problems caused by its catchment area – chronic unemployment, sub-standard housing and drug abuse are prevalent – the school exists to serve that community. The curriculum leans towards a local base, with studies of the area, its problems and needs being carried out by many classes. Pupils contribute regularly to the community newspaper and participate in local arts festivals. One class has worked with a locally based communication-skills working-party to produce their own video film, which won an international prize in Japan, while all classes make regular use of a youth retreat in a nearby rural village, often on a residential basis. Visits using the school minibus, and the nearby seashore, provide additional habitats for study. Parents are made welcome in the school. A community room is permanently at their disposal, and the nursery class has purpose-built accommodation for mothers.

In a recent submission to the Schools Curriculum Award, it was stated that

our curriculum has been devised to meet our own particular needs. Academic goals and literacy do not weigh heavily as a priority amongst the majority of the families we serve. This in itself has influenced our curriculum planning. While we seek to stretch our pupils we have to be realistic about goals being attainable ... it is challenging to develop an effective curricular strategy for children whose needs are unlikely to be met elsewhere.

It is within this framework, backed by a favourable allocation of specialist remedial and consultative staff from the local authority, that the school seeks to ensure that the individual pupil's difficulties are met by an appropriate educational response. Many strategies are used in bringing diversity into the classroom. I shall consider five issues here to illustrate how provision was made in specific instances:

1   relating remedial programmes more closely to pupils' own background
    and interests;
2   taking the pressure off basic skills;
3   introducing a wider range of media;
4   co-operative work between remedial, class and subject specialist teachers;
5   interdisciplinary work.

RELATING REMEDIAL PROGRAMMES MORE CLOSELY TO THE CHILDREN'S OWN BACKGROUND AND INTERESTS

For all children this strategy is desirable; for Sean it was essential. By the time he was nine, his future within both the family unit (he had been fostered by his grandparents) and the mainstream school was in jeopardy. Serious trouble out of school was accompanied by school reports stating, 'Sean refuses to work ... has an enquiring mind, but little perseverance.' He was brought to us in a last-ditch attempt to meet his needs. Residential care was the next stage. The remedial programme we devised for Sean just *had* to work; there was no room for error.

We saw him as a boy of above-average ability who needed support all hours of the day, as an individual as well as one of a group. Four main educational aims were identified: to foster existing skills in a stimulating or challenging context, to extend linguistic skills, to introduce him to a wider range of leisure reading-matter, and to encourage both practical and physical aptitudes which could be developed as hobbies. Unless these were related to Sean's whole lifestyle as well as his capabilities, we realized that the programme would be a dead duck.

For a boy who responded most readily to the off-beat, the bizarre or the controversial, standard textbooks held little appeal. Newspaper articles, pop magazines and television programmes (soap operas as well as documentaries) became valuable resources. The aim here was to stimulate critical faculties and reflection rather than blind acceptance of majority opinion. Sean loathed writing. The tape-recorder, painting, clay modelling and drama replaced the pencil as the most frequent media for recording.

A. MATTERS OF FACT

Write True or False after each of the following statements –

1) The music of The Clash is soft and happy. *False* ✓
2) There are five people in the group. *False* ✓
3) Joe Strummer is the lead singer. *true* ✓
4) Mick Jones plays guitar. *true* ✓
5) Mick's parents got divorced when he was young. *true* ✓
6) The Clash want things to stay as they are. *false* ✓

B. MATTERS OF OPINION.

Be ready to discuss the following with me. Think about it..........

1) Are the Clash right to be so angry? *Yes – it's not fair that only the rich people get jobs and the poor people don't. Everyone should get a job from the Government.*

2) Is it fair that so many young people have no job? *No, because they won't have any money of their own.*

3) Are you for, or against, the National Front? *"For", because I don't like niggers.* *

4) Was it right that Mick only saw his father once a year? *No, because he needed parents to house him and feed him and look after him. **.*

5) Were the times The Clash thought difficult and hard **really** hard? *Not really. They wouldn't like someone dying, or being run over, or going blind.* ✓

Figure 14.1

Figure 14.1 is an example of the type of material used in oral work with Sean. He read an article on the rock group *The Clash*, he wrote the answers to section A, then discussed section B. After the session, his teacher pencilled in the main points which Sean had made in the discussions.

Sean's outlook on life is illuminated by this poem he wrote, entitled 'When I am old':

> When I am old, I'll race down to the betting office,
> And back a pound double on Troy.
> I'll buy a motor bike, and work on an oil-rig,
> And wear a pair of twenty-incher DMs,
> I'll sunbathe in the garden,

Shoot chickens and squirrels, to eat with nuts and sweets.
I'll jump on people, play cards,
And gamble my money away.
I'll read books, and buy a cat,
And get my ears pierced through about five times.

A physical-education programme for Sean included inventive work with apparatus, movement to music and games skills, as well as outdoor activities, including canoeing and putting. Drama sessions were particularly successful, as Sean loved using theatrical make-up, and in routines was quick to establish himself as a 'clever feed' type.

His grandparents and social worker became teachers, giving swimming-instruction, and extending the language and communication skills fostered in the classroom by participating in evening theatre-workshop sessions. Together we encouraged Sean to read more widely, and his social worker arranged family expeditions to the local library. Since the child's difficulties were caused by circumstances outside school as well as in the classroom, an extended network of support was necessary. This working-together of all the adults featuring largely in Sean's life was undoubtedly made easier by the established philosophy and practice of the school, where easy relationships already existed and stereotyped roles were not seen as particularly relevant, nor professional boundaries as under threat.

TAKING THE PRESSURE OFF BASIC SKILLS

In other cases, a remedial strategy may have to be far more specific, and home in on an issue such as basic-skills practice. This raises the question of the weighting given to basic-skills work within the individual curriculum. The danger is that for some pupils, particularly those requiring long-term remedial support, programmes can become overloaded in this direction, often with a disproportionate phonic content. Jill, a pupil who was hemiplegic and had many learning difficulties, had been following this restricted type of curriculum. She performed competently with familiar mechanical work which she enjoyed, but worked largely on her own in the classroom. Figure 14.2 provides a typical example.

The strategy used in Jill's case was to shift the emphasis towards oral language, supported by both speech therapist and drama specialist, to link written language more closely to class topic work – Jill particularly enjoyed letter-writing to celebrities – rather than the phonic workbook and language lab.

Figure 14.3 gives an example of such work. As part of their environmental-studies programme, the class had visited a local Georgian house. Jill enjoyed this, but the worksheets provided were inappropriate for her. This differentiated work focused on what Jill actually saw.

Figure 14.2

It was also decided to develop Jill's work in PE. From being completely non-participating in the gym, Jill progressed to the stage where, kitted out in a new leotard, she would attempt most activities. Group work was encouraged whenever possible. Learning became a more stimulating and sociable experience for her, and, in her mother's words, she became better able to cope with the 'hurly-burly' of school life.

Sometimes continued practice in the basic skills on the same scale may be considered desirable, and reducing the pressure may rather be a matter of setting that practice within a more relevant learning context. Jason, a P2 pupil, was felt by both his parents and class-teacher to be under-achieving in language and number work. However, his good performance in motor skills, his creativity, and his enjoyment of environmental studies compensated happily for those weaker areas.

Phonic and number workbooks were set aside, and teacher-devised material linked to environmental studies took over. Word patterns, measurement, computation and classification (Jason's particular difficulty with the concept of belonging was affecting many areas) were all developed within the current topic of 'Myself'. Games and activity items, such as the step-by-step maths apparatus, were chosen for their immediate visual appeal as well as their intrinsic value, and used extensively for reinforcement. Success with a programme of this kind can often help influence teachers' attitudes and approaches, particularly where these have been syllabus-oriented, or restricted in their use of resources. Jason's teacher was quick to see the advantages of this approach, using differentiated content, for all the pupils in her class.

The master and his family lived upstairs .

The servants lived downstairs.

Life was not the same in the two parts of the house.

UPSTAIRS	DOWNSTAIRS
They drank _tea_ and _wine_ from china _cups_ and crystal _glasses_	They drank _beer_ and _ale_ from thick _mugs_
There were _carpets_ on the floors.	The floors were bare _stone_
They slept in comfortable _beds_	They slept on the _floor_ or in the _cellar_
The rooms were lit by _wax_ candles	They only had _tallow_ candles.

wine	cups	glasses	mugs	floor	stone	
tea	beds	wax	carpets	ale	beer	cellar	tallow

Figure 14.3

INTRODUCING A WIDER RANGE OF MEDIA INTO EVERYDAY STUDY

The usefulness of this strategy can be seen quite clearly in the case of Freddy, a ten-year-old boy whose hands had been badly damaged in infancy when he had thrust them into an electric fire. He had no fingers, but two thumb stumps and thick 'mitts'. His physical handicap was accompanied by a disinterest in school, considered by his parents and teachers as a greater obstacle to learning. He was aggressive to other children, and as a result was not readily accepted in group activities. The educational psychologist questioned whether mainstream education was in the long term feasible. Although Freddy was able to write extremely neatly, this was a tiring procedure for him and could not be sustained for any length of time.

The first stage in Freddy's remediation programme was to teach him to touch type. After a slow start he gradually became competent and much of his recording was done through this medium. The logical development was to extend this skill to the computer keyboard, an activity which was deliberately fostered in a small-group situation. Freddy took to the keyboard like a duck to water, and with his considerable head start was soon able to instruct the others in his group. The support was very much a two-way affair.

Widening the range of media has certainly made Freddy less dependent on the written word as a channel of communication. The social interaction was particularly welcome. The head teacher claimed that any strategy that resulted in Freddy's working profitably and peaceably with his peers was little short of miraculous. But the most far-reaching consequence was the extended curriculum to which he now had access. He had hitherto seen much of his school work as pretty irrelevant, and, having recognized this, his class-teacher could now offer him a more acceptable curriculum, tailor-made to his needs. Moreover, this was using a medium where real dialogue was possible. The computer is sometimes little more than a diversion in the classroom; for this pupil it satisfied a very real need.

CO-OPERATIVE WORK BETWEEN REMEDIAL, CLASS AND SUBJECT-SPECIALIST TEACHERS

Andy's experiences in his last year of primary school demonstrate how co-operative work between teaching-staff can bear fruit. The oldest boy in the school, he was orally confident and 'a bit interested in most things', as he put it, but had made a bare start in reading and writing. His co-ordination was poor. He lolled about in his chair, wriggled, and frequently knocked things over. On meeting him for the first time, the immediate impression was of his frustration and poor self-image.

Fairly drastic action was needed. Our educational aims were limited to two: to get reading off the ground, and to isolate any one strength we could identify, and build on it. Andy had previously had to complete many mechanical exercises (see, for example, figure 14.4) which had little connection with his interests.

In reading, the inappropriate phonic approach was discarded. One aspect of the class's current environmental-studies topic was selected by Andy himself, and, using an appropriate core book as a base, alternative reading strategies were developed, linked to the Fernald approach to writing words. In one instance, Andy chose motorbikes, within the main theme of transport, and we used Manxman books as core material. This work was fairly intensive, with continual overworking of the word and verbalizing. We found it most profitable for the remedial teacher to train Andy in these techniques, while the class-teacher was to develop them through a language experience approach in the classroom. He compiled his own reading-books, gathering much of the

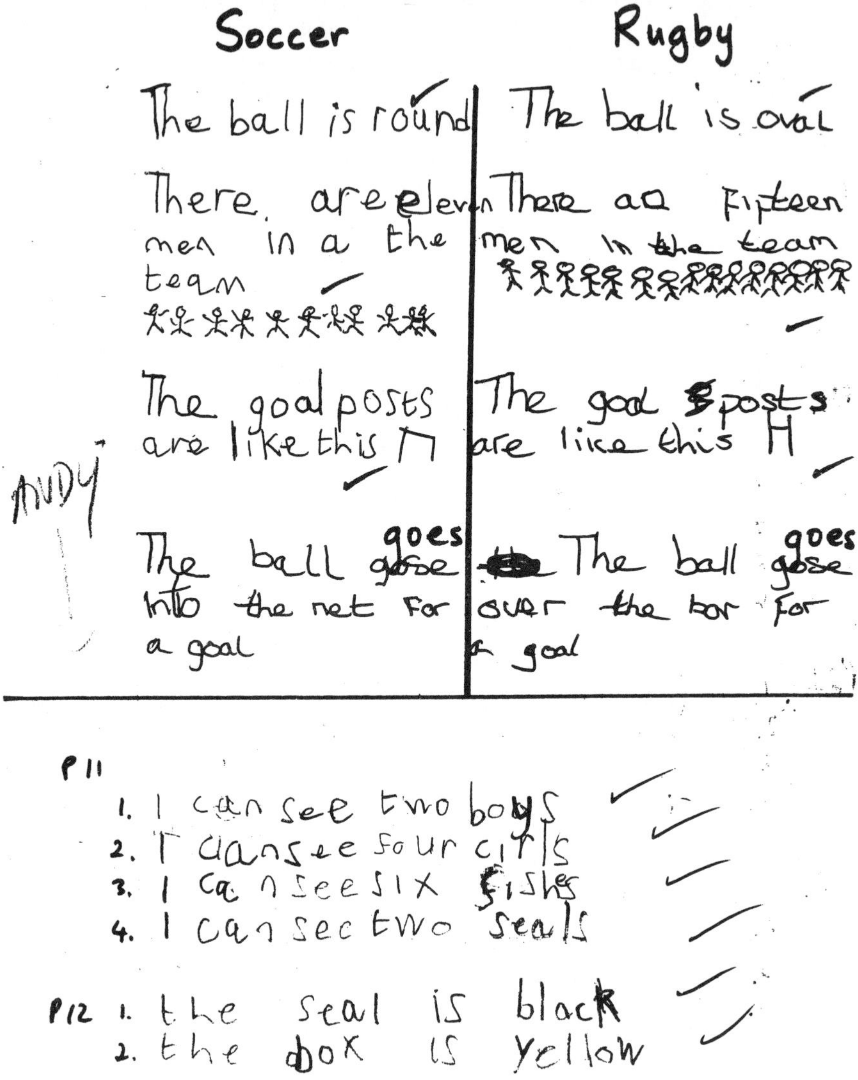

Soccer | Rugby

The ball is round | The ball is oval

There are eleven | There aa fifteen
men in a the | men in the team
team

The goal posts | The goal posts
are like this ⊓ | are like this ⊓

The ball goes | The ball goes
into the net for | over the bar for
a goal | a goal

AnDy

P11
1. I can see two boys
2. I can see four girls
3. I can see six fishes
4. I can see two seals

P12
1. the seal is black
2. the box is yellow

Figure 14.4

source material first-hand on class outings. Figure 14.5 reproduces two pages from 'My own book of motorbikes' written by Andy. In collating his information, he had visited a local motorbike centre, and had interviewed the owner.

The same theme was in turn developed by the drama specialist, who found that Andy could contribute ideas, retain new vocabulary, and plan and execute routines with a partner. Perhaps the most satisfying outcome for all of us was the occasion when Andy stayed behind after school to get down on paper what he felt like in role as a steam engine. It was the first time that anybody had heard him express a desire to write spontaneously.

In her exploration of the theme through imaginative movement, the PE specialist identified Andy's greatest strength, and we were able to fulfil our second aim. He proved amazingly agile in the gym, and the inventive movement was accompanied by mastery of complex skills. Badges were won, and Andy blossomed, with the new-found confidence spilling over to all his work. The school was now providing a more consistent level of support, and each teacher could build on her colleagues' successes. A wider curriculum was being presented in a more appropriate manner. Restricting our aims to a realistic level, focusing on a common theme, and concentrating on Andy's strengths rather than his weaknesses were the keystones of this co-operative response to need.

INTERDISCIPLINARY WORK

Relating different areas of the curriculum within an individual programme usually has the initial effect of stimulating the pupil's interest and kindling motivation. The work then acquires a new relevance as it is set in a wider context, with the different aspects brought together in harmony. In the first instance it is the pupil who benefits. There are, however, considerable advantages for the teacher as well.

Observing Andy in the gym, we found that, although he could hit a ball hard with a bat, he had no sensitivity in controlling force, and we thought of his poor pencil control. We found that his auditory recall was so poor that he had difficulty in repeating even simple rhythms, and we thought of his difficulties in blending and word-building. These observations had a direct bearing on the programme that was ultimately devised for him.

We had noted the lack of confidence with which Jill faced new learning situations, and wanted a clearer idea of the factors that led to her meeting them successfully. Her performance in drama sessions was monitored closely, and we were particularly interested in the degree to which she depended on teacher direction, group support and an extended time scale to assimilate new ideas. Our findings were then applied to other parts of her curriculum, making it more closely match her learning-style.

Jason found it very hard to tell the difference between certain sounds. It was through a specific skills progression devised by the music specialist that this difficulty was tackled. Her structured programme, including, for example, discrimination games using a variety of contrasting instruments, was developed to use language-related material by the class-teacher. Reading was the first area to benefit from the improved perceptual skills.

The most expensive bike in the shop was the Kawasaki Z1300. It is the biggest bike in the world and it costs £3.200. The man sells one of these bikes every month. Here it is

Z1300

£ 3,200

Figure 14.5 (this page and opposite) Two pages from 'My own book of motorbikes'

These examples illustrate how an interdisciplinary approach can help the school to meet the pupil's need in a more effective way. The teacher is given the opportunity to assess that need in the context of overall performance, and her interpretation of a suitable educational response should therefore be

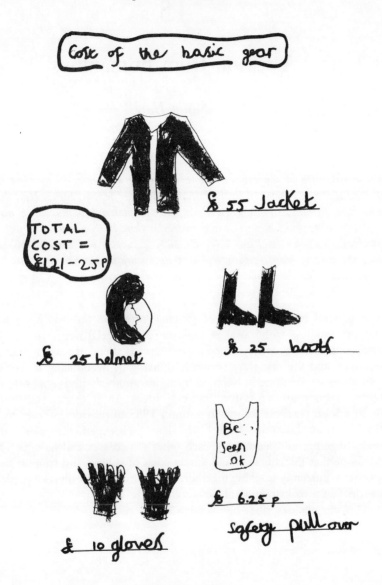

Figure 14.5 cont'd

more authoritative, and realistic in its aims. Moreover, observation of a child's performance in one area, particularly where the focus is on successful performance, can suggest possible approaches or methods in another. Specific skills may be developed most effectively in one area, producing a ripple effect across the curriculum.

15

A lesson from humanities

Susan Hart

The contribution of support teachers to preventing difficulties in learning is most effective if they are involved in the initial planning of lessons. Susan Hart describes a number of strategies to change a lesson plan and materials to make them accessible to a class as a whole, as well as to a particular child likely to encounter difficulties. Involvement at this level can only take place if support and subject/class-teachers have the time to plan together, and if a close working partnership exists between them. Susan Hart concludes by discussing these wider issues.

The general trend in special educational provision towards more in-class support and less withdrawal of children with special needs meant, in our area, that most secondary schools were already doing at least some support teaching, and the rest were seriously thinking of introducing it. Yet all the schools were operating in isolation from one another with no opportunity for mutual support and cross-fertilization of ideas. An in-service course was set up at a local teachers' centre in autumn 1985 to provide a forum in which teachers from different schools could share their experiences, clarify the key issues together and learn from each other's successes and failures. Despite our hope that the course would attract pairs of subject and support teachers who were currently teaching together, only one of the twenty-two participants was in fact a mainstream subject-teacher.

This chapter describes one session of the course.

ACTIVITY BASED ON 'KIDNAPPED'

In this session, the group had agreed to focus on the role of the support teacher in lesson-planning. One of the course-members, Sue Gyde, and myself had recently revised a lesson in some detail and taught it together to her mainstream humanities class. We agreed to present this lesson to the group, and to explain the changes we had thought necessary. We planned an initial activity which would encourage course-members to formulate their own ideas and pool suggestions before we offered ours.

They were given a set of learning-materials, a brief outline of the aims of the lesson and a description of a child whose needs they should take into account. Working in pairs, they were to discuss how the lesson might need to be modified and what kinds of support might be required. These suggestions were then to be listed in terms of those that would be appropriate for the class as a whole and those just for the individual child, or others with similar difficulties.

The lesson was part of a series of introductory lessons about Italy, leading to a study of volcanoes and the fall of Pompeii. The class, a mixed-ability group of eleven-year-olds, had already studied pictures and maps of the country, and the aim of this lesson was to provide a purposeful context for further map study, this time using a written rather than a visual stimulus.

At the start of the lesson, the pupils would be told the story of a kidnap happening in Rome. Two young Italian children have been kidnapped on their way home from school. Six kidnap notes have been discovered, but no one knows in what order they were dropped. Working collaboratively in groups of four, the children have to study the notes (four of which are reproduced in figure 15.1) for relevant clues, work out an order together, and use the information in each note to locate a likely spot on their map. They then plot the kidnappers' route round Italy and, using information from the final note, predict their hiding-place, using grid references to locate the exact spot.

Besides relating the materials to pupils of their own, the teachers were asked to take into account one particular child, a brief description of whom was provided, who would be present during the lesson; the aim was to provide a common focus for discussion. 'Danny' was described as having a very poor view of himself as a learner, following a long history of learning failure, and hence as having little motivation for learning. While he expects print to make sense, he can read only very simple material. He finds writing of any sort painfully difficult.

Modifications to the lesson for the whole class

Most groups attempted to do the task themselves in order to see the kinds of demands it made on the children, and found it very difficult! Some thought that it was an interesting idea which would motivate most of the children to meet the challenge. Others felt that frustration was likely to set in for the majority within minutes. Either way, it was difficult to see how a child who could barely read would be able to cope at all. Most people agreed that ideally modifications to the lesson would be needed for the class as a whole.

Groups produced a number of suggestions as to how the lesson might be revised to make it more accessible to all children. These very closely mirrored the modifications which Sue and I had made and which we then outlined to the group.

They grabbed us as we were coming home from school today. They pushed us into a car and gagged us. We were screaming our heads off. We think they went north. We travelled for several hours. Then we stopped in the mountains for a drink. I said I wanted to go to the toilet and now I'm going to throw this on the floor and hope somebody finds it. We are all right but we are scared and

clue number:

grid reference:

We have left the mountains now and driven down to the coast. It's much warmer here and we can smell the sea. Are you coming to rescue us? They are quite kind to us now but we don't get proper food to eat and our clothes are getting dirty and we want to come home. Have they asked for money yet? The place we're in now seems to have a lot of rivers. People travel by boat instead of car or bus. I

clue number:

grid reference:

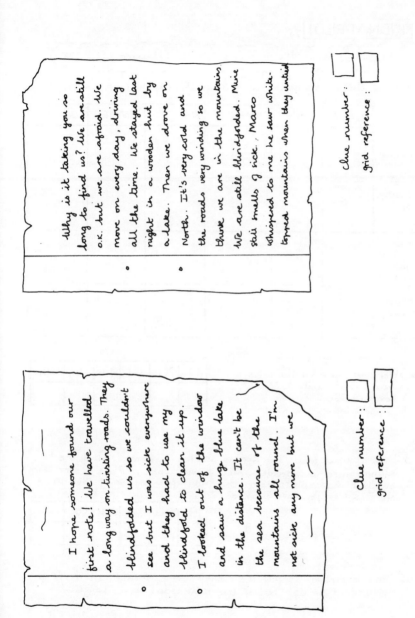

Figure 15.1 Four notes used in 'Kidnapped'

KIDNAPPED! ☆

Can you follow the clues and find the kidnappers' hideout?

1. Read the kidnap notes. Write down the important 'clue' words.

Kind of clue	Note A	Note B	Note C	Note D	Note E	Note F
land, Surroundings						
direction going -						
when - beginning middle end of kidnap						
other clues						

☆

2. Work out the order the notes were sent in. Write it in the boxes in pencil.

1st	2nd	3rd	4th	5th	6th

☆

3. Look at your map. The kidnap started in Rome. Read the 1st kidnap note and decide where it was written. Place a star there on your map. Write down the grid reference. Don't stick the stars on till you have checked.

grid ref. ↳

1st	2nd	3rd	4th	5th	6th

☆

4. Draw a cartoon strip of the kidnap story. Then finish it off in your own words. Say if the kidnappers were caught!

Figure 15.2 'Kidnapped': worksheet to assist note-taking

Course members' ideas	*Our ideas*
Teacher might read kidnap notes out loud to whole class	Sue read out all the notes (in the wrong order) to give a 'flavour' of the content
Guidance from teacher about the sorts of clues to look for; underline key words, etc.	Note-taking chart (figure 15.2) and guidance on stages of task to work through
Extra motivation of some kind to help them meet the challenge	Giving parts in story to each child and 'catching' kidnappers
Deciding most tricky parts of activity and arranging to stop class at intervals to share findings	

Two areas for modification are worth describing in more detail.

Motivation.   To increase the children's involvement with the task we had decided to give each child a part in the story. As they arrived, they were each given a slip of paper with the name of a character on it, such as 'kidnapper', 'detective', 'reporter', 'police dog', 'parent', 'accomplice'. This got a buzz of talk going about who everybody was and what was going to happen. Sue, as the subject-teacher, then told the class the story of the kidnap and explained that the kidnappers would only get caught if a group managed to locate their hiding-place on the map at the end of the lesson. We hoped that this would give them a stronger sense of purpose and encourage them to weigh up all the available evidence as carefully as possible.

Help with strategies for problem-solving.   We agreed with the course-members' conclusion that the demands of the lesson as it stood were inappropriate for a first-year class. Collaborative group activities need to be designed so that the children are able to support each other through the task by drawing on each other's resources. If just the right amount of support is provided, then the activity opens up different learning opportunities to different children in the group so that everyone can learn something in the process of completing the task.

We thought that the most effective form of support to build into the lesson for the class as a whole would be some help in understanding how to set about tackling the problem. The worksheet which we devised, reproduced in figure 15.2, was intended to help the children see more clearly the different stages they needed to work through. The note-taking chart showed them the kinds of clues to look for, and helped them organize a format for their note-taking which they could use to put the kidnap notes in sequence.

Making lessons more accessible for children with special needs need not mean that confident learners in the class will be deprived of material that will challenge them. In this case, the operations which need to be carried out collaboratively in order to solve the problem have not themselves been simplified. We have merely made the task more *intelligible* by making explicit the actual processes involved. At the same time, by building in opportunities to select and use information in a purposeful way, the activity has been enriched for the class as a whole.

Modifications to meet individual needs

The modifications described so far, however, would not be of much help for our case-study child Danny, unless some additional support were provided to give him access to the information in the text. Even if the notes were read out loud, he could not be expected to recall the details contained in each one. The activity assumes that groups will reread the notes together, reading intensively for specific information, as well as scanning, cross-referencing and making inferences and judgements. Even in a collaborative situation, it would need a supreme effort on Danny's part to join in at all. Course-members felt that it was more likely he would opt out, perhaps masking the fact with disruptive behaviour, or else just fading quietly into the background. Without further support, he would almost certainly leave the lesson having chalked up yet another failure to hasten the downward spiral of his self-esteem.

No one felt, however, that Danny would be better off by being withdrawn or given something entirely different to do. To use support in that way is short-sighted, since there will never be enough support teachers to offer the support that is needed in all areas of the curriculum at once. The best interventions are those which have a lasting effect, so that the child can learn whether there is a support teacher present or not. With this purpose in mind, the following suggestions for 'permanent' changes at the individual level were made by course members and ourselves.

Course members' modifications	*Our modifications*
Provide simplified version of text with picture clues for 'poor readers' to use	Colour-coded keyword cards to assist listening, reading and note-taking
Record text on tape and have recorders and headsets available for children to use if they wish	Motivation: make Danny a kidnapper to guarantee participation in lesson
Ensure child is sitting with supportive and motivated group	
Get teacher to increase amount of praise and encouragement, and frequency of attention during lesson	

Keyword cards. These consisted of twenty-four cards, each containing a word or phrase colour-coded according to the type of clue provided. They were intended to provide Danny with a means of responding to and recalling the key information contained in each note as it was read out. We thought that having something specific to do while listening would help him to focus his thoughts, that the colour-coding would help him identify the words swiftly, and that the cards, once sorted, would enable him to contribute to the group discussion and complete his chart.

We hoped that this extra support would mean that Danny, and children with similar reading difficulties, would be able to take a full part in the group activity. He would have the opportunity of working independently and using reading for learning at a level he could cope with. Since he would not be so reliant on the help of others, he could gain some sense of achievement and control over his own learning. Most importantly, perhaps, we should have avoided one alternative 'solution' often presented with the best of intentions for children with reading difficulties: namely, giving them something to do that does not require them to read at all. There is a problem, of course, about providing supplementary materials for a few children in a class. Unless, as in the best primary classrooms, the children are used to everybody doing different things, it is probably better, if possible, to avoid modifications which draw attention to particular children. In this case, the problem might be overcome by providing one set of keyword cards for each group, leaving it up to the individual children whether the cards should be used as suggested for Danny, or as a checking-device later on.

GENERAL ISSUES

Three important questions emerged from the analysis of this lesson. These formed the basis of discussion for the remainder of the session.

Time for planning

A good deal of despair was voiced about how realistic it was to think in terms of making such major changes to materials and teaching-methods, even if we were conscious of the need to do so, when so little time was available for planning. Many of us were supporting in a number of different subject areas, with different teachers and with different year groups. Even if our free-period allocation were entirely devoted to lesson-planning, we should not be able to manage more than a minimal degree of liaison with each teacher. Most of the time, we were lucky if we managed to track down the subject-teacher to discover what the following lesson was to be about, let alone have sight of the learning-materials in advance. Yet all the time we were aware that providing on-the-spot support was not really getting to the root of the problem. Was the solution, as some proposed, to do just a little support teaching but do it really well, with thorough planning and review, and so make a strong impact in one particular curriculum area? Or was it better to build a broader base across the curriculum, and so work with more teachers but develop more slowly? Whatever the strategy adopted, it seemed important that support teaching should be seen not as an end in itself but in terms of the contribution it has to make towards achieving the aims of special-education provision as a whole. It is in the context of those aims that any decisions about support teaching need to be made.

Negotiating with colleagues

Even were time available for joint planning and review of lessons, however, it was by no means generally accepted that the support teacher's role should involve such a close partnership with subject-teachers. Negotiating possible modifications to learning-materials and teaching-methods was felt to be a highly sensitive issue which needed very careful handling. Some of those present felt that, unless they were *specialists* in the subject in which they were supporting, they were not qualified to question teaching-methods and materials, and thought it unlikely that subject-teachers would be prepared to accept their suggestions. Others argued that many of the causes of learning difficulties are common to all subject areas, and in some cases not to be a specialist can be a positive advantage in learning to experience the curriculum from the child's point of view.

There was a general feeling that we should wait until we had got to know the teacher well before we risked opening up sensitive areas for discussion. Even then, it might be best to focus on specific children's difficulties to start with, and prepare materials to help them in the classroom, inviting the subject-teacher to help in evaluating their effectiveness, rather than tackling curricular issues head-on.

It was agreed that most could be achieved when the teachers themselves approached us for assistance and defined their own needs. However, one familiar problem is that the areas where children are experiencing most difficulty are usually those where the support teacher's assistance is the least welcome. It was difficult to know whether to begin there or with those teachers who warmly welcomed our help. The group identified four factors which need to be taken into account when deciding the kinds of modification which may successfully be aimed at in any given situation.

1 The degree of trust, co-operation and mutual respect existing between the two teachers.
2 The scope of the support teacher's role as defined implicitly or explicitly between the two teachers.
3 The willingness of the subject-teacher to undertake joint planning, and the time available to both teachers in which to do it.

4   The degree of acceptance by the subject-teacher of responsibility for preventing learning difficulties, and willingness to experiment with different approaches.

Questioning the learning-task itself

The third issue was the support teacher's dilemma when faced with the situation of having to help children do a task which is itself of dubious value. One teacher described, for example, a subject in which the children were regularly asked to copy down large amounts of writing from the blackboard.

If this support teacher was content to define her task in terms of what help these children need to carry out this activity, then she might decide to provide 'lasting-effect' support in one of a number of ways. On an individual level, she might ensure that children in difficulties were sitting next to children who could write clearly, so that they could copy from their books, or she might provide them with the text printed on a worksheet to make copying easier. At the whole-class level, the teacher might be asked to write more clearly, perhaps using coloured chalks, or have the text to be copied printed on sheets for everyone, instead of merely written on the board.

However, the real question which needed to be raised was why these children, indeed any of the children, were copying at all. Surely there was a more productive way for them to be spending their time? If the role of being supportive to the curriculum comes into conflict with the role of promoting children's learning, but the support teacher does not at that point question the learning-task itself, then in effect support teaching is helping to *reinforce and perpetuate an inappropriate curriculum.*

The problems experienced by the poorest achievers in school often highlight aspects of the curriculum which are inappropriate not just for them but for everybody in the class. Strategies which make learning easier for them, such as more collaboration, more group discussion, more shared reading- and writing-activities, a greater variety of approaches and choice of tasks, are already widely recognized as being beneficial for all. The role of the support teacher can therefore serve as an important trigger in bringing about changes which will enhance the curriculum as a whole, as well as enabling it to provide for a wider range of individual needs.

It would be unrealistic, however, and probably counter-productive, to suggest that every time support teachers are faced with such a situation they should always adopt a critical rather than a supportive stance towards the curriculum. The important questions for us to resolve, therefore, are to what extent and under what circumstances we should do so, and how we might foster a collaborative teaching-relationship which will allow such issues to be tackled.

CONCLUSION

The course-members' evaluation indicated that it was the opportunity to share ideas in a supportive environment which had been the most valuable aspect of the course. It is becoming increasingly evident that success in meeting special needs in mainstream education is likely to depend to a great extent on the schools' ability to organize for collaborative teamwork among staff. More specifically, in relation to support teaching, discussion between the two teachers who are working together to clarify precisely what they are trying to achieve is a necessary precondition for any effective support work. It is the basis on which all the rest depends.

16

The Kent face: introducing mixed-ability maths

Peter Kyne

This chapter presents an example of the involvement of learning-support staff at all stages in the reform of its teaching approach by a subject department. In their search for methods that would allow them to respond flexibly to all pupils in the early stages of secondary mathematics, staff at Auchterderran Junior High School, Fife, chose to use the Kent Mathematics Project, an individualized scheme published by Ward Lock Educational (1978 and subsequently). Peter Kyne, the principal learning-support teacher, was closely involved in the planning of the curriculum change. Coincidentally, the approach to maths-teaching chosen by the department also enhanced the role of learning-support teachers, since it heralded a shift away from lessons dominated by whole-class teaching. As a result, the subject and learning-support teachers could work on near equal terms in the classroom.

I like Kent Mathematics because you're doing what you are capable of doing. You aren't kept behind. I think you learn a lot more by the cards than a book. Plus you do something different each day and if you are working from the board or a book you would be doing decimals, fractions, division ect. for days on end. I also hate doing tapes I think they are waste of time and you don't learn much from them any way. The teachers are very slow at getting to you for marking your card or if you are stuck.

These are the comments of a first-year pupil at Auchterderran Junior High School in Fife. She is describing the Kent Mathematics Project, which we have introduced for our mixed-ability teaching-groups. The school population is around 400 and the average class size in the first and second years is twenty-seven; in later years, around twenty-one. The school does not cater for pupils beyond 'O' grades, though modules prepared for the '16–18' Development Programme are available for Christmas leavers. Pupils who are capable of higher grades are enrolled in the local six-year comprehensive at the end of either their second or their fourth year. This selection procedure does stigmatize the school as being unable to teach more able children, and consequently many parents enroll their children directly at the comprehensive. This has led to a gradual decline in the school roll. Eventually amalgamation will take place between this and another junior high school to form a second six-year comprehensive.

When I came to the school two and a half years ago, as head of a department of three remedial teachers, children were withdrawn for maths and for French in large groups of ten to fifteen pupils, with limited diagnosis of their learning difficulties. Withdrawal is an invitation for pupils to become alienated from class-teachers, who are generally excluded from the remediation of their pupils. The need for teachers to adapt their teaching-materials and methods is removed at the same time as the less able pupils. Those most likely to have problems with the current materials and methods are withdrawn from their classrooms, and because they have been withdrawn those children are likely to return to an unchanged situation. Consequently withdrawal can be self-perpetuating. Perhaps the most insidious effect of withdrawing children is its continuation when it is not needed. After a school has spent considerable time and resources equipping a specialized area, any organizational arrangement that means this area becomes redundant is liable to be rejected. Suitable clients will be found to justify the staffing and equipment of this area. It is unlikely that the area will become activated only if and when suitable clients emerge. Withdrawn pupils can often receive an education that is unrelated to their normal classwork and restricted to practice in the basic skills, which can become a repetition of past failures, but any gain in the basic skills by children who are withdrawn is at the expense of the monastic separation and segregation of themselves and their teachers.

In response to these problems, and as part of the school's wider response to Fife's new policy on learning difficulties (described by Glenys Andrews in chapter 8), it was decided in consultation with the principal teacher of mathematics that few if any pupils would be withdrawn from their normal classes. In that first year of change no pupils were withdrawn. Where necessary, pupils were provided with alternative materials and methods within the ordinary classroom.

When I approached the mathematics department about reducing the amount of withdrawal that was taking place, as a first step towards limiting withdrawal to the relatively few pupils who would require help on an individual basis, I found the department sympathetic though not wholly convinced that withdrawal was not the correct method for dealing with less able pupils. We were, however, obliged by the Fife policy to make certain decisions regarding curriculum for mixed-ability teaching, as the remedial teacher's role was now seen to be that of helping subject-teachers discharge their responsibilities towards pupils who experience difficulties in learning. Accordingly we agreed that withdrawal would be necessary only on a few occasions, provided that we could produce materials to suit the wide range of ability.

PROVIDING MATERIALS FOR ALL: DISCOVERING THE KENT
MATHEMATICS PROJECT

Mathematics is a subject in which topics or concepts are repeated at levels of gradually increasing difficulty. The content of our curriculum was similar to that outlined in the 1984 document of the Fife Region Mathematics Curriculum Committee. For example:

First year	*Second year*
Flow charts	Percentages
Whole number	Scale drawing/constructions
Solids and shapes	Statistics
Money	Integers
Co-ordinates	Shape
Graphs	Volume
Angles	Special percentages and arithmetic
Equations and formulae	Transformations
Decimals	Distributive law
Calculator	Time distance speed
Tiling and symmetry	Parallel lines and angles
Length	Linear equations
Time	Square roots
Area	Equations of lines
Fractions	
Negative numbers	
Statistics	

Guidelines for each topic were also given.

These lists, which are not in any teaching order, were adopted as the basic content of our curriculum for the two years. However, we found it difficult to make, collate and modify a large amount of material at so many different levels, and it was difficult to simplify some topics without bastardizing the concept so completely that it was not worth teaching at the lower levels.

The pupils were given a preliminary test at the beginning of each topic and this dictated the level at which they would follow the course. This effectively meant that each class was organized into sub-groups and at the beginning of each topic this allowed for group work. As the children worked on a topic, some progressed faster than others, so group work became impossible and the children were tutored individually.

Our method of organizing the curriculum was still rate-dependent. If we stopped teaching a topic too soon the less able pupils would not get enough time; if we taught a topic for too long, the more able children began to mark time, became bored or we ran out of extension material. These difficulties led us to become interested in the Kent Mathematics Project (KMP) as a possible answer to these problems. This scheme aims, in the words of the 'Teachers' Guide', to

provide a concept framework for mathematics for nine to sixteen year olds. [It] is divided into nine levels and the concepts progress in complexity and sophistication upwards through these levels, because the material has been validated and moderated on this basis. The position of a task in the framework is therefore an identification of the level of mathematics learning in an objectively designed structure of concept developments ...

It seemed that the KMP was organizing the curriculum in the way we desired and offered the breadth of material required to cope with the spread of mathematical attainment that confronts teachers in secondary schools. After a visit to a Glasgow school that was using the KMP we adopted the scheme.

THE KENT MATHEMATICS PROJECT IN PRACTICE

Pupils' views

Here are some more comments by pupils who have been working with Kent materials for a year.

I like using Kent Mathematics Project because you can do everything at your own steady pace instead of hurrying along with the rest of the class. I don't think the answers should be on the back because all the people in the class who are on high colours are the ones who usually look at the answers. Also I think that we should go out and get our cards in a more orderly fashion instead of everybody running out and knocking things over, banging into people and things like that.

After you have done a certain amount of cards you always do a test but I think that is stupid, I think that after we have done all the cards in one box that we should have one huge big test.

Half of the cards that we use tell us a lot so we learn something more on every card we do. And it is good that when we have finished a card the teacher asks us a question on the card we have just done so then we can recap on the things we done.

I like tenths mathamatics because it alows you to play games in it and it is a very good way of learning maths. But I think Mr K and Mr J. take to long coming round to you you sit for ages with your hand up and still nobody comes but eventually you get someone to come and help you. But I think mathematic is excellent and it helps you a lot in your adding take away multiplication Divide and money.

The reason why I enjoy Kent Mathematics project is you get a different choice to choose from. I also like the test you get when you finish all your cards. The only think I dont like is when you have to wait to get your card signed. As you lose a lot of time up.

These pupils have a number of criticisms of the way the scheme operates in lessons – mainly that they have to wait a long time to obtain help or to get a teacher's signature before moving on to the next card. But their comments are favourable on the whole, appreciating the variety of tasks, the games and the individualized pace. The pupils are in charge of their own record-keeping, so they can see how they are progressing. Even though some are sceptical about this, referring to the opportunity for 'cheating', this has been a powerful motivating force.

In general the KMP scheme is working well. The bulk of the children are progressing satisfactorily at their individual rates. Most of the less able children are working well, though some are finding it difficult to take responsibility for their own learning and organize themselves and the materials they require. For a very small group of two or three pupils we occasionally revert to more formalized teaching-methods.

Teaching co-operatively

Teachers have traditionally felt themselves to be autonomous within their own classes: it is therefore understandable that problems can exist when two teachers are working together. Remedial departments have often been isolated and independent of the main school, almost miniature kingdoms. It can be as difficult for remedial teachers to leave this territory as it is for class-teachers to accept them. Both teachers in the partnership may find it difficult to give or accept constructive criticism. The remedial teacher may be expected to deal only with the least able children and be thought not to have the necessary skills to deal with the average or the most able children. If the partnership contains a junior and senior member, the junior partner may resent being perceived by some pupils as a second-class teacher, which can damage self-esteem and classroom discipline. However, in our case these problems have been identified, which is the first stage in overcoming them. The introduction of the KMP has reduced some problems and eliminated others.

During the complete reorganization of the curriculum in S1 and S2 the workload has been shared. This joint responsibility has meant that the remedial teacher has become more than an extra pair of hands and indeed may not always be in the classroom as this time may be more profitably spent constructing alternative learning materials.

I have illustrated my concept of stages in collaborative teaching in figure 16.1 and how this is linked to consultancy, which can occur in the classroom or more formally during departmental meetings, or at a particular time on the timetable set aside for it. Using the present individualized scheme, a learning-support service can be provided either by one-to-one teaching as part of a partnership or by some form of consultancy.

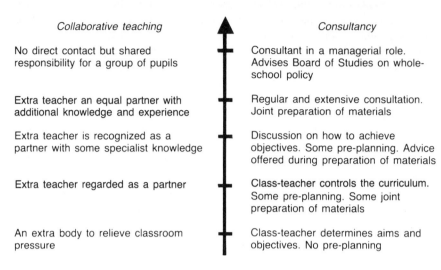

Figure 16.1 Stages in co-operative teaching

The lay-out of the Mathematics Department

Teaching occurs in two rooms that have had a connecting door specially provided. This door enables the remedial specialist who is team teaching with the subject specialist to cover two classes at once. The desks and chairs are arranged in rows. This may seem very regimented, but a flow of movement does occur in the classrooms. Children leave their seats to get material, go to the listening-area or to a partner's desk to play a game. The teachers also move around, to pupils who need help or to have their work marked. Rarely is a teacher at his/her desk. When the classes were arranged less formally it was found that this movement was made very difficult, with chairs blocking the few passageways that existed.

New power points have been provided, and the children seem able to set up and manipulate the tape recorders effectively, even if a tape has to be wound on to a particular point. The taped lessons are popular and are able to take the place of tuition on a small group or individual basis. The games area is a small area of free floor space that the children can use for activities that require movement, such as turning from north to south.

Problems

Assessment. Assessment is a key problem. It is very tempting to mark a child's work indicating that it has been completed without asking some searching question or for an example to be attempted under supervision. At the end of a group of tasks the pupils are given a short diagnostic test. On average pupils sit about three of these a term. If a pupil scores badly on a test then there are various outcomes. The next group of tasks allocated may be less difficult or the pupil could be tutored on certain topics by the subject specialist or remedial teacher before progressing. Some pupils' difficulties may seem so acute that they are placed on the 'L' material. This material was designed by the Schools Council project for very slow learners in the secondary school. The outcome of any assessment has not yet been standardized by the teachers involved. In some cases a pupil will repeat the same work; in others alternative material will be found from a bank that we are in the process of compiling, so pupils with varying degrees of mastery may be allowed to progress differently depending on the views of their teachers. A major problem is the amount of help needed by the pupils and the fact that they may have to wait some time for it. At least with the KMP, individual difficulties do come to the fore and the children do ask for help, so the teachers know what the problems are. In whole-class teaching it can seem that everyone has understood when many pupils do not, and do not want to say so.

Organizing the materials for constant use. Far more material is now being used in the classroom and it has to be available at all times. This has caused maintenance, security and organizational problems. The material is stored in plastic boxes which act as the drawers in an open-fronted cabinet. Most pupils will look carefully through these trays for the item they require, while some fake a cursory look and then tell their teacher it is not there. In time, pupils become more able to organize themselves and the materials and work independently. Damage does occur to items – not through vandalism, but because pupils adapt materials: thus the black and white die ends up with numbers on it and the numbered die ends up black and white. The normal wear and tear on material – plastic boxes splitting, connections breaking and items going missing – can be irritating. However, the use of concrete materials must add to if not partially create the children's enjoyment for maths, though it may be difficult for a teacher to summon up much enthusiasm for the umpteenth cardboard tetrahedron to be presented to him this year!

Class size. Although the KMP does cater for every child, this in itself causes difficulties, as the children demand and need more time on an individual basis. Because of this, class size is a limiting factor. It is doubtful if the KMP would be a suitable choice for mixed-ability classes unless more than one teacher could be timetabled into the classroom.

CONCLUSION

When remedial teachers are involved in the design, organization and presentation of the curriculum from the beginning, then change can be effected so that the less able need not be withdrawn from normal classes and teachers can more effectively perform their new role to recognize the range and diversity of learning difficulties; to design or select appropriate teaching programmes; and to select and display a suitable range of methods.

Although problems remain and there are questions still to be answered, we hope that by adopting a versatile curricular model and individualized learning-materials we have created an appropriate context for the co-operative teaching of mathematics to pupils of widely differing abilities.

17

Gaining access to science

Hellen Matthews and Jim Presly

Science in the first two years at Dyce Academy is taught using individual and group methods in a large open-plan laboratory, with the active participation of remedial staff. One of the advantages of collaborative work for subject-teachers is the opportunity to gain a non-specialist's perspective on the difficulties that pupils face. Hellen Matthews and Jim Presly, respectively principal teachers of remedial education and biology, describe some of the skills and abilities that pupils need in order to learn in their science curriculum. Few of these skills are exclusively scientific. They range from simple self-confidence to the ability to decode two-dimensional illustrations of three-dimensional objects. Many such skills are required in other subjects, and the remedial teacher brings valuable knowledge of pupils' work elsewhere, which can be exploited to good effect in science.

The development of Standard Grade science courses in Scotland provided a unique opportunity for people engaged in science-teaching to scrutinize their aims, methodology and course content. The development of criterion-referenced assessment forced teachers to develop realistic learning goals for pupils within three broad ability bands (Credit, General and Foundation) with particular emphasis in the early stages of course development on those pupils (Foundation) known to have wide-ranging learning difficulties.

Science staff in pilot projects had to ask, 'What core and option topics in science is it appropriate for these pupils to study?' 'What level of complexity is appropriate within that study?' 'What skills do the pupils have to have in order to achieve specified learning outcomes?' Criterion-referenced assessment has produced a very detailed analysis of a range of learning processes and practical skills, which have valuable applications far beyond the science laboratory, and not only for Standard Grade pupils but for pupils in S1 and S2 as well.

Science in S1 and S2 at Dyce Academy is taught by individual and group work and the course is continuous across the two years. Pupils acquire many of the basic skills necessary for scientific work while exploring, by means of integrated units of work, key areas in physics, chemistry and biology. The constant overlap of these three disciplines is continually stressed, so that, for example, the study of energy includes the study of photosynthesis, and the study of gases the process of respiration. Each topic consists of core and extensions; extensions usually provide further emphasis on the main teaching-point, more complex experimental work, or work demanding greater inferential skills. Each section is succeeded by a short written test which seeks in part 1 to establish knowledge of the topic and in part 2 to test understanding and inferential skills.

To succeed with what is for many their first acquaintance with science, pupils in S1 and S2 must be helped to acquire a complex of intellectual, physical and psychological skills. To proceed at all, pupils have to have a work ethic; they have to have sufficient confidence in themselves to work both independently and co-operatively, and, in an open laboratory, to ignore disruptive stimuli. An S1 or S2 science lab is, at any moment, alive with diverse activities, and pupils have to be able to concentrate on their particular investigation, however interesting someone else's is. The resulting work rate which a child achieves is inevitably a compromise generated by the interplay of the child's ability, inner drive and motivation, and encouragement or pressure from teaching-staff to achieve his or her best performance.

After an introductory period, pupils have to develop the organizational skills necessary to carry out their experimental work. They have to know where equipment is stored, to be able to choose appropriate apparatus, to sequence its use correctly, and to organize and use their own work space safely. To proceed safely requires awareness of potential hazards, a knowledge of how to avoid accidents (e.g. in the wearing of goggles) and a respect for the safety of everyone in the lab, including themselves.

Science is a valuable subject even in putting children safely in situations where there is, in the best possible way, no escape from things which some may think 'risky'. Some children lack physical skills or are poor at manipulative tasks, perhaps because they have had a very sheltered upbringing with an excessive emphasis on safety. Such children have to be helped to see that they can do these things, with a spin-off in the growth in general self-confidence which may follow. It is one of the rewards of working in science to see children become more self-confident and carry out tasks which they may not, at one time, have believed they could manage.

Another prerequisite of any work in a lab based on written workguides is the ability to read with understanding and to follow written instructions, whether they are directing the pupil to set up an experiment or to find reference material in the library. Reading is also essential for information retrieval through research. If a pupil cannot read adequately, there is immediately a major problem.

Competence in a wide range of language activities apart from reading is also demanded. The pattern of work is usually from written instruction to experimental work back to further written material for evaluation. Linguistic, as well as numerical, recording-skills are important here: conclusions often have to be expressed in writing either by cloze procedure or in extended writing. Pupils who have an inadequate grasp of written syntax often make mistakes with the cloze passages, but can give the correct explanation orally. It is important to be able to talk to a partner for experimental work, to the class-teacher when explaining either a success or a problem, and to the technician in order to collect important pieces of experimental material and equipment. Some children also have problems doing these things, not because they cannot find the words, but because they lack the self-confidence to go and ask.

One first-year pupil recently explained his failure to collect equipment like this: 'I've already asked the technician for something this period and I didn't think that I should bother her again.' It should be said that the technician in question was far from fearsome. Strong support is necessary from all staff involved in a science lab to help develop self-confidence. Other psychological skills are involved too: more generalized decision-making, independence of thought and action, and self-reliance all have a part to play.

For the conduct of experimental work itself, complex observational and conceptual skills are required. There is, for example, a difference between observing and observing accurately. One area which requires much practice is the reading of various kinds of scale. Here, the basic structure or concept of the scale, whether it be the divisions on a thermometer or the dual-scale system of a beam balance with 10-gram intervals on the top and 1-gram intervals on the bottom, has to be understood before meaningful readings can be taken.

Deficiency in basic arithmetical skills can lead to all kinds of problems. Equally difficult is the scale on a thermometer: for example, difficulties often arise with its positive and negative numbers, although this can often be explained by reference to work on positive and negative numbers in mathematics.

Dealing with abstractions poses difficulties for many people, not just twelve- and thirteen-year-olds, and elementary science makes demands here too. Pupils must, for example, be able to translate two-dimensional drawings of apparatus or structures into three-dimensional reality, and *vice versa*. Visualizing molecular packing is also difficult in this way, as is any discussion of how atoms combine, what 'size' they are and so on. Concepts in physics pose difficulties too: *energy*, for example, is an abstraction. The model of a hydroelectric dam which pupils study in order to explain energy transformations is very difficult for some. They will grasp, for example, that moving water means kinetic energy is available. Isn't it understandably baffling, therefore (if you've been told that the particles in a liquid are constantly moving anyway), that once that same water is sitting behind a dam wall it has 'gravitational potential energy' and, once it begins to flow down through the dam, it once again has kinetic energy? Even at this elementary stage, science demands subtle thinking. It is one important role of the remedial teacher in a science lab to try to get the pupil to explain what it is he 'can't see' and then to lead him back through the process step by step.

Introductory biology involves some very enjoyable elementary work on classification. All pupils who have been through primary school in recent years are familiar with set theory and Venn diagrams, knowledge which is very useful in appreciating, for example, the principles of constructing a biological key. The connection is not usually apparent to pupils, and it is one of the advantages of having a remedial teacher 'floating' across the curriculum that she may use pupils' grasp of set theory to provide an analogy which helps them to see how to tackle the task.

Work on classification is also beset by simple linguistic problems, not necessarily of the pupil's making. In working on the basic division of vertebrates and invertebrates and having established that a starfish does not have a backbone, many pupils, when they come to record examples, will still, despite what they have had confirmed as correct, attempt to classify a starfish as a fish. This is very understandable. Visual similarity also creates problems here: isn't a snake like a worm? If a worm is known not to have a backbone, wouldn't common sense tell you that a snake doesn't have one either? Obviously, in a well-organized course, reference material and skeletons on display back up unit work; imagine how completely confusing this could be without visual aids.

Pupils who have not, in general, confidently grasped less familiar uses of concepts such as 'larger than'/'smaller than' or 'higher than'/'lower than', also come unstuck; the first lack gives rise to problems when it becomes necessary to arrange objects in size sequence, or to make evaluations on the basis of size (growing crystals is one example here). The second causes problems when experimenting with tuning-forks. Some children don't know what they are looking for, not because they are deaf, but because they don't understand 'higher' and 'lower' in the context of pitch unless they have already been introduced to it in music.

Manipulative skills are in constant use in a science lab in setting up and in using apparatus. All S1 pupils at Dyce are taught how to set up and use a microscope safely. When you consider the angling of the mirror to reflect light onto the stage, the preparation of a small slide, the placing of a coverslip, the finding of the slide material within the field of view, and the successful focusing of the lens, this becomes a process with many potential crisis points for children with poor manipulative skills. Add to this the need to be able physically to look down the microscope clearly and perhaps to draw the significant parts of what you see, particularly if you have never seen it before, and the task becomes very complex indeed.

On the other hand, certain specific disabilities, such as poor sight or hearing, are much less of a disadvantage in this kind of individualized learning than in class teaching. In whole-class teaching a child with poor sight must sit near the front; in individualized work, long-distance vision is not so important, nor is there any 'front' to sit at. Poor hearing is also less of a problem: there is very little whole-class discussion and talk with teachers usually happens individually or in small groups with all the speakers close to each other. For children for whom these disabilities may cause lack of confidence, and for those who lack confidence for other reasons, individualized learning is much less stressful, helping to build confidence in ability to do science, if not public speaking as well.

So far, we have tried to show something of the range of skills needed in a science lab, to give examples of the ways in which pupils come unstuck when they lack these skills and to touch on the question, 'What can staff – remedial or subject staff – do about it?' Maximum use of staff resources requires further discussion.

Sharing in the construction of workguides and worksheets, and being involved in planning and evaluation of teaching approaches is one important aspect of the work of the remedial specialist. It is helpful too for subject and remedial specialists to adopt complementary roles. If the subject specialist is primarily concerned with a 'subject-first' approach, the remedial specialist's first concern should be with strategies for learning, and this should, in turn, lead to a co-operative scrutiny of the whys, whats and hows of pupils' classroom experience.

Individualized learning leaves far more teacher time available for lengthy group or individual tutorials than would a whole-class approach, where one child's difficulty could hold up everyone. The great advantage of individualized learning, provided the workguides/worksheets are well produced, is that many pupils can at any one time be getting on with their work while attention, sometimes lengthy, is given to a few. Individualized learning has several other advantageous group effects: if pupils within a lab are working across a range of activities at any one time, all that anyone knows about anyone else is that they are either on the same or on a different piece of work. Since pupils tend to gravitate to pupils of like ability to form friendships, the group around any one table, having been chosen by the children themselves, is less likely to contain children hostile to each other or of very different abilities. There is much less friction between groups and individuals than there would be with whole-class teaching where a child who was struggling could, to his or her great embarrassment, be constantly exposed. Also, since the rate of progress of different pupils within a group is often similar, intensive teaching can sometimes be conducted for the whole group at once, allowing for relaxed participation and discussion and economical use of teacher time. We believe that the informality of individualized learning encourages children to seek help in a relaxed way. The particular role of the remedial teacher working across the curriculum may be that she or he is aware of difficulties which the child may have in, for example, language or mathematics which are bound to impinge on work in science; conversely, the remedial teacher who works across the curriculum may, in order to elucidate a point to a child or even a whole class, draw by analogy on understanding which she knows has been explored in other subjects. Liaison among remedial teachers within the department spreads information about pupils who have difficulties and members of staff can be on the alert for problems when they arise.

It can be seen from all the foregoing that most remedial work in science can easily take place in the lab, provided it is properly set up for individualized learning: the extra teacher–pupil dialogue is just one other activity. All pupils, including the very able, are guaranteed the teacher's individual attention for some of the time, as their progress through a unit is punctuated by check-points at which they must stop and have their work discussed by a member of staff, who will then revise or extend learning appropriately.

We have no doubt that doing science, quite apart from its intrinsic interest and educational value, is also important in building confidence; it surely makes some of the most complex demands of any subject area.

18

Team teaching by leaps and bounds

Muriel Adams

Remedial teachers working by withdrawing children have a readily identifiable role. They are, by and large, teachers of basic literacy. In co-operative work, the differences between the roles of mainstream and support teachers can become elusive. This becomes a positive benefit, as Muriel Adams shows, for it liberates both teachers to offer whatever skills they happen to have which are called for in a given lesson. All lessons require many more abilities of pupils than those which are the focus of attention in the teacher's mind. A mistaken assumption about the pupils' background skill and knowledge can wreak havoc in a well-planned lesson. The flexibility of teaching-roles described here also allows for prompt responses to such discoveries.

The beginning of the session saw a considerable change in the way my timetable was organized, resulting in a substantial part of my time in both schools being spent within classrooms, with only a very few pupils withdrawn for their remedial instruction. This arrangement allowed me to spend sixteen blocks of forty-five minutes to one hour with each of eleven classes. The time spent with a class has been used in several ways. For example, individual pupils with specific needs in reading, language and related skills are catered for, as well as pupils with a similar need in maths and number, and some involvement with environmental-studies projects has emerged. Leaving aside basic literacy and numeracy, my time in the classroom is spent on practical maths and, to a lesser extent, contributing to the environmental project of the moment. It is on these two topics that I wish to focus.

PRACTICAL MATHS

The presence of a second teacher in the classroom during a practical-maths session is obviously very desirable. Recently I have been seized upon more than once to work with a group of children on a topic such as length or volume. There we were in the corridor, the P4 boys and I, estimating then measuring a hop, a jump forward, jump backwards, a bunny jump. A bunny jump? 'Miss! What's a bunny jump?' Well! Sometimes actions do speak louder than words and so there followed the *modus operandi* demonstrated by myself (appropriately clad, I'm glad to say) observed in stunned silence, but, to their credit, with not even the merest hint of a suppressed giggle, by my gang of four, and only briefly interrupted by the even more than usually ubiquitous janitor and one passing parent.

Lesson one. Be prepared to discover that sometimes a pupil's difficulty stems from a failure to perform the basic task rather than with any difficulty related to the mathematical topic itself. In fact two of the boys of this particular group had been identified as 'non-hoppers' during PE lessons, and our gymnastic efforts in the corridor gave them a welcome chance to practise their hopping with some purpose, in this case executing a hop that was long enough to measure.

The volume work with a P5 class is noteworthy too. My group on this occasion consisted of three boys and one girl, three of them relative newcomers to the school and one 'slow learner'. The task was to find the capacity of a bucket using bottle A (small), bottle B (1 litre) and bottle C (large), and then to estimate the relative capacity of a number of containers of varying sizes. To perform this task satisfactorily I had noted that manipulative skills, past experience, recording- and tallying-skills and an ability to estimate and make inferences would all be necessary. Not one of my heterogeneous group of four this time was found to be proficient in all departments. In the bucket-filling operation one boy encountered great difficulty in judging when to turn the tap off. Pouring was a clumsy, 'directed towards himself' operation for another. Estimation and inference were quite fanciful to the point of being absurd, and none of the four could keep a tally of the number of times the smaller container's contents were poured into the bucket.

It does seem inappropriate somehow to attempt to put right in forty-five minutes what a lifetime of ten years in the wilderness has failed to impart in the way of manipulative skills and the certain knowledge that if you persist in pouring inwards towards yourself you will end up with a very wet front. Bearing in mind that estimation and inference can only become more realistic in the wake of past experience, I considered the only contribution that I could feasibly offer was an introduction to tallying. In the event the process was grasped and, dare I say, mastered without incident, much to their satisfaction. All four gained in confidence as their turn to record on the blackboard came round. It is a skill that they will be confident in using next time it is required of them, perhaps in the context of their environmental studies.

Lesson two. Assorted children bring assorted skills to a group lesson because of their assorted backgrounds; in this case one boy's development was temporarily arrested by the sudden death of his mother just before he started school, and at least one of the group would be denied the pleasure of a cuddle in the sink or bath due to domestic pressures of time and tidiness.

Time alone will not solve such problems and you cannot put the clock back. Moving school and moving house are hazardous adventures when you're in primary school. While you may have 'done' some aspects of the curriculum ahead of your new schoolmates, there is equally every chance they will have 'done' some things ahead of you.

ENVIRONMENTAL STUDIES

The involvement I mentioned earlier with a P5 environmental-studies project was a first for me in two ways. First, it arose from consultation with the class-teacher at the planning-stage, and, secondly, my contribution in this instance was 'national dance'.

During some discussion about project work, the teacher showed me the flow diagram she had produced for the term's proposed environmental-studies project on the countries of the European Economic Community, with particular reference to France and Italy. The art work would consist of towers and mosaics. There would be customs, food and climate discussed, but it was my chance remark about national dances that seemed to strike a chord. I have a friend who has not only a great interest in but also an exhaustive collection of dance and music, and together we found an example of both French and Italian dances which seemed within the capabilities of the class. The easier of the two, fortuitously, (for France was the first country they were to study) was the French peasant dance, and so we began.

The first session went well. With the class-teacher at the piano, we practised galops (slipping steps) and skips until they were acceptable. The children all managed reasonably well, and the initial boisterous leaping around soon gave way to a more silent and controlled if exhausted measure. The dance is performed in a circle with hands joined – boy, girl, boy, girl, alternately – and, while this slipped swiftly over the 'find a partner' problem, it did nothing to persuade them to join hands. However, with much cajoling and coaxing, and wiping of hands on skirts and trousers, we finally connected as a circle. From then on, they worked well on the peasant dance. When it was as good as it was ever going to be, the class-teacher and I switched roles, and I played the piano while she watched. If there was a problem, it was that of maintaining the size and shape of the circle throughout the dance. I made use of games-court markings on the floor of the hall to counteract this, and the children soon found that if they kept their circle within the square the whole thing was a great deal easier.

Flushed with our success with the French dance, we ventured forth into the saltarello, a traditional Italian dance immortalized by Mendelssohn in his Italian Symphony. Two new hazards appeared in this one: a springing step and taking partners *and* hands. A springing step closely resembles a controlled run really, and yes, you've guessed, it was in the beginning more of a runaway stampede. Even when their saltarello was well-nigh perfect, good enough certainly to be performed for the head teacher, there was always the feeling, on my part at any rate, that there was a stampede in there trying desperately to build up to a breakneck speed. I think we achieved civilized control by means of concentration (they had to do thirty-two springing steps to start the dance) and the judicious pairing of 'sensible' girls with potentially 'wild' boys.

Lesson three. An exercise of this sort gives pupils the opportunity to perfect and perform while at the same time moulding a class of individuals into a group with a common purpose.

In summing up, it is clear that remedial teaching has come some way since the days of 'Janet and John in the medical room', and perhaps co-operative teaching too is reaching beyond the bounds of producing suitable worksheets for groups of pupils (identified or otherwise) within the classroom, for involvement at the planning-stage can open up so many avenues of exploration where two teachers really are better than one.

19

Getting to know you...: a co-operative teaching partnership

Will Swann

Plans for co-operative teaching are put into practice by people with individual histories and personalities. The development of an effective teaching-relationship between a mainstream and a support teacher involves meshing two styles and two personalities. This chapter describes the development of one partnership, set in the context of the histories, personalities and educational beliefs of the two partners. Despite differing priorities and perceptions, these two teachers were able to establish a close working-relationship. Amongst the factors that helped were their initially positive attitude towards co-operative work, their ability to discuss problems openly as they arose, and their self-confidence, which grew with mutual support.

Mary Morton was at the end of her first year of remedial teaching. It followed a career built on frustration and rethinking. She qualified in 1977 as a biology-teacher and then spent her two-year probationary period in an Edinburgh comprehensive. At the end, she left intent on giving up teaching and feeling utterly disillusioned: 'I couldn't understand how everyone wasn't performing the way I wanted them to perform, because I thought at that time I was quite a good teacher. I couldn't understand why children failed ... I just found it incredibly frustrating.'

Looking back, she feels that she never thought about the children as individuals, and just saw her job as teaching a lesson. She blames her teacher training, her own schooling, and herself. Her training concentrated almost exclusively on preparing her to teach biology to 'O' level and Higher standard, and her education at a senior secondary school isolated her from less able children: 'I don't think I ever realized that there were children who didn't get anything out of school ... I was pitching it too high for an awful lot of the kids and had been totally unaware of it. I suppose it was my fault, but I didn't know what to do about it.'

She spent six months in France as an au pair, and then returned to do a secretarial course. She found the six months in her first (and only) secretarial job worse than teaching had ever been. She had felt unsupported and isolated as a teacher; now she was totally dependent. If she was given no work, she had nothing to do. It forced her back into teaching.

She applied to Grampian Region, and worked in an Aberdeen comprehensive for six months as a business-studies teacher. This time she felt
rather differently. She spent a lot of time with less successful children, and
enjoyed it. Somehow, she was no longer driven by the same expectations of
children and herself that had led to earlier disappointments: 'I saw that it
wasn't particularly the bright child that I was interested in. They get by
anyway. I didn't have the same to offer them.' After she left, a number of
pupils typed her letters saying that they looked on her not just as a teacher,
but also as a friend.

During her time at this school she was invited to apply to train as a
remedial teacher, and, under the system operating in Grampian, she would
spend a year on secondment to the remedial team serving a family of schools
before doing a full-time Diploma in Learning Difficulties.

It took only a week to decide that she liked the school she was seconded
to, principally because the children are such a socially diverse group. She is
a committed and explicit supporter of comprehensive education, a belief that
stems in part from her own educational history:

I was the only person in the village where I lived who went to the senior secondary,
and all the rest of them went to the junior secondary. My school must have been 7
miles away from where I lived, and for a period of time I didn't have any friends
who lived in the village any more. I found myself in an extremely strange situation
in that the people that I was at school with were all living five or ten miles away.
The other people who didn't go to my school were 'the thickos', and that was
extremely bad for me.

For similar reasons, she would like to see mixed-ability teaching extended,
and she has worked with groups in which the most and least able children
have co-operated successfully. On the other hand, she believes that mixed-
ability teaching has often been imposed on teachers who were ill-prepared
to cope with it.

She sees herself as a teacher of children, not subjects: 'I really like the
kids. It's not the subject, I'm not particularly interested in the subject at all.
I like the reaction between myself and the children. I like to be friendly with
the kids, but at the same time they would still say I was a "hard bitch".'

At other times, she describes herself less colourfully as a 'fairly strong
disciplinarian':

I have standards that the children would have to work within. Not silence. I dislike
silence in class. I hate it. Whenever the kids were working and doing it silently I
used to say to them, 'It's OK, you can discuss it with the person next to you.' I hate
that idea of teaching where I set a piece of work and they all sit and do it. It makes
me feel completely uncomfortable.

Her first year of co-operative teaching has ranged, she says, 'from the
sublime to the ridiculous':

There have been situations where I've been misused and abused, in that people have
taken me for granted. They've gone off and left me for period after period. I've not

really known what the class has been doing. I've managed to take the class and get by. I wouldn't allow it to happen if I knew that I'd be staying here.

This doesn't mean that co-operative work without such blatant abuses is straightforward. Mary has encountered problems when for various reasons her own approach to teaching has not matched her subject colleague's. She still finds teaching frustrating, but her frustrations are now with other teachers: 'When I'm team-teaching, and I think that's not a very good way to do it ... or don't let him do this, or pay attention to what the kids are doing, or get more involved with the children ...'

She has also found it difficult to cope with classes where the subject-teacher has had what she perceives as a discipline problem: 'I've been in classes where the kids have been incredibly insolent to the teachers, and that puts me in an embarrassing situation. The teacher's just backed off. What you want to do is butt in, but you can't.' This difficulty has also rubbed off on her relationship with the children:

You see them in so many different situations; the kids don't know where you're at because you're in a situation where they're allowed to carry on and be insolent, then you're in a situation where they're all under the thumb. They find it difficult to relate to you because they don't know what you're like.

This, in turn, she also finds frustrating. Although she is committed to the idea of co-operative teaching, it has meant the loss of continuous contact with and responsibility for groups of children. Nevertheless she believes her work now puts her in a good position to help children with difficulties. They need, she believes, a lot of individual help and suitable materials, and she is now in a position to provide both.

Simon Castle's working-career began with two years in a bank. But he had, from the age of fifteen or sixteen, liked the idea of teaching. In his late teens he worked as a cub- and scout-leader. His initial preference was to teach PE, but, since he suspected that the prospects for promotion might be limited, he decided to go in for business studies. After a four-year degree course at a college of higher education, he took a postgraduate certificate of education and then got his first job at his present school, where he has been for four years now.

The business-studies department, in which he is now the longest-serving member, only offers courses from S3 onwards. Simon currently has classes in both S3 and S4 doing 'O'-level and CSE courses, an S5 crash course in secretarial studies at 'O'-level, and an accounts class. He has also recently been involved in the development of the new Standard Grade course in social and vocational skills. Although he prefers the economics and accounts aspects of business studies, he has found himself teaching mainly typing and office practice. As he remarked, 'I've adapted to that.'

His experience of starting teaching is typical of many of his colleagues.

His teacher-training course provided little by way of practical help with the job: 'At times, I thought it was a waste of time, but I did learn to type. Secretarial studies was new to me. That was the best part of the course, along with going out to schools on teaching-practice.' He feels the course was particularly poor at preparing him to teach children with difficulties.

As a probationer, he found that nearly all the classes he was allocated were lower-ability pupils. Only one out of six were doing an 'O'-level syllabus. This didn't worry him at the time, but, looking back now, he feels hard done by. Exam classes and exam results are an important part of the job for him.

There's job satisfaction when you've got an older class, whereby you can see them learning; and then especially when you find out in the O-grades and Highers that they've passed. That's one of the first things I do in August is find out the results. It's nice to know if you've taught them.

He derives pleasure too from teaching children not doing 'O'-level courses when they are keen to learn, but he feels constrained in his relationships with them by the pressures of the syllabus and the final exam on the horizon: 'You see the lower-ability kids in a better light once their exams are over and just before they leave; you tend to get along a lot better with them on an informal basis – chatting away about what they're going to do when they leave; they really like that.' It pleased him greatly that some children in his last CSE class came back to school to visit him and tell him what they were doing.

Another important part of his initiation into teaching will be familiar to many of his colleagues. He was told by friends and his head of department to be strict with children at first. 'If you're not hard with the kids initially, they'll try and run over you like mad. If you hit them hard for the first two or three weeks, you hopefully hold them.' He remembers one group in his first year of teaching which he treated 'easy' for the first month and then found it difficult to control. For Simon, this was an important lesson: 'If it's not in your nature, it's quite difficult to be hard. You don't know what the limit is. It wasn't in my nature, but I'm getting better at it.'

He likes to maintain certain definite rules in the classroom, including not eating and not shouting out. He prefers children to put their hand up, but admits that with some pupils, because of their uninhibited keenness, it is very difficult for them. Nevertheless, he doesn't like classes to be entirely unresponsive. His current crash-course group are extremely quiet and he gets no feedback at all from them. Paradoxically, he finds this hard to manage after his CSE S4 group: 'It's nice to have a class that's a bit more rowdy to keep you on your toes.'

Working at his present school suits him. He enjoys the company of other members of staff and finds the school's location, close to university sports facilities, convenient for training for his principal leisure activity: running. Although teaching can be wearing, especially six to eight weeks into a term, he has never got up in the morning and regretted the fact that he has to teach. Yet he does not want to stay an assistant teacher too long. He applied unsuccessfully for the position of principal teacher in his department, and is on the look-out for promotion.

Before he began working with Mary, he had had no experience of team teaching. The last person who had been in one of his lessons had been his teaching-practice supervisor. Nevertheless, it was he who took the initiative and approached his principal teacher when he heard about the development of co-operative teaching. This was mainly because he could see that there were three or four children in the group who were very slow. He felt they could complete the course successfully with a little more help, but he didn't think he could give them the time they required.

The class that Simon and Mary worked with for a year were in the second and final year of a CSE Mode 3 course in commercial practice and office organization, which ran over seven twenty-minute periods per week. The course involves topics such as finding a job, telephone use, duplicating and copying, banking and postal services and typing. Of the eighteen in the group, twelve were boys.

In the first year of the course, pupils worked mainly from a workbook with tasks and teaching-content set out in detail. In the second year, the group worked mainly on long assignments and revision. In this year, there was no class teaching: children worked at their own pace.

In this context, Mary's work consisted of monitoring and supporting individual children, helping with problems such as understanding instructions; providing extension exercises for the more able children who finished work well ahead of the others, providing revision material such as word searches and crosswords, which were particularly used on the last period on Friday afternoon; withdrawing groups of two or three children who were often absent, to help them catch up.

With such apparently differing styles, views and personalities one might expect Simon and Mary to have found it difficult to work together. Mary comes across in conversation as extrovert and boisterous, making her points forcefully, and reacting to challenges. Simon seems much quieter and more reserved. Yet Mary disagrees:

I don't think Simon is a different personality from me. He's very much like me. He's good fun, but I don't think he's sure enough of himself yet, perhaps. I don't think the kids could ever work out what Simon was like, because he doesn't give an awful lot of himself to the kids ...

After the first lesson, Simon and I discovered we had a lot of mutual friends, so I suppose we moved on very quickly from being the polite façade to just being ourselves. I said Simon shouldn't wear a tie. Both myself and his wife take Simon by the tie and he just does what we tell him to do. No, that's not actually true ...

Together, Simon and Mary talked about the way their mutual relationship, and their relationship with the children developed:

Simon On the first day, I just tried to settle them as usual and I think I did introduce you. I remember you kept saying, 'I hope you're not embarrassed', but I wasn't. It didn't really bother me.

Mary For a long time the children didn't know who I was. Maybe they knew my name, but they didn't know what my role was at all, and that created a number of problems for me.

Simon That was my mistake. I still taught them the way I used to beforehand. I'd talk and they would be sitting down; we'd get one or two to read parts of the book, and I'd ask them questions. It was really just myself and pupils; Mary really wasn't involved at all.

Mary We talked about that.

Simon We talked about it ... well, *you* talked about it.

Mary I *told* him, I didn't have any role in that situation, I was just going to be standing there. I had slight discipline problems in that Simon would maybe go and fetch something from the cupboard, as soon as he left the kids were getting incredibly high ... All I was trying to say was that if you were going to teach in that way there wasn't a place for me.

Simon A lot of teachers would say, 'Look, you've got to conform.' I'd like to think I'm not like that ... I think the kids thought you were a student.

Mary I resolved that by saying maybe I should try to take them and you go out. There was a lot of friction initially in the class because I knew this could be a breaking-point. I had to do something. I was worried every time Simon went out of the classroom because I knew the kids would start misbehaving and boys would say dirty things. So I took the class and I resolved it. It wasn't very nice because I did have to shout at them and did have to say to them that I was there because Mr Castle thought most of them could do OK in their exam but that they were a big group and with a little bit of extra help they could all get through. I did have a few battles with one of the girls, but eventually she became very friendly with me. They *did* think I was a student. It's very difficult to say, 'This is Miss Morton; she's the new remedial teacher', because that kind of puts kids off a little. But otherwise they don't know who you are.

Simon After that we still had to keep tabs on them, but it certainly wasn't so bad.

The discussion then moved on from overcoming initial difficulties, to the style of co-operation that eventually emerged.

Simon I would introduce the lesson. I might read over the work, tell them what they should be doing. After that we'd both go round the class.

Mary Sometimes I would ask questions if Simon was talking and I would ask the question the kids should be asking if some point wasn't as clear as it should be. I would answer questions as well when he was asking the kids. Sometimes I took the role of the child, sometimes the role of the teacher ...

I took the assignment book away so that I knew what it was about, but we didn't discuss it before the lesson, because very rarely were you teaching to the class.

Simon It was straightforward enough ...

Mary Well that's what Simon thinks! *I* understood it OK; but Simon thinks it was straightforward, the kids didn't. It took a lot of explanation. It's the kind of thing that the teacher thinks is no problem, when in fact there were a lot of problems in it ...

Towards the end, when the assignments were almost finished, I took some of the kids, because there were quite a lot of absentees, and I would go into the small room and work with the four or five who were behind.

Simon With Mary helping out with those three or four pupils, it helped me to get on with the rest and do revision for their exam.

The issue of control and discipline was never very far from their minds and surfaced repeatedly in the discussion.

Simon When we began on the assignments, fortunately the kids quite like doing things for themselves. They work at different paces; they move around from the calculators to the machine room. It was good having two teachers, because you could make sure they were not just messing around. I might be in the machine room with a group and Mary would be in the main room with the rest of them. If I was on my own, even if I bawled at them they'd be up to mischief. You couldn't leave them to themselves.

Mary I always felt Simon was awfully anxious about the children's behaviour. I remember that was something that concerned you. You kept asking, 'What were they like? Were they OK?' Simon's ideas are obviously different from mine because I never ever thought the kids were out of control at all.

Simon I think my expectations are higher than yours. I tried to be harder with them, probably through my experience in the first year.

Mary I would say that you toned down.

Simon I probably did.

Mary Did you not feel more relaxed with the kids having another person in the class? You didn't have to be on top of them all the time.

Simon I probably eased from being as hard as I was initially. I still kept that distance from them really. You were probably closer to them than I was. You would sit on the desk and chat to them, whereas I wouldn't do that. The only time I would do that was after they finished their final exams.

Mary Team teaching changes your relationship with the kids. That was something that Simon found a bit of a problem – that I seemed to be more friendly with the kids, which meant that he felt the kids saw him in comparison as more of an ogre.

Simon I used to think I was the baddie, you were the goodie.

Mary But if I hadn't been there, you would still have been considered as the baddie, wouldn't you? Or was it the kids comparing my relationship to them with yours?

Simon I think if you weren't there I wouldn't have eased so much.

Mary I was seeing the kids in other places, and I know they could be unruly, but I didn't think they were unruly at all. I felt they were the kind of kids who could do with a lot of social chat. I think it's a shame if kids can't do that with teachers.

Finally, Simon and Mary recalled the kind of to and fro, easy relationship that they managed to build, and that helped to humanize them in the minds of the children.

Mary I think the kids like to have a man and a woman in the class. I've found that in general the male–female thing has been a better situation ...

We did have situations where myself and the girls were setting Simon up. You did exactly the same with the boys – give them all a laugh at me. When I was leaving they all asked what I was going to do, and you told the boys I was going for a job down at the amusement arcade … You told the boys I was running in a marathon.

And although most of the class probably knew that *Simon* was a marathon-runner, few could have suspected that Mary worked as a barmaid in the evenings.

20

Perceptions of consultancy

Tony Booth

In recent years various groups of teachers have been expected to exert on the school curriculum an influence that extends beyond the pupils they actually teach. They are expected to influence colleagues in developing language work or approaches to pastoral care, or anti-sexist education. Such a role has often been envisaged for remedial specialists too, though there has seldom been official sanction for it. But in Scotland all the new diploma courses for training teachers to deal with learning difficulties must now devote a considerable part of the course to teaching one of the 'four roles', that of 'consultancy'.

Whatever else it means, 'consultancy' stands for the involvement of remedial teachers in curriculum development in schools in its widest sense. In the national guidelines for Scottish colleges it is recognized as the 'hallmark of the new diplomas'. The term is also controversial. Many people dislike the connotations of arrogance associated with the idea of one group within the profession setting themselves up as consultants to the rest. They prefer to talk of 'consulting' or 'negotiating' with colleagues. Others resist the notion of the broader remit for remedial specialists entirely, wishing they would continue simply to 'take the pupils away'.

In an attempt to describe and examine the developments in training and practice in Scotland associated with the wider professional role for remedial teachers, I gathered a group of teachers together. In the edited discussion which follows they tried to pin down what they meant by consultancy, its relationship to other aspects of their work, the methods they employ and difficulties they encounter in trying to influence the curriculum in schools so as to reduce difficulties in learning. As these teachers make plain, for several of them the new expectations have involved a radical shift in the way they work. As one remarks, 'it's a complete change in your whole outlook'. However the tension between identifying particular children and attempting to foster inclusive curricula is handled differently by each of them.

I have divided the script of the discussion into eight sections, each centring on a particular question:

1 What is consultancy?
2 What skills do teachers need?

3 How do you get started?
4 What do you need to know about content?
5 Who has the power to change?
6 What are the limits of the role of learning-support teachers?
7 Can there be a whole school policy to reduce learning difficulties?
8 How much progress has been made?

I have commented myself where I feel the dialogue needs introduction or explication. The discussion is an examination of ideas and it is hoped it will stimulate the reader's own ideas. It represents the views and experiences of a small group of people, though in analysing the material I have been impressed by the range of points they covered.

1   WHAT IS CONSULTANCY?

The discussion started with an explanation of the relationship between co-operative teaching and 'consulting' and how one emerged from the other. It soon became clear that the planning and evaluation that some teachers call 'consultancy' others see as an integral part of co-operative teaching.

Kate   You can't say now I'm being a consultant, now I'm being a co-operative teacher, the two roles are so closely intertwined that you can't separate them.

Paul   You start off team teaching with the remedial specialist going into a classroom to help a mixed-ability class without defined goals, but after a number of weeks you start looking at areas where there are problems. Pupils who are having problems and why the pupils are having problems. And there I think you're moving into the realm of consultancy.

June   The main purpose of co-operative teaching in the secondary school is to make the curriculum more accessible. It sounds very pat, but basically your purpose in being there is to ensure that the curriculum, or at least a core element of it, is accessible to all pupils; that no one is falling through the net. I feel very strongly that no co-operative teaching should be taking place unless there has been a dialogue as to what you expect to come from it, and there should also be a time limit. At that time you review it and you say, 'Well, we've got half the way there', or 'This has come out of it'. It's terribly easy to fill up the departmental timetable with a block which says Monday, periods 3 and 7 you service those four English classes, and Tuesday, periods 2–4 you're there for these four maths classes. You rotate between the groups and you spend your time going round putting in dots and commas in the English class, and in the maths class you teach them to set it out correctly, find out why they did it wrong, and it goes on and on and on and on ... to no purpose at all. And that can be very frustrating. It's work that could be usefully done by well-motivated sixth-formers who want to put in a bit of service to the school.

Paul   Absolutely, I find that I have to really push this idea because some teachers see co-operative teaching as an end in itself. And in that case it ceases to become co-operative teaching, it becomes reducing class size effectively. I would put a time limit on it too.

Tessa   The problem of remedial teachers going into classes full of ideas about co-operative teaching and curriculum change and ending up as an auxiliary is very real.

Richard It's best to think of co-operative teaching as the starting-point and have your consultancy grow out of that. And then eventually you can reach a stage where you can even stop co-operative teaching and the consultancy can continue.

June You have to become a consultant as soon as you become openly critical of something. As soon as you go to a colleague with a criticism, however muted, you've got to be prepared to come up with an alternative.

Kate There's a problem with the word 'consultant'. It suggests that at a certain point you go into a little office, put on a white coat or a suit and *become* 'a consultant', as if it's up to others to come for your expertise. It's a two-way exploration of problems and issues and solutions rather than one person being the 'fount of all knowledge'.

Tessa But it is a complete change in your whole outlook. In the past, as remedial teachers you were concerned with your responsibility for your own pupils; now you are suddenly aware that, instead of just being responsible for children when they're with you, you are constantly looking for openings, to influence what they're taught the rest of the time. In fact the way all the pupils are taught.

Richard As your work in schools develops, then your understanding of consultancy becomes refined. In the early stages consultancy can be understood as a little more than just talking about the vocabulary of a worksheet. As things develop it becomes deciding on what are appropriate ways of presenting concepts or what is appropriate teaching-material for the whole range of pupils in the class.

Kate Once you give assent to the statement that 'the curriculum is the major source of learning difficulties and the point of potential cure', once you've done that then you have to operate as a consultant. You have to have an influence on the curriculum, so you have to work with subject colleagues. But as soon as you start touching the curriculum you realise that there are actually policy matters that have to be decided. You have to liaise with management staff to find support to push for change from chalk and talk to an approach that makes more allowance for individual differences.

Paul You're trying to prevent problems arising as opposed to attempting to patch up problems after the event. You've got to predict when problems are going to arise.

2 WHAT SKILLS DO TEACHERS NEED?

If for many teachers spending time consulting with others involved a new way of working, was this something they had to learn or did working in a new way simply bring out personal resources which were already at their disposal?

June If it's not new skills you are gaining, then you've got to develop keenly skills which were very dormant – management skills and interpersonal skills which really weren't called on at all in the traditional role for remedial teaching. You have to develop the skill of being able to plan and proceed at the right pace in discussions with people. You have to develop skills to be able to get people to be able to see another point of view when they are quite entrenched in their position.

Kate You also have to develop skills in terms of working within structures and organizations and the implication of the structure and hierarchy. If you're looking at a particular department, you find out what's going on within the department, what relationships are like within the department, what relationships are like between management and the department. You're having to judge all these things.

June   There is another type of skill as well that I've become aware of, which is recognizing when the presenting problem is the tip of the iceberg and having a framework to trace it back. Instead of as you have been asked – 'fix this worksheet' – when in fact it's the concept that is inappropriate. I've learned to test out whether this is the real problem or is it something that is four stages further back and how to trace that back.

Paul   Yes, and also how to take the teacher with you as you go back. Because there's no point in you going back there on your own. You've got to take whoever you'll be working with along with you.

June   One of the skills that always bugged me is making a judgement as to when is the right time to do it. You very often get it wrong, and you go in either too soon, which generally means that you've got to go back again, or you leave it too long, by which time they feel that basically that what they're doing is all right and I think that's quite a finely honed skill. When is the teacher ready to take criticism as opposed to 'you're doing a great job'? I had to learn that on my feet. I could only really learn it by doing it, making my mistakes and going away and analysing them and saying 'Well I really made a right hash of that – I'd better be more sensitive next time.' It applies to management as well. When is the right time to go to them?

Richard There is a degree, I think, of staff-in-service. If a remedial specialist (I can't get my tongue round the new names) had worked with a subject-teacher, I would be very disappointed if that subject-teacher was not more sensitive, more aware, more skilled in dealing with the range of pupils in front of them, whatever area of the curriculum or at what level of the school they were working – that some insight had been imparted.

Kate   I think we can forget how important it is to learn how to manage your own time. Once you get this free remit to go and influence the curriculum you can kill yourself in a fortnight and destroy your credibility in three days by seeing far too much and getting involved in far too much. Once you've gone through a year of killing yourself and getting no further you have to start setting yourself a short-term goal.

Tessa   It's a wee bit different in the primary school. Consultancy starts at the end of the year with management discussing an overview of the whole school. I advise them about ordering up materials for the next year with certain children in mind. At the beginning of the year I decide where I'm going to work and how I'm going to work. At that time teachers who are getting children who we already know have problems ask me how we can help, what resources they need. Also seeing parents. It's a big thing in primary school, where parents are looking to help their children at home. You act as a sort of relay station between teachers, parents and other professionals. You have to process what you get from them and then feed it out in an appropriate way to different class-teachers and to management. That's quite a difficult skill to manage.

3   HOW DO YOU GET STARTED?

Once a teacher has been working with subject- or class-teachers as well as the school management for a considerable time, a pattern of work may have arisen which is rewarding for everyone. But getting a broader way of working off the ground may require considerable skill in itself.

Kate You identify areas where you are confident you can make an impression. For example, you look at all the science material that is being used in a class, and you recognize that you are able to identify particular problems in the language that's used, the layout of text, the quality of illustration, the number of experiments that are demonstrated, the access that the pupils have to materials, and so on. And you select elements – where you're sure you can negotiate for some change – that will demonstrate to the science-teacher that you have made the curriculum more accessible to particular youngsters within the class. Once you have been successful you know that's going to act as your sales-promotion material for the next department that you want a breakthrough in.

June In my school I write a timetable for myself and the others in the learning-support department and that's terrific, but to consult with people you need time and it's a very tricky matter when your timetable is up for public scrutiny to have periods when you've just got 'Consultancy' written on it, and you've got 'Consultancy' written in because you know the science department will need time, and it's a good time to meet them. The teachers see that you're not actually teaching kids and that can do a lot to ruin your credibility. So you've got to pretend you're seeing kids and sneak around doing consultancy in your spare time. ... You need time to do it and you don't get paid to do it because people don't see it as real work; management don't see it as real work.

Paul One of the most gratifying situations is when someone in a subject department says, 'Look, it's more important you are available to us at a consultancy level, than that you're tinkering with this class or that class.' That's ultimately where we would all like to be. But you're going to be at the tinkering-level for an awfully long time.

Richard One might set up a consultancy situation via a bit of observation in the classroom. You might not know what you're going to be doing beforehand at all. As a result you see whether you need to focus on particular pupils or whether you want to step back and encourage the teacher to move in, or whether you want to move right out and start negotiating with the school administration. The whole thing might start from an initial period of observation.

Tessa Before any kind of consultation can take place in a primary school you've first of all got to prove your credibility to both staff and management. You go in to the class in a very general way and you prove yourself as a teacher first and foremost. That's when teachers will approach you.

Paul I know this sounds terribly devious, but it may be that the teacher has asked you in in order to keep Willie and Jeannie and Annie, quiet and busy out of their hair, but you say, well I can come in for *x* weeks, or I will do it pro tem, and what you're really trying to judge is when have I established enough credibility to be able to say, 'Don't you think it would be good if we sat down *before* the lesson next week?', and then you're into the consultancy.

June I think there's another point worth considering though it can be hard to put it into practice. It's difficult for someone to effect changes within a school they've been in for a long time. As an agent of change in the past you may have gone all out for the old system and sold yourself and your reputation on it and then there's another general swing in education. Suddenly you're faced with telling them that you've been wrong all these years ... you think you've done the most wonderful work and you sit back for a moment and you turn round and there's another Inspectorate report over your shoulder which tells you how to do it better than you've been doing and you're faced with the problem of being an agent of change again. In my opinion it's best to move on somewhere else.

4 WHAT DO YOU NEED TO KNOW ABOUT CONTENT?

Disagreements arise about the extent to which support teachers need to be conversant with or should interfere with the content of lessons. Are they technologists operating on the curricula produced by others or should they be involved in planning what is taught as well as how it is put across?

Paul   I don't think you have to know that much about the content. I think what you need to have is a framework for investigating how the material is imparted to children.

Kate   Certainly I go into subjects where I don't have training in the subject. That's not a problem really, because I go in with a different cast of mind altogether. But inevitably you do get involved in thinking about whether the concepts that the teachers are aiming to get across are appropriate for the range of kids within a particular class and you end up talking about content.

June   It can be an advantage not to know too much about the subject because you're released from the assumptions the subject specialists make. ... I'm a rotten co-operative teacher in geography because it's my own subject and I get carried away with the discipline. Some of the best co-operative teaching I ever did was in biology, and what I know about biology you could write on the back of a stamp because I never did it. I could see very clearly where the kids didn't understand because it was where I didn't understand either. I was working with lower groups. The content of the lessons was set by the biology department, but they seemed to have given up hope that these pupils would ever cope with it. The staff were going through the motions of trying to teach them in the hope that maybe the odd one here and there would pick it up. I found they were assuming knowledge that the children didn't have and they were not really seeing what the children did know. They were appealing to the wrong pool of knowledge. I worked with them to get them to tap into this background knowledge and by rewriting the material we did in fact get the concepts that we wanted. We actually used the same experiments as the rest of the year group but we did it in a slightly different way and certainly with different worksheets.

Richard One of the very first things we ask is, why are you teaching the thing, why do you think they need to know it?

Paul   You have to know people really well before you're asking them, 'Why are you doing this?' There's another way of asking, 'Why are you doing this?', and that is, 'I don't know anything about physics. Could you tell me why you're doing this?'

June   I don't think I would start there. I think that if you get to the point of saying, 'Should you be teaching this?', then you have already worked with the department concerned on the language, the presentation, the rate, the differentiation of the curriculum. It is only if you have good rapport with somebody from the subject side that you should begin to question the relevance of the content.

Tessa   In a primary school you really do have to know what's going on in the core curriculum from one end to the other, and, yes, I would say it's my job to go in and give advice on it. For example, at the moment we have the new text book of *SPMG* coming in here – it's a Scottish primary maths that we use in my region – and I've had to look at the textbooks and consider all the implications that they raise for practical maths. I'm concerned that practical maths will be thrown out of the door.

5   WHO HAS THE POWER TO CHANGE TEACHERS?

To the extent that remedial teachers have changed into learning-support specialists, something has facilitated the change. These teachers point to the Scottish Inspectorate report of 1978 as well as the groundswell amongst teachers themselves. They recognize a new status given to dealing with learning difficulties and are keen to make the most of it while it lasts. But they are aware of the limited effect they can have without support from head teachers, other senior staff and local-education-authority policies.

Paul   ... It depended on the changing attitude of the remedial teachers and to some extent the real nerve of the remedial teachers.

June   I don't know that we needed to change our attitude. We recognized that the pupil was not getting appropriate help in this subject or that subject. I think what tended to happen was the subject-department barrier came down and you did what you could outside the subject for the child. You negotiated with the child, you saw the parents, you did all these things. You did everything bar interfere with the subject, and you sat and you grumbled and you moaned and you said, 'It's all no use because the minute he gets back into that room it'll all be undone and he'll be as diffident as ever by next week.' I think the big change has been there's been a remedial specialist following the child back in and taking those views, the work, the advice, along in the class. Because, as we also knew before, that wasn't the only child who needed it. I think it's getting through the subject-department barrier that's new, not that I didn't know what to do before, but I tended to do nothing about it because I felt shut out.

Richard   The principal teacher (remedial) in the secondary hasn't got the clout. You're only dealing, if you're lucky, with your equals. Secondary departments are difficult little eggs to get into because they're autonomous. And traditionally nobody, except the Inspectorate, and they soon go away, interferes with what happens within the confines of the department. But, having said that, compared to primary there are rather more chinks for us, because there are more of them. The secondary head teacher's an autonomous beast, but the primary head teacher is even more autonomous, because the kingdom is more defined. There's fewer outlying districts where they can break down the great big wall.

Kate   But at least in primary you're not subject to the same constraints as far as the curriculum is concerned; you don't have the exam board and the whole exam structure sitting on top of you.

Tessa   Yes, but unless you have got a head teacher who is prepared to say, 'You need that time, I'm prepared to give it to you', then it's a wash-out. All right, you've got your quarter-past-three, but that quarter-past-three you depend on also to keep up to date with children that you're no longer seeing, or children who you are seeing, and want to keep the teacher totally up to date with what you're doing. There's so many other things to be done during it that you need time to see that teacher during the school day and you need your head teacher to be backing you.

Richard Everything depends on how much power the management in a given school invest in you.

Paul Let me give you an example from my own school. A new head teacher arrived last year and he has abolished the remedial class and introduced total mixed-ability classes throughout the first year. This year the big job of my department is to promote mixed-ability teaching for mixed-ability classes. There is this impetus of the change taking place. Most teachers are now very keen to do it. It's a very very big job, and we're having to move fairly cautiously, but it's pleasant because we're not fighting people to do it. They're keen to co-operate even though they've taken mixed-ability work on board for the first time. It's really very pleasant. We still have the old system working, higher up the school. We still have the class in the second year, but it ought not to happen again.

Tessa Within the last few years my experience has been that people anxious for promotion have been coming along and making a point of getting to know about learning difficulties. When they get the little chit which says, 'You have been invited for an interview on ...', their first port of call very frequently thereafter is up to see the old remedial teacher: 'Tell me about remedial teaching and I have a class in twenty minutes.' It is becoming more and more of a high-profile area in terms of career prospects, and everybody is being expected to be able to say the statutory four sentences on remedial work, and if you can actually write on your CV 'I have been involved in co-operative teaching' – or in planning, or whatever – 'with our learning-support services', this is the good thing. It's easy to laugh at it, but I don't think we should lightly spurn it, because it is there and it looks as if it's going to continue to be there for a few years.

6 WHAT ARE THE LIMITS OF THE ROLE OF LEARNING-SUPPORT TEACHERS?

When one group of teachers redefine their role, this brings them into potential conflict with a whole host of people with whom their new position can overlap. The problem can become more acute when the new role is broader, less specialist. Unlike some other professions, in schools the least specialist posts are at the top of the hierarchy. So, having a view on every area of the curriculum as well as on the organization of the school can place learning-support teachers in an unusual position. As one teacher remarked for primary schools, 'One of the major difficulties in some regions is how you reconcile having somebody like a learning difficulty specialist in the same school as an assistant head, because a lot of the job conflicts.'

In training in Scotland there has been a firm distinction between quali-fications to reduce the learning difficulties of pupils in the mainstream and those for supporting pupils of low ability or with disabilities or deviant behaviour who might be the subject of Records (like Statements in England

and Wales). In actual practice, however, remedial or learning-support teachers frequently do take on responsibility for pupils with a variety of difficulties that are traditionally outside their remit. The organizational absurdity of the coexistence of remedial and special needs departments within a single school are often resolved by having a single head of department.

Paul In my region we have special classes in mainstream schools. In my school we have a group of pupils who have been called up until now the 'mildly mentally handicapped'. My title is Principal Teacher in Charge of Remedial and Special Education. Children who have been partially hearing or visually impaired have either gone out of the region if the case is severe enough, or, if it's not too severe, we have the children in our school. I have a monitoring-job there, and with one child in the early days we had quite a big input, because a member of my department was the only one who could understand what he said.

A number of teachers have recognized that dealing with the curriculum implications of the disability of a pupil is an integral part of providing access to an appropriate curriculum for the same pupil. Teachers in this group were aware that, because these implications had not necessarily been taken on board by the authorities within or beyond the school, life could be made difficult for them.

June You need to have a co-ordinating role. If you have a visiting teacher for the deaf or a peripatetic specialist, you will be the person in the school with whom they will liaise; you will then channel their expertise to other subject-teachers and class-teachers and you will raise the implications of their vision or hearing impairment in your discussion about curriculum development, their position in class and so on. Your commitment at a professional level would make you take that aboard, but there needs to be a written statement in a school. Liaising with these people is part of your responsibility.

Kate It really has to be within the policy. I worked in a school with pupils who had various levels of visual impairment and also a number of pupils who had physical disabilities. All of these had implications for provision across the curriculum. Initially the liaison was going to be between guidance staff and external agencies. Provision was going to take account of pastoral considerations, but it was not taking account of curriculum implications. It really had to be thrashed out that, if there were all these curriculum implications, then liaison with these external agencies was to be done by your learning difficulties specialists, who would then transmit information across the curriculum.

Attention is drawn, then, to potential overlap, particularly at secondary level, with a parallel group of guidance or pastoral-care staff in catering for pupils with disabilities. But, as one of the teachers remarked earlier, this could be the 'tip of the iceberg'. The heart of the job of pastoral-care staff is in overseeing discipline in the school. Many people would argue that disaffection in school as much as difficulties in learning can be attributed to the nature of the curriculum and that it is there that one should look first for a solution. Yet this is not an aspect which is widely included in the new training in Scotland.

The teachers in the discussion group were initially concerned at being overwhelmed with work if problems of discipline became part of their remit, though they had no doubt that a new relationship with guidance staff had to be forged and even that guidance staff were treading the same expanding path as themselves. To rethink their relationship with guidance staff, perhaps they need to follow through the implications of the logic of their own professional development. For, if they wish to shift the focus of their initiative in learning difficulties from pupils to curricula, and if curricular problems exacerbate disaffection, then they are already operating on the disaffection of pupils. Did they agree that disaffection might be a good or even the best signal that there was something wrong with the curriculum?

June   Not always, no ... Very many pupils who could easily cope with what is being presented to them are disaffected.

Paul   You couldn't look after the needs of disaffected and disruptive pupils because you could lose every iota of your time, lose all possibility of affecting the system.

Tessa   You have to distinguish between taking on the job of salvaging discipline problems and taking on youngsters who have learning problems because of some severe social or emotional disturbance.

Richard   If you get the relationship between a remedial department and the guidance department right it's marvellous, but if you get it wrong it's catastrophic. You can write policies until you run out of paper, but there's so many areas where you overlap. It has got to be on a level of professional co-operation as opposed to a level of professional rivalry. If you're not very careful, things can go sadly adrift.

Paul   We have two very different cases on the go at the moment. One child was identified last year as having learning difficulties in certain subjects and so he was given support from a remedial teacher. He had been truanting, but when he received remedial support it stopped. Last week one of the games-teachers came to me and said, 'This child has started truanting again.' He was clearly relating the taking-away of remedial support to the truanting. And that may be; he may still be having difficulties that require some support, so we are coming in and are prepared to help him.

There is another boy in the fourth year who had remedial support about three years back. He truants off and on and gets into a lot of trouble. In our opinion he can cope with the work that he's being given. But his older brother spent most of his last year being suspended from school. There is a family and social and cultural image involved here. I don't think it would be a valid use of remedial teachers' time to do too much in that case. So we're not taking that up. The guidance staff are being asked to cope with the social aspect of the second boy's case.

Tessa   In the Primary 6 class there are several difficult children who – not necessarily very bad children, but who can't work alone, they want somebody with them. I'm being used there as a kind of buffer. By working with that particular group I am providing them with what they need at the moment with the hope that we will withdraw it later on. It's taken the sting out of a situation while the teacher is feeling threatened.

June   But we do have to recognize that the guidance system is moving in a way which closely parallels what has happened in remedial education. They're moving away from simply looking at individual pupils, at the end product of the system. They're looking at the processes within the curriculum, at its content and at ways of training staff to make curricula less disaffecting. It's interesting that two groups of staff are moving in a similar way. Hopefully it will create a wider net within which the children can be helped.

7   CAN THERE BE A WHOLE-SCHOOL POLICY TO REDUCE DIFFICULTIES IN LEARNING?

While the notion of a 'whole-school policy' has become a catchphrase of the 1980s, it's not at all clear what it means and whether it is attainable. It is clear from the discussion that learning-support staff need in turn the support of their colleagues and in particular the senior management of the school. But how reasonable is it to expect agreement on approaches to learning difficulties within the school when in a school of six teachers there may be six different views of education expressed?

June   I'm trying, just now, to write a policy for the school on pupils with learning difficulties. I am finding that it impinges on so many different aspects of the school and involves everybody from the janitor to the head teacher. It's incredibly difficult to get it on paper.

Paul   While I think it has to be pushed by management, I think it has to have its bones fleshed out among the staff. Otherwise you've not got a school policy. You've just got people paying lip service to it, but really you have tissue rejection.

Richard Yes it has to be something which is developed in the whole school. Even if six people can have six different opinions you have to find some common ground. They must agree that it's their job to teach all their pupils.

June   You have to begin to lay down broad issues like mixed-ability work, minimal withdrawal.

Kate   There are certain philosophical principles to which a school must be committed, and once the school management has made such a commitment on paper then that becomes your basis for negotiation on every practicality through years of battling and challenging, wheeling and dealing.

But if whole-school policies depend on your making a statement of fundamental beliefs, then to what extent is it reasonable to expect agreement on fundamental beliefs about education? When we tried to formulate the fundamental belief on which our courses on learning difficulties should rest, we came down to a principle of equality of value: that pupils are of equal worth irrespective of their ability, disability, background, skin colour, sex or attainment. But, once state it in that way, we recognize that it is not a recipe for agreement.

Kate The learning difficulties specialist who thinks that, eventually, they won't have to manage conflict over this policy is really crazy. It is going to come to fundamental clashes. You could wait until the third millennium in any secondary school if you didn't change the staff, and you still wouldn't get a consensus. There has to be a point where management say, 'This is the way we are going to do it.'

Tessa In some regions it is part of regional policy to insist that each school has its own policy for pupils with learning difficulties.

June I don't really think we should be debating a policy about pupils who have learning difficulties. I think we should be trying to define how to avoid learning difficulties. In my school I'm trying to push people right away from the deficit model of the child into looking at, really looking at, the curriculum and its differentiation.

Paul Once you're into the deficit model of saying, 'The child who cannot ...', it's destructive; and yet, when you define and describe and lay out areas of responsibility, it is so very, very difficult to avoid the pupil-deficit model.

8   HOW MUCH PROGRESS HAS BEEN MADE?

During the discussion there was an emphasis on what the teachers wanted to happen in the schools. They were aware though of the very many barriers that exist to creating curricula accessible to the full range of pupils in the school. It was easy for management and other staff to pay lip service to change: 'People say they're accepting it but really they are rejecting it. They just carry on as before.' There was little doubt that these teachers had seen a change in practice, but there was little point in painting an over-rosy picture which would contribute to the lip service paid by those resisting the developments.

Tessa The attitude is still there. Even since the Inspectorate report, class-teachers are not in the habit of saying, 'The buck stops here' ... It's not so much that they necessarily want you to do your knitting in the wee cupboard, it's just that they personally don't want to have to take the responsibility for seeing that a child is appropriately educated.

June It's in the secondary school as well. 'You're the reading-teacher ... take him away ... he shouldn't be in that class.' I've had students over from training-college and they've said exactly the same thing. 'Is there not somewhere else they can send so-and-so? He shouldn't be in that class'. If you get that sort of statement from youngsters who are currently in training, you still have a long way to go.

Paul There's an inclination for management to use us to deflect pressure from themselves. They say, 'Oh, here's Mr or Mrs So-and-so, straight back from the Diploma in Learning Difficulties. She knows what she's talking about; why, she's been shooting her mouth off about it all the time she's been away, so let's get her to do it.'

21

The place of withdrawal

Hellen Matthews

In this chapter Hellen Matthews, a principal remedial teacher in Aberdeen, discusses attitudes to withdrawal of pupils experiencing difficulties in learning both before and after the introduction of a policy emphasizing support in mainstream classes. She suggests that initially there was an overreaction: no withdrawal at any cost. She argues for a reassessment of the most effective settings for learning for pupils on particular tasks, and suggests that this may not always be the mainstream classroom; what matters is less the fact of withdrawal, than the purposes it serves.

Discussion about the withdrawal of pupils for remedial help from the secondary-school classes is often dogged by misunderstanding. In the past in Grampian Region, the withdrawal of pupils from class on a regular basis for extra help in language and mathematics denied them complete class participation and access to the whole curriculum. A decision to withdraw them was often made on admission to secondary school if they had experienced difficulties in their primary school. Withdrawal usually occurred during modern-languages periods. It was automatically assumed that those who were 'poor' at English and maths would be 'poor' at modern languages (often without this hypothesis being tested in individual cases) and their parents were 'advised' against their participation. In schools which had no such definite policy on withdrawal and no in-class remedial teaching, pupils were withdrawn haphazardly and very often from subjects, such as PE, art and music, which one might argue they particularly needed to experience, precisely because there they could interact freed from the handicap of poor language and number skills. Any system of remedial help which devalues aesthetic subjects is even less justifiable than withdrawal from a foreign language, where it could be thought that a pupil who is poor in native language skills might well have difficulty – although this remains controversial. Nevertheless, both these systems, along with the older system of 'the backward class', run entirely counter to the philosophy of comprehensive education, which seeks to end divisions among children and to give similar curricular opportunities to all.

In primary schools, practices similar to those in secondary schools prevailed. The remedial teacher was often told that a pupil could quite easily skip choir, drama, art or swimming to make time for extra help: in other words, that these subjects were less important features of the curriculum. As a practising remedial teacher who had trained as an English-teacher, I found myself unable to implement such a policy, and in one catchment area where I worked I simply refused to withdraw children on this basis in both primary and secondary schools. It seemed to me quite wrong that a child whose problems stemmed in part from limited experience of the world should be given less than others, and end up with a school curriculum consisting of a relentless diet of language and number activities divorced from the context of a varied and stimulating curriculum.

The problems associated with early withdrawal of pupils from areas of the curriculum were compounded at a later stage in the secondary school. When pupils made decisions about subject choices for third- to fifth-year courses some were excluded from the foreign-language options. Many traditionally organized remedial departments found themselves with groups of fourteen- to sixteen-year-olds for whom as many as six periods a week of work had to be provided. However well-intentioned, courses thus devised existed for negative reasons, and the cynical might say that at least some of the rash of 'basic' or 'social' skills courses which emerged were a direct result of this problem. Working in the field at that time, it was my belief that the basic-skills course could not be justified as a course for a few selected in this way, particularly in a socially deprived catchment area where social-skills training should have been available to all across the curriculum in an integrated way.

In 1977 Grampian Region published a document which recommended an end to the existing policy of withdrawal (Grampian Regional Council Education Committee, 1977). The response of schools varied in part according to the staffing available for cross-curricular support. But at present, within schools which have remedial support within their classes, the debate about withdrawal has entirely shifted ground. This has been assisted by the arrival of *Tour de France* and other oral/aural-approach foreign-language courses which offer some scope for individual learning (see chapter 36).

Now, when we discuss 'withdrawal' within this region we are speaking about precisely which settings are most appropriate for support in class, either in a quiet area of the classroom or in another room. The decisions made should be common-sense ones, taking account of the following kinds of consideration.

1 How easily distracted is the pupil with the tasks in hand?
2 Will the dialogue which the pupil and I shall share interfere with other talk going on in the classroom? Will our work be distracting to the other teacher or the rest of the class, either because of conversations cutting across each other or because the rest of the class is working quietly?
3 Will being overheard possibly embarrass the pupil being helped?

The fact that the pupil may for some reason (e.g. prolonged absence) be doing completely different work is not in itself a sufficient reason for removing to another room, and pressure to do this becomes less where teaching-styles permit group or individual learning.

There is a further question of how to assess the pattern of withdrawal for pupils with severe learning difficulties as the 'Parents' Charter' in the 1981 Education (Scotland) Act brings increasing numbers of such children into mainstream schools.

One would hope that that particular phase in the wake of the Region's 'no-withdrawal' policy when teachers confused concepts of 'withdrawal' and felt they could never take a child to another room even if that would have been the best setting has now passed, and that common sense prevails. After all, pupils are still withdrawn repeatedly for individual music lessons, for example – would anyone suggest that trumpet lessons should take place in class? Since these pupils do miss class work as a consequence, this could be seen as very controversial!

The following examples illustrate different ways of dealing with learning difficulties in my school.

1   I would not withdraw a child in S1/S2 science here, as I cannot imagine a reason for it. The apparatus, the individualized style of learning, where all children in the laboratory are doing different things anyway, and the privacy which this situation generates, all point to in-class tutorial work (see chapter 17).

2   With *Tour de France* I often withdraw that group of pupils who have made low scores on the current criterion-referenced assessment. The course allows for revision and reassessment and, since *Tour de France* is a largely oral/aural course, to conduct such revision within the classroom where other work is going on would simply subject all pupils and staff to auditory interference: a quiet, separate room is much more satisfactory for everyone.

3   If, following an assessment in mathematics, a number of pupils reveal difficulties (despite in-class support) in a particular topic through which they have just worked, I withdraw them as a group for reasons of economy. I even, if numbers are small, withdraw pupils with similar difficulties across two mathematics classes taking place simultaneously. Here the setting may be either another part of a large maths area or another room, depending on need for boards, equipment, and so on. Following the 'remedial' session, pupils return to their maths classes and continue with their work, which is in any case individualized. On a day-to-day basis, individual help within the class is also given. Two points should be noted. Both settings for help – in and out of the classroom, individually or with other pupils – are commonplace and there is no fixed pool of 'remedial' pupils. A very able pupil having difficulty may also receive my help: our system aims to offer maximum flexibility.

A common-sense approach to learning-support derives from basic considerations about what is the best working-environment for the pupil. An environment full of noise and distraction which requires a constant filtering of irrelevant information is not a good learning-environment for most people. In making decisions as teachers, we should give some thought to how we learn most effectively ourselves and seek to establish an environment of equal quality for our pupils.

REFERENCE

Grampian Regional Council Education Committee 1977: *Working Party Report on Remedial Education in Secondary Schools*. Aberdeen: Grampian Regional Council.

Integrating Special Education

22

The policy and practice of integration

Tony Booth

This chapter provides an introduction to the theory and practice of integration and examines the extent to which integration is part of government policy. It argues for a conception of integration which is linked to the development of comprehensive community primary and secondary schools and views segregation as a form of selection which involves the devaluation of some groups of pupils. Further detailed discussion of this issue can be found in Integrating Special Education *(Booth and Potts, 1983) and in the third volume of 'Curricula for All', Including Pupils with Disabilities.*

WHAT IS INTEGRATION IN EDUCATION?

I define integration in education as *the process of increasing the participation of children and young people, their families, communities and teachers in the educational and social life of ordinary schools and colleges.* Usually integration is taken to refer only to the process of bringing children with disabilities or educational handicaps from special into ordinary schools. But a definition of integration as a *process* without any end point highlights the possibilities for a further increase in the participation of children with disabilities once they are within the ordinary school. Can they join in ordinary lessons? Can they have and determine rewarding social contacts with other children? Can they play as significant a role in school life as other children? But if we are willing to examine the degree to which we permit the participation of children with disabilities, then it makes sense to do the same for *all* children and to increase the extent to which all children receive an appropriate education irrespective of their class, sex, colour, background, culture or disability. The process of integration, then, involves no less than the creation of a comprehensive system of nursery, primary, secondary and further education in which 'comprehensive' means 'for all'.

My definition of integration also includes parents and teachers as well as the community in which the school is located. It would, after all, be inconsistent to ask how schools respond to the needs, interests and choices of pupils without doing the same for all their participants. What lessons do children receive about the value or function of their participation if their teachers exert no control over their own work? But there is also a more specific reason for including adults. Most people with disabilities are adults, particularly old people, and our failure to make schools accessible excludes them from participation in their children's or grandchildren's education, as well as from community facilities based in schools. Most significantly, a lack of access precludes people with disabilities from working as teachers, school secretaries, educational advisers and support professionals. In considering integration within education we must take a new look at the inclusion of people with disabilities in work both inside and outside schools.

Integration can be seen, then, as part of a process in which schools increasingly respond to the needs of their communities and in which communities have an increasing role in determining the nature and content of schooling. Whilst some form of community schooling is the ultimate goal of such a process, achieving the goal involves many steps. It is *change* in the direction of increasing participation, rather than any particular form of educational provision, which defines integration. The education for some groups of children with disabilities might be supported by a centralized resource base in the ordinary school as one step in returning them from segregated schooling. Whether or not it is feasible or desirable for all children to attend their neighbourhood schools can only be determined as the integration process is implemented.

Any increase in the involvement of communities in education entails a transfer of power to the consumers from the providers. On such a view, integration is an essentially political process.

WHY ARE CHILDREN IN SPECIAL SCHOOLS?

I find it useful to divide into two sorts the arguments commonly used to justify the exclusion of children with disabilities from ordinary schools. The first sort, *centralization* arguments, highlight the efficiency with which resources can be deployed. They concern a perceived need to centralize specialist equipment, teachers and support services for some children. Now, while such arguments are frequently taken to imply a need for separate special schooling, they cannot be used legitimately in that way. For the physical centralization of resources and the grouping-together of 'special' children and teachers can occur within ordinary schools as easily as on a separate site.

Valid arguments for segregated schooling, on the other hand, must justify the isolation of groups of children as an essential feature of their education, and these, *isolation* arguments, form the second sort. The isolation of children may be advocated for their protection or our own or because their isolation brings a positive benefit to them or the people that work with them. Separate education for 'mentally handicapped' children is frequently justified on the grounds that they need protection from the harshness and competitiveness of ordinary schools. Frequently, children are assigned to schools for the 'maladjusted' for the sake of the safety and peace of mind of children and teachers in the ordinary schools. Some people, including many deaf adults, argue that deaf children need to be isolated from the hearing world in order to develop a sense of community as well as proficiency as sign-language users. (I have examined the cogency of such arguments in Booth, 1983.)

Of course, there are historical reasons for the existence of special schooling which have nothing to do with the logic of arguments used in its favour and these help to account for some of the confusions that have arisen. The misapplication of arguments for centralizing resources depends on the confounding of 'special provision' and 'special placement'. Special provision can be delivered to any site. Such a confusion may have arisen partly because it has suited the professionals involved in the education of children with disabilities to believe that their assignment to a special place guaranteed their receipt of 'special treatment'.

SEGREGATION AND SELECTION

The existence of special schooling can best be understood as dependent on the same selection philosophy or political ideology which underpinned the sorting of children by an eleven-plus examination into grammar and secondary-modern schools. Such a philosophy has two main strands: first, that children could and should be divided into homogeneous groupings which require a uniform style of education; secondly, that such education should take place in separate buildings. It is important to note that the second aspect of selection does not follow from the first; the separation of children into homogeneous groupings does not entail that such groups require separate buildings for their education. The justification for such separation in the case of grammar schools is that it is easier to surround distinct buildings with an aura of high status for both pupils and teachers and thus make them serve as an educational carrot.

A consequence of applying a selection philosophy at the upper end of the ability range is that segregated schooling for children of 'low ability' will serve as an educational stick; separate schools for children with 'moderate' and 'severe' learning difficulties will have low status and attendance at them will be perceived as a punishment. There can be little doubt that schools for pupils designated as having moderate learning difficulties, whose pupils are predominantly working-class, have been frequently regarded in this way, and a considerable amount of 'persuasion' has been needed to discourage parents from resisting transfer of their children to them. Sally Tomlinson (1982) has described such schools as providing a stigmatized education without credentials for working-class children which plays a part in legitimating and reproducing the class structure.

At first sight it might seem that there is less stigma attached to other groups. Placement in schools for pupils designated as having severe learning difficulties is often seen as an inevitable consequence of a label assigned to a child at birth or shortly afterwards and may meet with less resistance and hence *appear to be* subject to less compulsion. However there is evidence against such an interpretation. Where parents have challenged the appropriateness of such schooling for their children, the forces for compulsion have been revealed. The attempts of one group of parents to persuade their local education authority to provide a class in an ordinary school were summarily dismissed by the authority on the basis of false claims about the abilities of the children and the 'unrealistic attitudes' of the parents to them (see Booth and Statham, 1982; Burrows, 1983). The stigmatized nature of such education is also powerfully revealed by the alacrity with which parents will accept a redefinition of their child as having moderate learning difficulties and their disappointment if this process is reversed. It is shown too by the vigilance with which some heads of schools for moderate learning difficulties keep out children, such as those with Down's syndrome, who they think 'look' mentally handicapped. An interesting comment on the attitude to two groups of pupils was shown by one local education authority which sited a unit for pregnant schoolgirls in the grounds of one of their schools for pupils with severe learning difficulties.

Nor should such schools be regarded as always being a haven of acceptance for their pupils; since they are at the extreme of a system of schooling based on selection by ability it is hardly surprising that rigid segregation often operates within them. The profoundly and multiply handicapped children, known as the 'special-care' group, often have no contact at all with the rest of the school. At one school there were several sub-divisions even within 'special care' (Corbett, 1982). When the school opened in 1971 the special-care department contained two undifferentiated groups. By 1977 these had been subdivided to form groups for immobile, semi-mobile, problem and hyperactive children and had been joined by a new group formed from children 'presenting behaviour problems' in the rest of the school. Staff in the department felt that they had reduced status in the school and welfare assistants rotated their duties there, regarding it as 'serving their time'. Suggestion by the head teacher that some special-care children be included with other groups part-time met with strong resistance. Staff argued that it would disrupt the lessons of the '*normal*' mentally handicapped pupils.

WHO CAN AND SHOULD BE INCLUDED IN ORDINARY SCHOOLS?

The extent to which it is *possible* to include children with disabilities within ordinary schools can be assessed to a great extent simply by considering the nature of the arguments for and against it. After all, how could it be more difficult physically to locate a given degree of specialist support within an ordinary school rather than in a separate and distant building? But a view on the possibility of integration can also be informed by practice. Examples of the successful integration of children with almost any given disability irrespective of severity, can be found somewhere in the United Kingdom.[1]

Clearly, children who are effectively educated in an ordinary school in one area could be so in another comparable area. The vast majority of children in special schools, therefore, could be transferred with their special provision into ordinary schools. Segregated education for children with moderate learning difficulties, which has always included pupils whose problems overlap precisely with uncategorized pupils in ordinary schools and which accounts for by far the largest group of special schools, could simply disappear and the specialist resources which were released as a result would benefit a far wider group. There are many reports of schemes and approaches to integration and such reports indicate that children can be included within ordinary schools irrespective of the severity of their disability. There are particular resistances to integration in the case of deaf education, pupils with severe learning difficulties and the disaffected and disruptive.

The integration of the deaf raises some of the most searching questions, because many deaf adults are violently opposed to it. They see integration as an assault on their communities, identities and language. For example, Paddy Ladd (1981) has argued,

My experience of mainstreaming in England ... leads me to believe that it is ... the most dangerous move yet against the early development of a deaf person's character, confidence and basic sense of identity. Forceful, clumsy attempts to mainstream not only deny the facts about being deaf but destroy much that deaf people and their friends have worked so hard to create and may in the last resort be seen as genocidal.

Ladd uses 'genocidal' in a literal sense to refer to the practice of advising parents against having children or to have an abortion if their offspring are likely to be deaf.

There has recently been a suppression of the use of sign language in education for the deaf in the United Kingdom and a consequent exclusion of deaf adults from the teaching-profession. The official means of communication in most schools for the deaf has been spoken English, and there have been deliberate efforts to prevent children signing, a practice which often reasserted itself the moment the teacher's back was turned. It is argued that, in preventing deaf children from using the language of the deaf community, teachers have sometimes stunted the growth of their ideas and vocabulary and impaired their ability to read and write.

I am convinced that deaf children need contact with other sign-language users and that deaf adults should not be excluded from the teaching-profession, though I think they have something to offer all children. One possible solution is to centralize provision so that a campus is shared with an ordinary school and interpreting-support is provided.

A consideration of the integration of the deaf highlights the necessity for seeing integration as an acceptance or celebration of diversity rather than an attempt to fit all pupils into a narrow definition of normality.

The number of children designated as having severe learning difficulties who are included in ordinary schools is disproportionately small, but there are examples of the inclusion of such children, both individually and in groups. Since 1971 groups of young children with severe mental handicaps have attended ordinary schools in Bromley. In 1974 all such pupils in South Derbyshire began to attend ordinary schools for the duration of their schooling irrespective of the severity of their difficulties. In South Oxfordshire a school for children with severe learning difficulties has placed a class group of children in the infant department, and another in the junior department, of a neighbouring primary school, and a third group in a nearby comprehensive secondary school. None of these schools can be regarded as educational perfection; the participation of the children could be enhanced considerably in all of them. Yet, in each case parents, teachers and pupils are pleased with the system of education. Pupils in South Oxfordshire have even objected to the insistence that they return to their special school on a Friday afternoon for an assembly. The changes that have been taking place in Springfield Junior School in South Derbyshire are described in chapter 25.

Perhaps the greatest challenge is posed by children who are disaffected or present discipline problems and are sent to 'disruptive units' or schools for the 'maladjusted'.

There can be little doubt that a concerted policy could begin to reduce the burgeoning exclusion of children to disruptive units or maladjusted provision. The excluded children do not form a homogeneous group. Children have been suspended from school for having long hair or protesting about sexist literature as well as for fighting or disrupting lessons (Grunsell, 1980). The problems of discipline, disruption and disaffection cannot be made to disappear but the only appropriate way to tackle them is by an authority-wide policy which starts from an assumption that such problems cannot be solved by removing an ever-increasing number of pupils from the schools. The head in a large community comprehensive in an impoverished area of Glasgow argued against the setting-up of units for disruptive pupils on the grounds that 'teachers are only human. They'll always be able to find ten more pupils they would be happier without.' If a freeze were put on the setting-up of new segregated provision and all the time and energy currently expended on referring children, assessing them and moving them out of ordinary schools were spent instead on reducing exclusion rates, then we could gradually redirect resources for the majority of these pupils back into their schools. In the Glasgow school I mentioned they have introduced a school panel where parents and children who are experiencing difficulties with their education attempt to work out with their teachers and others how schooling can be made to satisfy their needs. Rob Grunsell (1985) has been working on materials for school-based in-service education which could form part of a local-education-authority policy on reducing suspension, disaffection and referral to maladjusted provision and disruptive units (see also the approach taken in Booth and Coulby ed. 1987).

Of course, knowledge about who *can* be included in ordinary schools cannot actually determine decisions about who *should* attend them. For whether one favours a principle of integration or one of segregation must remain a moral choice. In fact it is the values one brings to an examination of integration schemes which influence the lessons derived from them. For, depending on one's initial assumptions, problems in integration can be viewed as evidence of failure or as a challenge to be overcome.

WHAT IS GOVERNMENT POLICY TOWARDS INTEGRATION?

I define policy as a co-ordinated attempt to control the direction of practice. It involves the elaboration of a set of principles and a plan on which actions might be based and also a definite intention and commitment to implement such a scheme. Adherence to integration *in principle* entails a desire for integration in practice; but this consistency of intention and action has not been a dominant feature of government policies towards education. In assessing government policy, as I have defined it, one has to look both at official rhetoric and at the reality of government actions.

In education we are used to working with approaches to policy-making which fall far short of a coherent strategy for change. In fact the very notion of such policy-making runs counter to a national educational slogan for local autonomy. In one common approach, policies may be identified with written documents such as a government circular or a curriculum plan for a school. But the trouble with this view is that it assumes a correspondence between public documents and the private intentions, as well as the public actions, of their authors which is rarely realized. Furthermore, official papers cannot be prescriptions; they simply do not contain sufficient detail to be unambiguously interpreted.

On a second view, officials might describe the policy of a local education authority or government department by cataloguing local or national practice. But such an approach may involve the deception that what is going on is the product of a rational design. It may also obscure the fact that officials do attempt actively to create policies in a direction which they would like to remain hidden and hence beyond criticism. As one senior educational administrator remarked at a conference, 'I didn't get where I am today by committing myself'.

In understanding policies towards integration it should be clear that government discussions and documents have not linked the participation of children with disabilities in ordinary schools to the development of comprehensive education. Although the movement to comprehensive schooling was given impetus by Circular 10/65 (Department of Education and Science, 1965), which suggested that comprehensive schools might contain 'the whole ability range', this circular was issued at a time of unprecedented expansion of segregated special provision. In looking at government policies towards integration, then, we can ask two distinct questions. What are government policies towards the inclusion of children from segregated schooling? What are government policies towards the development of comprehensive education? The answers to each of these questions throws light on the other.

What is government policy towards the inclusion of children from
special schools?

Since the early 1950s central-government documents about integration have suggested that a principle of integration is official government policy.[2] Through the 1970s a series of documents and books claimed not only adherence to a principle of integration but also that such a principle *was being implemented*.[3]

However, for almost all categories of special provision the numbers of children in special schools grew considerably throughout this period, and into the 1980s.[4]

Has the 1981 Education Act, implemented from 1 April 1983 (Good Friday and All Fools Day), created a new push towards integration? It was written, apparently, in the false belief that there was already a general national move towards integration. Clearly a law required to encourage and regulate a trend would be written differently from one intended to initiate it. Although a superficial reading of the words of the Act might lead one to suppose that the law did imply a new movement of children from special into ordinary schools, that would not appear to have been the intention of those who wrote it. Section 2 of the 1981 Act actually replaced section 10 of the 1976 Act (which was never implemented) because section 10 was regarded as too integrationist.[5] The fact that the 1980 White Paper and the 1981 Education Act went on to include words which were virtually identical to those in the 1976 Act is mystifying in the extreme. It is made only marginally less so by knowing that discussions about integration have been misleading by tradition. The 1982 Act followed on the Warnock Report, whose chairperson, Mary Warnock, remarked, 'People have said we fudged the issue of integration, but we fudged it as a matter of policy' (*Times Education Supplement*, 25 May 1978).

In Circular 1/83, which contains the Department of Education and Science directive on how assessments of special needs are to be interpreted and implemented, there is a section on 'placement' but integration is not mentioned at all (Department of Education and Science, 1983). One senior HM Inspector closely concerned with this circular suggested at a recent conference that he preferred the word 'placement' to 'integration'. Furthermore, administrators at the Department have been specifically disclaiming that the Act is integrationist. At local-government level the policy intentions and actions of officials about integration appear equally guarded. Most local education authorities who returned a questionnaire to the Advisory Centre for Education and the Spastics Society (1983) showed no inclination to change their present segregated system of special education. In a further survey, of information that local education authorities have given parents about their rights under the 1981 Education Act, few mentioned integration at all (Rogers, 1986).

It is still possible that the letter of the 1981 Act may yet be enforced by pressure groups so that it gives a fresh impetus towards integration. But the unintended consequences of a law cannot amount to government policy.

What is government policy towards comprehensive education?

In the United Kingdom, unlike most other developed nations, whether or not children should be selected by ability for different kinds of school remains a significant issue. Comprehensive secondary schools have never been introduced in Northern Ireland and grammar schools remain in many areas of England. But even within comprehensive schools the ethos of grammar schools and the social and academic divisions on which they depend are still common (Sayer, 1983). In the United Kingdom the answer to the question 'What is government policy towards comprehensive education?' may appear to be self-evident, for opponents and proponents of such education divide along party-political lines. Yet clearly the answer is more complex, for the nature of comprehensive education has never been defined by government. Does it imply groupings mixed by ability? Does it require curricula adapted to the interests and backgrounds and cultures of pupils? Does it imply power-sharing of education with the communities of the school?

The present government favours selection by ability and a return to selective schooling. It is also opposed to mixed-ability grouping. In the *Times Educational Supplement* for 18 March 1983, Stuart Sexton, political adviser to Sir Keith Joseph, was reported as saying, 'The government is doing its best to encourage setting and streaming at the top end of the primary school.' He also admitted that, when assessing the educational grounds for closing a school, one of the determining factors was whether it had mixed-ability teaching. He said that the government should not condone a system of mixed-ability teaching wherever such teaching was avoidable. Now, whether or not this orthodoxy percolates through the Department of Education and Science and local-education-authority administrations or to the schools is another matter, but the intentions are clear. And there is some evidence of its adoption by HM Inspectorate. In an otherwise favourable report on a comprehensive school in Sheffield, published in the same edition of the *Times Educational Supplement*, the Inspectorate stated that it was 'particularly worried by mixed-ability teaching in the first two years in many subjects'.

Obviously a Conservative government with such views about selective education would not curtail segregated schooling for children with mental handicaps *because* of adherence to a comprehensive ideal. And before a Labour administration did so for that reason it would have to make a new link in its thinking between comprehensive education and selection by low ability or disability. It would also need to spell out the implications of a non-selective philosophy for the organization and curricula *within* so-called comprehensive schools.

CONCLUDING REMARK

The overwhelming conclusion is that where integration does not happen it is because people with the power to make the changes do not want children with disabilities in ordinary schools. The forces for segregation still predominate over the forces for integration. These forces are not based on medical or educational facts about children with disabilities. Instead they concern values of selection and achievement which lie at the heart of our social structure.

It is commonly believed that the education system can and should provide pupils with an equality of opportunity to achieve wealth and status in society. Such a view depends in turn on the pretence that education could provide pupils with a fresh start and the beliefs that they should compete for limited rewards and that they can do so on equal terms. That we should be forced to acknowledge the ordinariness of a group of pupils who, for example, are incompetent through no fault of their own, may challenge such cherished views. The presence of such pupils in ordinary schools is a constant reminder not only that people have unequal starting-positions but also that the available opportunities depend on who controls the definition of success. Expanding the opportunities of these pupils, then, involves us in giving up ours.

NOTES

1 A bibliography of integration schemes in the UK can be found in the appendix to Booth and Potts (1983); see also Booth and Statham (1982) and Hegarty and Pocklington (1981, 1982).

2 In 1954 it was stated in Ministry of Education Circular 276 that 'no handicapped child should be sent to a special school who can be satisfactorily educated in an ordinary school'. In section 2 of the 1981 Education Act the terminology had changed but the message was the same; it became the duty of local education authorities making special provision for a child 'to secure that he is educated in

an ordinary school' provided it is compatible with his or her needs, the needs of others and with 'the efficient use of resources'.

3 For example, in the White Paper heralding the 1981 Education Act it was stated that 'An increasing number of LEAs and teachers are tackling in ordinary schools the additional needs of children, particularly those with physical and sensory handicaps in every age group. ... The Government intends that the process of planned and sensible integration of handicapped children into ordinary schools should continue' (Department of Education and Science, 1980, pp. 9, 13). See also Department of Education and Science (1974, p. 3; 1978, p. 99), and Chazan et al. (1980, p. 122).

4 I have analysed these trends, the reasons for them and the gap between official rhetoric and reality detail, in Booth (1981). Will Swann (1985) followed up this analysis and documented the continued expansion of segregated provision into the 1980s.

5 As expressed in the 1980 White Paper: 'For some children with special needs association, or full association, with other children is the wrong solution and to impose it would be unfair to the child, his parents, other children and the taxpayer...(Department of Education and Science, 1980, p. 13). Accordingly the Government did not propose to bring into force section 10 of the Education Act, 1976.

REFERENCES

Advisory Centre for Education/Spastics Society 1983: Slow progress on integration, *WHERE*, 187, 5–6.

Booth, T. 1981: Demystifying integration. In W. Swann (ed.), *The Practice of Special Education*, Oxford: Basil Blackwell.

—— 1983: Integrating special education. In Booth and Potts (1983).

Booth, T. and Coulby, D. (eds) 1987: *Curricula for All: producing and reducing disaffection*. Milton Keynes: Open University Press.

Booth, T. and Potts, P. (eds) 1983: *Integrating Special Education*. Oxford: Basil Blackwell.

Booth, T. and Statham, J. 1982: *The Nature of Special Education*. London, Croom Helm.

Burrows, L. 1983: *Integration at Sancton Wood: some lessons to be learned*. London: Centre for Studies on Integration in Education.

Chazan, M., Laing, A. F., Shackleton Bailey, M. and Jones, G. 1980: *Some of our Children*. London: Open Books.

Corbett, J. 1982: A case study of the development of the 'special care' department within an ESN(S) school from 1971–82. Unpublished paper.

Department of Education and Science 1965: *The Organisation of Secondary Education*, Circular 10/65. London: HMSO.

—— 1974: *Integrating Handicapped Children*, White Paper. London: HMSO.

—— 1978: *Special Educational Needs* (Warnock Report). London: HMSO.

—— 1980: *Special Needs in Education*, White Paper. London: HMSO.

—— 1983: *Assessments and Statements of Special Educational Needs*, Circular 1/83. London: HMSO.

Grunsell, R. 1980: *Beyond Control? Schools and Suspension*. London: Chameleon Books.

—— 1985: *Finding answers to disruption: a discussion pack for secondary teachers*, Schools Council Pamphlet Series, London, Longmans.

Hegarty, S. and Pocklington, K. 1981: *Educating Pupils with Special Needs in the Ordinary School*. Windsor: NFER/Nelson.

—— 1982: *Integration in Action*. Windsor: NFER/Nelson.

Ladd, P. 1981: The erosion of social and self-identity by the mainstream: a personal experience. In G. Montgomery (ed.), *The Integration and Disintegration of the Deaf in Society*, Edinburgh: Scottish Workshop Publications.

Rogers, R. 1986: *Caught in the Act: what LEAs tell parents under the 1981 Education Act*, London: Centre for Studies on Integration in Education.

Sayer, J. 1983: A comprehensive school for all. In Booth and Potts (1983).

Swann, W. 1985: Is the integration of children with special needs happening? *Oxford Review of Education*, 11.3, 3–18.

Tomlinson, S. 1982: *A Sociology of Special Education*. London: Routledge and Kegan Paul.

23

Making a start: small steps towards integration

Jan Moore and Carmen Renwick

This chapter reports on the collaborative teaching of Jan Moore, head of special needs at a comprehensive school, and Carmen Renwick, senior teacher with responsibility for the leavers' programme at a special school for pupils categorized as having learning difficulties. They have been working with a group containing a mix of pupils from their schools and based in the comprehensive. They see it as a first but important stage in breaking down the separation between the special and mainstream schools.

When Chesterton School needed a course for a group of pupils pursuing non-examination English work, the head of special needs (Jan Moore) decided to investigate the RSA (Royal Society of Arts) Practical Communications Skills course. The RSA Practical Profile Schemes have been developed in conjunction with the Inner London Education Authority. They are a series of assessment mechanisms which can be applied in a variety of learning situations, and which give each student the possibility of a certificate. The profile schemes do not provide a syllabus or a course content. They are templates which can be set over existing courses; for example, the Complete Profile may show that a student has demonstrated the ability to read straightforward printed texts, locate information in a library, interpret and make use of pictorial and graphic information, take instructions, give instructions, make and carry out arrangements. The senior teacher with responsibility for the leavers' programme at a local special school (Carmen Renwick) was introduced to Jan Moore so that extended links could be made with the two schools. Pupils were already attending classes in personal and social development, woodwork and needlework at the comprehensive, so they were familiar with the school. The RSA course was attractive as it seemed to allow the freedom to develop a course that was relevant to senior pupils from the special school – for example, topics of interest which developed a wide range of 'survival skills' and the like.

During the early discussions it became apparent that not only did the two groups of pupils have common needs, but we also shared common ideas about children with special needs and their teaching. We decided to teach the special-school class of fifteen-year-olds with the non-examination group as a single unit. The group was to be taught in the mainstream school, but later, at the group's request, a weekly session was held at the special school.

The group from the Lady Adrian School is made up of thirteen fifteen-year-old pupils with reading-ages of five years to ten years. Three of the group have severe social and communication problems; one boy has a welfare assistant who attends all the English sessions. There is one boy from India in the group, who has been in England for two years and who came to the special school because of his apparent 'learning difficulties'. As he learns to read, write and speak English with more confidence, it becomes clear that his problem is not one of lack of ability. Another pupil in the group is more able to speak English, but has a violent temper at times, which can frighten the 'toughest' pupil. There are several lively, attractive girls who are at ease socially, and two boys who lack a great deal of self-confidence and find the mainstream classes very daunting. One other boy, who is a regular truant, finds it difficult to feel involved in his school life at all.

The group from the mainstream class contains eleven boys and three girls. Amongst them are two Indian pupils, some lively boys who are constantly 'on report', and several who regularly truant. In fact, they are a typical 'bottom' English set! It is hardly surprising that the headmaster of the comprehensive, while giving the 'go ahead', had reservations about the amount of work involved.

Of course, a system which excludes groups of students from the mainstream of its life, labels them as 'non-exam', 'special needs', 'non-academic', 'behaviourally difficult', 'English as second language', and so on, is far from ideal. However, the process of reintegrating these pupils within their 'comprehensive' school is at present a slow one and in the meantime they still need to be taught. We felt that the special-school pupils would benefit from working with other pupils and staff. Previously these pupils had been taught by one teacher for all their lessons, exclusively in their own school. Under new leadership this has been changing rapidly.

Six pupils from the special school have just passed their CSE in art, one pupil with a grade 1. They attended art lessons with a fourth-year exam group at another local comprehensive school. They worked with the head of department, who had high expectations and demanded high standards from them. The quality of their work improved beyond recognition. We felt we would harness these high expectations with the new RSA course. Often, special-school pupils have not been expected to enter examinations, and setting such precedents is always highly motivating for both staff and pupils.

We planned the new English course over two terms and sent it to the RSA Examining Board to be validated. We started the course in September 1985 and it will run for five terms. The course is topic based; topics include 'Yourself and others', 'The media', 'Local studies', 'Leisure' and 'The world of work'. We had no special textbooks or money when we started, so much of the work was initially worksheet-based, adapted to children's different reading-levels. As we got to know the group better we were able to encourage a wider range of communication. On the first topic, 'Yourself and others', we included the making of bar charts of the birthplaces of the pupils, family trees (where appropriate), questionnaires, art posters on their likes and dislikes, fashion drawings exploring the pupils' fashion styles, and special-interest folders which each pupil had to present to the class orally. When pupils could not write down their thoughts, they would dictate to our welfare assistant, who acted as a scribe.

Initially the two groups worked in separate halves of the classroom, but gradually there has been a shift to more voluntary mixed seating-arrangements, to some extent according to pupils' background. The boys and girls began to take an interest in each other. The mainstream boys were delighted that the girls were impressed by them! These boys' image in the comprehensive had not encouraged their own fourth-year girls to spend much time with them.

Their first task was to complete a form with their personal details. Wayne, from the mainstream school, put up his hand and asked how to spell his address. The atmosphere immediately changed as the special-school pupils looked in disbelief. They were not the only ones with spelling problems. William, a popular mainstream boy with high 'street credibility', reminded his teacher that he never could spell his school's name and so could she put it on the board? The 'visiting' pupils relaxed even more.

After a request to our local education authority for more funding we now possess five tape-recorders, three school cameras and a video camera. This has made a great difference to our latest project, 'Local studies'. Groups of pupils have been out and about in the locality taking photographs of local buildings, people and street signs. The films have been developed by the husband of one of us, who is a professional photographer. One group of special-school pupils interviewed the headmaster of another local special school, and another group talked to health workers at a family-planning clinic. Three boys worked with old people in a local home, and recorded their experiences on tape. Interviewing-techniques and the use of the video were discussed in the classroom. Pupils were encouraged to write their own letters, make their own phone calls, and be as independent as possible.

It became apparent that our least able pupils needed more personal help, and we were able to achieve a maximum of eight volunteer helpers during one halcyon month. They came from the local college of further education, the university and its department of education, and there were local youngsters from the Volunteer Centre. The classroom became an adult 'workshop', as children were able to write, tape-record, discuss, look up references in the library, go out into the community and seek advice when necessary. Unfortunately the helpers have not been consistent, owing to their other commitments, but we shall try to make closer links with our local education institutions in time for the start of next term.

Part of our course included a three-day residential course. Seven pupils from each group paid £17 to work and live together. We should have liked all the pupils to attend, so next year we shall try to raise funds in order to pay for the visit ourselves. The theme was 'Communications' and included treasure trails and town trails in Bury St Edmunds, photography, video-making, eating out and generally getting on together.

Some friendships between the two groups blossomed on one memorable evening 'eating out' at a local restaurant. The girls from the special-school class wore so much make-up, tight clothing and perfume in order to impress the Chesterton boys that they produced a stunned silence from everyone in the restaurant. I have never seen the girls take such an interest in themselves before. So much for the hidden curriculum.

One boy from the special school found it necessary to compete with the comprehensive boys on every occasion and became very anxious and angry. At an animal auction in Bury two staff had physically to restrain him from attacking another boy. He damaged his hand as he hit a wall in his uncontrolled temper. Amazingly the comprehensive group ignored him, and boys who were regarded at school as 'immature' were able to discuss this pupil's problems with their own teacher with much maturity and understanding. This greater tolerance of each others' weaknesses has been one of the outstanding features of this mixed and sometimes disaffected group.

The highlight of our stay for the pupils was undoubtedly roller-skating. At the end of two hours, boys and girls from both schools were helping each other as they in turn fell, picked themselves up, and learned new skills. We recorded this on video and were able to discuss the dynamics of the group when we returned to base. This mutual sharing of experiences, which included one girl from the special school teaching the mainstream teacher to skate, has made the group much closer, and much easier to teach.

We have learned a great deal as teachers this year, as we have had to adopt varied teaching-methods according to the needs of the pupils. We had expected far too much written work from the pupils in the past and it has been difficult to restrain ourselves from listening to a tape of a pupil and saying, 'Now write down this, or this.' The tape has to stand as a valid means of communication in itself, as does a videotape, or a photograph, or a map-reading exercise, or an interview, or a child's part in a group discussion. The recording of the RSA objectives has proved time-consuming and easy to forget in the demanding hurly-burly of the class. We are determined to do better next term now the group are operating in a more relaxed fashion, but it would be a lot easier with extra staff and built-in planning and assessment sessions, which have been non-existent so far.

The whole experiment has become a normal part of the schools now and it has been taken for granted that we shall start a new group of fourth-years on the course next school year. Other schools have shown an interest in the course and have asked to observe lessons. We have had many visitors and were amused that our ordinary, noisy class should be thought to be unusual or special. One can only see it as different if one compares the classes acting in segregated institutions. Those are the places to visit in order to compare.

Working together has motivated both of us professionally and has allowed us to teach a so called 'difficult' group with more confidence. We can support each other to avoid confrontations with these pupils, and, because as teachers we are both fairly informal in our style, we have been able to work together harmoniously throughout the year. The audio-visual aids have enabled even the weakest pupils to participate, and the atmosphere of mutual acceptance among all pupils has enabled even the shyest pupils to talk more freely in class. We were impressed by how quickly this happened. We expect the pupils to succeed at their level, and this, we believe, makes them more motivated and caring about their folders of work. They seem proud of their course, and parents have talked to me about them with some interest.

Small-group work coupled with community involvement, extra support helpers, extra audio-visual equipment and extra teaching-time will establish a course which we hope will be accepted by mixed-ability classes in English in the next few years. A teacher from the English department with a similar group next year and pupils with physical disabilities from a nearby special school may also join in.

Since this chapter was written there have been considerable developments between the two schools. With the advent of GCSE, all groups studying English in the fourth year at Chesterton are mixed-ability; the 'bottom set' has been abolished. The pupils from the special school opt for course modules offered by different teachers, in the same way as other pupils. The success of the work described in this chapter contributed to giving teachers the confidence to make these changes.

24

Support for Mark: the learning experience of a six-year-old with partial sight

Will Swann

Mark is a pupil in a first school. This chapter describes him and the way he learns. He has partial sight, but, as the chapter makes clear, it becomes impossible to unravel the effects of his disability on his education. He has the assistance of a welfare assistant at school, and by looking in detail at the support he receives it becomes clear that the support is a response to his needs, whatever their source.

MARK AND HIS SCHOOL

Mark is a very likeable little boy. His oval, slightly dimpled, bespectacled face and soft voice would make him a strong contender for the part of an angelic schoolboy in an Ealing comedy. His mother said of him, 'He's so innocent; he would never lie ... he's not devious at all. If he's broken something he can't say his brother did it ... *he* did it!' Not that he is every grown-up's vision of the perfect child; like the film version of the schoolboy, Mark has his own independent streak. If there is something he'd rather not do in class, he may roll back and put his legs in the air, or wander off to find something more appealing. And there are times when he has tried his parents' patience, once to the point when they began to wonder if he wasn't 'showing all the signs of hyperactivity'. He's an excellent conversationalist, although he may appear shy on first encounters or in front of a group, partly because he rarely looks people in the face. Perhaps his favourite activities at school are stories and singing. For a while in songs he was a little echo, half a bar behind everyone else; now he has caught up.

Mark was born with cataracts in both eyes, which were removed at the age of fourteen weeks. He was left with a severe visual impairment. In his first six months his sight was restricted to light and dark, until he was fitted with contact lenses. He wore these until he was four, and he now wears glasses. The severity of his impairment is not clear. He attends a national eye hospital twice a year and on most visits his prescription is changed. The hospital staff have said that he has no effective sight without his glasses, but he is able to move around his home with ease before he puts his glasses on in the morning. He has adequate vision up to two metres with his glasses on. When he reads, he does not hold the material close up to him, but print must be reasonably large. His close vision can be surprisingly good. When the class hatched some ducks, Mark noticed that they had small black patches under their wings, and recorded this in a picture.

His distance vision is much poorer, although his ability to make use of it depends on where he is and what he is asked to do. In unfamiliar settings he can experience great difficulty. On his first visit to a neighbour's garden he was, according to his parents, 'a walking disaster', but after exploration he learns the layout of new places quickly. Yet he can also make surprising use of his distance vision. At the age of three and a half, he learned to recognize letters from the street signs around his home, which has given him an abiding interest in road signs. His parents have found that he notices details, such as shop signs, at some distance from him. In school, when he was asked to read the time from a wall clock some twelve feet away from him, he did so successfully a number of times.

Mark attended a playgroup for six months when he was three, then the local education authority recommended that he attend the nursery attached to the local first school. He spent five terms in the nursery, one more than the rest of his age group, because his teachers felt that he still needed plenty of free play, and that his concentration was too limited for the more formal work of the main school. He began in the reception class after Easter 1985 and stayed there for two terms, taught by Andrea Linton. He moved on to a new class and a new teacher, Janet Tyerman, in January 1986.

In class, Mark has the support of a full-time welfare assistant, Jane Bryant. She is also responsible for helping Darren, who has Perthe's Disease, a condition which requires him to wear a large and restricting plaster cast around his hips and upper legs. Darren needs little or no support in the classroom but requires help to move around the school and to use the toilet. In the classroom, Jane's time is largely devoted to Mark, although occasionally she works with other children in small groups. Mark's teachers are also assisted by a peripatetic teacher of the visually impaired who visits the school periodically to monitor Mark's progress, advise the staff and provide any resources they need.

MARK'S LEARNING EXPERIENCE AND THE IMPACT OF HIS IMPAIRMENT

Coping with classroom routines

Most activities in a busy infant classroom call for some ability to work unsupervised. Mark is limited in his ability to do this, although he has made considerable progress. In many tasks his attention needs to be regularly refocused. For example, in completing an addition workcard, I noticed that he would often stop work the moment Jane's attention turned to another child. Such interruptions were always very brief, but could perhaps have been more serious without Jane there.

In whole-class activities, which are only a small part of Mark's day, he may appear not to be attending. For example, during a story, while the rest of the class were sitting up listening with considerable interest, Mark spent most of his time looking at the floor, playing with vents of the wall heater or lying on his back with his head under a table. But this does not mean he was not paying attention. I asked his father to ask Mark that evening if there had been a story and what it was about. Mark could recall the storyline in some detail. There is thus a danger in judging Mark's behaviour by conventional standards. The rest of the class looked towards the book because there were interesting pictures to be seen. Since Mark was some seven feet away he could have seen little of them.

Mark also encountered some problems not because he failed to grasp the concepts he was dealing with, but because he didn't follow the procedure required by the task as his teacher defined it. One of Mark's tasks that I observed was a series of additions by one. He first had to set out counters to represent the sum on a 'set-space' mat. Then he had to make the sum on the mat using numerals written on small card squares, and finally write the sum in his book. For '5 + 1 = ' Mark filled the set space with the correct number of counters, then took a 6 from the box of numerals and put it under the group of five counters. He had solved the mathematical problem, but made a procedural error, which was corrected by Jane. In recording this sum in his book, Mark began to write on the line he had written the previous sum on. He noticed the error, and said to himself, 'I don't start there.' As he wrote the sum on the correct line he left out the equals sign, and again corrected himself immediately. So, although he made these minor procedural errors, Mark was also able to monitor his work closely. One of Mark's characteristics mentioned repeatedly by his teachers was his 'tendency to rush ahead', and they may have had in mind such errors. In the addition work it caused little difficulty, since the routine was familiar to both Mark and Jane.

In an unfamiliar context, the gap between Mark's interpretation of what he should do and the rules of the task defined by the adults could create more serious communication failures. Mark was playing a game with Alan and Natalie, assisted by Jane. On the floor between them was an outline drawing of a boat, divided into three sections. On each, three spots were marked. A die was supplied with faces either blank or marked '1p'. The object of the game was to collect toy 1p coins until the player had two, then to exchange them for a 2p coin which could be placed on one of the spots in the section of the boat allocated to that player. The winner was the first person to cover all their spots. The arithmetic here presented no problems to any of the children. Mark experienced difficulties in this game which neither of his fellow players encountered. Throughout he was the subject of much more explanation and checking from Jane than either of the other two children. For example, after Mark had thrown his second 1p, there followed considerable confusion. Mark should have picked another 1p coin, then exchanged his two 1p coins for a 2p coin to put on the boat. Instead he put his only 1p coin straight onto the boat, possibly in response to a comment from Alan that his section of the boat was still empty. His 'jumping the gun' was the beginning of an interchange between Jane and Mark in which Jane tried to ensure that Mark understood the rules, but it was not clear exactly whether or how Mark was confused. In the end Mark resorted to following Jane's directions to the letter. This episode is not significant in its own right, but an accumulation of such events in Mark's school day could begin to create frustration. In fact they were rare events, and in the second game the confusion was much reduced.

Writing and moving

Like many pupils, when Mark began in the nursery he was unable to control a pencil effectively and most of his work would appear as a random scribble. In Andrea's class, children progress from tracing over the teacher's script, to copying underneath, to independent writing. When I observed Mark, he was at the second stage in this progression. All the other children in his class

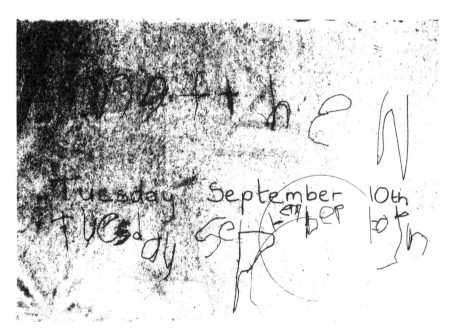

Figure 24.1

had moved on to independent writing. Figures 24.1–24.3 show the progress he made during the autumn and early spring terms, 1985–6.

Mark has difficulty controlling his hands for other purposes as well. He finds scissors very hard to use. This is clear from his attempt to cut a straight line round the edge of the darker triangles in Figure 24.2. During a television programme, the class was asked to draw letters in the air with their 'magic pencils' (their index fingers). Mark held his finger out, somewhat crooked, with his hand close to his face, and said, 'I can't see my magic pencil.' As the other children drew expansive letters in the air, Mark's hand was still and his finger-tip moved slightly. During a rehearsal for a performance of Cinderella the class was asked to clap with two fingers. Mark succeeded only in clapping with his fists clenched, until Andrea intervened and formed Mark's hands into the correct position. He was then able to carry on briefly.

Early Autumn Term. Sept .

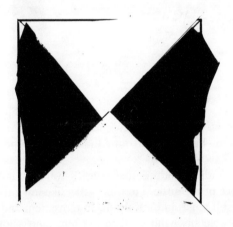

This square was

made from 4 triangles

Figure 24.2

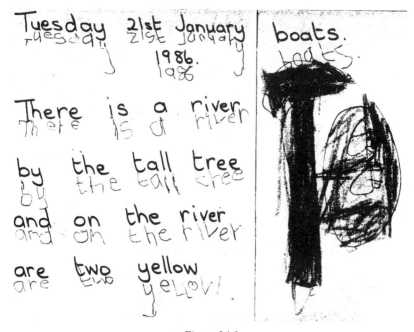

Figure 24.3

When this exercise was repeated a few minutes later, Mark could be seen forcing the fingers of his left hand into the correct shape using his right hand.

In the nursery, Andrea noticed that Mark's walking and running were unusual, being more of a shuffle. He now walks like any other six-year-old, but his running is still tense and uncertain. In movement and PE, he initially needed Andrea to hold his hand even to get him onto a low bench. Since then, his progress has been considerable. His visual impairment is more likely to play a direct role here. His difficulty in seeing obstacles and in judging distance and depth may have made him less confident and limited his opportunities to develop many skills. His impairment also denies him the opportunity to learn by observation, so that in movement lessons he cannot readily see what other children are doing.

Social life

When Mark first started in the nursery, he was in Andrea's words, 'a real loner', a description with which his parents agree. He now joins in games with other children and occasionally organizes others to play with him. However, he has no close friends, and only rarely do children come to play with him. He plays a great deal with his younger brother, Oliver.

His social position was evident one morning during register. Children were already sitting chatting on the carpet when Mark came in and sat down. Rather than join a conversation he played with a toy telephone. During the register Mark had one brief conversation with Alan, in contrast to the general quiet talk around him. His only other social contact at that time was when a girl nipped him in the back of the neck. But Mark was not completely isolated by any means: I observed him striking up short conversations on several occasions.

The origins of the pattern of Mark's social life are complex. His parents said he shares few interests with other children of his age. He watches very little television, and the most popular programmes, such as *The A Team*, are too fast for him to follow. He has only recently begun to look at his parents when talking to them. Andrea sometimes had to turn his face towards her, especially when she wanted to indicate she was cross. She also found that when Mark had bumped into someone he was unaware that he had hurt them. His impairment has prevented him from registering and copying some facial expressions and gestures. But this has not marginalized him or provoked any hostility. Children are in general very kind and considerate to him. If teachers notice that any pupil has a particular and unfamiliar style of inter-action, then this may be an area where they can actively help others to understand and accept differences.

The place of an impairment

In all probability, Mark's learning-style, patterns of attention, movement, writing and social relationships have been affected by his visual impairment, but it is impossible to say how in any precise way. They have been affected by many other factors as well. It is not possible to disentangle these various influences, and, even if it were, it is not clear that this would be of any use to his education. Many children without any visual impairment have similar learning patterns and difficulties and they may need similar help. In some instances, as we shall see, Mark was provided with support which was designed to surmount limitations imposed by his impairment. In many more instances the support he was given was a response to needs which may or may not have derived from his impairment.

THE NATURE OF SUPPORT

The word 'support' suggests something out of the ordinary. All children in all classrooms receive support from adults and other children: it is usually referred to as 'teaching'. Many of the methods that Andrea used with Mark were exactly those she used with other children, but Mark would often need more help at each stage. For much of the time the support Mark received was different only in degree. Occasionally it was different in kind. Some aspects of the support were very obvious; other aspects only became apparent when they ceased temporarily.

Personal contact

Both his teacher and his welfare assistant worked individually with Mark. The bulk of this work was taken by Jane Bryant. Her skilled and patient teaching was indicated during a seventy-minute individual typing-lesson with Mark. This was the second time that Mark had ever used the typewriter.

Mark was writing to Father Christmas. He said what he wanted to write, Jane wrote it down and they sat down at the typewriter, on the carpet in the classroom. As they turned to each word, Jane got Mark to identify the first letter and find the appropriate page in his alphabetic wordbook. She wrote out the word and they then typed it. A typical example was 'Dear':

Jane asks Mark to find the right page for 'Dear'.

Jane What does 'Dear' start with?
Mark Duh

Mark turns the pages of the wordbook from the front and goes past 'D'. Jane tells him he has gone too far and asks him to go back to the beginning and start again, sounding each letter. He finds 'D' this time and Jane writes 'Dear' in the book, pointing out that it has a capital. Jane holds down the shift key as Mark hits the 'D', too lightly at first and then, after Jane prompts him, with enough force. Jane then points to the next letter of 'Dear' in the wordbook and tells Mark it is on the top line of the keyboard. Mark finds the 'E' and types it. The sequence is repeated for 'A'. Mark then finds 'R' without a prompt. Jane tells Mark he needs a space and shows him how to make one using the space bar.

Within this two-minute sequence Mark uses many skills, but he cannot manage alone. Before a letter is typed, Jane lets him search through the wordbook freely; then, when he makes a mistake, she takes him back through the sequence and gets him to sound each letter. Thus, having given Mark an opportunity to use a faster but more difficult method, she takes him to a slower but easier method. Once typing begins, Jane reduces the complexity of the task by operating the shift key for Mark. As he types the 'e' and 'a' she limits the work he has to do by telling him which line to find the letters on. Jane prompts Mark about the space bar.

Over the course of the lesson, Jane's prompts were modified moment by moment in response to what Mark did. Support was steadily withdrawn as Mark learned. For example, the shift key was used six times. On the first four occasions, Jane told Mark that 'Dear' had a capital, and then held down the shift key without telling him what it was for. On arriving at the word 'want', Mark pointed to the shift key and asked Jane to press it. Jane replied, 'No, it's not the beginning of a sentence.' By this stage, Mark knew the function of the key, but had not yet co-ordinated it with the conventions of capital letters. On the next occasion Jane said, 'It's a new sentence, so it's a capital. How do you make a capital?' Mark pressed down the shift key and released it. Jane then got him to press it down again and held his hand down on it while he typed 'L'. When Mark came to type his own name, he spontaneously held down the shift key as he typed 'M'. Jane then removed his hand before he typed 'a'.

Andrea was conscious of the possibility that Mark could become dependent on Jane and made sure that each day Mark spent some of the time working apart from her.

Less obvious but significant support came from the other children in the class, predominantly the girls. For example, Mark played a dancer in *Cinderella*, partnered by Dawn. After their scene was over, Dawn reached out for Mark's hand and led him off. When the scene was rehearsed again, Mark took up the wrong place on stage, and was moved by Dawn and another girl. As the dance set off, and Mark was the last to start, Dawn took his hands and they began. When they rehearsed the final bow, everyone except Mark came to the front of the stage. Dawn turned round, called him, then led him to the front. On many other occasions Mark was 'kept in line' by the girls.

Setting-up

All the children in Mark's class were able to use their time profitably because their teacher had planned the activities in detail and organized the room and tables so there was no 'hanging around'. Teachers were in school at around 8.00 a.m., setting up the room. Before Mark came into the room in the morning to do the addition work described earlier, Andrea had already made detailed arrangements. The table was laid out with the group's workcards and materials: a box of coloured counters, a box of the numbers 1 to 10 written on small squares of card, pencils and crayons, and the set-space mats. At Mark's place was a workbook that Andrea had specially prepared. Mark had earlier done this activity using standard squared paper and had found it difficult to write in the small squares. Today the paper was marked in larger squares. The date was already written in large black letters at the top of his page. This had not been done for any other child. Six prominent pink dots were marked to indicate where Mark should record his sums, and Mark's pencil, sheathed in a rubber grip, had been placed on his book, another detail not provided for the others.

Various other adjustments were made on an *ad hoc* basis. For example, Andrea had provided a piece of white card with a slot cut out for Mark to use with his reading-book. This showed only one line of print at a time. In earlier maths work, Andrea had given Mark numbers written on pieces of sticky paper to bypass his writing difficulty.

When the class sat on the floor round Andrea for singing and other activities, Mark always sat close to her. This not only gave him a better chance to see but also allowed Andrea to help him with any difficult tasks, such as finger games. She also checked regularly that Mark had understood instructions issued to the class. Many children were individually addressed in this way, but Mark's name predominated. There was no evidence that he or anyone else found this obtrusive.

Providing a purposeful environment

A general busyness pervaded Mark's class. Work was extensively individualized, although all the children pursued a common path. Mark was seldom reluctant to engage in an activity, and he appeared to find his school life purposeful. The importance of this environment only became clear when it was changed. I watched Mark in two hymn-practice sessions. These took place in the school hall and involved the whole school. On both occasions, Mark's participation was tenuous. In the second session Mark did not sing any of the songs. When the school was learning new songs, the majority of his class was similarly inactive. However, even when the class was fully engaged in a clapping song, Mark was a silent non-participant. Instead he diverted himself by rocking, fiddling with the jumper of the girl next to him, rolling his head, playing with his socks, dribbling, and blowing bubbles with his saliva. This was enough to provoke alarmed looks from the girl next to him. Such episodes were not typical, but they are among the most telling for showing what might happen in a less supportive setting.

Tolerating difference

Although Mark's behaviour in hymn practice was eventually the subject of adult attention, at many other times his idiosyncrasies were simply disregarded. For example, Mark frequently hummed as he worked and was rarely checked for this, although it was at times obtrusive. On one occasion Mark passed a few minutes between activities by running back and forth in a rather jerky manner in one corner of the room. This went unremarked and probably unnoticed in the general diversity of the room. During the story described earlier, most of Mark's apparent inattention was ignored.

The system of support

The term 'system' is apposite because the various levels that I have described need to be assessed in relation to each other. The personal support that Jane provided during the typing-lesson was important because it enabled Mark to achieve something he found meaningful. Throughout the long and painstaking lesson Mark never lost sight of the purpose of the exercise, and never tired of it. The end product was shown to Andrea with some satisfaction. This support gained its value from being part of a more general task which

Mark valued. This relationship has its mirror image, for the general tolerance which allowed Mark to take part in his school gained some of its value because it gave him access to more specific valuable experiences.

CONCLUSION

A number of other children on Mark's table were also finding their work difficult. Mark, with Jane's near full-time help, completed his addition work-card with all errors dealt with before the sums were finally recorded. In the same time other children barely began the task. If support resources were to be shared out on the basis of educational need rather than disability, then Mark's advocates would find themselves with a great deal of competition. This is not to argue that Mark should be deprived of his resources. Jane's presence in particular was important to his continued success. But others would have found it useful as well. Despite her key role, Jane, like most welfare assistants, was very poorly paid. All welfare assistants employed by this local education authority were at the time on one-term contracts. The attractions of such staffing for authorities seeking greater 'cost efficiency' are considerable. The possibility that a greater use of ancillary staff may develop when or if children are integrated from special schools is one that some teachers see as a threat. They are themselves seriously underpaid by comparison with their colleagues in other developed countries. Teaching children such as Mark raises serious political questions. The development of coherent policy backed by adequate finance is the most pervasive form of support that children with disabilities and their teachers should be given.

25

Extending primary practice: Springfield Junior School

Tony Booth and Anne Jones

What can be learnt about integration by extending primary practice? The first part of this chapter is a cautionary tale about the search for models of good practice and describes the ideas for integration that an American visitor took away from a visit to Oxfordshire primary schools in the mid-1970s. The second part describes the way a group of teachers have built on their experience of primary teaching to break down the barriers between three distinct sections of a school in which 'mainstream' pupils and pupils categorized as having moderate and severe learning difficulties were educated.

MODELS FOR INTEGRATION

Most people who have taken an interest in integration have experienced a desire to point to models of good practice to allay the doubts of those who think it preferable or safer to segregate some pupils in special schools. One feature of such models is that they are usually far away either in terms of physical distance or from the current working-conditions of the audience and they can provide as much of a defence against change as a reason for it. Schools, too, are always in a state of flux and we do them a disservice by characterizing one snapshot, taken from one vantage point under one set of viewing conditions, as their ideal state.

One of the features of the voyage in search of good practice is that one often encounters people travelling in the opposite direction. Thus when Tony Booth was looking at schools in Oslo which would reflect the progress towards integration in Norway, he was directed to one high school where children with disabilities were included within groups of pupils engaged in a project-based curriculum taught by teams of teachers. He asked where he would find similar schools elsewhere and the immediate response was 'Countesthorpe in Leicestershire'.

Similarly, considerable attention has been paid to the efforts towards integration in the USA, particularly since the implementation of new legislation in the late 1970s (see Booth, 1982; Shearer and Vaughan, 1985). We have found it interesting to read an account by an American (Levine, 1979) who drew inspiration from a reverse trip across the Atlantic. He wanted to find sources of ideas to help him answer one of the key questions for integration: what forms of classroom organization permit teachers to tolerate differences between pupils? His attention had been drawn to the Plowden Report (Central Advisory Council for Education, 1967), which, he claimed, made a link between integration and the progressive primary schools.

He spent the year 1974–5 studying the Oxfordshire primary school and noting those features which made it possible to 'integrate children who have a wide variety of educational and personal needs into the same classroom':

In general, in the classrooms that I observed, the rooms were usually richly endowed with a variety of materials, and often the display of children's work was beautiful and visually exciting. The classrooms typically allowed a large measure of freedom of choice for the children. Usually, there were multiple activities taking place. Sometimes the activities were widely varied, and sometimes it was variation on a common theme (e.g. different kinds of work in mathematics, or choice in a project topic and how the topic was to be developed). In many of the classrooms, children were allowed to speak to each other most of the time. Similarly, children were free to move about as they wished. Although the crowded physical arrangements of desks limited free movement in some of the rooms, children did not have to sit at their desks all day. Many of the schools incorporated two or more grade levels within the same classroom. In one school, children from ages four to eleven were integrated into the same group under the same team of teachers, and in another school, the group ranged from ages seven to eleven. (Levine, 1979, p. 173)

He drew attention to the way team teaching could foster the adaptability required to cater for diversity and to the importance of playing down the competitiveness between pupils:

It was my impression that the team-teaching offered the teachers the greatest flexibility in the ways in which they could use their time and in the way they could devote themselves to individual children. It seemed to have great potential for integrating children at all levels into the same working environment. …

It is my belief that the noncompetitive atmosphere is a critical factor in allowing teachers to cater to individual differences, making it possible to have special children tolerated, if not totally accepted, in the normal environment. (pp. 190, 176)

We have given some space to these observations to remind us of the familiarity of the questions at the heart of the process of integration. How can a diversity of activities take place in the same classroom? How can the attention of a mixed group of pupils be sustained? How can pupils of different abilities and backgrounds feel comfortable together? There may be no great mystery to these questions or the answers to them. As Levine observed of one child,

In one classroom, a boy was working very diligently at a typewriter. The teacher had identified him as a nonreader. In fact, the teacher had been told by the boy's parents that he would literally vomit if forced to read. The child had been given the task of preparing a stencil, containing word lists that other children in the class would be using. Although the child was unable to read, he was able to match letters on a typewriter keyboard with those on a word list and slowly copy each word.

I was in that classroom for approximately one hour, and I did not see the child so much as move off his seat, even though the rules of the class allowed the children to move freely throughout the classroom. Another child, working on something completely different, would look over his shoulder every now and then and offer suggestions or help him to find his place in the list. That nonreader was dealing with symbolic materials, was making letter discriminations, and was dealing with letter combinations. The task that he had been assigned was a real one, since others in the class would be using the materials that he was producing. He had a place in the classroom and could feel that he was making his contribution. (p. 185)

To many of us Levine's account of English practice may look rosy-eyed and highlight the difficulties of anyone gaining an overall picture of practice in another country. It is difficult enough as a visitor to a single school to come away with a picture that any of the main participants would recognize. In recent years the pattern of American litigation or Italian political will or Scandinavian comprehensive education has been cited to explain the greater progress these countries have made on integration. Yet Levine asked his American readers to 'take into account cultural characteristics of British society that make it easier for special children to be accepted' (p. 193). However, he did argue that his observations should be used to indicate 'the principles that can be applied' rather than expecting that the British primary school could be 'transposed to the American scene'.

In the remainder of this chapter we shall look at the way the teachers in one junior school have followed a similar path to the American traveller: how they have attempted to apply principles of primary practice to develop the process of integration in their school. If a comprehensive school is to be defined as one which includes pupils 'over the whole ability range', then Springfield Junior must be one of very few comprehensive schools. The school has incorporated junior-age children designated as having moderate learning difficulties and pupils aged two to sixteen said to have severe learning difficulties. These include some children with profound handicaps, who have no speech and little mobility – the so-called 'special-care' group. Like any school, Springfield Road is staffed by real people, and has its own history and therefore its own particular set of human and historical advantages and handicaps. It would be absurd to suggest that the transposition of such characteristics to other schools is desirable or possible, and equally naïve to reject what can be learnt from it because it is constrained by its imperfections. We have not attempted to capture the whole school in this brief account. Even to create the illusion that we were doing so would take a far longer piece and might in any case involve an unacceptable degree of intrusion into the lives of people working there. We suggest that one can learn most by considering how the school is changing from what it was to what it might become, and we have tried to illustrate some features of that process.

SPRINGFIELD JUNIOR SCHOOL

The background

The school opened in 1937 as a junior mixed and infant school. In 1967 it lost its younger pupils to a new infant school in the area. Later, this absence of infant-age pupils was to place a limitation on the mixing of young children with 'severe learning difficulties'. When the authority was expanding seg-regated provision in the late 1960s, it chose Springfield with its extensive grounds as the site for a unit catering for forty pupils with moderate learning difficulties (the 'M' unit). These were pupils drawn from local junior schools with the usual bias towards pupils whom for one reason or another the schools found difficult to teach. They were housed in their own block of classrooms next to the main school and functioned as a mini-special school.

In 1974 the local authority responded to its recent statutory duty to take responsibility for pupils with 'severe learning difficulties' by creating a second mini-special school in a further new unit (the 'S' unit), this time for thirty-five pupils. Children were included in this unit from the age of two years, and, while the majority moved on to similar provision at the neighbouring comprehensive, children with profound disabilities could, in theory, remain at the school until they were nineteen. There was no suggestion at the time that these pupils should be integrated, and even today, while the integration of such pupils within Springfield is supported by the local education authority, the major part of provision for pupils with severe learning difficulties in the county is in special schools. Two 'new' special schools for such pupils have been built and filled since the Springfield unit was opened.

Both of the units had a teacher-in-charge, and, even though all their staff were attached to the one school, they retain considerable independence with separate funds and separate curricula. Up to 1981 there was relatively little mixing between the three groups of pupils and there was considerable resistance to such movements by some teaching-staff, both within and outside the units. As the school secretary, one of the longest-serving members of staff, recalls, 'It was operated as three schools before. It wasn't just a feeling, it actually was ... the capitation allowance was divided ... Integration then was dinner in the hall and some play in the playground and that was that...'

Now and then there were attempts by staff to create greater involvement of the separate groups but these faltered for lack of support. An NFER report on the school drew attention to the missed opportunities for integration in the school (Hegarty and Pocklington, 1982). But it would be a mistake to think that the ordinary school base made no difference to the pupils and their families. One obvious tangible benefit had been the building of a swimming-pool for the use of the whole school with funds raised primarily by parents of the group in the 'unit' for severe learning difficulties. Despite the limited contact between pupils, parents of this group felt an acceptance of their children within the community that they would not have expected had they been isolated for their education. Siblings of different abilities could attend the same school. There were also less obvious results, such as the acceptance displayed by a young man who lived in a nearby guesthouse, who had gone through Springfield Junior and the comprehensive school and could talk in a relaxed and sensitive way about people with mental handicaps.

The winds of change

However, from the beginning of 1982 the school started to undergo rapid changes. A new head teacher, Ian Mitchell, was appointed whose concern and brief it was to create a single school from the three parts. The school secretary described the scene before and after the winds of change:

Life was very calm in those days. We'd always got money left over at the end of the financial year – and nice orderly things like that. Then Ian walked through the door and we've never stopped since ... I've seen more of the handicapped children than I'd ever seen before. They're a lot closer to me. They're up and down this corridor now. Before you actually had to go over and see them, which is division not integration. We, all of us, are in together now. In the past you were teaching-staff and non-teaching-staff and the division was great – not great in a good sense – it was there: for instance, non-teaching-staff didn't attend staff-meetings. Now we do. You have to think twice before you remember who's a teacher and who isn't. I like that. I'm busier than I've ever been in my life, which is how I like it. If I was a parent of a handicapped child, this would be where I'd like him or her to come.

Ian Mitchell's early interest in teaching had been in working on fieldtrips with primary pupils:

I went to college in the West Midlands, which had an outdoor pursuits centre where we worked with difficult youngsters from an Approved School and I thought it was something that could be done with primary pupils. I put an advert in the *Primary Education Journal* offering my interest in outdoor pursuits in primary schools (in those days you couldn't get teachers ...) and they put mine right next to an advert for someone like me at a school in Leicestershire. We used to take every class away for a week with a fortnight's pre-work and a week's follow-up. We gradually merged that activity with sport for all clubs on a couple of afternoons a week, with parents and others joining in. The standard of reading and maths were really good in the school despite all this lunatic stuff. Some of us began to think standards were good because of it ...

Figure 25.1 shows the staffing-changes which took place between January 1982 and September 1983. A new deputy head, Anne Jones, was appointed in September 1982 who shared the head's background and commitment to mixed-ability teaching and learning. She revealed the chance nature of her appointment:

I had posted my application in the school postbox in the wall and when I had dropped off an area sports receipt to one of the staff Ian came leaping out to say he hadn't had an applciation from me. They never used that postbox. They had to get my application out with a hammer and chisel! Then the morning of the interview my car wouldn't start and I was frantically ringing round for a taxi to get here. So I breezed in thinking someone was trying to tell me something ...

Anne Jones's ideas were developed in her early posts teaching religious education in a secondary school: 'It was a case of she's last in, she can do RE ... But it was a place where everyone was involved in planning and where people used to swap groups and sit in on each other's lessons.'

Appointed pre-1982

Teacher-in-charge ('M' Unit)
Two Scale 3 (10–11)
Scale 2 (Remedial 10–11)
Two Scale 2S ('M' unit)
Two Scale 1S ('S' unit)

↓

**Head teacher appointed
January 1982**

↓

Appointed Autumn 1982

Deputy head teacher
Teacher-in-charge ('S' Unit)
Two Scale 1 (9 and 7–9)

↓

Appointed Spring 1983

Scale 1S (7–11)

↓

Appointed Autumn 1983

Scale 1 (7–9)

Figure 25.1 Teaching-appointments 1982–3

She then taught a lower-ability group in a streamed primary school: 'I was the youngest member of staff and did things like skip out in the yard and throw balls at children and played games with them which in those long dark days just weren't thought of ... no one would speak to me in the staffroom.'

She rejected streaming and the constraints of the classroom walls: 'I don't like a specific age range or four walls around me ... children are children to me whoever and wherever they are.'

Soon after Anne Jones joined the school the head of the 'unit' for pupils with 'severe learning difficulties' left to become head of a special school. Her place was taken by Lana, a member of her staff with the greatest interest in breaking down the barriers between groups. As she said,

I had set my mind on integration since I first came. It used to be a matter of pushing for a change in attitude from this end and it was an uphill task. But with Ian coming he's done the job for me in the mainstream ... My finances have gone into the main school fund. I'm still happy to do fund-raising – we've a sponsored swim going at the moment. But instead of raising money for a 'unit' it's for the whole school. If we're sharing the curriculum, let's share other things as well.

The plans for integrating the three parts of the school have been developed largely by the head, deputy head and head of the former 'S' unit, all of whom shared an interest in sport and outside activity. One of the early moves was to break down the distinctions between physical parts of the school. The junior group moved from the 'S' unit into the main area of the school and a group of seven-to-nine-year-olds from the main school took their place. The head teacher shifted his office across. Access to the staffroom for the whole school, which had been housed in the 'S' unit since it was built, was made through the special-care class, and a porch was added to it to prevent draughts.

The first attempt to enable pupils with diverse abilities to learn together was a 'club' session on two afternoons a week where all staff offered a wide range of craft, games and sports activities to mixed groups. These, according to the head, were a success for 'most of the pupils and some of the staff'. For some staff they appeared as an appendage to the curriculum; others felt that certain of the activities excluded pupils because they were competitive.

Inevitably 'outdoor pursuits' and school trips figure prominently in the early mixing of groups. Parents were encouraged to join in, as one parent governor, a local policeman, explained:

We are encouraged to come to the school any time. I'm a parent governor but there's an open invitation to all the parents to participate in the classes ... I actually went away with a group of pupils on a school trip.

I'd met one or two of the youngsters before in the course of my job, not for anything serious, and I kept an eye out for them in particular. I couldn't believe it. They were the ones who were hanging back to help the slower ones. It's really working very well. Some of the boys who would like to think of themselves as so-called hard cases were busy using their strength to help the handicapped children ...

We went on walks ... not just walking past things but taking notes, we looked at animal traps and pond dipping. They thought that was great. You take a net and dip it in the water and empty out what you catch in a bucket. We caught a few little newts and freshwater shrimps. We looked at the microbes under a microscope when we got back ...

The mentally handicapped children get as much out of it as any of them. More probably. They didn't miss out on anything. If necessary we would ferry some of the slower ones about at the end of the week, but at the beginning they managed very well under their own steam. We did a trip to a 'watered slough', I think it was called, 100 yards long, dark inside. All the children thought it was really exciting ... The field-study centre was about 100 or so yards from the hostel itself. We did that walk, singing each morning. A beautiful walk in the fresh air.

There are some parents who through ignorance are under the impression that I was originally, that if there are handicapped children in the school their children will suffer educationally. If more of them would take advantage of visiting the school they'd see the benefits that the children are gaining through their experience of life and of helping others. It works both ways. They all get something out of it.

I know my daughter is happy to come here each morning. Could you say more than that? I wasn't always happy to go to school, but she never misses a day ...

In order to increase the mixing of staff and pupils, each member of staff was asked to work out whom they might like to work with for which activities in the week. This voluntary choice began to break down the reluctance of teachers who were reticent about change. Team teaching started in a variety of areas of the school. One group of staff set up a shared-project afternoon described by Anne Jones in the dissertation she wrote about the school for her in-service degree of Bachelor of Education (Jones, 1983) and the following account of the project is drawn from there.

Developing project work

The project work was planned in the summer of 1983 and took place in the autumn term. It involved four teachers, a welfare assistant, a trainee nursery nurse and two parents working with forty-five pupils. (Since he began pushing for integrated groups, the head teacher of Springfield has sometimes been asked where his extra staff came from. In fact, he is staffed in accordance with county policies for mainstream and special schools. Using staff flexibly enables all groups to be reduced in size.) Of these forty-five pupils, twenty-nine were from Anne's mainstream group of seven-to-nine-year-olds. Nine pupils (aged eight to ten) had been categorized as having moderate and seven (aged seven to eleven) as having severe learning difficulties. Four mixed groups were established, each with one teacher and another adult. The adults met together to plan the course and started by stating their overall aim: 'to provide a topic approach to the curriculum that enables children of varying abilities and interests to work alongside each other and share experiences'.

They chose water as a topic because of its accessibility and because it could provide a range of experience from play to scientific investigation. They drew up charts of the possible areas they could cover, and, as the whole universe began to emerge from the pool of ideas, they made a selection from them. They charted the resources (figure 25.2) on which the experience of pupils could be based. Anne set about finding out more about the interests and abilities of the pupils in her group with whom she was less familiar. She made lists of activities and investigations for the children to conduct which she tested out in the privacy of her own bathroom, creating rumours about a religious revival as cries of 'Oh God, are you still in there?' echoed round the neighbourhood. She collected together a range of objects whose relationship with water would be put to the test and which would also provide a focus of interest for touching and questioning.

The project proper started with all groups and helpers together in a communal 'splash-in' in the school swimming-pool, and the excitement of this activity was used to trigger a brainstorming session back in the classroom

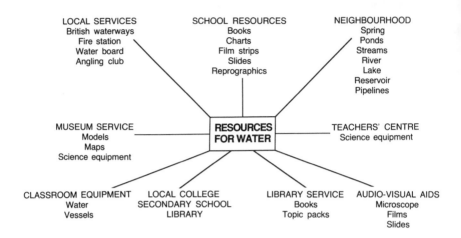

Figure 25.2 Resources for water

to produce lists of words associated with water. Then, in the smaller groups, pupils made a personal statement within a drawn raindrop: a drawing or their own collection of words. These were all mounted and displayed to indicate an acceptance of each pupil's efforts. Anne's group familiarized themselves with her collection of objects; they picked them up, looked at them, talked about them. One of the least able pupils promptly left the room and returned with a building-brick from his class base and proudly placed it in the display.

Subsequent sessions were built around a key idea that would extend the scientific skills and provide relevant experience for all. Together they classified and observed, tested objects for floating, produced theories, took risks about being right or wrong. Mark reported that his stone 'splashed and went to the bottom'. Classified as having moderate learning difficulties, his estimation of his teacher plummeted when she asked whether his stone had floated or sunk. 'Sank', he replied, but clearly thought she ought to know the answer already. Another child suggested that they record their estimations of whether objects would float or sink in overlapping hoops 'like in sets in maths'.

The personal investigations of one pupil with a coconut at home prompted subsequent experiments of how the enclosure of air in an object increased buoyancy. They discovered a way of testing objects to see whether they contained air by submerging them and squeezing them. Not all pupils grasped that this had anything to do with science or coconuts. But the highlight of the session was one 'less-able' pupil's discovery 'I float when I've got arm-bands on...because I've blown them up and there's air in.'

The way in which the thinking of pupils was extended by mixing the groups was brought home in a discussion with three of the pupils classified as having moderate learning difficulties. Our conversation was proceeding falteringly when we were joined by a pupil from Anne's class who insisted in joining in as he always spent that time with these friends. The conversation turned to their project group and they all started reminiscing about the discoveries they had made, swapping stories about the experiments they had done at home.

The next session looked at degrees of submergence of floating objects. Inflated balloons were compared with ice cubes. Egg boxes were loaded with marbles. Icebergs, plimsoll lines and the Titanic were raised. Subsequent sessions involved shaping plasticine boats and dissolving and suspension.

The project ended with each child, if able, showing or reporting something that he or she had learnt during the sessions. One girl waited her turn with growing excitement until she was able to explain how she used water to make her Ribena drink, and others recognized this as 'a great step forward' for her. Like all the sessions, this one provided opportunities for assessing 'how to do better next time', particularly about timing activities and about how to make the shared basis of the lesson a common interest and experience of as many pupils as possible. It was clear that the open style of investigation, discussion and recording was one in which variations in ability were relatively unimportant and which generated considerable enthusiasm from the pupils:

'What are we doing now that we've finished water?'
'When can we start?'
'Can we come next week?'
'I like working in here.'
'The children are nice.'
'We did lots more talking ...'

In fact the topic period was extended to five occasions in the week, and the group tackled 'communication' for their next project. As Anne Jones reports, it was the practice of working with the pupils which provided the best and only justification that was needed for integrating in this way:

Some visiting special educators asked me to justify what I was doing with my group. At the time we were engaged in looking at ... instruments for communication, telephone, radio, CB, TV, walkie-talkie, torch. The children had made their own telephones using tin cans and string. One of the children [categorized as having severe learning difficulties] lifted up a telephone receiver and started a conversation, he then went to another telephone and carried on the conversation as if he were someone else. This was a great step forward in his language development. While this was in progress another child was concerning himself with how sound waves travel, how they are picked up by the ears and messages sent to the brain. Surely this one example shows that the diverse needs of each of these children were being met ... (Jones, 1983, p. 112)

Building on the changes

As the teachers gained experience of mixed groups, they gradually thought less about the 'nagging doubt' that there was something 'special' that some pupils were missing out on. In fact, as they expanded the range of activities in which pupils were involved, some pupils revealed surprising capacities, as Ian Mitchell recalled:

We took Roger Vincent, a junior kid from the severe learning difficulties area, camping. He has a way of holding his head on one side and twitching which separated him from other kids. Other kids had some empathy for him but they didn't do a lot with Roger – we did some drama up in the Peak District about a nineteenth-century cotton mill, acting out a play by a local author. We did a plan of the action and to our surprise Roger was better at drawing plans than some others in the main part of the school. Roger suddenly found himself held in esteem by other kids for a talent they hadn't expected.

Ian Mitchell advocated a move away from 'teacher-dominated' lessons for all pupils, whether these were produced by class teaching or individualized instruction. When asked to prepare a curriculum statement for the local authority his instinct was to say, 'This school doesn't have a curriculum', but he relented in favour of a set of experiences of the world and cultural life in which all pupils could share.

The final dissolution of the units was tackled by sorting out teacher teams using the advantage of the relatively small numbers in each class as an inducement to reluctant staff. As Anne Jones remarked, 'We looked at boxes on a piece of paper with arrows showing what teachers and groups might do together. Everyone could see themselves fitting into the framework somewhere.'

The head and deputy head recognized that 'coping with a diversity of staff' was as important and as difficult as responding to a diversity of pupils. Yet, almost three years after the arrival of the new head teacher, the 'units' had virtually disappeared. The extra teaching-assistants from the special units along with the teachers had all been used to create relatively small mixed teaching-groups usually with more than one adult.

The former 'S' unit is left with its nursery and infant-age children, who were always going to be an anomaly from their introduction into the school after it had ceased to have its own infant department. But they do share teaching-periods with a fourth-year group, who also work with the special-care class. Other pupils have been brought into the spacious special-care area for a variety of activities. There is a helpful interest by pupils in the difficulties some of these children face. They are keen to be with them at breaks and lunchtimes. One group of pupils designed a computer program to help some of the younger children, and others are involved in reading stories and thinking and planning about the progress they can make.

Tony Booth talked to almost all staff-members – both teachers and others, including the road-crossing supervisor – as well as parents and pupils. Virtually all the people he spoke to supported the changes that had taken place. There were some who, while arguing strongly that integration was good for all the pupils, were suspicious of or antagonistic to the informal atmosphere of the progressive primary school that went with it, summed up in the phrase which a few of them used: 'I may be old-fashioned but ...'. There were also a couple of staff whose educational philosophy was simply opposed to unstreamed classes. The support for selection was put most strongly by one teacher who said, 'I rue the day when this county abolished the eleven-plus. I think we should be more concerned about fostering the needs of the gifted than with the needs of pupils of low ability.'

Others would argue that the move away from a teacher-controlled curriculum is the very change that ought to permit the education of the brightest pupils to flourish. One parent of such a child told Howard Sharron when he wrote about the school (Sharron, 1985) how glad she was of the mix of abilities her son experienced:

I really can't work out who gains the most, the normal children or the handicapped ones. Nicholas has only been here two years but he has literally blossomed.

It has given him a sense of responsibility; he plays very carefully with the children and is very perceptive about their needs. I feel it has also helped Nicholas come to terms with himself – to understand that he can't be good at everything and that he has to try, like the disabled children, very hard to master things he is having difficulty with. I think he is getting a wonderfully broad education. (Sharron, 1985)

There are many directions in which the school might develop. Some of the staff question whether it is necessary to bring in pupils to Springfield from other schools, particularly those who are classified as having moderate learning difficulties. They argue that, ideally, they should be supported in their own schools. The teacher with the main responsibility for severe learning difficulties has argued that attendance at their neighbourhood school should be the aim for all.

Equally the notion of creating the school as a haven of non-competitiveness, in which the value placed on pupils is not a reflection of their cleverness or physical skills or the way they look, is an ideal which can be only very imperfectly fulfilled. The pupils in a mixed group were asked to describe their fathers. Here is a selection of their written portraits, which reveal some of their, and possibly their teachers', priorities:

My dad

My dad is brilliant he is kind and handsome. He is nice big and strong. He is fair and an expert at different things. My dad is brainy and funny and he is good.

My dad is happy and nice and fantastic and brilliant and fun and my dad is an expert. My dad makes lorrys and mends lorys and my dad lets me go to bed late.

My dad is wonderful and brave and I think he is the best dad in the world. And he is very good fun he is smart and handsome and most of all he is brainy and loving and strong and he is an energetic adventurous runner.

I love my dad he is a mechanic and he is exciting   He can give me a piggy back. He is wonderful. He has got black hair he is a bit funny he is brainy and he is brave he is nice.

REFERENCES

Booth, T. 1982: National perspectives. Unit 10 of E241, *Special Needs in Education*, Milton Keynes: Open University Press.

Central Advisory Council for Education 1967: *Children and their Primary Schools* (Plowden Report). London: HMSO.

Jones, A. 1983: *The curriculum implications and practice of integrating children with special educational needs in ordinary schools*. In-service B. Ed. dissertation, Derbyshire College of Higher Education/University of Nottingham.

Hegarty, S. and Pocklington, K. 1982: *Integration in Action*. Windsor: NFER/Nelson.

Levine, M. 1979: Some observations on the integration of handicapped children in British primary schools. In S. J. Meisels (ed.), *Special Education and Development*, Baltimore: University Park Press.

Shearer, A. and Vaughan, M. 1986: *Mainstreaming in Massachussetts*. London: Centre for Studies of Integration in Education.

Sharron, H. 1985: The most integrated school in Britain. *Times Educational Supplement*, 25 Oct 1985.

26

Switching off the alarm: the integration of students with disabilities into a further-education college

Jenny Corbett

This chapter is about the changes that occurred in the education of students with disabilities at 'Fraser College'. Jenny Corbett describes her experience as a lecturer with responsibilities for special needs. The first year of this scheme was one of great difficulty. But two years later, after the introduction of sensible planning and the development of a system of provision to meet the needs of staff and students, the students with disabilities were an integral part of the college.

Fraser College is a large technical college on a busy main road, where the constant roar of traffic outside competes with the voices inside. The whole ambience could hardly provide a more dramatic contrast with the borough's sheltered special school for physically disabled pupils, tucked into a side road, serving a small, exclusive population. The special-school pupils grow used to seeing the same few faces of staff and peers, from the age of five to sixteen, the cosy familiarity providing a cushioned security from a harsh world outside. In Fraser College the bewildering range of staff and students could never provide the same secure familiarity, but could compensate with rich and varied stimulation.

There are five departments in the main college, plus the community-service unit. The building department, with ninety staff, offers a wide range of building and mechanical-engineering services, City and Guilds craft and advanced craft certificate courses, and recruits students from well beyond the borough. The department of business and administrative studies provides a wide range of courses preparing students for careers in commerce, industry and local government, and has about thirty-five staff. The department of engineering, with an average annual enrolment of 650, and a staff of thirty-eight, caters for the needs of the engineering-industry through a range of craft and technician-style further-education courses. It too draws students from beyond the borough. The department of environmental health and science is organized into three main areas: environmental health, GCE and computing. Most of the GCE 'A'-level work of the college is in this department, and there are currently some 250 full-time students and about fifty staff in the department. The department of health, hairdressing and floristry has a full-time teaching staff of twenty-nine, assisted by some thirty-five part-time teachers. There are over 300 full-time and above 500 part-time students, mainly recruited from nearby areas but with a few from much further afield. This department trains beauty therapists, florists and hair-dressers, nursery nurses, teachers in further education, dental-surgery assist-ants and nurses.

In contrast to the size and scope of these five, extensive departments, the community-service unit has only ten staff, with a senior lecturer in charge, instead of a head of department. The courses include a core course of general basic education and a choice of options based on the art-and-craft aspects of the curriculum.

This is the diverse environment into which the students with disabilities were to be integrated. Each department functions separately and has its own flavour and atmosphere, so entering the college is like coming onto a campus which links five separate schools or sixth-form colleges, but this large college offered these students enormous diversity, contrast and interest, and exposure to many aspects of life.

A PILOT SCHEME: SEPTEMBER 1981 TO JULY 1982

The pilot scheme was the result of a collective decision taken by the borough Education Department, Fraser College and the school for physically handi-capped children. The Lees School had been integrating children into main-stream schools for ten years, and the head teacher was both sufficiently experienced and determinedly enthusiastic to extend this integration into further education. It was intended to encourage deaf students to enter the college as well, with the support of peripatetic teachers already experienced in integrated provision. These two groups of students appeared to be selected on the basis of prior attendance at special schools which were already well practised in integration and which could offer suitable support. It was assumed that they could be easily assimilated into the curriculum offered within the college.

Despite the best of intentions, the pilot scheme managed to suffer all the mistakes common to many integration schemes. First, the students were introduced *before* the necessary physical alterations to the building had been made. The resulting disasters were inevitable. The students in wheelchairs were simply unable to get to some of their classrooms, and ended up sitting in a corridor, evidence to all of a foolish lack of foresight. Toilet facilities were woefully inadequate, and resulted in a student having to be sent home if unable to cope with the restricted resources available. Such discomfort and embarrassment did nothing to integrate the students with disabilities into their new environment.

Secondly, staff were often ill-informed. This lack of clear information filtering through to all levels created tension and unhappy confusion. Some staff felt betrayed by the lack of preparation they had been given to cope with the learning problems of students with, for example, spina bifida and hydrocephalus; they felt deceived by promises of 'physically handicapped but bright students'. One lecturer turned up for a class to find a student in a wheelchair whom nobody had told him was coming and whom he knew nothing about. This clumsy incident caused obvious distress to both lecturer and student, and displays the crudest problem of integration – fear of the unknown.

A well-defined policy on integration was not drawn up until three years after planning had taken place, and the role of students with disabilities and their liaison tutor was obscure. Throughout the first two years of the scheme, those directly involved felt insecure and uncertain of their position within Fraser College. They were *in* the college, but not a *part* of the college. A borough policy on students with special needs in further education had not been established, so there were no guidelines on which to work.

The fourth mistake was that initial support was not maintained. After much discussion, planning and crisis-supporting through the stormy pilot year, the degree of encouragement and guidance from the local education authority was gradually lessened until, as the scheme began to progress successfully, support was almost non-existent. Support through crisis is valuable. Support through experimental educational development is surely essential, if policies are to be implemented and new schemes given credibility. Yet those who helped to establish new developments did not seem prepared to see them through the early stages into a secure framework.

In its wake the pilot scheme left dissatisfied students, able neither to get to the rooms they wanted nor study the subjects they chose; frustrated lecturers, feeling ill-equipped to cope satisfactorily; and a progressively unsettled union, hostile to the evidence of blunders around them. A welfare assistant remarked,

We were rejected by everyone at the beginning. There was a lot of bickering and fighting. I don't think anyone expected it to last and they thought it would only be tried for a year. Our students used to eat their lunch outside the canteen. They wouldn't use it. There was no base for handicapped students.

As a culmination of the year's disasters the liaison tutor for students with disabilities resigned at the end of August, leaving the two welfare assistants to cope with the four students arriving in the autumn term.

ALMOST ON THE ROCKS: AUTUMN TERM 1982

The autumn term of 1982 began with an active protest from the local branch of NATFHE (the National Association of Teachers in Further and Higher

Education); it was a direct result of the troubled pilot year. To focus attention on the problems, NATFHE refused to allow the four students with disabilities who had enrolled for the 1982–3 session to start the term when all the other students started. After three weeks of local publicity, causing local newspaper headlines such as 'College row over disabled', NATFHE relented and allowed the students in, having been able to draw maximum attention to their grievances. A NATFHE member remarked,

> There is an attempt to make the unions appear the villains of this piece. The disabled students last year spent a lot of time stuck out in corridors. There are no proper sluicing facilities. We've got a medical room as big as a toilet. How the hell do you look after people with special needs with these kinds of conditions?

For the students with disabilities this was the worst possible start to a college career. Two of them even experienced prejudice from fellow students, who would not lend them any course notes from the first three weeks, leaving them despairingly unable to catch up lost ground. Two students were on a course which required 'O'-level maths qualifications, which they both lacked. Another boy wanted to study subjects in rooms he could not reach, so he compromised by joining a course for which he was ill-qualified and under-motivated. Accepting students with disabilities onto courses which would have rejected them had they been 'normal' students seems patently absurd. It was unfair on teachers, expected to cover material in limited hours; unfair on fellow students, anxious to keep up a pace towards exams; and, above all, grossly unfair on the students with disabilities, who had to endure the frustrations of failure on top of their other problems.

This stormy period will be remembered as the time of frequent fire alarms but no fires. Just as the welfare assistants had taken two students in wheelchairs to the fifth floor for their class, the fire bell would ring. Two members of staff were allocated to each disabled student to carry them down in emergencies. They would have to run from all over the building to reach the students. The whole experience served to draw embarrassing attention to the students in wheelchairs and their vulnerability. John, a student with muscular dystrophy, recalled,

> The atmosphere was terrible. There were arguments all the time. I'm not taking sides between the unions and the administration. But the bitterness and lack of flexibility was incredible. I asked if I could attend lectures on the third floor but I was shunted up to the fourth and sometimes the fifth. There were arguments over who should move a table. The caretakers said it wasn't their job; the lecturers said they wouldn't do it. I'm not blaming everyone. Some people were very helpful, but all the hassle was getting me down.

By the end of this miserable term, two students with disabilities, including John, who was to study 'A'-levels, had dropped out, with subsequent publicity in the press: 'A disabled student who needs a wheelchair has dropped out of his course at Fraser College because he can't stand the rows.' Rumours spreading through special schools in the borough painted Fraser College with a fiendishly tarred brush. Only two students with disabilities remained. One welfare assistant remarked, 'It was terrible. I never want to go through that again. We felt that we were completely unwanted.'

It was at this lowest ebb that I entered the scene, to replace the liaison lecturer who had left in August 1982. My trepidation was considerable, as the whole college seemed to be waiting to see if this ill-fated scheme would sink or swim.

WHO NEEDS FRASER COLLEGE? JANUARY 1983 – JULY 1983

In January 1983 the only link between Fraser College and potential students with disabilities was the Lees School, which had six school-leavers in its senior class, not all of whom would seek Fraser College for further education. The education office felt that once the scheme was well-established there would emerge many potential students from all over the borough, yet the tarnished reputation had already done much damage to public relations between college and community, and people were slow to forget. Remarkably, while desperately seeking to extend positive links in the community, I was approached by the specialist college for young people with disabilities in the next-door borough, a head of a school for maladjusted children, and the head of the Lees School: all wanted part-time attendance for some of their students at the college. Thus two boys who enjoyed art at the specialist college came to attend art classes with support workers; two girls came to join floristry students once a week; one boy joined a brick-laying class; and another boy joined a computer class.

This period, where students with disabilities were joining classes they were enthusiastic about, had a significant impact on 'labelling'. Of the six students with disabilities four had physical disabilities; one was a student with moderate learning difficulties and a physical disability; and one had 'behavioural problems'. Each of the four with physical disabilities had very different problems. The criterion for entry for these first part-time students was their capacity to cope with the classes and to enjoy the work. They managed to challenge their labels, to the delight of teachers. James, from the school for maladjusted children, was the only one of this group who failed to complete the term, having giving up on school and college attendance simultaneously. Yet, when he attended brick-laying classes his conduct was exemplary. I was sceptical when he told me of his previous experience in building, but he proved to be a very competent worker. His biggest obstacle to progress at college was his very poor reading- and writing-ability. Teachers found James quiet, courteous and eager, but needing constant repetition of instructions. Susan and Clare soon settled into their floristry class, where they worked alongside an experienced floristry student, who helped them. These girls continued to attend college classes for the following year, gaining in confidence and skill. Philip and Tom, who attended art classes, developed a very good relationship with the teacher and enjoyed their sessions. Tom was able to come to art classes for another year and, despite misgivings from staff at Fraser College and his specialist college, insisted on sitting 'O'-level art, which he passed with a 'B' grade. As a teacher from his specialist college said, 'The Toms of this world are the exceptions and not the rule, and, as such, are valuable tools in the integration policy.' Brian, who attended computer classes, became a full-time student at Fraser College, having already got to know the place and some people.

This period of part-time integration was very successful for this group of students. The development of staff attitudes and their growing ability to cope served also as a pointer to the future. To illustrate the severity of disability which teachers encountered, Tom had quadraplegia, used an electric wheel-chair, had very poor use of one hand and restricted use of the other, and, with no speech, communicated with his Canon communicator. Not only did the art-teacher learn to communicate with him and to develop his artistic ability, but she so enjoyed the experience that she has continued to teach students with disabilities ever since. Susan, with learning difficulties and hemiplegia, which hampered her work in floristry, became a popular student at the college who worked alongside the far more capable florists, gaining confidence from the reassurance of the teacher. Neither of these teachers had taught students with disabilities before, but both were skilled teachers who approached these students with confident sensitivity.

What became clear during this period, and the months that followed, was that a skilled, successful teacher is more likely to be able to assimilate students with disabilities into his/her group than an insecure, weak teacher who is already struggling to cope with the class. It was also apparent that the college teachers often set much more ambitious targets for these students than they had been used to at the special school, and would approach them on entirely different terms from those typical of their specialist teachers. Even if they were expecting too much, they could not fail to stimulate interest and alertness.

One of the unexpected features which teachers at Fraser College dis-covered was that severity of disability was unrelated to performance. 'Some students with severe handicaps try hard and make a better effort at a task than those with mild handicaps. It's really a question of personality every time', one teacher remarked. Gradually the 'disabled' image began to blur, and teachers saw these students as young people first, 'disabled' second.

CREATING A CURRICULUM: SEPTEMBER 1983 – JULY 1984

At Fraser College the emphasis is on vocational courses, where specific practical skills are involved, or on academic courses, where preliminary qualifications are required. The community-service unit is the only section of Fraser College which offers more basic courses on very flexible terms. In the pilot scheme of 1981–2, the unit took four students onto its basic courses. After this experimental period, the lecturers concerned decided that the students with disabilities were not suitable, because 'The unit follows a very precise programme of training for a particular type of student.' This may, on the surface, appear to be a rigidly harsh judgement, yet it reveals a crucial area of controversy which cannot be ignored. The 'particular type of student' is a student whose needs may be for improved literacy and numeracy, enhanced job prospects, or a reintroduction to education after bringing up children. These needs require a particular approach, and are not comparable to the 'special needs' of students leaving a school for physically handicapped children, who will have experienced a restricted curriculum and may have had long periods in hospital, and may be emotionally immature for their age. I think it essential that the student with special needs should have ample opportunity to mix socially and educationally with as wide a spectrum of the student population as is practical. Where the lack of basic courses prevents this, then a curriculum has to be created.

The curriculum for these students with special needs was constructed with specific aims in mind: to reinforce basic subject areas, such as maths, English and science, so to compensate for time lost through frequent hospital stays; to extend recreational interests, through subjects such as music, art, computer skills, PE and drama; and to develop practical skills for daily use (through cookery, for instance). The course, which began in September 1983, was called a 'general education' or 'bridging' course and was intended to serve as a one-year stage between school and other courses at college. In the autumn term of 1983 the course had three full-time students, all recent special-school leavers, and thirteen part-time students, who ranged from those still at special school, to young people living in self-contained flats in a hostel, to members of a local day centre, aged twenty-four to forty-five. After the first term, lecturers were asked to comment on the progress of these students. While many comments were positive, there were certain problems which recurred:

'They need a lot of prompting.'
'They do seem to find recall a problem.'
'They never volunteer answers or ask questions.'
'They sometimes fall asleep on Friday afternoons.'
'She has certain difficulties with co-ordination of left and right hands and some perceptual difficulties.'
'She reads every word, even the full stops, and occasionally goes off on a little mental walk-about.'

As liaison lecturer, I had to reassure staff that these were natural problems and not any reflection on the inadequacy of their teaching.

Some lecturers had a remarkable capacity to take on a diverse range of abilities, with positive enthusiasm. The computer-teacher, for example, took on more students, until there were eleven in the group, one to each computer.

Within this group there were two boys who worked on their own programs with the teacher's guidance, several students who needed constant help with the keyboard, and others who were still in the very basic stages of improving manual dexterity. This lecturer, not trained for 'special needs', had a natural skill with students, relaxing them and displaying great sensitivity underneath his witty manner. 'That man's a genius!' declared one of the mature students who attended his classes. This teacher was exceptional, but others were eager to learn, and one of the exciting spin-offs of integration has been the exchange of teaching-methods between mainstream and special-education staff. Mainstream teachers have come to these students without preconceived notions, and, even if expectations have often been too high, the dynamism of a novel approach and demanding tasks has been noticeably effective. This was particularly illustrated in the case of Tom, the student with severe disabilities who attended art classes, who was inspired by his artist lecturer to reach for the heights, and, with superhuman effort, attained a good pass at 'O'-level and a prize from the college for 'application'. Mainstream teaching gives students from special schools or colleges a challenging taste of exacting goals to aim for, which they were unlikely to have met before, and some of the students rise to this challenge. A forty-five-year-old student from the day centre attended cookery classes for a year, and then began to be 'catering-manager' at her day centre, having visibly developed self-confidence and alertness through the course of the year.

A special course established to accommodate a specific group of students is not the ideal form of integration. Students on the bridging-course did join other classes for cookery, computer study or music, but this only formed a small part of their course. It would be preferable for these students to be fully integrated with other school-leavers. The course has, however, served two purposes: it has been a valuable stepping-stone between school and college, as illustrated by two boys who attended last year and are now well established in a course in the engineering department; and it has enabled a wide range of students of all ages to attend part-time, students who otherwise would have had no entry into further education.

ALL CHANGE: SEPTEMBER 1984 – JULY 1985

Attitudes within Fraser College changed dramatically over this year. Students with disabilities became an integral part of the college community. Staff and students progressed from awkward embarrassment to positive acceptance, opening doors, holding lifts, offering help when asked, with the ease of familiarity. This, and the increased intake of students with disabilities, from twenty in 1983–4 to forty in 1984–5, led to a more confident, independent and authoritative approach from this group of students, who became a *significant* minority. Most members of the college community came in contact with these students in the course of a week's activities, and all the tension surrounding the pilot scheme evaporated into a tolerant atmosphere. All the provisions demanded by NATFHE are now well established and in daily use. There had been no end of fire alarms when there were only four students in wheelchairs in the college; now that there were over twenty students in wheelchairs, there were no fire alarms.

Teaching for Diversity

27

A sense of wonder: science and technology in primary schools

Alan Ward

To some, science is something for experts. Alan Ward is concerned here to take science into the heart of the curriculum of the primary school. He discusses the way science projects arise out of the ordinary questions of pupils. He also argues for the linking of imaginative and investigatory work.

The primary school is a comprehensive, taking its students from the local community. Much of the work is done by groups of individuals, although a teacher may organize the children according to their abilities for subjects demanding a progression of relatively complex skills, such as mathematics and English language. However, most group work is done by brighter and less able children co-operating in a common task, with the teacher acting as leader and guide. The project might be taking a traffic census, making a pond, producing a play for assembly, or constructing a hot-air balloon. Projects involve a variety of different kinds of intelligence, such as reasoning, facility with words or numbers, physical abilities, sensitivity to other people's feelings, mechanical insight, and various artistic talents.

All of these are almost never found in a single person, yet they each have value. When children of 'mixed abilities' are encouraged to work together, they are given opportunities to learn socially important lessons about sharing their (equally valued) skills, and the acquisition of mutual respect. Simple studies in science and technology are particularly apt.

PAPER JACK AND DIANA'S EYES

Some years ago the Association for Science Education began to publish a thrice-yearly bulletin, *ASE Primary Science*, under the editorship of Dr Helen Rapson. This is a collection of actual infant and junior science and technology case studies, and it provides exemplary models of group work in state schools. In the Spring 1983 edition there was a fascinating account of how a project started after children aged seven and eight complained that their feet felt cold (Eastland and Harris, 1983). Their teacher told them about a local tramp called Paper Jack, who used to keep warm by wrapping newspapers around himself. The children went outside, to feel the cold of −5° Celsius, then they returned indoors, to 'put newspapers under our jumper, in our boots and on our head'. Afterwards, out again in the freezing weather, the children said they felt nice and warm. Ivan drew neat pictures and Mlungisi, who did a fair test by putting newspaper in only one of his wellingtons, wrote, 'My foot without the newspaper was very cold but my foot with the newspaper was very warm.' Shared experience led to careful work on heat insulators, on the use of thermometers, on the wisdom of putting on winter clothing in layers, on thermos flasks and lagging pipes, nicely combining meaningful science and technology with compassion for Paper Jack.

Nowadays it is fashionable to stress the skills employed to do science, rather than to concentrate on a special body of knowledge, although there is pressure from teachers who want more official guidance on curriculum content. Emphasis on skills, the so-called 'process' approach, means getting the children to answer questions through planned investigation. Ideally the questions should be the children's own. Key skills are: observation using all the senses; measuring; comparing similarities and differences; making records in words, pictures, models and numbers; predicting; posing precise questions; identifying variable factors which might affect the result of a test; and fair testing itself. At the same time, children are encouraged in certain attitudes, such as curiosity, originality and perseverance. Primary science may be defined as developing inquiring minds, urging scientific approaches to problems and applying scientific skills.

A charming example of a child's questions that led to a satisfactory conclusion was reported in the Summer 1984 number of *ASE Primary Science* (Taggart, 1984). It concerned Diana's eyes. Infants in a London school wondered if Diana, who had the biggest eyes in the class, could see furthest. The children unrolled a measuring-tape away from a wall in the playground, and the child to be tested stood by the wall. Other children, who had written words on cards, approached the wall and stopped next to the tape when Diana read the cards correctly. But 'It was not a fair test because some words were big and some were small. Some colours were easy to see and some were hard to see.' Katie's summary of criticism led to a second test. But next time, as Diana wrote herself, 'Some words were not spelt right and some were long and some were short.' Finally the children devised a test with a number four centimetres high, written in pencil, and Katie pronounced this a fair test: 'because we pressed hard and it was nice and big and we all knew the numbers'. Toby reported that 'Katie could see furthest and Diana who has the biggest eyes came 4th.' Notice how this example illustrates all the criteria for a process approach. Also see how it was relevant to the children's spontaneous curiosity, and reflect on how it focuses objectively on individuals' physical differences. The case study is published with a six-year-old's drawing of two smiling children (boy and girl) doing the experiment. It is auspicious for future self-motivation and deeper learning when children associate happy feelings with their work.

When I am working with large groups of children, during my various science 'happenings' (practical lecture–dialogues) in schools, teachers regularly comment on my propensity for picking 'difficult' children from the audience. I do not quite understand how I manage to do this, since the children are unknown to me before I begin and I am reluctant to damage my intuition by being too self-analytical. However, I am generally told how surprisingly well a child has reacted, perhaps answering a question appropriately, or assisting with an experiment. I am assured that my science happenings help to improve children's self-confidence and self-esteem. Practical science is so useful for doing this because science and technology are intrinsically interesting and varied; enthusiasm on the part of the teacher is essential.

I remember working with a small group of children in a children's hospital. My topic was 'Paper helicopters'. One of the infants was actually being 'potted' while the lesson was in progress. Yet the children participated, to the extent of making rough models that worked, and their teachers were pleased with the interest and progress. Science is for everybody. But what is understood by 'science', the process, not necessarily the content, has to be defined and appreciated by teachers who are not often scientists by training.

On another occasion teachers gasped with anticipation when I picked out a junior boy with mild spasticity to do an experiment with a glass of water. I soon realized why the teachers were uneasy: the child's movements were awkward, but I managed to prop him up and support him sufficiently for him to achieve success. I am certain that the most important aim of education should be to get students to enjoy learning. There are teachers well qualified to train future scientists and technicians; indeed, secondary science-teaching seems dedicated to these ends. But national science education is a waste of time if attention is not given to the majority of people who will never be scientific professionals. In a world dependent upon technology, in which technology is frequently a political issue (noisy airports, farming-policies, atmospheric pollution, nuclear weapons, automation *versus* jobs) everyone must have some interest and knowledge in, and tolerance of, science.

EXPLANATIONS

Children of differing intellectual abilities will, of course, interpret phenomena in ways compatible with their levels of understanding. Years ago, when I was trying out ideas about teaching the concept of force to juniors, I gave the children in a fourth-year class (aged about eleven) some activities on using magnetism and the upthrust of water to affect the heaviness of objects, as felt by the kinaesthetic senses, feeling how muscle resistances change when things are grasped and lifted. Less able children could describe what it felt like to lower an object fastened to a string into deep water: 'When you put a brick in the water with some string around the brick, it feels much lighter and if you take it out again it feels heavy.' Or, as another child wrote, 'It immediately feels light because there is hardly any gravity on it ....' Or, 'In water the brick weighs less – when you pull it out it will weigh more ....'

A child with deeper scientific understanding appreciated that 'the water was forcing the brick out'. Applying this to zoology, Suzy wrote, 'Insects can't grow very big because their skeletons are weak and cannot hold the weight, but lobsters can because they live in water and the water helps to support them.' Responding to the magnet activity, Rory wrote, 'When the magnet got closer I could feel the tin lid much heavier – because the magnet was pulling the lid to it.' But Rory's extended explanation was incorrect: 'This was making the force of gravity more ...' The writings were often accompanied by drawings that showed, as a cartoonist tries to do, the invisible forces operating.

One of the main difficulties with present-day primary science-teaching, when children are expected to suggest explanations for what they observe, is that the explanations may be utterly wrong. In many cases, a teacher, through lack of knowledge, is unable to judge whether a child's ideas are acceptable in textbook terms. (The non-specialist primary teacher has 'mixed abilities' for the wide range of subjects to be taught.) This is a controversial matter. Children can check their findings and ideas with textbooks or other expert opinion. But, somehow or other, teachers must get over the idea that knowledge is always limited by the prevailing consensus. Facts and explanations are constantly being updated as more evidence is found. Teachers find this responsibility daunting. They may feel that it undermines the bedrock of their authority, but many continue to seek truth by the practice of healthy doubting.

In a society haunted by technological artefacts (videos, digital watches, laser light-show machines, home computers), children want to know how these work. Information about advanced technological systems, written clearly, in plain words, with metaphors well chosen for children, must be available, alongside the simpler forms of practical crafts and technical investigations possible for youngsters working on projects in mixed-ability groups. It is reasonable to let them study home-made watermills, rubber-powered vehicles, the strengths of cardboard bridges, the effects of friction, doll's-house lighting-circuits, paper gliders, water rockets, and polystyrene hovercraft worked by hairdrier fans. These technologies are accessible to direct juvenile understanding. Even so, there are dangers for teachers who are unwise enough to initiate subtle explanations.

The effect of an airstream on a flat wing shape that is converted into an aerofoil can be observed. But will juniors be able to cope with the idea that faster air travelling over the camber of the wing exerts lower pressure on the wing's top surface – the Bernoulli effect? Careful observations and measurements that, as far as the children can tell, are always true in their experience – *these are adequate explanations*.

Young readers can take their pick of simply written books about complicated high technology, and teachers are advised to read the books. A child whose conventional academic skills are limited, but who can read, may be well informed about space shuttles, robots, communications satellites, nuclear power, holography and biotechnology, and so be a challenge to a teacher who is unacquainted with this knowledge. The sheer variety of predigested information available for children is amazing. Cheap, attractively presented books about virtually everything are so abundant in bookshops and libraries that nobody has an excuse to stay ignorant. By valuing the efforts all children make to learn, whatever their abilities may or may not be, an enthusiastic class-teacher can inspire them to want to go on adding to their capacity for thought and understanding in this complex world.

THE OBJECT LESSON

The Victorian object lesson is a suitable form for mixed-ability teaching. From time to time a teacher can present an elaborately prepared class lesson about a difficult subject of topical interest, such as North Sea oil extraction, the circulation of the blood, why a compass points to the earth's magnetic poles, the solar system (with a scale model on the playing-field) or how television works. These are what I call Sunday-newspaper colour-supplement lessons, but they involve demonstrations and children participating, as well as an array of audio-visual aids. Planning them motivates a teacher to research new knowledge. An object lesson must be devised in ways that lead to lively discussions involving every child, if that is possible. Skilful programming of questions will attract responses from less able children, and every child is expected to write and draw something arising from the lesson. I think it is silly and sentimental not to expect children to struggle with putting their thoughts on paper; drawings can count as 'picture writing'.

My favourite object lesson is about 'How we see the pictures on TV'. I begin by asking the children to imagine that they are inside a television tube. I stand at the back of the room and use a stick as an 'electron pencil' to scan from side to side and top to bottom of the 'screen' (the front of the class) to 'build up a picture by activating light-emitting chemical dots or dashes called phosphors'. To reinforce the notion of scanning, I have secretly set up a silent slide projector (prefocused to a distance of about one metre) which is throwing light rays over to a part of the room where the children do not notice them. When I wag the white-painted stick where the projector is focusing, the children are thrilled to see a magical materialization of Mickey Mouse. Then I explain how they see the whole image by persistence of vision. It is then possible to talk about how actual television pictures are built up from three scanning beams, activating red, green and blue lights.

I pass around little multicoloured spinning-tops for the children to operate on trays, to show how primary colours can be mixed to make other colours. Then, at the end of the lesson, the children make up their own flick-book paper movies to show how television images are animated. After this lesson an eleven-year-old wrote,

Persistence of vision is when you look at a picture and others very quickly. The picture stays in your brain (or mind) for a twelfth of a second, then it goes, but before it's gone the next picture comes so they mix. You can see the pictures of the television screen because there is an electron pencil which scans the screen firing phosphors which make the screen light up. The electron pencil does the odd numbers (lines) first and then the even numbers. There are 25 pictures in a second. Also a screen has 625 lines.

That was from a child of fair to average ability.

Relevance of my lesson to a child's previous experience, and evidence of enthusiasm for the theme, are captured by another quotation, from one of the less able children:

Inside a television there is an electron pencil in which tiny particuls called phosphors build up 625 lines a second which makes 25 pictures. The primary light colours are red, green and blue. Once when I went into the lounge my dad was fiddleing about with the television there were three knobs on one side of the television. My dad pressed a knob and it went a primary red colour the whole picture on the television went all shades of red he pressed a blue and it went all shades of blue then he pressed the green one and it went all shades of green. Sometimes when Mum has got her hover on and I'm watching television the picture has lots of broken lines.

Compare the last two quotations with this, from an able child:

Persistence of vision means that the picture lingers in our brain for 1/12th of a second. If lots of pictures are shown quickly the pictures in the brain overlap forming moving pictures. You can show this with a thaumatrope. On one side of a piece of card could be a fish and on the other side could be a bowl. On television there are 625 lines to make a picture. A beam of electricity containing electrons goes along all these lines, odd numbers first. On the black and white television there is one electron pencil. It works along the lines of phosphors – chemical dots which glow when the electron pencil reaches them – given different signals from space. This varys the beam from the electron pencil so producing the different shades on the screen. On the colour television there are three electron pencils each of them putting one of the three primary light colours on the screen. But these colours are mixed to form lots of other colours.

Several children, without being asked, worked out how many scanning lines would occur in an hour (56,250,000, close to the limit of a pocket-calculator display). The third child quoted wrote that 'Although the set would likely go bust in a year the electron pencil would cover 492,750,000,000 lines.'

AND WONDER ...

The demands upon teachers' nervous energy, patience, stamina and intellectual versatility are increasing at an alarming rate. With minimal resources, teachers are expected to organize what amount to original investigations, not to mention craft work, which is also a form of technical problem-solving. They are asked to stimulate children to think creatively by asking questions phrased in ways that will not predetermine 'right' or 'wrong' answers. Yet, to what extent can the average primary-school teacher evaluate truly novel answers? Many teachers long for structure. But, whatever the future for curriculum change, teaching-strategies can always be devised to serve the varied needs of children who are not always selected for class or group work on the basis of their supposed abilities.

I shall finish with two more infant voices. After one of my science happenings, on 'Bubbles', a brilliant but modest Gloucestershire teacher of six-year-olds held sessions in which all her children experimented with soap bubbles. She gave me thirty pieces of written work, all unique, ranging in length from one to several pages. Two of her mixed-ability infants expressed their interest and learning in very different ways. First, the 'technician':

How you can blow out a candle flame with a bubble

We had to light a candle but we had to make sure that the candle was standing on the saucer properly because if it fell over it might start a fire then we had to blow a big bubble with the top of a washing-up liquid bottle. When we had blown a bubble we put our finger on the hole we blew through. Then we put the bubble near the flame of the candle then took are finger off the hole. The air that was inside the bubble escaped and blew the candle flame out.

Second, the 'poet':

A bubble

a bubble is beautiful and shiny
we can blow big bubbles
and we can blow very tiny bubbles
bubbles are round
their shape is a sphere
in the tiny bubble you can see reflections
and you can see all the colours of the rainbow
bubbles float gently to the ground
they pop
they burst
they disappear

Science can also inspire a child's sense of wonder.

REFERENCES

Eastland, W. and Harris, R. 1983: What to do with the Times Ed? *ASE Primary Science*, 10 (Spring 1983).
Taggart, B. 1984: A fair test – devised by infants. *ASE Primary Science*, 14 (Summer 1984).

28

Using maths to make things happen: the mystery of the forgotten shower unit

Gill Blake

Many children still learn mathematics in a very abstract way. They have few opportunities to relate the skills they are taught to their own experience, even to realize that the skills they are taught might be of some value. This approach to mathematics was adopted by the Open University course Mathematics across the Curriculum. *As part of her work on this course, Gill Blake organized a real problem-solving project with her mixed-ability class of ten- and eleven-year-olds in a middle school. She wanted a project that would be meaningful to all the children, and which would involve the use of a wide range of mathematical skills.*

POSING THE PROBLEM

As a way of assessing the interests and feelings of my class, I held a discussion during which I questioned them about various aspects of school life and life in the villages where they live. One problem was mentioned by almost every child: the school's changing-rooms and washing-facilities. When our school building was completed three years ago, the money ran out before the shower rooms and changing-rooms could be completed. They remained as empty shells with bare walls, without heating or lighting, used for storing waste paper and netball goals. As the older children did not like changing in open classrooms, they crammed into the toilets to change, where the smell was none too pleasant and space was minimal. Others changed in classrooms. The only washing-facilities after games were two sinks in the toilets; there were no towels – only automatic hand-driers.

The children were not the only people to feel strongly about the situation. Parents had already complained about the state their children arrived home in; school managers had all commented on the problem. Any improvement would also be bound to help the various community groups who used the school's sports facilities.

So not only would the children be motivated by the problem, but there was a real chance of making changes. I envisaged that evidence collected by the children might force a decision on the future of the shower unit, or lead to an improvement in other facilities. At the very least, the matter would be brought to public attention.

PLANNING THE PROJECT

As the children returned from changing after their PE lesson, moaning and groaning about being squashed, having nowhere to put their clothes and so on, I decided to start the ball rolling: 'Why were the changing-facilities unsatisfactory? What could be done about them? Could you do anything about it?' The class leapt on the problem with the greed of a hungry crocodile! Later on, I learnt from parents that the children went home full of indignation and determined to rectify this scandalous state of affairs.

Over two long brainstorming sessions, we wrote ideas up on the board and finally shaped them into a topic web around a definite central challenge. Every child contributed. At this stage I put plenty of time at the children's disposal, so that, although I tried to cut down rambling discussion, I did not frustrate them with 'cut-off' times. Towards the end of the two sessions I did intervene to some extent to question some of the headings on the board which seemed to me to be tangential. Ideas were then grouped into tasks that groups could tackle. I allowed the class to change their minds about groupings until they were absolutely satisfied with the tasks. My intervention here was minimal. When it came to the wording of the central challenge, the children voted for one which I did not particularly favour, but which has

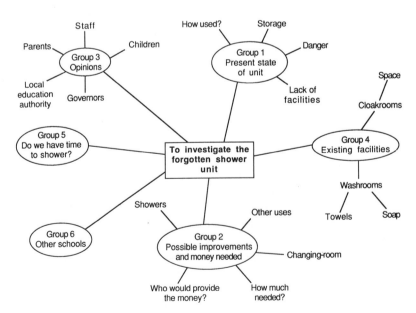

Figure 28.1 The plan of the project

since proved very suitable. I was relieved to see that the final arrangement (shown in figure 28.1) corresponded quite closely to the planning I had done beforehand.

I allowed the six groups to form on friendship lines, as this generally provided a cross-section of ability and sex. As they settled down to plan their investigations I became mainly a moving 'observer, encouraging discussion and occasionally intervening with questions to clarify their thinking. Their first task was to outline the questions to ask, and then work out what information they would need to collect. In the process some groups divided to tackle separate questions, some more closely interrelated than others. Towards the end of this planning-stage, we returned to base for group reports, final orders and a general rallying-cry of 'Take it calmly!' Each group now knew what the others were up to.

My role as a facilitator now came to the fore. Before the children went out to collect data, I had to make arrangements for their visits to other classes, their interviews with individuals and their measuring escapades, keeping the head well-informed of the proceedings. The children presented me with lists of resources they needed, so I made sure they were ready for each session. Now that I knew the way their investigations were leading, I could compare the mathematical and problem-solving skills which each group would need with those I knew they already had, to see what was missing. Thus I gave a 'skill-getting' session to a group who were planning scale drawings, and similar sessions to the groups tackling questionnaires, timing and averaging. One group, a pair of boys, needed help with the problem of what to say to a teacher when you wanted to ask his class some questions. They felt happier when they had written out a little speech to make! Figure 28.2 shows the skills areas that the six groups were involved in using.

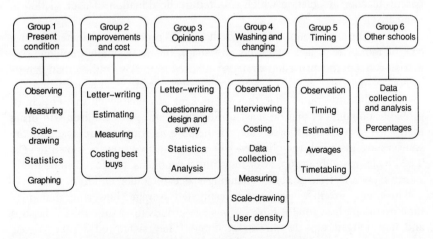

Figure 28.2 Skills required for each group

RESULTS

The group investigating the present state of the unit provided two large scale drawings of the two main sections of the shower unit. One marked with large red stars the dangers, such as loose flooring, holes and tatty carpets. The other marked all the things stored or poking out in a dangerous fashion. This group also found out how many accidents had happened in one unit this year and found that over half the users had suffered minor injuries. One of the governors brought a polaroid camera and photographed the main dangers in the unit to show the local education authority – much to the children's glee. This group's evidence carried great weight with the governors.

The improvements and costing group showed great initiative. They wrote to a local builder, whose estimate for the completion of the unit was £6,000. This seemed too much for us to raise, especially as, in reply to a child's letter, the local education authority wrote saying that for the moment no more money was available for our school. Two of the girls set about costing conversion of the unit into an art room, a general practical room or a changing- and washroom. It was found that these would cost considerably less than the showers. For the costing the children used not only school catalogues, but also ones of their own. They developed a good eye for a bargain. Their final report is reproduced in figure 28.3. The boys from this group found another shed which they considered could house the waste paper and made suggestions for storing the other equipment more safely.

The opinions group spent their time designing, sending, collecting and analysing questionnaires and trying to justify to other children why they or their parents hadn't been chosen as part of the random sample! Their biggest problem was analysing the results sensibly, but they did come up with a clear yes vote from parents and children. They also wrote the letter to the parent–teacher association which resulted in the donation of over £1,000 to our cause!

The washroom group discovered that most problems originated from a lack of money (e.g. lack of towels and soap), but were finally implementing a trial run on the provision and use of proper towels (rather than hand-driers), which they found that most children preferred. They washed the towels daily and found that they were kept reasonably clean. The most probable outcome is that, at least during the winter, the children will bring their own towels, and the caretaker is helping us with storage space. If the showers are installed, the children will automatically bring their own towels. The changing-room group, after their initial problems, produced some interesting facts and figures about changing-space for older children.

The timing group worked out an estimated average showering/changing-time by timing how long it took various age groups to change for PE lessons and how long it took to shower at home. They suggested a rota to ease congestion and timing-problems for taking showers. It was interesting that this group started with the assumption that, if each child took 10 minutes to

Final Recommendations
Money and conversion of Unit Group

Our group set out to find out
how much a shower unit would
cost, compared with the cost of a
Practical Room, and an Art Room.
We did this by looking in catalogue's
to find things suitable for each room.
David S got a letter from Burrell's
the builder, and it said the shower-
unit would cost £6000. It would
take about 4-6 weeks to install
We wrote to the L.E.A to see if
they planned to finish our unit, but
they explained that there wasn't
enough money at the moment and
other schools were in greater need
eg they still had outside toilets
We discovered that the practical room would
cost about £500.00 The art room would cost
£222.80 much less than the shower-unit would
cost. We recomended that the practical room would
be the best idea. In the class we had a
vote and we had first and second choice.
We gave two points for first choice and
one point for second choice. 15 children chose
the shower unit for first choice, and 0 (pee)
children for second choice. Six children chose the
changing-rooms for first choice, and 15 for second
choice. 4 children chose the practical room
for first choise and 10 chose it for second
choice.
So the points were:
Showers 30 points, Changing Rooms 27 points
Practical Room 18 points. Although the shower
unit gained the most points we decided
that if £6000.00 seemed too much to raise,
after talking to the P.T.A and the managers,
we would try to have the changing rooms
built instead.

Kim Hards
Vivienne Harding.

Figure 28.3 Improvements and costing group: final report

shower, then a class of 26 would take 26 × 10 minutes! However, they did show eventually that, with a rota system, lesson times would not be affected to any great extent.

Trevor and Stuart, the two boys investigating other schools, had to be persuaded that they could not visit every school in Norfolk, so contented themselves with contacts in other schools supplying information. This group's evidence, depicted in figure 28.4, may seem the least productive and convincing, but their personal development through the project was the most marked.

Other Schools Group.

We (Trevor and Stuart) set out to find proof so we could have the long lost showers which were going to have until the L·E·A ran out of money. We went to each class to see if they had contact with children in Norfolk schools and schools in other parts of Britain. We made a table to show our results. Out of 22 schools with which we made contact 12 had showers and 10 did not have showers so 54% of these school have showers. In Norfolk out of the 17 schools, 10 had shower units, so that is 59%. Because more than half of the schools have showers we think we have a right to have them too.

Figure 28.4 Other-schools group: final report

LEARNING THROUGH THE PROJECT

The class's main strengths throughout the problem-solving process were their enthusiasm, perseverance and total involvement. They also had good discussion skills, which they demonstrated in the 'together' times, listening to each others' ideas and making positive suggestions. Their weaknesses showed themselves at various times, though not dramatically. They sometimes had problems co-operating in their small groups, unsupervised by an adult. There were occasional quarrels, problems of people being left out and dominance problems which I had to deal with. The children were generally shy when having to make contact with adults about important matters and would often ask me what to say. Both of these points will improve with practice; more opportunities for working in groups and making contact with adults can easily be arranged. Most groups also had difficulties organizing the data which they collected and had their trays full of pieces of paper, many of which could have been discarded. General organizational tasks in the future will improve this.

The skills and abilities required for the project could generally be foreseen, so I had made provision for them. Some things did need further development: for instance, planning; organizing how and when information should be collected, so that opportunities would not keep slipping by; and the best ways of presenting information so that it would both be convincing and have visual impact. The report-writing stage also produced some problems. I think accurate reporting is extremely important, so I shall certainly develop that in further work.

Throughout the project I was able to gain interesting insights into each child, as the class worked in an atmosphere which gave them greater scope than usual for using their strengths and discovering their weaknesses.

Kim was a leading light in the money and improvements groups, where her tasks included writing a letter to the local education authority; costing the conversion of the unit; calculating paint coverage, flooring-area, size of fitments; estimating and comparing costs; and, finally, preparing a written report of recommendations (figure 28.3). Trever was the noisier and less able member of the 'other-schools' pairing. This relatively minor task made great demands on him, such as formulating a speech to make to other classes, questions to ask children, drawing up a record sheet, reorganizing information, sorting into categories, looking up maps and calculating percentages. Finally he managed to write a report (figure 28.4). A record of their progress can be seen in figures 28.5 and 28.6.

Kim needed encouragement in her general attitudes. She is a shy girl but has well-formulated ideas which are worth sharing, and I shall continue to encourage her to communicate with adults and other children as she has had to do during the project. Her confidence needs continually building up. Her working-partner was often Kim's mouthpiece to the rest of the class. Kim's confidence certainly grew during the project, and was given a marvellous boost when she received a long and sympathetic reply to the letter she had written to the local authority. Kim is an able mathematician and needed little in the way of new skills, but she had to be helped to apply her

	KIM				TREVER			
	Confident	Unsure	Needed and used	Taught or reinforced	Confident	Unsure	Needed and used	Taught or reinforced
Counting	✓		✓		✓		✓	
Addition	✓		✓		✓		✓	
Subtraction	✓		✓		✓		✓	
Multiplication	✓		✓		✓		✓	
Division	✓		✓		✓		✓	
Fractions	✓					✓		
Ratios		✓				✓	✓	✓
Percentages	✓					✓	✓	✓
Measuring	✓		✓	✓		✓		
Comparing	✓		✓			✓	✓	✓
Estimating	✓		✓			✓		
Organizing data		✓	✓	✓		✓	✓	✓
Statistical work		✓	✓	✓		✓	✓	✓
Making graphs	✓					✓		
Spatial awareness	✓		✓			✓		
Planning	✓			✓			✓	✓

Figure 28.5 Mathematical skills in Kim and Trever's project work

	KIM				TREVER			
	Confident	Unsure	Needed and used	Taught or reinforced	Confident	Unsure	Needed and used	Taught or reinforced
Interest in work	✓				✓			
Ability to discuss		✓	✓	✓		✓	✓	✓
Ability to explain		✓	✓	✓		✓	✓	✓
Ability to define problem	✓		✓	✓		✓	✓	✓
Ability to make decisions		✓	✓	✓		✓	✓	✓
Confidence in tackling work	✓		✓	✓		✓	✓	✓
Analysing data	✓		✓	✓		✓	✓	✓
Letter-writing	✓		✓	✓		✓	✓	✓
Reporting		✓	✓	✓		✓	✓	✓

Figure 28.6 Other skills and attitudes in Kim and Trever's project work

skills to the task. For example, she knew how to calculate area but needed prompting to find out how much paint was needed to cover the unit walls.

Trever may be full of chatter but he lacks confidence in his ability to contribute anything in a class where everyone is cleverer than he is. The fact that he and his friend were doing an investigation all on their own boosted his morale from the word go. Trever needed help with such basic tasks as drawing up a sheet on which to record information. Having made one or two suggestions, Trever drew up four different sheets before being satisfied that he had an appropriate one. He needed special help in sorting and organizing data and discarding irrelevant or repetitive information. I had to discuss his findings with him before he could draw any conclusions from them, and this talking about what he had done certainly helped him to sort out ideas in his own head. Like Kim, Trever gained confidence from the whole exercise because he had contributed something. He learned certain specific skills such as sorting according to given criteria and calculating percentages using a calculator. He became more able to talk to adults and even made 'phone calls at home for the project. His reading of his final report was a real thrill.

I wanted the class to reach a firm recommendation on the basis of the group reports because I knew the school governors were meeting within the next week and our aim was to put pressure on them. The main decision to be made was whether to press for a shower unit, or to try for some other improvement to facilities. The money and improvements group put the facts before us, recommending that the unit be made into a practical room. We discussed methods of voting on the options and came up with a simple weighting-procedure: 2 points for first-choice vote, 1 point for second choice. The result was 30 points for the showers, 27 points for changing/washrooms and 18 points for art or practical room. I was amazed at how well the majority decision was accepted by everyone, even the group whose recommendation had been turned down. This was due, I think, to the fact that the children chose their own voting-method.

So, the children presented their recommendation and reports to the head, who put them before the managers, who put them before the Education Officer and local MP. Now we had to play a waiting-game. As I was shortly to lose this class, I saw that I would have to forge firm links between the various parties and the children, so that they would not have to work through me. But this had already begun to happen: the secretary of the parent–teacher association came to tell the class that they were willing to put £1,000 towards the unit. She did not tell me to tell the class, or even tell me first. The MP and Education Officer have arranged to see the class, not me. I can foresee that 'making it happen' will take some time, but, now that the children have convinced a number of significant groups, they are not working alone.

29

Personalizing the past: oral history in schools

Sallie Purkis

Sallie Purkis describes an approach to history based on the personal reminiscences and lives of the people who live within the communities of children at school. Oral history reduces the emphasis on writing and reading and is hence accessible to pupils of a wide spread of attainment. In the examples Sallie Purkis cites, all the children were encouraged to be active and creative, and may, as a result, have gained a sense of control over the production of their own knowledge. By being the historians of their own (or any other) community, they may have come to reflect more deeply on why it is as it is, and how it might be different.

If the new language of images were used differently, it would, through its use, confer a new kind of power. Within it we could begin to define our experiences more precisely in areas where words are inadequate. Not only personal experience, but also the essential historical experience of our relation to the past: that is to say the experience of seeking to give meaning to our lives, of trying to understand the history of which we can become the active agents. A people or class which is cut off from its own past is far less free to choose and to act as a people or class than one that has been able to situate itself in history.

John Berger, Ways of Seeing

WHY 'HISTORY'?

The case for including history in a curriculum for all is a strong one. First, it is a subject exclusively concerned with human beings and human experience. Together with geography, it helps provide some explanation of how and why we find ourselves where we are. Without a time perspective, the essential human questions, 'Who am I?', 'Where am I?', cannot be satisfactorily answered. Individuals and groups have a psychological need for some knowledge of their roots and origins and, without it, only exist in a state of partial social amnesia. Indeed, it is this very craving for some link between present and past which is a powerful factor in engaging those who enjoy history long after they have ceased to study it at school. Besides being concerned with roots and change, history is also about power, authority and social control, concepts of some significance when seeking to understand the present.

The skills-based approach to history-teaching has since the 1970s forced teachers to re-examine exactly what they teach and why. Attention has been drawn to the inherent bias in many historical sources, and objectives have gone beyond the regurgitation of content to awareness of teaching for conceptual understanding of change and continuity, similarity and difference, cause and consequence. The shortcomings of textbook versions of the past have also been revealed, particularly those which still resemble versions of *Our Island Story*, popular in Victorian and Edwardian classrooms (see Purvis, 1980b; Steedman, 1984). Many, too, now recognize the inappropriateness of an anglocentric, male-dominated approach in a society which seeks to promote equality, and it can be seen that the traditional history syllabus is discriminatory in its reflection of the lives of the majority of people in the past. For too long it has been preoccupied with the affairs of a small minority rather than people in general. That minority were rulers rather than ruled, entrepreneurs rather than workers, and men rather than women. Members of ethnic minority groups, whether black or white, rarely appear except as supporting players. In fact what is remarkable about much school history is not what is in, but what has been left out. School history has often succeeded in alienating a considerable proportion of the population.

PERSONALIZING THE PAST

Personalizing the past is a way of elevating to a central position in the school curriculum the life experiences of ordinary people; that is, those most likely to have been the ancestors of the pupils, teachers and their parents, whether 'half-timers' in Halifax, agricultural workers in East Anglia, or Afro-Caribbean mothers in Brixton.

For inspiration and resources, schools that adopt this approach will look inwards to their families and local communities, thus releasing into the classroom historical knowledge that will challenge the accepted notion of what is valid history. People, places and events will be selected for study not because they can be justified in the school curriculum in terms of their contribution to the growth of a national identity, but because of their accessibility, relationship and relevance to the students undertaking the investigation. No claims are made that this is a value-free approach. Rather, emphasis will be placed on individuals previously regarded as 'unknown' or as unworthy of study. Procedures and materials will be introduced that might develop pupils' self-esteem, give meaning to the social and physical environment of the late twentieth century, celebrate the diversity of our society, and enable more people to 'engage the whole personality in a kind of dialogue with the past that shows us more clearly who we are' (Reeves, 1980).

There exist a number of possibilities within the framework of the school for studying the past at a personal level. For example, history, the history around us, as the Schools Council History Project 13–16 calls it (Schools Council, 1976), has been recognized as good practice for more than thirty years. It offers opportunities for first-hand examination of evidence, usually in the form of buildings and associated documents, and makes the past more alive and real than a textbook's second-hand version. It encourages skills of observation and deduction and introduces pupils to a way of working which, for some, becomes a lifetime's interest.

Personal project work, whether carried out with an examination in view or simply for the satisfaction it brings, has been produced by students of all ages fired with an enthusiasm that is created by first-hand investigation and the opportunity to work on a small area of a neighbourhood that is already familiar. Family history is another personal approach. Steel and Taylor (1973) showed in their book *Family History in Schools* how personal timelines and family trees could introduce pupils to the history of the last hundred years, and sometimes more, by reconstructing the times through which members of their own family had lived. Personal memorabilia, documents and photographs from the family album could all be drawn on to identify change in both personal lifestyles and particular localities. As family disintegration became a more frequent feature of the lives of school pupils, many teachers felt that to pry too deeply into individual circumstances in the cause of a school history project might be, for some children, a painful and demoralizing experience; so the approach, at an intensely personal level, has gone out of favour. Nevertheless, when handled with sensitivity and with knowledge, and the agreement of the child's family, this method is still to be highly commended as relevant and fulfilling historical investigation.

A third type of project which has seen a significant growth in the past decade is the oral-history project, which personalizes the past by drawing on the memories of those who have lived through it. Variously described as the 'interview method' in social history, the 'life-history method', and 'the voice of the past', it introduces into the classroom authentic and vivid historical evidence that is readily available, whether the school is near a record office or not, and offers opportunities for creative and satisfying work. It is genuine 'do-it-yourself' history and is suitable for pupils at every stage of their education and of all abilities.

ORAL HISTORY IN SCHOOLS

A major source of information about oral-history projects in schools and colleges is *Oral History*, the journal of the Oral History Society. I have drawn examples from the Oral History in Schools section, which I edit, to illustrate how the past can be given personal significance for those involved. Most school projects, of course, may never be published, but this in no way diminishes their value, which lies essentially in their personal and local connections.

Cutler's Brook School, Bristol[1]

Val Moore and Paul Morris, employed under a grant from the Manpower Services Commission to organize School and Community Involvement Projects (SCIP), successfully introduced oral history into one school as a way of bringing young and old together.

It involved a third year junior class from Cutler's Brook School in the St Werburgh's district in an investigation of what life was like in the 1930s.

The greater part of one day per week was given over to the project for a period of six weeks. In the morning, the Community Service volunteers took some archival material from newspapers and old photographs deposited in the Central Public Library. In addition they read each week from some of the working-class autobiographies that have been published by Bristol Broadsides. These seemed to capture the children's attention very effectively, possibly because of the sometimes humorous content and the vital way in which the writers put across their life experiences.

After lunch, the children were taken to the Horley Road OAPs Club, where they were introduced to four enthusiastic pensioners who willingly answered their questions about their schooldays, their working lives, their social activities and how they lived through the Blitz.

Back in class the children were debriefed, partly to see what they had learned, and partly to give the different groups a chance to exchange information. The children also wrote some pieces on what they had learned. It was interesting to see how their memories of what they learned that week were subjective in the same way as the memories of the old folk were looking back over fifty years. Little details which captured the imagination are more real than facts and figures and the official version of history it seems.

At the end of the six weeks, two of the pensioners were able to accept the children's invitation to lunch at school – a lunch they had helped prepare themselves.

Mrs Helen Shipway, the head teacher of Cutler's Brook, noted the progress the children made over the weeks in their ability to talk and exchange views with people two generations removed from themselves. On their return to school, they eagerly volunteered to tell her about life fifty years before. She comments, 'It was obvious that the 1930s had become real – an era to which they could now relate – living history and not something to read about or copy from a book.'

She also noticed a change in attitude towards the children from the elderly respondents. Those who had previously had little to do with the local children were now remarking how friendly they were and how interesting it was to talk about them.

A report on this project has appeared in *SCIP Ahead*, the newsletter of the SCIP, and published by the Bristol CSV Centre, 13 Midland Road, Bristol 2.

Grove and Arbury Schools, Cambridge[2]

Carol Jones introduced her class of seven- and eight-year-olds at the Grove Junior School to oral history. She writes,

At first sight a large council estate, built over the last thirty years, seems to offer little potential as a subject for historical survey. However my class of seven- to nine-year-olds were enthusiastic about the idea of finding out about their own locality.

The children started their investigation by asking parents and neighbours for their memories of 'The day I moved in', and we were off to a good start when Helen brought in a photograph of her sister as a baby in which we could see builders still working on houses in the background. We invited Helen's mother to school, where she talked to two children armed with a tape-recorder. The class were fascinated by her account of coping with unmade roads, no bus service or local shops. From this moment, the advantages of using oral evidence were apparent. It gave stimulus to the development of language skills, listening, making assumptions, speculating and questioning. Written records were made after several tapes had been listened to, children selecting and organizing the aspects of the evidence that interested them particularly. This opportunity for language development was an interesting and highly desirable aspect of the project. As the primary resource was oral, all the material was readily available to readers and non-readers alike. The latter were able to make a pictorial record of their findings. All the taped sessions led to lively discussion.

The children started on their own research, seeking out parents and friends who had a story to tell about Arbury. In this way we were able to record Mrs Lark, who had organized the petition for a play space on the estate and who, after long and difficult negotiations with the council, had won the present playing-field for the children. Her story of how amenities were promised yet never materialized provoked thoughtful discussion on ways of improving facilities, and perhaps her final words, 'We learnt whatever you want on Arbury, you've got to fight for', may have sown a seed of social consciousness in the minds of even such young children.

An older person came into school and told us how she could remember when the area was farmland and nurseries and Alice discovered that the old farm cottage was still standing, now surrounded by new housing and so modernized as to escape detection. The children interviewed the present owners and we took photographs of the stable still standing in the back garden. We were loaned photographs of the cottage in its original state. Afterwards, the whole class were invited along to view our 'ancient building' and shown the place where once a tall tree had stood where a nightingale sang every night. These discoveries of a rural past led to interesting discussion about priorities. Was it more desirable to provide housing for a lot of people than accommodate a few?

We were amazed at the wealth of photographic evidence we unearthed of the school in various stages of development, the old farm buildings, the roads as grassy tracks and all within the living memory of many of their parents. The local history library, the Cambridgeshire Collection, rephotographed many of our pictures for inclusion in their permanent collection.

The topic was both enjoyable and valuable in that children were able to be the experts, making genuine discoveries. The knowledge that many ordinary people known to them had played a part in the development of the estate gave the children a feeling of identity within this growing community, in which the experiences of their own families were part of the history of their own locality. Oral history revealed a hidden and interesting story about familiar places.

Gwen Chambers used oral history at Arbury Primary School with her class of eleven-year-olds. She writes,

My class of eleven-year-olds were disbelieving when I told them we were going to investigate the history of their part of Cambridge. They were well aware that hundreds of tourists from all parts of the world flock to see the historic buildings; equally aware that these tourists never penetrate the fortresses of the Arbury estate. They listened politely when I explained that many seemingly ordinary people have interesting stories to tell, but were obviously not convinced.

I felt that the best way to start the work was to involve every child directly at the very beginning, so a practical session was organized taking up a whole school morning. After suitable briefing, groups of children went out to interview and record local residents, some of whom had lived on the perimeter of the area in houses built in the thirties. One group visited an old farmhouse and the remainder recorded in school a lady telling of the achievement involved in building a nearby street of houses by a self-build group. The change in the children's attitude after this morning was dramatic. Excited groups sped back into the classroom, clutching their precious tapes, photographs, hand-drawn maps and even one of the original French tiles from the farmhouse roof. They could hardly wait to tell the others about their discoveries and the rest of the morning was spent in exchanging information and discussion. Later we listened to the tapes and followed up some aspects in greater detail.

The children's interest and enthusiasm were maintained by further visits to people in their homes and talks in the classroom. Our general assistant spoke of her childhood when the area was still country and she and her friends played in the fields and copses and fished for newts and frogspawn in the local pond – now filled in and the site of a bus shelter. Another day, one of the children's grandmothers showed us a series of slides showing every stage in the demolition of the farmhouse which once stood opposite the school, and the building of the houses which stand there now.

We soon discovered that many of the people living in the new houses had always lived nearby and that the land had been farmed by a family still living on the estate, one member of which was actually in the class. Tina's father agreed to let me talk to him one evening and the result was a fascinating account of land use and farming-methods until comparatively recent times.

The children learned an enormous amount about the area and will never again regard history as the story of the remote past made by important people. They became confident in handling resource material of many kinds. In addition to all our taped material, we acquired many photographs, newspaper cuttings, programmes, building-materials. These were supplemented by pictures from the Cambridgeshire Collection, showing horse-drawn milk floats and ploughing with horses and traction engines, which had been mentioned in our interviews.

In addition to this, the work developed many language skills and this was a valuable aspect. The children learned to formulate open-ended questions, to listen and assess information. They collated information and passed it on to each other clearly and concisely and had many lively discussions. Because the source material was almost entirely oral and pictorial, it was freely available to all, regardless of ability. All were able to strip cartoon sequences of the self-build housing scheme, from the first meeting in the Anchor to the final housewarming party, complete with paper hats and straws. The class as a whole decided what caption should go with each frame and two of the abler children made a transcript of the tape to accompany the drawings.

The class produced a wealth of written work, factual accounts, imaginative re-creations, poetry and artwork, including a large fabric collage, 'On the farm'. At the exhibition, all these things were accompanied by quotations or complete transcripts of the tapes.

The children had a great sense of personal involvement in the work and a strong sense of belonging to the community was built up. They became aware for the first time that the old country life had had to be destroyed before the new estate could be built, and that the new area needed a positive approach by those who live there. They themselves concluded that the desperate need for homes had led to unimaginative planning and they went a step further by producing many excellent and practicable suggestions for improving the area and making the best use of the open spaces which still exist.

By using oral history as a means of studying their locality, the children learned many valuable lessons, not the least of which is that history is a continuing process of which they themselves are a part.

Highwood Secondary Modern School, Gloucestershire[3]

At Highwood Secondary Modern School, Nailsworth, Gloucestershire, Sally Mullen, an English-teacher, has found oral history a useful way of encouraging her pupils to acquire and develop their vocabulary and to learn to talk fluently and confidently. She writes,

I use oral-history tapes extensively in English and find the children quickly pick up the techniques involved when making their own tapes for each other. Childhood is a major theme in my second-year work programme and it is central to many of our class readers. The Bristol People's Oral History tapes tell of true childhood experiences and when used selectively they impart information about life in the last eighty years.

As a prototype for their own tapes the oral-history collection is stimulating. I have found that the children are surprisingly adept in the techniques of interviewing. A few reminders about test recording and positioning are usually all that is necessary to ensure a good recording, and practically all the children are familiar with tape-recorders and cassettes even if they do not own them. They are good interviewers and elderly people respond to children differently than to adults. The information or memories recalled to a small child seem somehow more enthusiastic and lively.

The themes which the children have used are, firstly, exploring childhood fears. After class discussion based on our own personal fears – for example, the dark, closed doors, spiders, graveyards, etc. – we compiled questionnaires for our respondents. This was done in pairs and then as a class exchanging and swapping exciting or original questions. Homework involved selecting the respondent and making the tape. The following week's lessons involved listening to individual children's tapes. The children were seated in an informal and relaxed way and the child whose tape was being played was responsible for setting up the equipment and briefly introducing their tape and the respondent. After hearing the tape once, the usual request was to hear it again. The children enjoyed listening to them, enjoyed the lesson, which was controlled by the child whose tape was playing, and to some extent my role as teacher/ guide was eclipsed. In fact I was forgotten.

Part of the discussion after hearing the tape was to assess whether the interviewee enjoyed the experience. Questions were posed such as 'Was the making of the tape useful and interesting?', 'Was it an enjoyable activity?'

Another theme which the children are working on at the moment is that of local ghost stories. In groups the children are gathering local tales and each group is involved in selecting the tellers, working out how and when to record, and learning about how to make a tape co-operatively rather than individually. Another group is working on 'sound-effects', which we are using to introduce each separate story. This tape will then be part of the school resource and other classes will be able to use it.

The third theme on which we are working is schooling. We have listened to tapes on school in the past. The children have talked to parents and friends about school, and we have had class discussion about school as a basis for compiling the questionnaire. We have also enacted some school scenes in drama based on true experiences. Adrian had suggested we include a question on nicknames; Richard put down one on school bullies; Wendy, who is often late, included a question on what would happen to latecomers. These tapes will soon be finished and we hope that perhaps we could swap tapes with other schools in the hope that a useful and interesting resource may be available to us which is made by the children for the children.

PREPARING FOR PROJECT WORK

From these accounts it is possible to draw up a few practical guidelines for anyone attempting a school project for the first time.

1 Select a small and manageable topic, particularly at the first attempt – e.g. 'Going to the doctors'.
2 Plan carefully: who will be interviewed, by whom, where? What questions will be asked in order to accumulate evidence appropriate to the topic?
3 Draw up an interview schedule, or flexible framework in the classroom with the students.
4 Select the best equipment at your disposal. Although any kind of tape-recorder can be used, a separate microphone cuts out background noise.
5 Practise handling the machinery and interviewing each other in school. Set standards for *good* interviews.
6 When going out to interview, remind the pupils that they are collecting evidence of all kinds. List all borrowed photographs as they come into school and have copies made if possible.
7 Transcribe all interview materials, though not all teachers agree that this is necessary. It can be done in groups of two or three pupils.
8 Remind the class that they are writing history. Discuss the difference between evidence and history. Compare interviews, look for other forms of evidence.
9 Work on editing and the final presentation of material.
10 Write to thank all who have taken part and invite them to any public event.

COMMUNITY EDUCATION

The opportunities for putting the work of the school on public display should not be neglected, particularly since members of the local community will have been closely involved in the enterprise. Such co-operation promotes and fosters links between school and the world outside the gate, not simply in terms of good neighbourliness – 'Come in and let's get to know each other better' – but also in curricular terms. What the school is actually communicating is, 'Your knowledge and your experience are valid and have a place in our curriculum.'

The personal contacts between people from different generations will probably remain strong. People are intrinsically interesting and there seems to be an ease of communication between pupils and their grandparents' generation that is not always evident when dealing with their own parents.

Old people, too, have time on their hands and can benefit just as much from interviews as can the pupils undertaking the investigation. Putting the two generations together, for a purpose, gives each a common goal and is particularly valuable in developing those social skills which schools believe to be an important part of their pupils' education. They are developed naturally by this kind of practice.

ORAL HISTORY ACROSS THE CURRICULUM

Although emphasis has been laid in this chapter on oral history in the history classroom, it obviously lends itself to work right across the curriculum. In English lessons, for example, teachers have utilized the life-history recording as a means whereby slower-learning pupils and those for whom English is not their mother tongue can be helped to get their own reminiscences first onto tape and then onto paper. Recorded life histories have also been studied alongside written autobiography, which in turn has inspired personal writing and poetry. Geography-teachers have also used reminiscence to trace the development of a locality, particularly one that has undergone extensive redevelopment. People who spent their childhood in other parts of the world have also been called into school to give first-hand information about their homeland.

Social studies, general studies and voluntary work schemes have also found oral history a useful resource, and, when school students visit old peoples' homes or clubs, reminiscence can be one way of establishing contact. In this way, recording the details of working life over the past fifty years, for example, and comparing the experiences of three generations, will be appropriate for many prevocational and work-experience courses, and the interview material can be assessed for examination purposes.

CONCLUSIONS

Personalizing the past has many educational advantages, not least the acqui-sition and practice of a range of skills: talking, interviewing, transcribing, editing. The final report of a project could be a piece of writing, a booklet, or an exhibition. Tape-slide units, radio programmes and even plays have been produced as the end products of oral-history work (see chapter 37, 'The Making of Motherland').

Handling tapes and tape-recorders also aids the development of motor skills, often an area where pupils have proved to be more skilled than teachers, in much the same way as with computer literacy.

Finally, all the historical skills encouraged by the new history movement can be examined by using oral evidence. Some of the questions to be asked are about the nature of the evidence, how reliable it is, how it fits in with other kinds of evidence, and how it might be conserved. Questions that illuminate the key concepts of change, difference and cause cannot fail to come up in the discussion of life-history testimonies, and students will be forced to ask questions such as 'why?', 'when?' and 'where?' as they confront the evidence they have collected.

Passive learning in the history classroom can be incredibly dull for both teacher and pupil, however intrinsically interesting the topic. Oral-history projects are not only opportunities for active learning, with a great deal of responsibility being put on the student; they are also creative. Pupils collect historical material that has not been retrieved before, for opportunities to talk about their past experience usually remind respondents of back-up documents and photographs which they have in their drawers, but which they have never thought would be of interest to other people. Such items, together with public documents such as census returns, maps and newspaper extracts, help students to put their oral evidence into context and so to pull a piece of genuine history together. Oral-history projects lend themselves to current models of assessment, whether self-evaluation, school- or college-based monitoring, or external validation is required. Diligence and application to the task will be evident in the final presentation, but, where appropriate, skills and concepts can also be identified, graded and tested. The greatest reward, however, is likely to be in the student's growing self-esteem, as the flexibility of an oral-history project allows realistic goals to be set for pupils of all ages and ability.

NOTES

1 *Oral History*, 11, 1 (1983), 7–8. A report on this project has appeared in *SCIP Ahead*, the newsletter of the SCIP, and published by the Bristol CSV Centre, 13 Midland Road, Bristol 2.
2 *Oral History*, 8, 2 (1980), 13–15.
3 *Oral History*, 11, 1 (1983), 8–9.

REFERENCES AND FURTHER READING

Adams, C. 1982: *Ordinary Lives*, London: Virago.
Beddoe, D. 1984: *Discovering Women's History*. London: Pandora.
Cleaver, E. 1985: Oral history at Thurston Upper School. *Oral History*, 13 (1), 11–13.
Dodgson, E. 1984a: From oral history to drama. *Oral History*, 12 (1), 47–53.
—— 1984b: *Motherland*. London: Heinemann Educational.
Humphries, S. 1984: *The Handbook of Oral History*. London: Inter-Action Imprint.
Purvis, S. 1980a: *Oral History in Schools*. Colchester: Oral History Society (available from Department of Sociology, Essex University).
—— 1980b: The unacceptable face of history? *Teaching History*, 26, 34–5.
—— 1983: Arbury is where we live. *History Today*, 33 (June), 29–32.
Reekes, A. 1980: Oral history and the Raj. *Teaching History*, 27, 4–5.
Reeves, M. 1980: *Why History?* London: Longman.
Ross, A. 1984: Children becoming historians: an oral history project in a primary school. *Oral History*, 12 (2), 21–31.

Schools Council 1976: *History around Us: some guidelines for teachers*. Edinburgh: Holmes-McDougall.
Steedman, C. 1984: Battlegrounds: history in primary schools. *History Workshop*, 17, 107–112.
Steel, D. and Taylor, L. 1973: *Family History in Schools*. Chichester: Phillimore.
Thompson, P. 1978: *The Voice of the Past*. Oxford: Oxford University Press.

PACKS FOR TEACHERS

Voices from the Past. Tapes, slides, transcripts and guidelines from the North West. Available from Dr Elizabeth Roberts, University of Lancaster.
Memories of the Twenties and Thirties. Workcards for secondary schools. Available from Help the Aged Education Department, PO Box 460, 16–18 St James Walk, London, EC1R 0BE.

30

Practising anti-racist teaching

Martin Francis

Martin Francis challenges the idea that anti-racist teaching should be thought of as a feature of school life separate from other parts of the curriculum. Rather it should simply be a dimension of all good practice. In this chapter, he concentrates on the way he has incorporated anti-racism in his primary practice through curriculum content and the choice of books, and, above all, by being willing to talk about children's attitudes and experiences. His reluctance to see anti-racism as isolated practice is reinforced by his inclusion of material on combating sexism.

The first problem that confronts the teacher, particularly in a classroom or school where there has been a tendency to shy away from tackling 'controversial' issues, is to find ways of estabishing an atmosphere in which they can be discussed. The organization of the classroom, provision of materials and teaching-styles are important here. By providing multiracial books, resources in childrens' mother tongues, anti-sexist display materials, 'alternative' sources of information (e.g. community newspapers), encouraging discussion and collaborative learning, you can influence the hidden curriculum so as to create an atmosphere in which anti-racist teaching can take place.

Without this background raising the issue of racism and trying to discuss it will come like a bolt from the blue – something completely different, threatening and accompanied by moral pressure. As we have worked on anti-racist teaching in the ALTARF (All London Teachers Against Racism and Fascism) primary workshop, it has become clear that in one sense we are merely talking about good primary practice – but in another we are talking about radical changes in the organization of schools, teaching-method and content. A content that challenges racism and sexism, that recognizes the ability of young children to think through issues themselves, that encourages them to argue, debate and organize, that takes established views and subjects them to rigorous examination cannot leave unexamined the hierarchical nature of schools, the relationship of the school to the local community. Possibly 'good progressive education' meant that anyway – but the sharper edge we are giving it cannot leave the school unscathed.

The progressive axiom of 'starting where the kids are', from their own experience, can be limited to starting a project on metamorphosis where a child brings in a caterpillar, but can be extended to include *Unpopular Education*'s idea of making the contradictions children experience themselves the object of study (Centre for Contemporary Cultural Studies, 1981). Over the past few years children have raised with me issues about sexism, racism, local housing, lead in petrol, the powerlessness of young people, unemployment and the nuclear bomb. These issues increasingly impinge on their world as they reach the age of eleven and we shall be failing the children if we do not take them up. One of our first tasks is to 'take the lid off' this experience.

In order successfully to 'take the lid off' the teacher has to have generated the kind of atmosphere in the classroom where children feel free to talk about their experiences, to express strong points of view, and feel able to disagree with each other and the teacher. The way the contradictions of modern society touch the children is often deeply personal and they have to be confident that they will be heard and taken seriously. This is a matter not just of the teacher's attitudes but also of the child knowing that the teacher or the school has taken on such issues in the past. Building up such an atmosphere is a slow process that goes backwards as well as forwards – particularly when the teacher her/himself is constrained by the school time-table, expectations of other staff, fear of a parental backlash. However, the primary school teacher with the close relationship she/he can develop with the class is in a better position than most.

When you have taken the lid off, you'll probably recoil at what you find – there will be all sorts of attitudes and ideas that will appear prejudiced, reactionary or just plain daft (not that such ideas are absent in teachers!) – but when you get down to discussion there will emerge ideas that are generous, thoughtful, open-minded, sorted-out. You now have the job of sorting out what kind of intervention you can make. You have on your side that it is *contradictions* you are looking at – the views of different children will contradict each other but they will also have individually within themselves contradictory views and interpretations of their experience. The children are involved in a continuous process of building up a picture of their world – feeding into that all sorts of disparate information and experience culled from friends, family, television, comics, books and school. You as a teacher can provide information and experience that can help them clarify things for themselves.

I have looked elsewhere (Francis, 1982) at the various approaches you can take in terms of concentric circles with the child's *personal* experience at the centre, moving out to *school*, the *community*, *national* events, *historical* events, *geographically* distanced events and perhaps even to totally *imagined* starting-points. In a sense we can start anywhere in this pattern. In a school with an ethnic-minority population the personal may be the best starting-point. In an all-white school, national, historical and geographical starting-points may be the wisest. The teacher's experience and confidence in raising the issue are also important, and those just embarking on this approach may be happiest with the more distanced starting-points.

Although in this chapter I am looking mainly at the anti-racist dimension, I shall also be looking at examples of anti-sexist and class/community issues. The concentric circles can be applied to all three areas.

PERSONAL EXPERIENCE

This is where you really 'take the lid off' and get children to talk about their own experience. Getting children to listen to their peers as others they can learn from is very important. They will often shut up for the authority figure (the teacher) but not for each other. I have found one way of getting over this is to sit in a circle and pass a stone around. You are only allowed to speak when you have the stone. Normally, the stone is passed clockwise or anti-clockwise so that all have a chance to speak. Other teachers have found this artificial and have a system where the stone is passed to anyone who wants it. The first way can certainly enable children to listen to each other and sometimes enables them to get beyond just talking off the top of their head. They have time to consider what they are going to say whilst waiting for the stone to come round. As far as possible the teacher should stick to the rules and not speak 'out of the stone'. If the stone method does not cut out male dominance, the group can be split into girls and boys and two groups run and this can also be done with larger classes.

I have tried to develop a tradition of discussion in the classroom so that a racist or sexist remark can be discussed in a setting which has become normal and comfortable – if discussion becomes merely a disciplinary device to deal with such remarks, it loses its educative function.

In these discussions I do not see myself as 'neutral' but express my own point of view. Again, where there is a tradition of disagreement and challenging, this shouldn't be a problem, although you cannot completely get away from the authority of the teacher. As I listen to tapes of my own classroom discussions, I am very aware of how often I am called 'sir' and how much is directed at me. There will always be something that pupils will profoundly disagree with you about, so that, if you get a feeling that they're waiting to 'please the teacher' with the 'right line', you pick a topic on which you're likely to disagree with most of the class. For me these have included Charles and Di's wedding (their reaction, 'Aaaaah ...'; mine, 'Ugh!') and television (they wanted more; I wanted less). It's important for teacher and pupil that the views you put forward are genuine.

Once pupils have got used to discussion and listening to each other, it is possible to have less structured discussions, split into smaller groups or develop techniques of 'reporting back'. This is a transcript of a discussion I had with a small group about a racist name-calling incident. Kim had called

John a racist name and, following an after-school discussion with me, had written a letter of apology.

John   Usually when it happens [being called a name] you just want to get the person that said it, really.

Me   You were really angry, and shaking and crying weren't you?

Kim   It weren't really only me that said it, it was Cheryl as well but Cheryl got out of it so that I got all the blame.

Me   But what do you feel about the way we dealt with that, was it better or not?

John   That's the best way to deal with it really. Have a talk with each child and see what you can do and when you can see which one is right or which wrong let that person who is wrong say they're sorry or whatever ...

Me   Kim, do you really think you were wrong that time?

Kim   Yeah.

Me   And what did you think when you wrote the letter to John? Did you *feel* that or were you just doing it because you were told to?

Kim   I weren't doing it because I was told to. I shouldn't have done it in the first place.

Me   What did you think John when you got the letter back?

John   Yes, it's all right but usually you can't take an apology for a few minutes can you? It sticks in your mind ... usually you don't like taking a letter, you like hearing it personally. Like when Kim gave me the letter I made her read it all out to me and say it first.

Lorraine You know when you tell teachers something, like if you had a fight, they look at you as if they don't know you, as if you came from Mars or Jupiter or something.

John   Yes, like you're an outerspacer, like they've never seen you before.

Later in the discussion I asked John if teachers tried to undertand what was happening to children:

John No, not really, they just deal with school and the rest of it's nothing to do with them.

The 'rest of it' is to do with racism in the community outside, the experience of being black, linking up with all the concentric circles I've outlined. It is also to do with the experience of being white and under pressure from racists:

Paul In some schools I've heard about, if some white kids don't want to join the NF, the NF beat them up. If they tell about what they're doing to the black people they make the white people join NF.

Jack When I tried to leave the NF they beat me up for no reason. They always do that ... They were too much violent and they were just beating up people and stabbing them and all that. They just started beating me up. They were calling me 'chicken' and 'nigger-lover' and all that.

In such discussions it's not just heavy issues such as that which come through, but also more positive ones where white children can hear black children expressing strong feelings about their language and culture:

Michael I will teach my children (patois). If someone comes up and speaks to my children in our language, I'll teach them our language so that they can say something back to them.

Me   Do you enjoy speaking patois?
Michael Yes, its's nice. Because of the kind of accent you speak in.
Me   Do you feel different when you're speaking patois, to when you're speaking English?
Michael It's as though I'm in a different world when I'm speaking it.

From an anti-sexist viewpoint, such discussions often centre on being called names such as 'cissy' or 'tomboy', but also on feelings and behaviour. Here again, the teacher is crucial and we *all* have our own direct experience to throw into the discussion. As a male teacher I'll take a group of boys while a female colleague takes the girls. You have to be prepared to sit down and be open – to talk about your own childhood and the kinds of fears and misconceptions you had and also about how often you cry, what you are still scared of. Lifting the lid off in this way reveals a whole can of worms.

If children are going to be as open and revealing about themselves as these quotations imply, it's clear that the school has to reciprocate by taking up the issues they raise. Such discussions are often painful (for different reasons) for both black and white children, and for both girls and boys. It would be a gross misuse of the trust placed in us if we took no action about them or saw the discussions as ends in themselves.

SCHOOL

Apart from pupil–pupil and staff–pupil relationships, there are also school-based issues of curriculum and resources. Multi-cultural and anti-racist education can sometimes get it wrong. The emphasis on slavery for example can push black people into the victim role, liberated by a white knight (Wilberforce, praised so wholeheartedly by the establishment recently and credited with the abolition of slavery by Mrs Thatcher), without recognizing the struggle of black people themselves. The following extract shows that an attempt to get beyond that still has problems:

Me   So what do you think about some of the things we've done? Have you enjoyed ... we've done a bit about Paul Robeson and Harriet Tubman ...?
Michael ... and Olaudah Equiano.
Jackie ... and Toussaint L'Ouverture.
Me   Did you talk to your parents about doing that sort of history?
Jean   I did.
Michael I've talked about that. They said they don't like people giving us that kind of history in that way. Because you never find them giving King Henry history in that way, like King Henry had to work on plantations and black people whipping him. They wouldn't give a history in that way. They only give it in coloured people's way wouldn't they?
Me   How should it be taught then?
Michael It should be taught in the same way white people's history is taught.
Me   But you can't change what happened can you?
Michael No, but there's still some history of black people hidden in the past but they don't want to record it ... I'm sure that there's a lot of black history but they

don't want to record it ... I'm sure that there's a lot of black history but they don't want us to know about it. They only let us know about King Henry, who was white and all those things.

Jackie Because if they did they think we might want to start it [the fight against white oppression?] again.

That conversation made me think about what I was doing, and it's salutary to check up on yourself in this way. It seemed that, despite my attempts, the image of slavery – plantation workers, whippings – was still the main one getting through. This is an important aspect of what happened but not the only one. This image was compounded at the time by the screening of the television film *Roots*, which aroused mixed feelings among black pupils in the class.

The resources of the school are also important and convey messages to children about the school's attitudes towards black peoples' presence in Britain and towards black pupils:

Mary In the books they show more white people and in the advertisements.
Ann Like we're not there. Like we're nothing.

Echoes of Lorraine and John feeling treated like 'outerspacers'!

Apart from the absence of black people in books, there is also the question of how they are portrayed when they are present. In ALTARF's BBC2 Open Door Programme, *Racism: the fourth r*[1] we showed Mara Chrystie taking up the issue of illustrations in the Dinosaur book *Going Swimming* with her class of infants. A child had objected to black people being coloured in grey in the pictures, and the class decided to write to the author:

Dear Jill,
I like the story but I don't like the pictures 'cos people are really brown and no people are really grey. When I go out in the street I don't see any grey people. I am a bit white and bit brown ....

The publishers were hurt, because they thought they were being accused of being racist, while others thought the issue was trivial. In fact it showed several fundamental aspects of anti-racist teaching: the teacher took the issue up after a child raised it (i.e. it was not dreamed up by oversensitive trendy teachers); the children made their own alternative book (demystifying books and showing the illustrations could be better) and the children were encouraged to see that their views were legitimate and to take action about them (writing to the author and publisher). The item shows that children can from a very early age be encouraged to be critical of learning-materials, and that even well-meaning publishers (Althea have an anti-racist policy) and schools (the books had gone through a screening process for racist/sexist content) can get it wrong.

Similarly I was pulled up by one of the pupils in my class last year. I am in charge of library and resources at my school and prided myself that I'd tried to get in some good anti-racist and anti-sexist books. However, Wendy thought differently: 'Well, I think there isn't enough black books in school. They've got *Peter and Jane* and they're white and they haven't got any books for black kids and if they have they're just silly books – they're not sensible.'

In fact we don't any longer have the Ladybird reading-scheme but use the Moon Individualized system to draw on a wide range of multiracial books. However, the remark about the black books being silly seemed to reflect a feeling that they failed to address the issue of racism – they were humorous or, like *Berron's Tooth*, cosy. Again, we do have books that address racism – mainly fiction for older juniors – but Wendy and her friends wanted something different:

So what we tried to do (which we never finished) we made up our own book after a programme about people getting jobs and racism. We did a book about jobs and drew pictures and we talked about why black people hadn't been getting jobs. Was it because of their colour or is it just because they're not qualified, and we got to the decision that it was because of their colour. So what we did was we got together, we had a discussion before we started making the book, and we just started writing it down and drawing pictures about it.

The fact that ten- and eleven-year-olds wanted a book that confronted contemporary racism in a factual way reveals not only their own political understanding but also the underassessment, by both teachers and publishers, of their ability to understand.

Obviously books should also be looked at in terms of sexist bias, but school issues go much wider. I surveyed my class and asked them questions about the suitability of books in the class for boys and girls, whether topics chosen for class study were generally oriented to boys' or girls' interests, whether I as a teacher spent more time with boys or girls, whether boys or girls were more often the cause of disruption in the class, whether the cleverest pupil in the class was a boy or a girl. The answers to the questions were not only informative to me as a teacher (in addition to girls' general satisfaction with books, and the fact that both boys and girls nominated a girl as the cleverest child, they revealed a perception by both girls and boys of sexist bias), but also formed the basis of a very full class discussion. The survey and discussion provided useful reference material when particular boys were being a nuisance later, and also helped me look at books and topics with more care.

The school structure itself can become the subject of study. Using a video camera borrowed from the local teachers' centre I did a project on jobs with first- and second-year juniors. We interviewed various workers in the school: teacher (male), secretary (female), cook (female). The children worked in groups to prepare the questions and these were pooled and the final list decided and allocated between the children. Informed by discussions we'd had about housework and male and female roles within that, and pay and promotion, the children asked not just about the job but also about the effects on home life. Did the female workers' husbands share the housework? Was it equal? They also asked about pay and whether the jobs paid enough. As a background to the project we had a wall display on jobs which asked pertinent questions about school. Why do boys and girls line up separately? Why don't we have a woman school-keeper? Why don't we have male dinner helpers? Similarly, questions can be asked about the proportion of black workers in the school, and one child asked the (black) nurse about whether her colour had made it harder for her to get a job.

Sometimes support from outside can be important in raising the issues in school. Theatre Kit produced a Girls' Project about two years ago. The show dealt with sexist stereotypes through sketches and pupils' participation and produced a strong sense of identity amongst the girls. The show was for girls only and that in itself was challenging for male staff and male pupils. Boys hung around the hall trying to see what was happening, and male teachers were shooed off by girl pupils. The boys were quite threatened at something for girls only (despite football, for instance, being mainly a boys-only activity). I had a discussion with the boys while the girls were attending the Girls' Project about why the play was a girls-only event and got onto wider discussion about sexism and sexuality. The girls came out of the show shouting 'Girls are powerful' and were on a real high for several days. As a result they formed their own girls' group and held discussions in the school library at lunchtimes, but had problems with harassment from other pupils, particularly boys. This caused discipline problems, as a result of which they were thrown out, and we had eventually to make space for the group's discussions during ordinary classtime. Obviously my role as a male teacher with the group was extremely limited, but I was able to invite a friend who is a feminist and interested in working with girls to come in occasionally to work with them while I worked with the boys.

It would be silly to pretend that such activities do not present problems for a school. They raise questions about staff–pupil relationships, teaching-style and democracy and may well be opposed by some staff (teaching and non-teaching) who are happier with old structures and relationships. They may also be opposed by others who see them as pseudo-democratic and a 'progressive cover' on structures and relationships that remain fundamentally unchanged. I would argue that there is space available to undertake some of these activities and that the pupils themselves will begin to work out whether they are a con.

NOTE

1 *Racism: the fourth r* (BBC2/ALTARF). Available on video (VHS format) from ALTARF, Room 216, Panther House, 38 Mount Pleasant, London WC1X 0AP.

REFERENCES

Centre for Contemporary Cultural Studies 1981: *Unpopular Education*. London: Hutchinson.
Francis, M. 1982: Anti-racist teaching in the primary school. *Cambridge Journal of Education*, 12.2, 130–8.

31

A tale of frogs: close encounters in primary environmental studies

David Boalch

Galleywall lies just south of the Thames, on the borders of Bermondsey and Rotherhithe. This may seem unlikely territory for a project on frogs. But, as David Boalch recounts, some very interested children met some no doubt surprised frogs in an ecological park near Tower Bridge. The result was a flood of observations, activities and learning from all the children.

THE WILLIAM CURTIS ECOLOGICAL PARK

The William Curtis Ecological Park covers an area of roughly two acres. It is in the shadow of Tower Bridge and directly opposite Traitors' Gate in the Tower of London. The great warship HMS Belfast is moored about a quarter of a mile upstream. Hundreds of thousands of commuters pass through London Bridge station. Thousands of vehicles rumble along nearby Tooley Street and yet, when you stand in the middle of the park, all you can hear is the rustling of the shrubs and trees, the call of birds, and the occasional 'eureka' cry from a child.

The idea for the park came from Max Nicholson, Chairman of the Ecological Parks Trust. The aim is to use temporarily unoccupied patches of land in city centres to bring nature and pieces of 'country life' to city-dwellers.

The park project was initiated in February 1977. The site, then a lorry park covered in sand, ash and gravel, was transformed with over 300 lorry-loads of topsoil from excavation sites all over London. This was piled and hollowed and a hole was dug for a pond. The design was by Lyndis Cole, a landscape architect. The site was then raked over and seeded, trees were planted, and the pool was lined with plastic by volunteers from the Southwark area.

The planned opening in May coincided with the two-hundredth anniversary of the publication by William Curtis, the eighteenth-century botanist who worked at the Chelsea Physick Gardens, of his *London Flora* (*Flora Londiniensis*). Since then the park has started to balance out its own micro-habitats. Some of the trees have died; others have been planted. Insects, frogs and fish abound in the pond and in the grass. New species are being found almost daily. The bushes and undergrowth provide nesting-sites for birds, and the area as a whole has provided a staging-point for a few rare visitors.

There were few seeded plants, but very soon others, blown in on the wind, or brought in with the topsoil from all over London, have come to colonize the park. Many rare species have arrived by one or other of these methods. The pond itself was originally filled with tap water, but was very quickly 'diluted' by rain and run-off from the surrounding buildings. It has now provided homes for millions of creatures, ranging from daphnia to dragonflies to duck.

One day – tomorrow or, perhaps, if we are lucky, in five years' time – the park will be reclaimed again. This time it will be used as a building-site for housing or factories. Already other areas have been adopted all over London, not only to provide a pinhead of countryside in the forest of the city, but also to be used as a rich source of material for urban children to study.

USING THE PARK AS AN EDUCATIONAL RESOURCE

A visit to the William Curtis Ecological Park requires a local bus trip, a deal of forward planning and the help of an ancillary worker. However, I chose to take the class there rather than on a walk round the school grounds, because I knew that some of the class had made previous visits and I was guaranteed a wealth of 'natural life' to study. The experiences gained there would easily relate to each child's home and school environment, and the art of close study would be enhanced. I had also made a close study of the park while on an in-service course.

Some of my class of top juniors had already visited the park. I inherited not only ideas from the teacher who had gone with them, but also a tank of rain water with two three-spined sticklebacks and some snails and leeches which had been dipped for in the pond. The children had used this tank to study many things, including the differences in the movements of the three types of living forms and the rate of evaporation. These previous visits proved to be a great starter for the class. They were familiar with the route to the park, the set-up of the park, and the resident staff. The first visit was to be exploratory. It was the first time that I had taken the class out and so I wanted to set the standards for behaviour on the journey and in the park. It proved to be very easy. They were all excited about going, and the ones who had been before had filled in the details for the others: 'You mustn't run around the place 'cos you won't see anything – and don't splash the water, it frightens the fish.' This statement from the lad who had been branded 'top of the school thugs' was quite a revelation. When we arrived we were greeted by Pam Morris, who explained the set-up of the park to the class and soon found that they had remembered most of it.

She then asked the children if they would like to take part in a conservation project with frogs. There was a short silence until 'conservation' had been fully grasped. We finally settled on Chris's definition of 'saving' and most agreed. There were two girls who didn't, Tracey and Niquomoi, who both said they hated frogs because they were 'slimy and horrible'. We agreed that they should each be paired with someone who was quite happy about frogs, and that they should do the recording. Each pair had to record where they had caught their frog. Paul said, 'But they will all be in the pond.' 'Why?' asked Pam. 'Because frogs live in water.' 'I'll talk to you again later about that when we have caught a few', replied Pam.

Before we started we told the children why they had been asked to take part in the project. Some boys had been climbing over the fences during the times when the park was not staffed. They had been catching the frogs and cutting off their legs to use as fishing-bait. This was greeted with universal condemnation: 'I'd cut *their* legs off', said Tracey, who didn't even like frogs. The frogs that had been caught were then transported by tube to Hampstead Heath and released.

The children then set off on the frog hunt armed with their recording-sheet and a clipboard in a plastic bag. By now it had started to pour with rain. This point is significant for a later part of the visit. Most children went toward the pond. Immediately they found that there were frogs and froglets hopping 'everywhere'. Handfuls of them were quickly rushed to the collecting-box. 'Miss, this frog's a different colour from the rest', said Jason. 'Oh good', said Pam. 'Why do you think that is so?' Before he could answer, Jim came over and said, 'It's a toad, miss, not a frog.' A second container was brought out for the toads.

The two 'shy' girls had started to enter into the spirit of things. They were acting as 'spotters' or 'flushers-out': the partner did the catching; they then did the recording. I had found several frogs and had taken one up to Niquomoi and asked if she wanted to touch it. Eventually she did. She then took the next step of holding it in her hands and taking it to the collecting-box. Of course there were screams when the froglets jumped out or wriggled, but within ten minutes both of the girls were catching and recording quite happily: the first success of the trip. The final tally was 223 frogs and three toads caught; of these only five were caught in the pond. When we later discussed the places where they had found the frogs, the class came up with four main areas: under stones in the rubble areas (this was 'best'), in the grass, under the trees, and in the bushes in the basement. None at all had been found in the sandy area and only five in the pond. This lack of frogs in the pond surprised most of the children, because books and frog stories invariably depict frogs as water-lovers. The class eventually discovered that frogs, although amphibians, really only come to ponds each year to mate. They are born in water – a fact the children had discovered from a visit the previous year, when spawn was collected and kept in the classroom – but as soon as they are big enough they come out onto land. The children did point out that the frogs had to stay wet, though, and this is why they had not been found in the sand, because it was too dry for them. They also realized that frogs leave the water because their major sources of food are found on land: slugs, flies, worms, and so on.

Since it had rained quite steadily, and as there was no shelter at the park where we could eat our packed lunch, we decided to go back to school. Most of the children were soaked through, even though they were wearing waterproof coats, so they changed into PE kit and spare clothes at school, to eat their lunch. The wet clothes were draped over the warm radiators in the class and the hall. It was while we were eating lunch that a very interesting series of events happened. Rachel came up to me and said, 'Brett has brought back a frog.' So I called for Brett and asked whether he had a frog. 'No, sir,' he replied very confidently. 'Thank you,' I said: 'go and sit down.' A couple of minutes later Michelle came up and said, 'He has sir – he's got them in his pocket.' Again I asked Brett, this time publicly, whether he had a frog in his pocket. 'No, sir.' 'Have you got more than one then?' I asked. 'Yes, sir,' he replied slowly. 'Go and get them,' I directed. He went very slowly to the hall and picked up his coat, which was steaming by this time from the heater. He came back with a very sheepish look on his face and two thumbnail-size froglets in his hand, both of whom looked very dry and dazed. 'What are we going to do now with them?' I asked the class as a body. 'We could keep them in the tank,' said Chris, 'and look after them till they are old enough to go.' 'But they don't live in water. We will have to put in something for them to crawl onto, like a stone,' came another answer. I agreed to do this until we had made sure that they were all right and could be released. The two frogs plopped into the water, swam a few strokes and immediately climbed out on to the rock which we had placed in the water. Another child put up her hand and said, 'I don't think Brett should have done that because he was taking them away from their home.' 'But we were doing that anyway,' replied Kerry. 'Yes, but only because they were being hurt and we were putting them back to a place that was good for them.' The class, however, agreed that Brett had done the wrong thing.

It wasn't until about half an hour later that Brett came up and confessed to having brought back three frogs, and when he had got the other two he had dropped the third one, which had immediately hopped off. 'Go and find it,' I said again rather crossly. 'Martin has got two as well,' he said, as a parting shot from the doorway. Martin turned very red as a howl of indignation came from the class. 'We might just as well have left them for those thugs to cut their legs off.' 'They'll be boiled alive on the radiator.' Martin brought in his two dry frogs and these were also put into the tank. They just lay on top of the water, but by the end of school they had both mounted the stone. Meanwhile, I had found Brett's other frog, very bunged up with dust in a corner of the hall. It too was despatched to the tank and had joined the other four on the stone by the end of school. The resident sticklebacks were a bit put out at first and spent a lot of time swimming fast around the tank, but they soon settled to the extra movement and only had an occasional 'sprint' when a frog jumped in off the stone.

Before the children went home, we continued to talk over the day's events, the reasons for moving the frogs, and about conservation projects in general. Many had heard about campaigns such as 'Save the Whale' and organizations such as the Royal Society for the Protection of Birds and Royal Society for the Prevention of Cruelty to Animals. Although not strictly conservation schemes, these were the nearest equivalents of which the children had some previous knowledge. We also discussed the captive frogs' food problem. 'I'll bring in some worms,' said one. 'So will I,' said another.

By a quarter to nine the next day, half of the class was in looking at the frogs and wanting to put four-inch worms down them. We compromised eventually by chopping them up into smaller pieces.

During the day there was a constant stream of children popping over to look at the frogs. They were fascinated by them, and even friends from other classes came to have a look. It was during one of these visits that someone noticed that two were missing. 'They must have hopped it, sir, like you keep telling us to do,' said the visitor. The few of us in the class groaned. We found one, but the other had totally disappeared, perhaps to a visiting pocket, but I never found out. This presented us with another problem: how to stop them escaping again. Someone suggested a cover, but it was quickly noticed that it would cut out the air, and we would not be able to see them. It was eventually decided, after some discussion, that a piece of clear plastic could be put over the end above the stone, because it was obvious that they had jumped from there, and not from the water. I was very pleased to note that I had a few children who were starting to think scientifically.

The next day we found two of the frogs floating on the water, both dead. This provoked some sadness in the class, but also gave us a chance to talk a little about the question of death. Quite a few had lost grandparents or knew of someone who had died recently. We had quite a good discussion on the question of whether plants died in the same ways as animals. The consensus was that they did die, but didn't go to heaven. The other two frogs lived for a couple more days, but they too died. They had provoked a lot of thought about lifestyles, colour, movement, food, habitat and moral questions, plus the welcome visits from children from other classes.

As a follow-up to the visit to the ecological park, I brought in a cloth frog that I had made at college. 'We could sew one like that', or 'We could do a flat one like in the infants.' This idea very quickly caught on. I got a set of Binka squares, some cotton, and started. I asked how the children were going to know on which line to sew. 'We could draw it first' was one reply. 'Jason did a good one yesterday,' said Chris; 'he could do it for us.' Jason agreed but could only draw small frogs. 'How can we make Jason's small frog bigger?' I asked. Someone suggested drawing with an enlarger attach-ment, like the one that they had at home. Someone else suggested using the overhead projector, which had been used to make large pictures for the last Christmas production. It worked very well. Jason drew on the plastic, it was enlarged to the correct size, and a copy was done on banda paper for everyone. The pupils then drew around the frog and started to stitch. The concentration involved in the activity produced the first ever ten-minute silence in the class.

I suggested a piece of written work which was to be looked at from the frogs' point of view. This again produced some very good pieces.

This one visit focusing on frogs produced a tremendous range of follow-up ideas. Apart from the observations in the tank, and moral debates, some excellent art work and written work evolved. Jason, who certainly has considerable difficulties in learning, became the key figure in the drawing: a role the children had never seen him play before. Jim, the school top dog, became the best catcher of frogs and all-round expert on them, and, incidentally, produced an excellent bit of sewing. It was his idea to put in a fly for the frog to catch with its tongue. It was also a topic that Gautam, a boy who has recently come from India, with very little English, could take a full part in alongside everyone else, giving tangible evidence of his learning.

I think the greatest success of the visit was the badgering of me with one question: 'When are we going again?'

32

A market-place for learning

Mary Caven

This chapter started as notes by Mary Caven on how she organizes her class in a primary school alongside another group in an open-plan double classroom. She describes the teamwork between teachers and between pupils, and the use she makes of 'life' outside school as a resource for project work and for developing pupils' powers of investigation. She looks at the way pupils who may have difficulties in written work or with reading are helped to remain an integral part of the activities of her group.

I work in an open-plan classroom with a group of twenty-seven children of mixed ability, aged between nine and eleven years. There is a similar group 'next door', and often their teacher, Jacqui, and I work together as a team with other teachers, parents, visitors, students and secondary children doing 'service projects'.

Children have access to all areas of school (there is no staffroom as such) including the stockroom. From an early age we teach them to be responsible for all school resources and they are very sensible about waste.

Parents are welcome at all times. They can come in and see the work in class, and can 'look at the books' before, during or after the school day. They are perhaps our most useful resource and give of their time generously, hearing readers, taking cooking-groups, coming on outings, sharing dance and drama skills and running after-school clubs.

We members of staff are all very aware of the need to work together and help each other. We all feel able to share our skills and acknowledge weaknesses. For instance, I'm hopeless at dance and Jacqui dislikes 'capacity' as a maths topic, so I take her class for capacity and she takes mine for dance!

A daily staff-meeting takes place after lunch, where discussions on all aspects of school life take place: everything from hall times to philosophy; from children to visitors; from work to pantomimes! After school each day I meet with my student, Anne, to assess the day and plan aspects of the following day.

After that Jacqui and I meet to see where and how our classes are working, what we're doing together and how we can help each other. We need to make sure, for instance, that, if one of us is planning a noisy activity, the other knows about it and can plan accordingly.

My class area is large, bright and carpeted. Most of the furniture is mobile, so that, should we be doing drama or dance, we can easily rearrange it. The children's work – painting, models, books – provides part of the decoration of the room. The children can work where they like in the room; there are no assigned seats.

There are maths textbooks and workcards from about ten different schemes in the maths area, which is outside my classroom. Teachers pick and choose from them to cover the maths topics they are organizing in their classes. Much of the work is practical and oral and most comes from topics the children are studying. As far as 'reading' in the morning is concerned, the children read any books they like, fact or fiction. We don't have a 'reading-scheme'.

Each child has a record book. It sets out his/her work for a week or more. It records in note form what the child has done and hopes to do. I give the children information on happenings during the week, such as outings and visits. I comment to individuals on their work and tell them what the next topic is in each area if it's appropriate. The record book is a forecast of and guide to the children's work as well as a record. But we refer to it as 'record-book work'.

On the basis that 'a piece of work is a better record than a record about that piece of work', we (as a school) also keep a representative sample of every child's work each term and put it in a special folder. It's a very simple way of seeing for ourselves, or showing parents, where progress is being made, or needs to be made. When the children leave school, they stick all their 'folder work' into a huge scrapbook to take on to their secondary school. The children themselves derive enormous satisfaction from examining their efforts at four years old through to eleven.

VERTICAL GROUPING

Working in a vertically grouped class has several advantages for children. It allows them at least a two-year learning-period, so there's no pressure to achieve some mythical common standard in ten months. It also gives them the security of having one teacher in one base for a longer period of time, with all the advantages that implies – for example, time to recognize strengths and weaknesses, time to build on these strengths and to provide support in weaker areas.

It presupposes that the class will be taught mostly as small groups or as individuals. The expectation is that children will help children learn, adults will help children learn, and children will help adults learn.

Because we encourage parents, ancillary helpers and students to take a full and active role in school life, we can teach in lots of small groups and

I can often teach individually. For instance, when we were working on the markets project described below, I left the computer work to Josh, who was able to organize the other children, being more knowledgeable than most of the adults involved. I could then sit with Jamie and encourage him, partly by acting as his secretary, to put his thoughts into poetic form.

WORKING CO-OPERATIVELY

Teaching a class involved in as many as fifteen to twenty different activities, and not all going on in the same room, I rely on the children helping each other, hearing each other read, giving each other spellings. I spend a lot of time emphasizing the fact that we are all different, that we are all strong and weak in different areas and that all of us need friends to help us (but that it is *not* helping if you do someone's work for them). The children are surprisingly responsible; they don't copy or plagiarize and often teach each other better than I do.

PROJECT WORK: CHANGE AND 'UP THE MARKET'

I plan a topic the term before I 'do' it and *very briefly* outline aspects of language, maths, and so on, that I hope to incorporate. Much of this never happens in practice, because once we start work the children have ideas which lead us in other directions. When the topic is under way, I use the weekends to 'rough out' topics for the following week, and each evening I add in details based on that day's experiences.

Our work on markets was part of a large on-going project called 'change'. As much as possible I use primary sources as initial stimulation, as extension and as a point of reference for learning. Here, I used the Livesey local history museum[1] with its exhibition called 'Up the market', based on street markets in London at the turn of the century. Almost everything we had looked at this term, such as puberty, Divali, land movements, and schools over the last eighty years, seemed to show *dramatic* change. I was hoping that markets might not have changed so obviously.

As a preparation for the museum visit we spent an afternoon talking and improvising on the theme of life at the turn of the century in our local area. It was a general and open-ended discussion to 'set an atmosphere'. I had been prepared to talk about the history of markets and had several stories and poems 'at my finger-tips', but, as so often happens, the discussion was sidetracked and the children went off at different tangents (the Industrial Revolution, cheap goods from other countries, the making of an empire) asking questions to which I didn't, then, have an answer.

At the museum, a mixture of drama, slide show and worksheets was offered as a way of capturing the children's attention and centring it on the markets of 1900. The children enjoyed the drama and the slides but only six opted to do the worksheets. Worksheets have a certain novelty value for my class, as I don't often use them on a museum visit. It seems to me that looking at the exhibition can become secondary as children scurry from case to case trying to fill in sentences and draw quick sketches in inadequately sized boxes. Most of the class concentrated on the exhibition and made drawings of what caught their attention.

During the next couple of weeks at schools the children tried to find out about changes in markets between 1900 and 1984 by comparing the exhibition with the Whitecross Street market, which is just outside the school gate.

To start them off I took them on a walk around nearby Smithfield (the wholesale meat market), through Whitecross Street, ending up in a modern covered-market area outside the new Safeway store. On returning to the classroom we decided to put our impressions into poetic form. Some children concentrated on Smithfield, others on markets generally, others on markets 100 years ago.

Smithfield in the 1830s

There I was standing in slime and blood,
My ears and eyes and nose are glued
to the grunting
to the slaughtering
and the smell of blood and offal.
The cutting up
the hanging up
the absolute disgust of Smithfield
the blood drips on the ground
bits of meat fall as the meat is cut
that's Smithfield

(Hannah M.)

Market Cries

Markets markets
Bring out your baskets
Lemons lemons
Get your melons
Toys toys
Play them with joy
Clothes clothes
With this robe
Games games
In this lane
Stalls stalls
By this wall
Markets markets
Come and buy

(Jamie O.)

Market Day

Market bustle
market hustle
barrows creaking
wheels squeaking
yelling voices
difficult choices
different smells
ringing bells
it's time to close
the market goes.

(Hannah B.)

Smithfield

Shouting, hollering
'Make way for the bummarees' they call,
The blood drips, the cattle cry as they drop to the ground,
The grime and offal smells
The dung is ankle thick as I pass the cruel and awesome sights
My blood runs cold, sheep, pig and cow hanging on hooks
The banging and clanging of the market meets my ears,
I could never forget the sights and smells
Still they call 'make way for the bummarees'.

(Katya M.)

We made a tape of the poems interspersed with market cries, which became the audio part of a classroom display 'Markets 1900–Markets 1984'. The 1984 visual display took the form of a series of photographic images based on David Hockney's idea of a 'joiner'. At the museum, there was a joiner of East Street market along one wall, so my class compiled a joiner from their own photographs of Whitecross Street market. The 1900 visual display took the form of detailed three-dimensional models – for example, of decorated barrows.

In groups, some formed by the children and others juggled by me, but all mixed-ability, the children set out working on a way to document social and economic changes. Using a word-processor, they constructed a questionnaire to be given to the market stallholders over the next few days. Much discussion centred on whether to ask personal questions, such as names and on where goods for sale were obtained, and how to classify responses. Ultimately the following form was agreed on:

We are trying to find out about the changes in markets over the years. Please could you help us by answering some of our questions?
Has your family traditionally worked in markets?
How long have you been working in this market?
Have you always sold these goods?
What is your busiest day?
What is your busiest time of day?

Do your customers come from around here or do they come from far away?
Do you always work here or do you work at other markets?
Is there any way you would like to improve the market?
Would you prefer the market to be under cover or out on the streets as it is today?
How do you attract customers?
Do you use special offers or cries?
Do you have regular customers?
Do you get your products from one of the big companies or wholesale markets like Smithfield or Covent Garden?
Have you noticed any changes in the time you have been working here?

Thank you for your co-operation.

I need hardly say that the discussion had to be reopened as soon as the first group returned from interviewing the stallholders, and revisions were made to the original questions. Then, once all the questionnaires were in, we had to rephrase the questions and reclassify the responses in order to construct a database for the computer. (We used the Factfile programme on the BBC computer.)

Through their regular contact with market stallholders, some children became specifically interested in price changes, and one group compared the price of a meal for a family of six in 1900 with the price for an equivalent meal for a similar family in 1984. It turned out to be cheaper to shop at Safeway the day they actually carried out the survey!

Having studied some of the local markets and catalogued some of the changes in photographs, pictures, models, poems, fact files, charts and diagrams, the general consensus of opinion was that markets hadn't changed *that* much. We next set about creating an assembly to pass on what we'd discovered and how we'd discovered it to the rest of the school. This usually leads to more input from the children, teachers, parents and visitors who are present at the assembly – and who knows where that will lead us?

As to what we learnt from the experience: between the twenty-eight of us, a million different things, and not all of them to do with markets or change. For example, Alex was horrified that there were so few parks in the area around the Livesey Museum. There were lots of flats but no green areas. He checked it in the A–Z! This led to a lively discussion about planning and planners.

HOW INDIVIDUAL CHILDREN FIT IN

Rachel

Rachel is a very quiet, shy child with difficulties in reading and writing. My initial aim was to make Rachel more confident about herself and everything she tried. She likes drawing and painting, so I started asking her to do special notices for wall displays and made sure I said, 'She does it better than me', so that others appreciated that fact. Then I began to ask her to do other notices, such as 'School Council Toy Sale', now with a group of children, suggesting that she organize the operation. Sometimes she managed; sometimes she had the ideas and the others organized themselves around her. Gradually she became more assertive, especially when someone ruined a poster she'd designed!

Meanwhile *any* language work she did was praised. As a school policy we often work on the basis of several drafts to perfect a piece of written work. The first draft for everyone is always scrappy and rough. Spelling and punctuation are not an issue at this stage. Rather we're aiming for fluency and style and trying to say what we want to say. This draft is read through to a friend, or me, or a group, depending on the child and the working situation, and the emphasis here is on *constructive* criticism. I use this phrase a lot in drama and PE sessions so that the children understand its meaning.

On the basis of that read-through, a second draft is attempted and more attention is paid to style and spelling (using words on wall displays, from friends, and dictionaries). Often words that they know are misspelled are circled/underlined by the children and they concentrate on these in the second draft. Again it is read through. If there are more suggestions, then a third draft can be worked at. If not, then a final copy can be produced as the child's best effort.

With Rachel I try to come in after the second read-through. I work with her on the third and final pieces. If obvious spelling and punctuation problems occur and recur in the piece I will point *some* out and work on them with her, probably reinforcing them later with a game.

I'd better emphasize at this point that not every piece of writing is rewritten. However, creative and scientific writing often needs to be reworked, if it's to be writing for and with meaning, and not just writing for writing's sake.

This process means that Rachel, like every child in the class, has legitimate and safe avenues for experimentation, and recourse to help without obviously coming up to the teacher for every word she cannot spell, a process that must destroy any fluency in a child's writing, never mind his/her confidence and self-esteem.

We have set up a 'paired reading' programme. Rachel reads daily to the same adult. Unfortunately this is not her mother, because she found listening to Rachel read very frustrating.

As lots of mothers are in school hearing readers, it's not obvious who is hearing whom read. I make sure that Rachel also reads to other people, but I depend on the paired reader building up a special relationship, making the experience as enjoyable and as helpful as possible. The fact that Rachel now asks to read small pieces in assembly shows how her confidence and reading have improved.

Jamie

Children are not categorized as 'remedial' in our school when they experience difficulties. We recognize that everyone may have special physical, social, emotional or educational needs. Jamie finds it hard to stick at a task for long or to put together his own piece of writing.

Jamie joined the school when he was eight and a half. He had come from a formal school, where as a lively child with a need for attention he had found himself in constant trouble. He was labelled as 'disruptive' and became determined to live up to his reputation. The first thing to do was to try and increase his own self-respect. He did not seem to care what others thought of him, he often destroyed work you praised, and he was unaffected by peer-group pressure.

It took one and a half terms to discover that he adored 'creepy-crawlies'. So I built a class project around that: 'Beasts and mini-beasts'. It was amazing! He needed to record what he caught, in which traps, for the class terrarium. He needed to note and draw plans of areas where caterpillars, spiders and particularly earwigs were active in the wild garden. He needed to read. He needed friends to help in the 'nest watch'. Suddenly he wanted to be the class expert. There was little time for antagonizing people; his enthusiasm was catching.

Coping with his reluctance to write was much harder. At first he reduced all writing to a minimum, and creative writing consisted of a few staccato sentences. Redrafting was tedious and drove both of us crazy. To get round this situation and to make the whole experience more positive for the other children, as well as for Jamie, I sometimes acted as Jamie's secretary, which made the process easier and more thoughtful. He gradually put in more effort and as time went on I withdrew. However, I am in the lucky position of having easy access to a word-processor and that was a tool Jamie appreciated. Redrafting on a word-processor is easy, and fun. Slowly, the quality of his work is improving. He is becoming more skilful and acknowledges how useful this is. I am now working on handwriting skills with Jamie. The Insect Club (his idea) needs an extraordinary number of notices, posters and books. Jamie is a much more stable member of the class now and a much happier person.

NOTE

1 The Livesey Museum, in the Old Kent Road, is supported by the London Borough of Southwark. Exhibitions are mounted annually and are designed with both an educational and a local community interest in mind. Schoolchildren contribute to the setting-up of an exhibition and their project work may be included in the exhibition as the year progresses.

33

Attractions of the North Pole:
learning together in humanities

Susan Hart and Stuart Scott

A common response to the introduction of more diverse teaching-groups has been the production of large quantities of individualized learning materials. The effect has been cynically referred to as 'death by a thousand worksheets'. In the ILEA (Inner London Education Authority) Collaborative Learning Project, Susan Hart and Stuart Scott looked for an alternative which would make children less dependent on teacher direction, and more dependent on, and able to use, their own ideas and skills. At the same time, they sought an approach that would require collaboration between pupils. Here they offer an example of their work.

Skill development should always be part of an activity that has meaning and purpose for the child. Yet, as recently as 1980, most of the provision made for 'remedial' and bilingual children involved withdrawing them to special classes and units, with the result that learning took place in an artificial context which had little or no link with regular classroom work. This conveyed the wrong messages to learners and teachers alike. It encouraged poor readers to see reading as a ritual which they did to please teachers but which had little to do with the rest of their lives; it gave those learning English as a second language (ESL) the impression that they had to master English before they could benefit from what the classroom had to offer; and it suggested to the subject-teachers that, since these pupils were getting help elsewhere, there was no need to consider ways of making their own teaching more appropriate. Finding that, as teachers of 'remedial' and bilingual pupils, we shared a similar dissatisfaction with these arrangements, we decided to work together to see what alternatives could be found.

We sensed that what our children needed was the sort of language experience fostered by the best primary practice where they could learn through interaction with other children. Reading and ESL support could then be provided within the classroom through the medium of their normal class activities. Yet we knew that the standard pattern of secondary teaching, in which pupils spend most of their time either listening or writing, was unlikely to provide an environment rich in opportunities for reading and language development. What we set out to do, therefore, was to look at alternative ways of organizing learning in the secondary classroom so that children would be motivated to read, write and talk together, while accepting the limits of the curriculum as defined by the subject areas at that time. We therefore arranged to teach a first-year mixed-ability humanities class the following year, and began to consider a range of different strategies which might encourage collaboration.

We were not happy about many of the approaches traditionally offered as ways of catering for different levels of ability, which tend to differentiate between children and isolate them from one another rather than getting them to work together. Individualized worksheets, workcards and project-based methods, for instance, have no in-built need to collaborate, and rely heavily on the very language skills our pupils lack. We thought, too, that simplifying reading-material often leads to texts which are so banal they are not worth reading. Offering alternative tasks to, say, the bottom third of the class cuts those pupils off from their peers, and can have much same 'labelling'-effect as if the children are withdrawn.

We soon discovered too that sets of information textbooks, no matter how attractively presented, were more likely to deaden than to stimulate discussion. The presence of thirty copies of the same book in the classroom implies a prepackaged view of knowledge which ignores what the children themselves have to offer the learning process. We believed it was important for pupils to express and explore ideas in their own words, using texts as something to be questioned and worked on rather than just assimilated.

We began to try out ways of getting children actively involved in talking and sharing what they knew about a topic before they went to books as sources of information. We looked for ways to help them extract and use ideas from books without slavishly copying everything down. We wanted to bring alive the impersonal information of textbooks through personalized studies of 'real' people that were rich in detail, and to help the children engage with the ideas and respond critically to their reading in ways other than writing.

It seemed that, if we were to achieve a lively involvement in language activities, then we would need to reduce drastically the role of teacher talk and whole-class 'discussion', and set the children working in small self-directed groups as much as possible. If these groups were to be able to work independently of the teacher, however, specially designed materials would be needed to stimulate and focus the discussion activities. We realized that we had to be especially careful, however, that any materials we produced were not too directive. We did not want to restrict the possibilities of collaborative group work. There was also the danger that the activities might become a substitute for books, instead of stimulating children to use and enjoy a wide range of resources, as we intended.

ANIMALS OF THE ARCTIC

An example of the kind of activity which we produced is explained below. This lesson is part of a unit of work on adaptation and survival, and the pupils are exploring what sources of food there might be in harsh conditions such as those of the Arctic.

The instructions for what they have to do are written down (see figure 33.1), and the children have to work this out together. The reading is shared and the activity can begin as soon as they understand the task, without having to wait for other groups to be ready, or for the teacher to explain. Having cards to hold and look at one by one, to read and talk about together, to sort and share, means that right away everyone can become involved. Children who would never speak in front of the whole class have a chance to talk and share what they already know. Starting the lesson in this way confirms to the children that what every child brings to the lesson is valued as a resource for others. Even if the bilingual pupil does not join in the initial interaction,

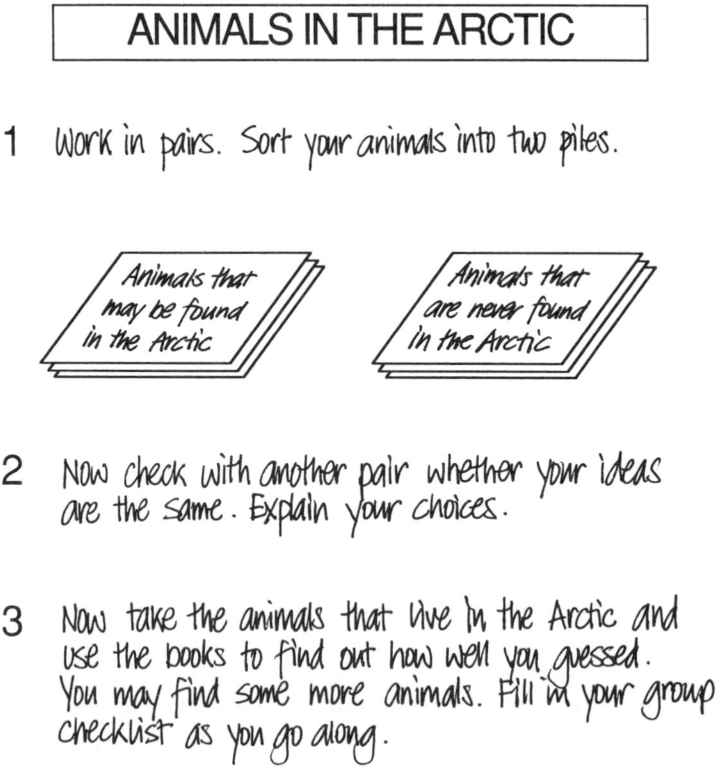

ANIMALS IN THE ARCTIC

1 Work in pairs. Sort your animals into two piles.

Animals that may be found in the Arctic

Animals that are never found in the Arctic

2 Now check with another pair whether your ideas are the same. Explain your choices.

3 Now take the animals that live in the Arctic and use the books to find out how well you guessed. You may find some more animals. Fill in your group checklist as you go along.

Figure 33.1

ANIMALS IN THE ARCTIC CHECKLIST

Name of animal	Found in Arctic	Not found in Arctic	Name of animal	Found in Arctic	Not found in Arctic
arctic foxes			snakes		
arctic hares			snow geese		
arctic terns			stoats		
beavers			toucans		
bats			vultures		
canada geese			walruses		
caribou			whales		
cod			wolves		
elephants					
frogs					
lemmings					
mice					
moles					
mosquitoes					
musk oxen					
planktonic animals					
polar bears					
ptarmigan					
ravens					
red squirrels					
robins					
seals					
sheep					
shrews					

Figure 33.2

he/she is able to perceive the purpose of the activity and has time to listen and reflect before joining in.

Within the limits defined by the topic, the children can also to some extent develop the activity in their own way. Because there are no tightly specified learning objectives, the children can begin from where they are and pursue their own concerns and interests. Language work is taking place at a variety of different levels. Children are identifying and describing the animals. They are using previous knowledge to explain and justify their decisions. They are speculating on which animals could survive in the Arctic and which could be hunted for food. It is up to them whether they raise issues such as migration, hibernation, warm- and cold-bloodedness or the possibility of animals being sources of dairy products, or to what depth these issues are explored.

When the children come to use the information books in the second part of the lesson to check their predictions, they know exactly what they are looking for. They learn to use books as tools for purposes which they have defined themselves, selecting from a wide range of resource books those titles most likely to meet their needs. They learn to use chapter headings and indexes confidently to locate information. They come to accept that no one book can answer all their questions, and begin to note discrepancies between books in the information presented. Besides using books to confirm and check what they already know, they search out more information and settle disagreements. They can follow up points of interest and questions that have arisen in discussion. They pass their findings on to each other and share interesting pictures, captions and passages together. Whatever their stage of reading development, everybody can use books to find information that will contribute to the work of the group.

Their combined efforts are recorded on a checklist (figure 33.2), which is designed to eliminate unnecessary writing. So often, information-gathering leads to verbatim copying. We wanted to encourage the kind of writing which follows reflection and discussion. Sometimes, writing might also be a group effort.

At the end of the lesson, the class come together as a group to share their findings. These can be presented visually against a backcloth Arctic landscape onto which pictures of the various animals can be placed. Gradually the picture is built up by representatives of each group. Since the result is knowledge produced by the class as a whole, not reproduced from textbook or teacher talk, it should hold personal meaning for everyone in the group.

ROLE OF THE TEACHER

Since we first began working with collaborative groups, we have come to recognize more clearly the significance of the teacher's role. At first, we were so concerned not to inhibit pupils' discussion by our presence that we tended to relegate the teacher to a management role, once the materials had been carefully designed and prepared in advance. Now we see that the teacher has two more essential tasks. First, teachers have to actively foster an atmosphere of co-operation by incorporating activities which build up a sense of trust within the group as a whole. Secondly, they have to learn how best to intervene in a group discussion and, without imposing their own concerns, assist the pupils in extending and developing their own thinking.

ROLE OF THE SUPPORT TEACHER

Classrooms organized on collaborative lines are ideal for effective support work. Both teachers can spend their time constructively working with groups for extended periods. ESL pupils and those with reading difficulties can be given support in their groups as they carry out the task. Sometimes groups may be withdrawn to work quietly elsewhere, but the same or related work is done and nobody misses anything.

COLLABORATIVE WORK AMONG TEACHERS

The principles behind collaborative work apply just as much to teachers as to pupils. Two teachers can help each other and learn a great deal through joint lesson-planning, talking over what happened and evaluating lessons together. When a reading- or ESL-teacher is involved, however, the partnership can be especially valuable. Our concerns for reading and language development combine with and complement the curricular concerns of the subject-teacher to everyone's advantage. As a model for in-service work, therefore, collaborative teaching between support teachers and subject-teachers has much to offer.

34

Integrated design and humanities at Bosworth College

Ross Phillips and Stephen Jones

In this chapter, Ross Phillips and Stephen Jones describe the teaching and learning in a course for fourth- and fifth-year secondary pupils that integrated work across two areas of the curriculum often taught in isolation. The course was built around projects taught by teams of staff from the two faculties involved. Students of all abilities participated. Despite the constraints of time, money, examinations and students' own expectations of dependency, the staff reported on the success of the approach.

INTRODUCTION

Bosworth College has always been fertile ground for curriculum innovation. By the end of the 1970s, a well-established core curriculum existed which, in some areas, integrated across a spectrum of separate disciplines. Although the school's architecture is often described as bizarre, with extremely narrow corridors and something of the feel of a factory, rooms have ample space for flexible approaches to teaching.

The design faculty and the humanities faculty both use Mode 3 (teacher produced and assessed) examination syllabuses. On entering the college for their final two years of compulsory schooling, students followed a core curriculum and selected several option subjects. In design, the core course led to an examination in foundation design, and in humanities to two separate examinations in English and community studies.

In the rest of this chapter we shall describe how a new course, which linked the design and humanities core courses together, emerged under the title 'HUF' (humanities and foundation design). The decision to go ahead led to groups of students working with a team of teachers for roughly one and a half days each week. Sessions included one whole morning and an entire afternoon. The team of teachers consisted of two from design and two from humanities, with a teacher from the supplementary-education department, responsible for supporting children who experience learning difficulties. This HUF team colonized an area of the design faculty as their base.

In what follows, we describe the work of one team, consisting of Alysoun Hancock, Stuart Hicking, Kalvin Turner, Ross Phillips and Steve Jones. There were several other teams operating as well.

WHAT HUF WAS LIKE

Not all students did HUF. Some in the same year groups followed the conventional separate core courses in core design and humanities. Those who did HUF covered a wide spectrum of abilities; a dozen or so students received help from a supplementary-education teacher in sessions outside HUF time. In itself, planning the organization of lessons with large numbers of students who had to move from, let us say, a workshop to a more conventional classroom required new thinking from staff. Making the nature of this integrated experience accessible to groups including students who couldn't or wouldn't read or write, as well as for those destined for academic futures after sixteen, proved difficult.

The students taking HUF were randomly allocated to five groups, each one attached to one member of the five-person teaching-team. These groups were used for registration and organizational purposes, and would work together for some of the time. On other occasions, other groupings emerged, and individuals would attach themselves to a particular teacher. The students were perceptive about teacher expertise. They turned to a teacher for advice on matters which did not always coincide with our own ideas of expertise. The student–teacher relationships which ultimately emerged began to cut across the school's pastoral system: HUF students frequently knew their teachers better than their tutors and used them in this way.

Examination results are by no means the most important measure of HUF's success or failure, but concern for public examinations in an upper school catering for ages fourteen to nineteen is a constant feature of life. From HUF it was possible to achieve up to GCE 'O'-level in design, English and community studies. Exam-entry patterns differed between subjects and between HUF and non-HUF students. They were differences and no more. An analysis of examination results in 1983 revealed that students following HUF did as well as their peers on the more conventional route through the curriculum.

Built into HUF, drawing heavily upon the school ethos, was the notion that students should organize their own time and be responsible for working to deadlines at their own pace. This carried over into decisions about examination entry, where individual students would discuss priorities and potential with staff before an entry was made. Often this process involved decisions about which exam or level of exam to concentrate on. This undoubtedly helped the least able, who, with their extra supplementary–education lessons, could on occasions pursue work which had been started in HUF for a specific qualification.

The public examination system imposes constraints over and above the need to keep an eye on the outcome. Even though the existence of Mode 3 affords considerable flexibility, continuous assessment and the examination board's requirements for descriptions of content curb teacher creativity. It was often necessary to curtail independent student inquiry and activity if this wandered from the prescribed syllabus.

During early discussions about HUF, there had been a sense that the humanities course dealt with similar topics to those in design. An example is the idea of shelter. In practice, few community-studies themes lent themselves to HUF very readily. Design-teachers in particular found topics such as family or education singularly uncreative. The solution to this problem was to plunge into huge projects where students might lead off into more conventional topics within a wider context. Selecting the study of an entire country and culture encouraged creative design work as well as the exploration of issues and themes. Two particularly successful projects of this nature were based upon Japan and China.

The China project

The eight-week course on China included pieces of work which could be used for English, community studies and design. Each student had to produce, as a minimum, an essay relating to Mao Tse Tung, an essay on an issue such as abortion or population, and a small piece of research into such things as living in a commune, sport, education, food, family life and medicine. Design work was based on an aspect of Chinese life, such as costume, calligraphy, kites, customs, religion, food or transport. The final presentation often ranged beyond the culture under study. All such work involved an examination of the history, as well as the design rationale for the subject. The presentation of folios undoubtedly revealed a Chinese influence.

Each student was given a diary to help guide and pace his/her work. It contained details of when introductions or lead lessons would take place. Students could thus opt for various routes, knowing when deadlines were up. Experience demonstrated that design leads were better early on in the project, since they led into long pieces of work. Introductions to essays could be spread more evenly over the time, so punctuating the students' progress through the course.

Some lead lessons involved the whole group; others were smaller affairs. We used simulations on some occasions; we would often split students into small groups to discuss a question and follow this with a large group report-back. On a number of occasions, teachers would deliberately take opposing positions to create conflict and a variety of interpretations. In HUF the notion of a lead lesson was slightly different from in previous practice. We were moving away from a didactic approach; often leads were used to show the possibilities available and were therefore put in after the start of a topic as we judged them necessary.

Lead lessons used a number of resources. Slides were often used for design work, but we also used videos, maps and posters. For China, for example, we gathered books, slides and cassettes from our own resource centre, a collection from the local education authority's resource centre, plus masks, kites, woks, cookery books and cooking-utensils. In addition, resources were built up from the students. Some brought back material from a doctor practising acupuncture; the local teachers' centre provided information on tea ceremonies, kite-making and calligraphy.

On top of this essential framework we introduced special sessions. This allowed flexibility in that we could add a film or a video if something suitable was available. Another example was a demonstration of the tea ceremony by a visiting teacher who had travelled to China. These sessions were also used to accommodate students who had finished their assignments or because they had to wait in the design faculty for pots to be fired, or paint to dry. At one stage we had a poet in residence, and these sessions were used by him to work with small groups.

Community art

Group work and discussion formed an important aspect of HUF. Although this was built into virtually all the work, one approach was particularly successful. It emerged as a result of a request from the design staff in the team. They wanted to give the students a brief to design a piece of sculpture to be housed in the local community. It was intended that students would not only be creating their own piece of sculpture, but also involving themselves in the broader issues of community arts projects as well. The problem for humanities was how to integrate. We decided to focus on the political and social problems involved in establishing a piece of community art. The intention was to encourage the view that, if their art was worthwhile, then the students would need certain skills to see it become a reality.

To begin the eight-week stretch, some students were briefed by design staff on modern community art, while others were taken by humanities teachers. By rotating the groups, all students began their work with the same set of lead lessons. In the humanities briefing, the students were deliberately organized into groups of four to six which contained students of all abilities and both sexes. Friendship groups were actively discouraged, and a quick lesson on the meaning of comprehensive education was slipped in. Once in these groups, the students were told to consider themselves as a community and work together until the end of the project. The plot they had to work through was as follows: the community had been bequeathed a substantial sum of money which, however, could only be spent on a piece of modern art; the money was not enough to cover the entire costs involved in such a project and the extra cash had to be raised from the local council. During the introductory session teachers took up various stances on this problem, pointing out, for example, the need in many communities for such things as

facilities for the old and infirm. After this, the groups had to produce various
pieces of work. The project was called 'Action file' and each student received
a set of instructions.

Action file

Plot: Your group has been given a sum of money to spend on improving your
           local environment by introducing some work of art.

Decisions: – How much money?
           – Where's it from?
           – What will it be spent on?

           – What is the community like?   { Private estate
                                                Council estate
                                                Inner city
                                                Rural

           – What characters are involved?
           – How does your campaign proceed?
           – Are there any demonstrations?
           – Does it succeed?

In eight weeks' time, every group must produce an *Action file* containing the
group's and individuals' pieces of work.

The file must include:

– 10 character sketches following examples given
– An outline of the community
– Newspaper coverage of the events
– Five letters
– Five pieces of descriptive writing
– A script to last 10–15 minutes when read aloud
– Artists' plans
– Location drawing and explanation
– Materials used
– Model of sculpture

   In the groups, tasks were allocated to individuals, and sensitivity towards
and support to the least able was apparent from the outset. Group files
developed containing the various aspects required, and more. Students were
encouraged to visit local council meetings, interview people in their own
community about the introduction of a piece of contemporary art in a locale,
and discuss alternative ways of spending a substantial sum of money. Oral
work was lively; full-scale debates were held. The individual student work
was varied, highly imaginative and successful.

THE EXPERIENCE OF A STUDENT WITH LEARNING DIFFICULTIES

From the student's perspective, Mark is a good example to look at. At the outset Mark was very anxious about school, and HUF in particular: the large open teaching-area, the number of students, a reluctance about writing and reading, and, to top it all, a dread of design. He was a big lad from a warm caring family living in one of the local villages. Tears were not an uncommon feature from Mark, and, although not so frequent by the end of the fifth year, there were moments.

Mark's lack of confidence meant that, when groups formed, he remained in his seat, fearing rejection. This resulted in his not belonging to any group. Unlike in sport, where the poor unfortunates are left huddled together because no team wants their 'talent', a lot of rejigging had to be done to get balanced groups. Mark was placed in a group where both he and the others felt comfortable.

Mark was a reluctant student mainly because he did not want ridicule for the standard of his work. He would have been quite content to let the group sort out the workload, a playscript, character descriptions, journalistic writing, creating and making a piece of art. The group were aware that he would not find it easy. In the early stages Mark got a lot of staff support, but we did not want to intervene to the extent of preventing the group from helping him. Groups knew that their files were to be reviewed half-way through and that they would not be accepted unless the work was complete from all members. This was a deliberate policy to create a situation where the group and not the teacher would create the pressure. This worked for most groups. In Mark's case, two members of his group spent quite a time encouraging and helping him. Over the weeks he produced a couple of character sketches using pictures from a magazine alongside a biography he created for them. His spelling was very poor and it took a long time to decipher his work. We used to get him to read through his work so that we could transcribe it for him to write up. Mark could not always successfully translate his work and near the end of the course we used a word-processor to good effect. He was embarrassed about his work and would not willingly share it with others; hence a reluctance to write.

This attitude was prevalent in design as well, and, in a subject where it is difficult to keep under wraps what is being produced, he was again reluctant. One of the design-teachers sent him out to collect some branches from trees around the school fields. From the collection of wood a suitable piece was chosen, and, with guidance and instruction from the teacher, Mark produced an original and good-quality piece of work. He cut up the small branch and attendant twigs into one-inch lengths, and then re-created nature's image by linking the wood with short lengths of wire. This simple yet effective idea was recognized by other students, and Mark benefited from the acknowledgement. In addition to the actual making, he also quite successfully produced some sketches of the sculpture and a plan showing its location.

Mark benefited from help from other students; they became aware of his difficulties and, for instance, taped the play the group were asked to produce instead of writing it out. One of the girls corrected his many mistakes. Nevertheless, there were still some – often other students with learning difficulties – who regarded him as 'Thicko', a label that had been attached to him well before he came to Bosworth. On one occasion he was very upset because one of the boys in the same literacy support group had torn up his character descriptions. This lad had seen Mark's efforts, told him they were 'crap' and thrown them in the bin. Talking to Mark we discovered that these were not isolated events; they had happened in his previous school and quite frequently in a science group which had a lot of low achievers in it.

CONCLUSION

When considering the success of the initiative we should also recognize the failings. The experience overwhelmed some students. In general, however, the students shared the triumphs and failures equally with staff, and, whatever their opinion of HUF, will not forget the two years. From the teachers' perspective, time was the critical factor and they never felt completely on top of the organization or monitoring of individual students. Should such ventures occur again or elsewhere, a real need is for extra time within the school day to cope with the load such a course imposes.

There is considerable potential in this approach. It brings together the pastoral and the academic. It brings together groups of teachers from different disciplines and as a consequence offers breadth to the students and increased awareness of other approaches to the staff. Planning-sessions are dynamic and do not rely on the energy or direction of one teacher: it keeps you on your toes. We were honest about the lessons we prepared and the criticism was constructive and fair.

Long blocks of time not only allowed us to get to know the students well but also gave us the space to develop new teaching-methods. A three-hour session on a Monday morning would push the limits of most didactic teachers! The students were encouraged to take some control over their learning by using the diaries and by our repeating leads. There were many times when we looked around and could only account for about half the group. Many would be in the resources centre or workshops downstairs; others conducting interviews around the college; small groups meeting in side rooms, some in Leicester. We also had our minority who worked very hard at doing nothing.

This year HUF is not in operation. This is sad but not surprising. Teacher-initiated courses do not obtain the funding and other resources they need. We were very envious of the support given to the Technical and Vocational

Education Initiative course, which began during our HUF work. This had the planning-time and money we desperately needed. As pupil numbers have declined so have numbers of teaching staff. The design staff in particular, who have lost many colleagues, felt that they could no longer support this initiative.

Perhaps the evolution of any new course needs time for reflection. The seeds have been sown and the teachers involved are convinced that the potential of this type of work is only just being realized.

35

Listening to music

Andrew Meredith

In theory, music lessons should be amongst the easiest in which to include all pupils. Yet music has often been taught as if it were really the property of an exclusive group. Here, Andrew Meredith describes his attempts to interest mixed-ability groups in music and concentrates on listening to and commenting on music. He breaks down the barriers between 'serious' and 'pop' music. By letting pupils know that their ideas matter more than their difficulties in writing, Andrew Meredith enables his pupils to respond sensitively and honestly.

INTRODUCTION

Nobody denies the pleasure that music can give, but how best to teach it to the wide range of children in school continues to be a challenge. What follows may suggest part of the answer.

In the early days of state education, singing was the main element in music lessons. The advent of the gramophone brought what was usually called 'music appreciation'; and more recently there has been much greater use of instruments in class. Here I am mainly concerned with approaches to listening. I shall refer to other activities in order to fill in the background against which listening takes place, and to assess briefly their value in a mixed-ability setting. We are interested here in the extent to which they put pupils in contact with real musical experiences, and what scope they provide for sensitive treatment of widely differing individuals. A more detailed history of music education can be found elsewhere, and books are available which give advice on teaching classes to sing, play and compose.

Singing is obviously a musical experience of the first order, involving our own body to make the sound. Although perfection is hard to achieve when a non-selective group perform together, the very act of joining voices can give confidence to the musically weak who on their own would be too shy to sing aloud. A tune does not have to be complex in structure and difficult in execution to give pleasure and satisfaction: those most amenable to repetition are often simplest in design. Some will find it hard to read words at speed, but hearing the rest of the class will help.

Instruments can be used either to make up your own music or to play what someone else has written. The latter involves learning to read and interpret specialized symbols. Differing abilities (when a class is to play together) can be accommodated by a variety of parts, from simple to complex, which nevertheless harmonize. Imparting these skills in such a context makes obvious demands on the resources and patience of the teacher – rather like showing a novice how to start the car in Piccadilly Circus – and becomes easier when more than one room (or corridor, etc.) is available.

Similar considerations apply when children are invited to compose: you cannot easily encourage one child to listen carefully to effects available on a violin while their neighbour tests out the cymbals! But if practical difficulties can be overcome, the educational potential is considerable, and the needs of different pupils can be met over a wide range of ability. Social skills are also given opportunities to develop. A detailed discussion of this approach, including practical suggestions about rooms and equipment, is found in Paynter and Aston (1970) and Paynter (1982).

Wherever possible, as the HM Inspectorate report *Music from 5 to 16* (Department of Education and Science, 1985) recommends, children should have a mixed diet of all these experiences, as far as facilities and timetables allow. The concentration on listening in the rest of this chapter is not intended to suggest its equivalent dominance in lessons.

LISTENING

Two main influences have affected the way pupils have been introduced to listening. One has been the view that, in order to enjoy – even more to 'appreciate' – music, we need to know something about it. The second, reinforcing the first, has been the existence of an examination at the end of the line and the consequent need to assemble facts which can be learned and tested. What happens to someone when they hear a piece of Beethoven is far more important than whether they know it was written in a key using three flats; but the latter is so much easier to identify, teach and subsequently examine.

The net effect of all this has been to hamper the communication which music itself might achieve directly, by mounting a barricade of introductory information and ready-made interpretation. If listening to Mendelssohn's Opus 26 has to be preceded by studying his biography, learning of his visit to Scotland and the Hebrides, and finally seeing slides of Fingal's Cave, there is not much room left in the listener's imagination for the music to do its work. A further lecture on 'sonata form', however interesting to the specialist, will do little to stimulate the average beginner.

Thus, despite the value in some contexts of background knowledge and technical analysis, they can nevertheless obscure the primacy of musical experience, and are not actually necessary: you can enjoy music, and make perceptive observations about its emotional content, without specialized knowledge or terminology. You don't have to be a chef to appreciate a good meal.

If we ask children for their subjective responses to the experience of actual sound, we make two discoveries: first, a wide variety of people can do this together; second, the experiences of these heterogeneous listeners do not vary as their capacity for intellectual apprehension might lead us to expect. Their emotional insights into and perceptions of the music do not run in parallel with other faculties. We are even likely to learn something.

To start this off, tell the listeners what to do when they hear the music. It will help, at first, to focus their attention towards a particular aspect of the music, using the simplest language possible to avoid confusion. To ask for an account of the emotional development of a piece, say, 'How does this music make you feel?'; and then, as a separate question, 'Does it change as it goes on?' To begin with, it may be easier to ask listeners to describe actual phenomena reminiscent of a corresponding effect: 'What does this music make you think of?' or, 'If this were the background to a film, what might be happening?' The answers 'Spooky' and 'I thought of ghosts' are obviously two ways of saying the same thing, and children should be encouraged to see this. It is wise to start with music whose effects are unequivocal and fairly obvious, and not to ask for multiple observations (but receive them gladly). Keep the music short and be satisfied at this stage with short answers.

How are answers best expressed? If the group is sufficiently small, spoken replies may suffice; in any case it helps to know what others think. But it can have drawbacks: as soon as one person has answered, others may be influenced before they have spoken. Time may not allow for everyone to be heard: some will be disappointed that their ideas were not taken into account. Adventurous thoughts may be embarrassing to say aloud. Knowledge that a written answer will be treated in confidence by the teacher is more likely to result in genuine, personal comments in which the listener lets down the armour and becomes vulnerable.

Written answers are subject to the obvious handicap of varied literacy. This can be overcome in part by our attitude. If we do not make accurate spelling important, pupils will be happier to put down a word which serves their purpose despite not being sure how to write it. In some cases it may be necessary to ask the writer immediately afterwards to translate their script while the meaning remains fresh in their memory. The teacher can insert words of interpretation between the lines for future reference. Part of a solution is to allow the drawing of either representative pictures or expressive shapes, to communicate what the music has inspired. It is important, however, to insist on a minimum of explanatory footnotes, even if these have to be added on in the manner described above: the meaning of some people's drawings may be far from self-evident.

Having got the children to record their ideas by these methods, it can be helpful to invite discussion. Sometimes they will take considerable pleasure in exchanging impressions, so long as it is voluntary and the shy are respected.

SOME EXAMPLES

There follow some examples of music used, and pupil responses with my comments. No such selection can be exhaustive, but it can give some idea of the nature and variety of possible answers.

Music composed with a royal occasion in mind makes a good start, often having characteristics which build confidence through ease of identification. Henry Purcell's music for the funeral procession of Queen Mary in 1695, with its slow solemnity and sombre tone will be found to communicate to most pupils either mourning or royalty, or both; and the comparison of answers, followed by revelation of the music's purpose, leads to some important realizations.

A similar effect in brighter colours will come from Handel's *Music for the Royal Fireworks* (1749); and the opening movement of Tippett's *Suite for the Birthday of Prince Charles* (1948) brought this from a boy of twelve who knew nothing of the title. I have used his own spellings:

The music sounds if it is a royal prossesion with the king and queen in a golden carriage, and in the second carriage is a beautiful princess, the soldiers are following the carriage in clean red suits and with shiny brass buttons and shiny silver helmets and there swords shinying in the sun, and at the end of piece of music which dye's down, it sounds if the royal family go in to there castle.

Figure 35.1 reproduces a less able pupil's response to the same music, and figure 35.2 his comment on the slow movement of a Beethoven sonata (Opus 26, no. 18) which has come to be known as the *Moonlight* (note that the corrections to spellings were inserted by a friend at the next desk this time).

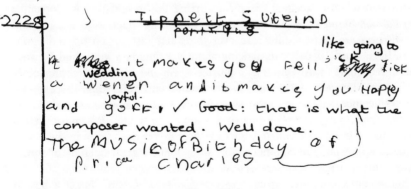

Figure 35.1

Interpretations reflecting a title given by the composer, or suggesting in some other way that the music has communicated as intended, can come from pieces whose effect might not have been thought so specific and

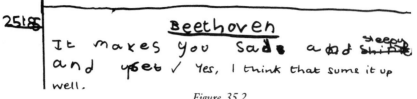

Figure 35.2

identifiable. Debussy's *The Sunken Cathedral* (1910) tries to describe, on the piano alone, the effect of a cathedral whose bells are caused to ring by underwater currents. The cathedral then rises up out of the water, and eventually resubmerges. Several members of a class, knowing nothing of the title, referred to being underwater and coming up and going down again; others referred to darkness, light and back to darkness in various scenes; and one boy, aged twelve, said, 'This represents a church under water and the water making the bells ring.'

Verdi's *Falstaff* (1893) includes a scene where the hero is lying under a Windsor oak at midnight, and is visited by fairies. The composer makes skilful use of violins to produce a light texture. Reproducing the notes on the piano sufficed to evoke from some twelve- and thirteen-year-olds responses such as 'someone walking in the woods', 'ballet and slow dancing', 'the leafs are coing [coming] down of the trees and pecalful [peaceful]', and 'a flock of angels flying about on stage is there seen in a play'. All that came from less than twenty seconds of music.

The Lark Ascending by Vaughan Williams (1914) commonly produces images such as 'a bird flying round and round in circuls', and 'butterflies floating away into paradise'. An excellent piece for stirring the imagination is Copland's *Appalachian Spring* (1944): 'It sounds like the spring which as just begun and the flowers are just bluming and everything has just woken up and lambs been born. Little people are dancing about very merry and excited because spring has come', was written by a fourteen-year-old who claimed previously to have no interest in listening to music and only undertook the exercise with reluctance. She is now more sympathetic. Of the same composer's music to *The Tender Land* (1954) a boy of the same age wrote, 'this music makes me think of great spectacular landscapes'; and you need to hear the actual piece to appreciate the comment, 'this sounds like a great opening of something, but then it gets softer because we can see what is hidden'.

Schumann's *Dreaming*, from *Scenes of Childhood* (1838), made a boy of twelve write, 'a sad piece of music, makes you think of your happy past and all the things you did', while another put, 'someone daydreaming and lost in his thoughts'.

It can be even more interesting to follow the thoughts of listeners to music which has no explicit title to suggest a 'good' answer. When I listen to Beethoven's Fifth Symphony (1808), I am aware of features of his character that could be exemplified in the style, and of theories about the philosophical meanings in his music, such as the suggestion that it symbolizes the 'thesis–antithesis–synthesis' of Hegel's dialectic. But no such foreknowledge preceded these comments by thirteen-year-olds: 'I think he was in an aggressive mood, and showing himself to be harsh yet also kind and forgiving'; 'like he was in two moods and didn't know which'; 'defiant'; 'trying to escape from evil' (Beethoven had in fact called the opening theme 'Fate knocks at the door'); and, from an older but less academic pupil, 'the man who wrote this must have been in a bad moude and then gon into a good moude and cep cange [kept changing] if he was in a good moude or bad moude. It cud be on a hore fime [horror film].'

The six-part ricercar from Bach's *Musical Offering* (1747) is a technical masterpiece which has been included for academic study as a set work for music-degree finals, and so it is not the sort of thing one would immediately think of playing to schoolchildren. Yet the response it can produce is heartfelt: 'It is deep, solemn – it gives you a warm feeling. At the end I was very comforted. It sort of went into me, I felt it inside' (from an eleven-year-old boy); and 'a sad sort of fearling, starting to briton up with the aperance of more instrements ... it left me with an empty feeling, and it was a lot quieteter around me, than when we first started' (another boy of the same age).

Whether or not the pupils enjoy the music will feature in their writings. This need not be discouraged (although it is unwise to ask for no more than that), as long as they are willing to reason about it constructively: otherwise you can end up with unhelpfully dismissive comments.

The divergence of attitudes to a given piece can result from various causes. An interesting example is over the issue of whether 'it all sounds the same'. One intelligent fourteen-year-old said that the first movement of Beethoven's Seventh Symphony (1811) was 'just about the same all the way through', while one of her friends 'liked it because it was different all the way through'. This contrast arises regularly. I think this is how: when we like a piece, the prevailing features don't offend us. We can spare attention for the changes. If we don't like it, these basic characteristics keep sticking out, causing irritation and diverting us from what is going on inside, as it were. The background obtrudes.

Different ideas may come from fastening onto different aspects of the same music. It is important to point this out, and as far as possible make each person feel that their contribution is valued and respected; and if their insight has shown us something, acknowledge it to them.

Figures 35.3 to 35.5 reproduce some comments by one boy of eleven whose difficulties in writing have not extinguished his imagination. Of the first movement of Mozart's Fortieth Symphony (1788) he says, 'it makes me feel like a ship on the sea and a storm came and it was getting bigger and smaller and bigger'; of 'Firth of Fifth', by Genesis (live recording 1977), 'the music makes me feel like a day awakening ... and it is very loud and I like

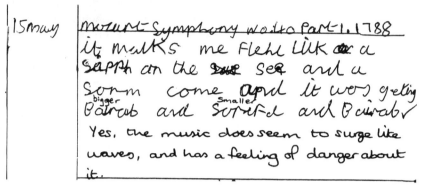

Figure 35.3

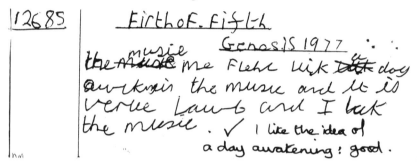

Figure 35.4

Figure 35.5

the music' (the music in fact becomes loud as it goes on); and of Wham's 'Careless whisper' (1984) just, 'the music is soft and it is ace and fab' – which gives a hint of the difficulties experienced when children try to say something constructive about music of this kind. As a girl of fourteen wrote, 'I find it hard to write about pop songs because you find yourself singing to it. There are also words in the song and I think that it puts you off writing.'

There are other problems, too: entrenched loyalties may be threatened if you ask young teenagers to criticize the style of their chosen peer group; and, if you have boys and girls together, a rapid polarization may develop. Identifying with a particular kind of pop music is often used as a means of

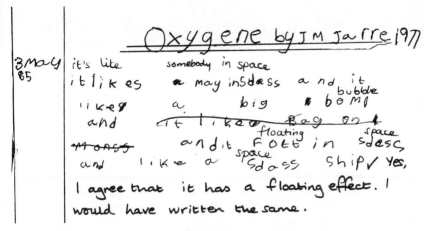

3 May
85
it's like somebody in space
it likes ~a~ may instkess a nd it bubble
likes a big bomb
and it liked Bag on a floating space
~~~~ and it fole in sdesc,
and like a Sdass Ship✓ Yes,
I agree that it has a floating effect. I
would have written the same.

Figure 35.6

establishing sex: boys are frightened of being associated with 'girls' groups', and so on. And, if you start to discuss the musical value of a song, it may lead to deep alienation.

Since the songs of the 'Top Ten' are usually designed, in their choices of rhythm and tempo, for dancing, and by their repetitions of catchy phrases aim to make one join in, the best way of using them in lessons is probably to encourage participation rather than enforce reflection. This can lead the pupils to try their hand at composition in a style with which they are familiar: I have been impressed by what can be produced with limited help.

The more imaginative comment on the track by Genesis (figure 35.4) comes from the music's greater length and the fact that it has more instrumental interludes and a less obvious message in the words. Music of that kind has considerable scope for stirring the imagination: figure 35.6 shows the response Jean-Michel Jarre's *Oxygène* (1977) obtained from the eleven-year-old girl previously quoted on Tippett and Beethoven.

I don't think I could have put it better than she did. If we can only give the music a chance, it can bring from young minds visions we might not have thought possible. Aesthetic experience seems to communicate deeply across barriers of traditional intelligence, bringing out a new race of imaginative, sensitive beings of whom we were formerly unaware.

REFERENCES

Department of Education and Science 1985: *Music from 5 to 16*, HM Inspectorate series 'Curriculum Matters', 4. London: HMSO.
Paynter, J. 1982: *Music in the Secondary School Curriculum*. Cambridge: Cambridge University Press.
Paynter, J. and Aston, P. 1970: *Sound and Silence*. Cambridge: Cambridge University Press.

36

French for all

Stewart Reid

Pupils who experience difficulties in learning are often withdrawn for remedial work during modern-languages periods, on the assumption that children who have difficulty in reading and writing their own language are unlikely to cope with another. This exclusion tells us something about the difficulty we attribute to the learning of the languages in our culture and the heavy reliance on written work. The Tour de France course, which is an aurally/orally based course, allows for diverse groups to be taught together. In this chapter, Stewart Reid describes how he has used a computer to help all pupils to practise and develop their skills in French.

It is interesting how my own career in modern languages has mirrored the changes that have taken place in this subject in the last twenty years. A typical product of a selective grammar school, I actually left teacher-training college to work at that very same school with the same sort of pupils who had been there seven years previously. Whilst I was teaching there, the school became a comprehensive and suddenly I and my colleagues in the department of modern languages were exposed to a range of pupils never previously encountered. Some (very few) of the best pupils in what in Scotland were called the junior secondary schools had sampled French or German or even done an 'O'-level, but, by and large, teachers of modern languages had only come in contact with the top 30 per cent of the school population. Now, literally overnight, we had to teach French and German to everyone – or almost everyone, for, as was the practice in most comprehensives at the time, pupils with learning difficulties were withdrawn in S1 and S2 to have extra English and maths. However, this has changed also, and in my present school (a comprehensive) all pupils in S1 and S2 without exception have French or German on their timetables.

These changes were a shock to most departments of modern languages, for our courses and books had been designed for a limited group of pupils, not for the broad spectrum we serve now. No surprise, then, when teachers found such courses – with their long lists of words to learn, their acres of grey French print, and poor quality of illustration – very difficult to sell to our average pupil, and just about useless for the pupil with learning difficulties.

Coming to terms with this situation has not been easy for the teacher: courses are now appearing – *Tour de France*,[1] for example – which are far better suited to today's pupil range. But there are still difficulties in the skills demanded by the nature of the subject. As in English-teaching, we can think about the four modes of learning and expressing the language: speaking, listening, reading and writing.

In any lesson the pupil might have to listen to a tape in the foreign language, answer questions in that language from the teacher, read a foreign-language text for comprehension or write down answers in English or the foreign language. All this entails not only learning new material but also recalling and using in context work of the previous lesson without recourse to notebook or textbook or even blackboard, perhaps in a dialogue situation. Clearly, for pupils with learning difficulties there are problems here; great demands are made on their concentration, retention and recall. In aural/oral work, of course, a lack of concentration is fatal, leading to comments such as these from pupils in an S1 French class: 'The teacher talks too fast', said Karen, and 'I think they talk too fast on the tape', from Paula. Concentrating on a strange foreign voice coming from a machine (the tape-recorder) has proved really difficult for some pupils, who find it all too easy to 'switch off' (themselves that is, not the tape-recorder). Repetition- as well as listening-skills come into play when the pupil is asked to imitate the teacher (or the voice on tape) in an effort to improve pronunciation. And the shy pupil can find this really daunting. When asked what they did not like in their French lessons, Karen, David and George said this: 'I don't like speaking in class. If you say something wrong, everybody will laugh at you'; 'I'm shy when I'm asked to speak French, everybody looks at me'; 'I cannot speak it right, they laugh at me.'

But imagine the teacher's difficulties if he or she concentrates on the efforts of one pupil in the midst of a question-and-answer session with the class: what are the other pupils to do during this time? Where do their attention and interest go?

In the early stages, written work in the foreign language will consist mostly of copying from the blackboard or course book, but even this causes great problems for some pupils. They meet accents, for example, for the first time: some pupils will have great difficulties putting them on the correct letter facing the correct way. Those who are slow at writing English will be even slower here. Recognition of new letter groups will be very slow, especially if the pupil who has barely grasped the rules of spelling in English suddenly sees these rules flouted in French.

Paula commented 'Writing down and spelling are the most difficult'; and David said, 'Finding the letters is the most difficult.' All in all, the modern-languages classroom can be a very confusing place for the pupil with learning difficulties. So what steps can be taken to alleviate the problems? One solution involves group methods, with work based on worksheets tailored to the group's or the individual's needs. But this is not an easy option for the teacher. Once the core of any lesson has been introduced to the class as a whole, the teacher will have to have ready a set of extension tasks for each of several ability groups. Few if any courses will have provided these for the teacher. Again, somehow, each group's activities will have to be orchestrated to such a fine level that all are ready at more or less the same point to stop one lesson and move to the next together. Add to this the problem we have in modern languages of *individual* testing of spoken ability, and it takes a great deal of hard work and administrative skill to bring it off successfully. Little wonder that some of us liken the experience to juggling with eggs – impressive if successful, but messy if you make a slip.

We have attempted to help all pupils practise and develop their French skills by working with the remedial teacher supporting the class and combining the better points of both the worksheet approach and the group method. The worksheets are electronic and involve group work with a computer, using programs that I have developed.

Each teacher in the department has a computer for his or her own room, as well as software written with the course and the ability levels of the class in mind. All pupils participate; there is no withdrawal of pupils with learning difficulties.

Pupils work at the computer either unsupervised or with a teacher; this may be in the classroom or in a small room adjoining. Groups can be of only two pupils or of several, and the smaller numbers seem to have helped the more retiring children: 'I am not shy because I am just myself' and 'I'm not shy at the computer because there's not much people there' were two typical comments received. One of the great attractions of computer software is that it can be designed to be tackled on several different levels. For example, the same program structure can contain different texts of varying difficulty; there can be several types of clue or help built in, which the pupil can call up or not; pupils can be given different amounts of time in which to give an answer, or no time limit at all. By such means it is possible for all pupils to be tackling the same program at the same time, though at different levels, and all in a package more easily administered and handled by the teacher than several worksheets.

Television itself, let alone television linked to a computer, is a great attention-grabber; with the small groups I find a greater level of concentration on the screen than ever there was on book or worksheet. Some pupils who found concentration difficult in whole-class teaching have surprised us greatly by what they can achieve in a small group before a television. This is not only because they are less shy here; it also has something to do with the nature of the medium itself. For example, the colour used in the programs attracts the eye, but is useful in other ways too. In the example illustrated in figure 36.1 the screen has been split up into sections of different background colour each serving a different function. Section 1 is blue and holds the

English text. Section 2 is green and displays the French question. Section 3 is cyan and displays the pupil's response (top line), corrects it and displays the computer's choice of a possible answer (bottom line). Section 4 is white and shows the scores gained by the pupil. Section 5 is red and is where the pupil's answer is typed in.

This is a complicated structure for the pupils, difficult to achieve on a worksheet. However, they have had few problems in finding the question, reading the text, typing then checking their answer and watching it being analysed. Pieces of text can be highlighted, reprinted in a different colour or deleted at will, all leading to a closer examination of the written word than we had previously experienced from pupils of all abilities.

But what of writing – or, more accurately, typing, since answers are now keyed in from a keyboard? Once the initial lack of familiarity with the layout of the keyboard has been surmounted (quite quickly now that so many have their own computers), greater concentration is evident in the forming of their words and phrases. There is another plus: correction by means of the delete key is very simple. Eleven answers are now at least readable and look good even if they are not correct!

The computer can easily parse sentences seeking either the 'basic answer' in what the pupil has written or something more detailed, and marking accordingly. It can allow the pupil another try at the answer, give spelling help, display the correct answer, give a mark and never shout! Karen said

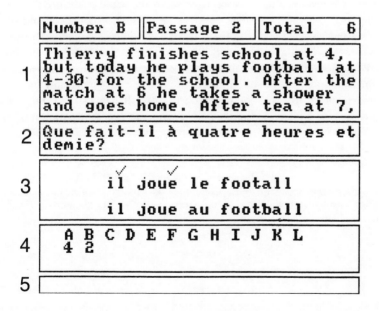

Figure 36.1

she enjoyed the computer because 'it can't talk back at you'. Reading-skills are developed also. One program can hold several texts of varying lengths, which can be rapidly called up on the screen to allow quick scanning for the gist or left on the screen for as long as required for more detailed study. Nor need this be a mute exercise: if the teacher is with the group, he or she can use the text on the screen as a source for reading aloud, repetition, and question and answer. Support teachers report that pupils with difficulties in whole-class teaching, who had tended to 'hide' or go silent, were completely different in group teaching with this new and different focus for their attention. One boy said he liked reading from the computer simply because it was 'more clear'.

We have found another way of grabbing attention and increasing involvement by using programs with a games structure, though these appear to appeal especially to the boys, who relish the competition involved. In general the pupils are highly motivated to do well, because of the sheer pleasure gained from working with the computer. Its use seems to help with the problems and consequent boredom some pupils find in the oral/aural approach: problems often bred of an inability to concentrate for long periods of whole-class teaching.

The computer buff tells us that the computer runs programs. How less daunting if we just considered them as a type of worksheet. The worksheet approach (it must be a new phenomenon, because I don't remember doing one as a pupil) comes from a praiseworthy desire to keep everybody working. But there are disadvantages, as we have seen: they take time to write, edit and print, especially if the teacher tries to cater with different sheets of paper for the several levels of ability in the class. They require marking afterwards: long and often boring work for the teacher. They tend to be very grey looking, owing to the price and difficulty of colour reproduction. I have found that the computer has provided solutions to these problems and has also encouraged me to use the group approach more: It has also led me to re-evaluate the use I made of the support teacher, to everybody's advantage.

NOTE

1 *Tour de France* (London: Heinemann Educational, 1981) is a French course developed by the Scottish Central Committee on Modern Languages, sponsored by the Consultative Committee on the Curriculum. It aims to cater for the full range of ability.

37

The making of *Motherland*

Elyse Dodgson

Motherland *was a school drama production of the highest order. It drew its strength from the deep personal involvement of all the pupils, and from Elyse Dodgson's commitment to a structure in which pupils could express, develop, extend and refine their own creative ideas. Through understanding and identifying with the troubles and achievement of an earlier generation of black women moving to a hostile, racist society, the girls who developed and performed* Motherland *gained not only a sense of their expressive power, but also a stronger sense of their own history.*

Vauxhall Manor School is a girls' comprehensive school in south London; the school population is represented by many different cultures, but the majority of pupils are of West Indian origin. As head of drama I have been concerned with exploring social and historical issues and developing materials that will inform this type of work. The issues that many of my pupils choose to explore are often directly related to their experiences of being female and black. It is because of this and my own commitment that much of my work in drama has been concerned with women's issues and what it means to be female in a wide variety of contexts and situations. In trying to explore critically the notion of cultural diversity, I work on materials that are related to some of the cultures represented within the school population. This preoccupation has extended beyond the classroom to intensive production work that has involved pupils of all ages in collaborative research and experiment. *Slave Girl* (Oval House Theatre, 1979) was about the female experience of slavery in nineteenth-century America; *Wicked Women* (Oval House and Cottesloe Theatre, 1980) looked at the persecution of women as witches in medieval Europe.

Personal testimony has always had an important part to play in this kind of drama work. The individual struggles, the triumphs, the frustrations and tragedies of other people's lives are for me what become the real substance of the drama. It is the introduction of these accounts into classroom work that engages my pupils most profoundly on an emotional level; they know that the work they are doing is based on real situations and the experience of real people. *Slave Girl* was derived from slave narratives in Gerda Lerner's *Black Women in White America* (1972) and from a rare autobiography of a female slave, Linda Brent's *Incidents in the Life of a Slave Girl* (1973). In *Wicked Women* we also used sources rich in this kind of documentation, including Henry Lea's *Materials Toward a History of Witchcraft* (1957) and accounts gathered by the late-nineteenth-century feminist Matilda Joslyn Gage in her *Woman, Church and State* (1972).[1]

In both these documentary dramas we recognized that we had not succeeded in using materials that were concerned with black women's experiences in Britain and this we very much wanted to do. However, few relevant materials were available. It took us very little time to discover that we should have to create our own. Last year we were given the opportunity to do so and our third work in the trilogy – *Motherland* – evolved.

In September 1981, Marcia Smith, a former pupil who had been involved in drama projects at the school and at the Oval House Theatre, was awarded a grant by the Greater London Council to interview her mother's generation of West Indian women in the local community. These interviews were to be used as the basis for a drama production. At the same time I was funded by the Inner London Education Authority to co-ordinate a school-focused in-service project. The purpose of this project was to develop materials which would help teachers to confront, through drama, issues in women's studies and multicultural education. Marcia and I decided to work together to explore the theme of the migration of West Indian women to Britain in the 1950s.

Just as slave mothers handed down their experiences of slavery to their daughters, so West Indian mothers have shown in the interviews that they have their own tale to tell about the hardship and discrimination they faced as early immigrants. Previously, however, no one valued these experiences sufficiently to document them. The idea of translating experiences from one generation to another caught our imagination and became the core of the West Indian Women's Project and its production of *Motherland*.

ELEMENTS IN THE PROCESS

It has become apparent that over the four years of work on all three plays the company has developed a distinct style of production. It was difficult at the time to untangle certain elements in the process. In retrospect, however, I can now see that the plays have been characterized by a number of elements. The most important are as follows.

1   *Ensemble.* The work is created and presented by the group rather than individual performers. From the beginning of the rehearsal period each member is expected to attend all rehearsals and take part in the experience of the whole play. All decisions are made through group discussions. In performance members of the cast establish and develop a variety of roles.

2   *Narrative.* There is always at least one narrator who tells the story that is taken, sometimes verbatim, from the testimony. In addition to the

narrator(s) a chorus reiterates and affirms various aspects of the tale. Both these devices contribute to the episodic structure of the plays.

3 *Ritual.* There is always a symbolic element to the drama, whereby the ritual is used to explore aspects of the materials that are difficult to express in more naturalistic terms or to make more powerful the group's own response to some of the subject matter.

4 *Song.* The songs work as interruptions to the play, prompting us to think about the meaning of the narrative. Written by the girls themselves, as a personal response to their work in the drama, the songs record their own attempt to come to terms with the significance of the materials.

A discussion of how these elements are used in the four phases of the rehearsal process may give some understanding of the potential and problems of this kind of work. These phases are not discrete; each new phase encompasses the previous one. What we are talking about is a process of building, not simply a linear progression. We worked on *Motherland* for nearly a year; having time is a crucial factor.

PHASE 1: ABSORBING

In this initial phase the emphasis is on becoming familiar with the topic and introducing the background materials to all those who are going to be part of the company. Marcia began interviewing the women, starting with her own mother and other female members of her family. At first the interviews were tentative and rather general, as was much of the early work in drama.

We began, during the autumn term, to publicize the formation of the company that would produce *Motherland*. This was open to all pupils, from the first to the sixth form. Up till this point only Marcia, myself and those in my upper-school drama groups had been involved in the research. Through drama we introduced the material to the others. At our very first meeting I worked in a role as a recruitment officer in Britain who had been sent to the West Indies to conduct a series of meetings about migration. Working previously in family groups, the company arrived at the meeting expressing hope but also a great deal of fear and doubt. In my role I could allay some of those doubts while at the same time giving the girls more information about the conditions in the West Indies at the time.

By the time we began to meet regularly for rehearsals a great deal of the subject matter had been absorbed. The elements that were to be a distinctive feature of the play were all in embryo, but it was the formation of the ensemble that was the crucial factor here. The groundwork had been prepared in previous years, as girls who had been in the other plays still adhered to the decision that each girl should have the opportunity of exploring a variety of roles regardless of her ethnic background. Thus each girl in the multiracial company began to take on roles of black and white women irrespective of her own colour. Most of our rules concerning reliability and commitment

which require young pupils to adopt a rigorous discipline were more effectively enforced by the girls rather than myself.

PHASE 2: EXPERIMENTING

This is not only the longest but, to me, the most important phase; the principle
of experimentation underlies all of the work, stressing the contribution of
each rehearsal to the final production. This phase incorporates all the
exploration we do on the theme through drama. In January 1982, we began
to meet for three two-hour sessions a week. We worked thematically, choosing
a particular aspect of the women's experiences to focus on. Marcia's interviews now included the mothers of over half the girls who were in the play.
The transcribed interviews and audio tapes fed directly into the rehearsals.
Among the themes we explored this way were

1 reasons for leaving
2 preparing and parting
3 the journey
4 arrival/first impressions
5 housing
6 working-conditions
7 childcare
8 relationships with the white community
9 relationships with men
10 education

We worked on these themes in many different ways: as a whole group with
the teacher in role, in smaller groups developing improvised work, individually
trying to re-create personal experiences and then writing about it. The
ensemble was being created as girls shared ideas with each other about the
meaning of the tapes and reflected upon their own interpretation of them
through drama. We worked through mime and movement, wrote verse and
told stories. Ritual had a great part to play in this phase, as the girls, having
learned how to operate the drama form with great skill, had the ability to
use symbols to create the high emotional point of a scene. Song too became
a powerful element. Excited by a particular aspect of the drama work, girls
would come back with new ideas – lyrics sometimes scribbled on crumpled
pieces of paper and melodies recorded on tapes. These all became part of
Motherland. The following is an account of how in a particular scene we
achieved this sense of involvement.

    The rehearsals were progressing slowly. I was beginning to feel a sense
of frustration, since there was not as yet any real emotional engagement with
the material. We were working on the theme of housing. It was clear from
the tapes and transcripts that many of the women found great difficulty in
looking for accommodation. This initial experience had a profound effect on

their changing attitude towards England as the mother country. Many described themselves as cold and tired, walking the strange streets with bags and suitcases trying to find a place to live. I dimmed the lights and asked half the girls to take on the role of landladies. The others were to gather their belonging as I read to them over and over again excerpts from the women's testimony on housing:

It was very cold ... everywhere looked strange, the buildings were grey ... the houses are like prisons ... I noticed the grey dull buildings ... how wet and dark everywhere is ... I couldn't believe it ... seeing houses without verandahs ... I couldn't believe it was London ... it was really cold.

I repeated the words from the testimony and the atmosphere changed as the girls, walking to my narration, become more involved in the roles of the weary and bewildered women. Every so often I asked them to stop at the door of a landlady. There was an exchange as they asked for accommodation and were turned away. I continued to read the testimony; their exhaustion intensified. I asked them to swap roles so everyone had a chance to be both the landlady and the women seeking accommodation. Introducing elements from the testimony into their improvised drama, the girls began to express their growing awareness of the women's experience:

Woman   Excuse me madam, I was passing your house and I see a vacancy sign and I was wondering if you still had a room?
Landlady   Yes I have a room.
Woman   Thank the Lord, I've been walking 2,000 miles.
Landlady   I'll tell you something. I've got three tenants already and they give me problems.
Woman   Me no give you no problem you know me promise you that.
Landlady   Do you have any children?
Woman   No children at all.
Landlady   Make sure you're out of my kitchen before I come home. Use my bathroom after I've gone to work. I don't want to see or hear you when I get to this house. No electric iron or heater unless I give you permission and I charge for it then. No visitors during the week – Sunday only. If you're not back in this house by ten don't bother to come back.
Woman   I'll remember that.
Landlady   Thirty shillings in advance, take it or leave it.
Woman   I'll take it.
Landlady   Come in.

When the scene was finally incorporated into the play, only half of the girls took part in it, but in this earlier phase each of them had the opportunity to experience the sense of isolation and despair that these women felt while looking for accommodation. I recorded or took detailed notes on all the rehearsals in this period. Many of the lines that came out of our explorations were eventually used in the play. In fact the structure of that early piece of drama, experimenting with the repetition of the narrative, proved so effective that it was woven into the final version of the scene.

We used the narrative element to link the various encounters. The ritual of the whole group talking, knocking, and freezing became a central image of the drama. The convention of black girls playing white women and white girls playing black women was firmly established during our work on this scene. At the next rehearsal one of the girls arrived with the words to a song that had been inspired by our work on housing. Several days later three others had put her words to music. It helped us all to come to terms with this experience:

> Searchin, wow I'm searchin
> Trying to find a place to rest
> Searchin keep on searchin
> England you put me to your test

> You're trying oh so very hard
> To see how far I'm gonna go
> And when I get there
> I'm gonna see, you'll break me up
> before I know

> I won't stop searchin, wow I'm searchin
> Tryin to find a place to rest
> Searchin keep on searchin
> England you put me to your test

> You think you're gonna chew me up
> That this is just some more black meat
> So listen here black woman
> Come along and take your back row seat.

PHASE 3: FORMING

By the end of the spring term we began to think more seriously about shaping the play. At this stage the experimenting was more vital than ever. Some things worked immediately and we knew that we wanted to incorporate them into the final product, while we were unsure about other ideas that we tried. At the heart of the project were the twenty-three women who had each by now been interviewed four or five times. We needed to meet with them as often as possible. Through a series of open rehearsals we shared with them our interpretation of their life stories. At the first open rehearsal we decided to select several aspects of our work in progress to show them. The women were visibly moved by what they saw, made suggestions, shared anecdotes and songs and pointed out anything that was inaccurate. The girls seemed hungry for information and continued to seek assurances from the women that they had 'got it right'. The open rehearsals reassured us that we were going in the right direction.

It was at this stage that we decided how we would use the narrative. The play would begin in the 1980s, with Marcia interviewing her mother and her

mother expressing doubts about the value of the play. In the final scene of
the play Marcia's mother agrees to give her life story, in the form of the
tape, back to her daughter. The narrative was now playing a crucial role in
shaping the sequence of the play.

At this point the whole ensemble began to address itself to the question
of form, as scenes were shaped, scrapped, juxtaposed and put into sequence.
We decided to tell the story chronologically beginning with the coronation
of Queen Elizabeth in 1953, and ending with the Nottingham and Notting
Hill 'riots' of 1958 and 1959. These were both events that people referred
to in the interviews. We also had to decide how to use male roles in the
play. In the past we had few males depicted in the plays and this was done
by a small change of costume. In *Motherland*, after much deliberation, we
decided against this convention. We wanted to concentrate exclusively on
the women's experience of immigration, although clearly this experience had
been to some extent shaped by their relations with men.

We began to get help from people who would eventually become our
production team. We had the tradition of wearing the same basic costume
with only some slight variation in shade or colour. Our designer, the head
of needlework, brought in ideas for the design and samples of material. The
girls chose a basic 1950s-style dress. Preliminary decisions were made about
the poster, the set, lighting and the musical accompaniment.

While beginning to visualize the play with its technical effects we were
still very much concerned with the internal life of *Motherland*. As we were
making crucial decisions that would affect the structure and perspective of
the play, our first consideration was not to lose sight of the main focus of
our work – this was a play about female experience. We had looked at
migration through the eyes of twenty-three West Indian women and in doing
that we had looked at many issues that affected their life deeply. Somehow
at this stage I felt we had been limited by our thematic approach. Childcare,
relationships with men and the importance of religion were not issues that
were separate events in the women's lives. They contributed to the quality
of life as a whole, every minute of every day. We all felt strongly that we
wanted to show the individual issues but somehow stress the effect that they
had on one life.

We achieved this in what we later called the dream sequence. This
emerged from an experimental session where we reviewed all the separate
incidents that had happened to one woman. Having spoken about the experience of one woman in one day, I asked each girl to create her own private
space and sit on a chair. She was to imagine it was the end of the day. It is
the first chance she has had to sit down on her own – the children are finally
asleep. I asked the girls to speak their thoughts out loud. It took some time,
but as one girl expressed herself others joined on. These lines spoken by all
the company were woven into the dance, poetry and song of the dream
sequence:

This is the first time I have had rest in weeks.
Look at this room; I'm sick of this hole.
The only thing that keeps me going is fear.
I feel guilty; they make you feel it's your fault.
The thought of tomorrow reminds me of today; today reminds me of yesterday.
I feel as if I want to scream; this isn't what I came here for.
I'm tired, so tired – I can sleep for a week.

Such expressions of identification with the women's lives could only come after a long and deep involvement with the material. The women's experience had finally become our own.

PHASE 4: POLISHING

This is the last phase (the final half of the summer term) and it is significant that throughout this period we were still absorbing new information – the interviews were still taking place. We were still experimenting: scenes were cut, additions were made, new ways were still being tried. We were still forming. We had our last rehearsal with the interviewees present just before we moved into the Oval House Theatre.

We had a working script for the last two months of rehearsal but we still had difficulty in deciding upon the final scene. Each of the previous plays had ended on a high and optimistic note. In *Slave Girl* through song and dance we told of the escape to freedom of Harriet Tubman and used her words to end the play: 'I'll never call any man master again.' In *Wicked Woman* each girl lit a candle in the name of a woman who had been persecuted as a witch and we sang, 'Everything that's hurt is healed again.' This time we felt the dialogue was still going on between the two generations of black women in our community and no one wanted to make such a final statement about the future of black women in British society. The girls decided they wanted to leave the play to represent the situation as it is in the present with all its complexities and contradictions. We decided to use the idea of flashback as a device to present the situation as it is today while relating it to the context of the past. The opening scene was set in the West Indies. The women spoke about their hopes of coming to England:

> England sweet England
> Is dere we g'wain live
> The air is so different
> But our labour we a give
> Even dough we know, the difference is big
> Sweet England, we're comin to live.

In the opening scenes the women were doing jobs that they would have done in the West Indies. In the closing scene the girls entered the same way, singing the same song; but this time they are relating to each other as mothers and daughters.

Marcia went out for her final round of interviews asking the women what advice they would give in the light of their own experiences. Testimony such as the following was incorporated into the play at this final stage:

I tried not to fight their battles for them but to prepare them for coming up against prejudice. I tried as much as possible to give them some values ... so I try to make them feel proud of being black and teaching as much as I could about their background.

At last we felt that we had made our statement. Through song the girls, in that last scene, expressed their meaning of the play for them. The mothers sang to their daughters,

> There's so much you don't know
> You've got to realise
> A black woman in this land
> You must fight to survive
> And so to help you
> I give you my life, my experience too
> Girl I hope you can make it through.

In conclusion I can only stress that through this kind of work in the classroom and within these projects there is a great emphasis on the use of materials. I believe that when work in drama is limited to the subjective response of pupils, when it does not introduce an element of fact, personal testimony and political analysis, we fail to give pupils the means to alter their perspective and make social change. Any such change should be informed by an understanding of the racism and sexism in our society. The work of the West Indian Women's Project has attempted to adopt an explicitly anti-racist and anti-sexist viewpoint.

NOTE

1 For a more detailed account of the use of social and historical materials in drama see my contribution to Nixon (1982).

REFERENCES

Brent, L. 1973: *Incidents in the Life of a Slave Girl*. New York: Harcourt Brace Jovanovich.
Gage, M. J. 1972: *Woman, Church and State*. New York: Arno Press.
Lea, H. 1957: *Materials Toward a History of Witchcraft*. New York: Thomas Yoseloff.
Lerner, G. (ed.) 1972: *Black Women in White America*. New York: Vintage Books.
Nixon, J. (ed.) 1982: *Drama and the Whole Curriculum*. London: Hutchinson.

38

Teaching history through drama

Jane Woodall, Terri Carey and Elyse Dodgson

Being a historian entails, amongst other things, thinking oneself into the personas of other people who inhabited other social, political and material worlds. It also entails the rigorous search for and questioning of evidence and its significance. The authors of this chapter describe an approach to teaching history with diverse secondary-aged groups which merges these two dimensions. In the process, they are mutually supported.

Teachers of history with mixed-ability groups face a challenge. To have any chance of success we need to select content areas which will be relevant to pupils who not only have, inevitably, varied interests and experiences but also a wide range of skills and educational needs. Moreover, we need to give consideration to the style in which the content is presented and be prepared to adopt teaching strategies which will engage pupils at various levels and allow each individual to develop her/his knowledge and skills at her/his own pace.

The history department at Vauxhall Manor, a girls' comprehensive school in south London, is committed to developing materials and techniques designed to challenge and stimulate pupils across the ability range. The department set up a Mode 3 CSE examination six years ago and more recently we have developed an innovative third-year course which adopts a multicultural approach to British history. This offers an historical perspective on migration to Britain from Celtic times to the present day, structured around a series of in-depth case studies which illustrate reasons for migration, compare the experiences of the migrant groups and assess the contribution of each to British society. The first case study focuses on the Roman occupation; the second on the growth of the black community in Britain, particularly on migration from the West Indies since the Second World War; and we plan further units on Irish and Jewish immigration.

Since September, the two history teachers involved in the third-year scheme, Jane Woodall and Terri Carey, have had the opportunity of working alongside a drama specialist, Elyse Dodgson. It has been a challenging experience for us all to see how we can teach history through drama and we have all been forced to question some of our assumptions about both subjects. We have not been concerned to make our teaching of history more dramatic, but, rather, have been concerned with how drama might be used to help all our pupils to gain a better understanding of historical events, personalities, concepts and skills – in short, to become better historians.

Our initial use of drama was, understandably, tentative and can be seen in the traditional mould of history role play. We tended to offer drama as one choice within a range of activities designed to promote empathy. For stimulus we relied on materials we had already produced. These consisted of a series of booklets, using both primary and secondary written and visual sources, devised around historical concepts and skills which encourage pupils to analyse events for themselves. Each booklet is supplemented by a range of other written and visual sources.

ROLE PLAY

The following sample of pupil activities is based on a series of workcards illustrating the principal groups that have migrated to Britain. Pupils are asked to carry out their own research into one of the groups before producing an empathetic account of the migrants' story:

Imagine you are one of the migrants in the picture. Tell your story, explaining why you have moved, your experiences on your journey, things that you will miss that you have left behind, things you might fear in the future or that you might be looking forward to.

You can write up your story as a *diary*, *play* or a *poem*, or you could draw some *cartoons* or *pictures*. You can use books to help you.

This type of role play has proved popular with pupils of all abilities. The children were undoubtedly exploring the past for themselves and through drama were coming to a deeper understanding of the infinitely complex interactions of history. The experience of the past meeting the experience of the present produced some powerful dramatic moments. However, we began to realize that drama had far greater potential than simply allowing children to re-create the known past. We saw that through drama pupils could begin to 'live through' historical incidents. The watershed came in a lesson called 'Conflict!', about the Romans' attempt to assert their cultural dominance over the Celts. The Roman position is given by one soldier, whom we have called Demetrius, in conversation with a Celtic warrior, whom we have named Loeg:

Now, when we Romans settle in Britain you Celts will have to give up your local quarrels and fights ... you'll be too busy working as slaves, building towns and roads – that'll stop your idle ways. You'll live in towns too instead of those country huts, and worship our Emperor instead of those Druid Gods of yours. You'll soon get used to having an army of occupation, and we'll make sure you pay your taxes ... I expect you'll learn to speak Latin like us, instead of that Celtic tongue of yours – you'll probably wear togas too!

Initially we presented this speech in writing on a worksheet. The pupils were told, 'Loeg goes back and tells his leader, Queen Boudicca, about his meeting with Demetrius. As a result a rebellion against the Romans is planned.' They were asked to 'Choose either (a) a conversation between Loeg and Boudicca; (b) a drama; (c) a story to show how and why they decide they do not want to be ruled by the Romans.'

We realized the limitations of this approach: we were handing over the event to the class, saying, 'This is what happened', leaving them little scope to develop their own interpretations. Although the pupils could choose to use the dramatic form, their role was simply to re-explain a historical event in their own words. Subsequently we decided to structure a drama which would enable pupils to work out the Celts' possible responses for themselves.

STRUCTURING A DRAMA

The pupils were asked to take on the role of Celtic village elders summoned to a meeting with Roman officialdom, represented by the teacher in role as a Roman centurion who makes Demetrius' speech. Left to their own historical devices, the 'village elders' responded in a variety of ways, ranging from open rebellion to retreat, and there were several who thought up sophisticated plots to subvert the Roman occupation. All their responses were plausible, given their own experiences and what they already knew about Roman and Celtic society. Equally important is that, having made their own decisions in role, the girls were more interested to learn about the decisions actually made by the Celts. Although our subsequent study of Boudicca's revolt demanded a great deal of the less able pupils, in that it used contemporary accounts from Tacitus, girls who had been involved in the drama were much more motivated to read and write about the extracts than those who had not 'lived through' the decision-making experience.

The success of this teaching technique gave us more confidence to work in role and in doing so we became increasingly aware of the potential for using drama to communicate historical information effectively. History cannot avoid being an information-giving subject. The problem – exacerbated in the mixed-ability classroom – lies in giving all pupils access to the information. In recent weeks we have gained sufficient expertise with working in role to dispense with written stimulus material in some lessons.

A MIGRATION STUDY

In our study of migration from the Caribbean, for example, we wanted to show that there were black people living in Britain long before the 1950s and to give our pupils, who came from diverse cultural backgrounds, some insight into the experiences of the black community in the past. By the eighteenth century, most black people living in this country were free but, perhaps inevitably, the majority faced terrible hardships and poverty. In the spring of 1786, after one of the worst winters on record, several prominent businessmen and politicians set up a Committee for the Relief of the Black Poor. The Committee adopted a plan to repatriate 'the blacks and people of colour' to Sierra Leone. The pupils were encouraged to take on the role of poor blacks; first they were asked to sit alone, eyes closed, and concentrate on their five senses while contemporary newspaper accounts describing the plight of the black poor were read to them. The girls were encouraged to describe their emotions aloud in a word or short sentence. These were some of their responses:

I'm feeling lonely.
I need somebody to be with me.
Why is it so cold?
I need warmth and heat.
I'm perishing.
I'm starving.
I cannot bear it.
Why am I alive?
Why am I suffering like this?
Why don't I just die?
I shouldn't be here.
Glad to be alive.
Who's going to help?
I've nobody to turn to.
How did I get here?
Will I ever get back?
Will I see the tomorrow?

They were then told that they had survived the winter and that, at last, there was a ray of hope as the Committee for the Relief of the Black Poor had called a meeting of the black community at one of their favourite meeting-places, outside the Yorkshire Sting, a pub in Lisson Grove, Paddington. The problem was now to convey the committee's proposals to the pupils. One teacher, Jane in this case, took on the role of Jonas Hanway, Chairman of the Committee, and read out a persuasive speech, based on primary sources, outlining the benefits of the repatriation scheme and encouraging each pupil to sign the document illustrated in figure 38.1, which is a simplified version of the 1786 original.

HISTORICAL ACCURACY

There was a great deal of debate in role about the pros and cons of the scheme, and Jonas Hanway was forced to answer many searching questions! Finally the pupils divided into groups of between three and five, representing either 'families' or 'friends' as they chose, and were asked to work out in role whether they would prefer to accept repatriation or remain to face continuing hardships in Britain. This raised the question of historical

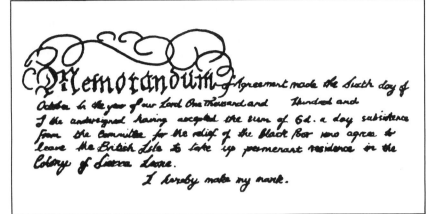

Figure 38.1

accuracy. Most of the girls in role initially decided to sign the memorandum – in fact most of the black community in the eighteenth century resisted. Only 441 out of an estimated 10,000 finally left the country for Sierra Leone. In this case the problem was resolved within the structure of the drama. Elyse, anticipating this situation, had researched for the role of Ottobah Cuguano, a leader of the black community employed by the Committee for the Relief of the Black Poor to recruit volunteers for repatriation. He quickly realized the problems inherent in the scheme and began to warn the black community. In role, Elyse voiced Cuguano's fears and advised the pupils to wait. The atmosphere was electric: the pupils in role were furious with Jonas Hanway, who was unable to answer Cuguano's allegations of corruption. At the climax of the drama one of the 'black poor' snatched the sheaf of memoranda from Jonas Hanway and the pupils proceeded to rip them up!

MARY SEACOLE

However, the question of historical accuracy is by no means a simple one and was raised again in our lesson about Mary Seacole. This example shows how drama can be used to enable pupils better to understand an individual in history. Mary Seacole was a little-known black nurse, a contemporary of Florence Nightingale, who, despite establishment opposition, went to the Crimea to nurse the wounded soldiers of the British Army. The drama was arranged so that the class had a problem to solve; this problem was the one that faced Mary Seacole. The teacher, in this case Terri, 'became' Mary Seacole and showed her being interviewed at the War Office. The government officials were played by the girls. Their responsibility was to find out about Mary Seacole's experience in nursing and to decide whether they would send her to the Crimea. Terri and Elyse had already done a lot of work with the class about nineteenth-century attitudes to women and had discussed the kind of questions an interviewing body of men might ask a black woman wanting to nurse British troops. The pupils were asked to prepare the room for the interview. The class worked well and asked questions such as 'How did you get here?', 'Where are you from?', 'What have you done in nursing?'

The teacher had to try and convey biographical information not only about the events of Mary Seacole's life but also about her personality. When asked to give their verdict on whether to send Mary or not, the class decided in her favour. The War Office came to precisely the opposite conclusion! Had our pupils been the ones interviewing Mary Seacole, history might have been different; as it was, they obviously found it difficult to sustain their roles as nineteenth-century men given their own experience as twentieth-century women. They empathized more with Mary Seacole than the War Office officials did. Does this type of 'mistake' in drama matter? We think not *provided* that the inaccuracy can be resolved in the drama or followed up in discussion. In this case the girls were forced to face the reality of nineteenth-century attitudes by contrasting them with their own decision within the drama. The impact was heightened as Terri, still in role as Mary Seacole, read extracts from her autobiography showing her feelings of anger, frustration and grief at being turned down. As a result the pupils were even more impressed to learn that Mary Seacole eventually decided to finance herself to nurse in the Crimea. This drama drew the pupils into a form of understanding and insight into a character which might otherwise have been denied them.

It seems to all of us that the experience of drama in history helps our pupils to become more historically aware. It affords them the opportunity to 'experience' events that happened in history – to learn history from the inside. Through empathizing with different people in different historical circumstances they get the chance to appreciate more fully points of view different from their own, and it seems to us all that the experience of drama in history helps our pupils to become more historically aware. It affords them the opportunity to 'experience' events that happened in history – to learn history *from the inside*. Drama can make the complexity of history real; bring back not only individual emotions, expectations and motives but also the social, economic and political constraints which shape history. By demonstrating for themselves the variety of possible outcomes of any historical situation and empathizing with different people in contrasting historical circumstances pupils have the chance to appreciate more fully points of view different from their own. We believe that these experiences can help break down cultural stereotyping and prejudice.

Using drama in history lessons also appears to motivate pupils to develop other skills and is particularly effective in developing co-operation in group work. We have noticed the confidence with which pupils discuss issues they have experienced through drama and the enthusiasm with which they approach writing about them. After a 'concrete' historical experience in role, pupils of all abilities readily recall detailed information and complex arguments. They seem to find the tasks of discussion and writing more worthwhile and are motivated to explore the topics in real depth.

In some of our lessons only one group works through drama and often presents their work to the class as an added stimulus. The most successful work, however, has taken place with the whole class working together with one or more teachers in role. When asked, many of our third-years agreed they preferred whole-group work, as 'more of us take part and people don't get left out'. They were very positive about the contribution of drama in general: 'It makes it more interesting, it gives you more experience'; 'You can experience what it was like in those days'; 'You enjoy it more when you're doing drama'; 'When you put drama and history together we know what we're doing. We're not making up silly things – we're doing actual things.' Working in role, each child has the opportunity to make a valuable contribution to the classwork in her own particular way. Through drama each child becomes more of a historian.

39

What's taught in geography? A critique of Geography for the Young School-Leaver

Dawn Gill

The 'hidden curriculum' generally refers to the ethos or climate of a school, as distinct from the formal curriculum. But much of the formal curriculum is hidden as well, simply by a lack of awareness of its significance. By looking closely at what one set of geography materials does and does not say about the Third World and about immigration into Britain, Dawn Gill has unearthed the unstated political attitudes of the authors. She argues that such material reinforces views of black people as incompetent and backward, and hides the role of Western countries in the exploitation of the Third World.

This chapter, when first published, formed part of a campaign by a number of teachers for the reform of Geography for the Young School-Leaver. The course has since been revised in the light of these criticisms.

Racism is a problem: Brixton, St Paul's, Finsbury Park; the National Front, the British Movement. The media seem almost obsessed with analysing the manifestations of racism – but little concerned with its causes. I feel that anti-racist educators should make a more determined effort to uncover the contributory factors to racism, and take on the task of publicizing the extent to which our school syllabuses and resources incorporate and perpetuate racist assumptions. It's a fact that some school geography courses foster racist attitudes. But to say so, without explaining how, is little more than sloganizing; to explain how takes time. It involves a consideration of syllabuses, teaching-materials and exam questions. But, unless we are prepared to look at the minutiae of what goes on in schools, we could be dealing with the manifestations of racism for ever.

This article makes the point that much geography-teaching still promotes the kinds of ignorance upon which racism is based. Many courses give credence to attitudes of white supremacy, but this is only the most obvious criticism. In many more subtle ways does the subject reflect and help to perpetuate the racism in society. It tends to use explanatory frameworks which fail to mention the trade relationships between First and Third Worlds as a reason for the relative poverty of the latter; it presents the notion that

Third World peoples are responsible for their own poverty and thus implicitly supports the view that they are ignorant or stupid; population growth, if mentioned in the texts at all, is rarely linked explicitly with levels of economic development – more often with hints that the uneducated are failing to use contraceptives; developing countries are presented as places which are important only because they provide us with certain commodities; urbanization is considered a major problem – its cause, immigration into cities; immigration is presented as an important cause of inner-city decline.

But it is not enough to generalize about school subjects and the ideas they present to pupils. If we want the syllabuses changed we must be specific. What, exactly, is being taught, to which children? I have chosen to consider here the content of two courses used in London schools. It is important to look at 'officially sanctioned' geography syllabuses because they determine what shall be taught in the upper school; and since the course content is considered valid by the examination boards it may also influence what is taught in the lower school.

Geography for the Young School-Leaver (GYSL) is a course, designed by the Schools Council, that many teachers have adopted because its concern for the problems of urban areas makes it relevant to inner-city education. Many schools offer Mode 3 syllabuses in Geography. Of eighteen Mode 3 geography syllabuses validated by the South Regional Examinations Board in 1981, thirteen were based on the GYSL syllabus. Another indication of GYSL's influence is that eighty-five of the 185 secondary schools controlled by the Inner London Education Authority use it as the basis of a Mode 2 course.

As the GYSL syllabus is used nationally, an examination of its content is perhaps more important than a study of other, more local syllabuses. Change in GYSL holds greater potential than does change in any other syllabus for influencing what is learned through geography in schools. For these reasons I have chosen to present a detailed analysis of GYSL in terms of its contributions to education for a multicultural society.

What ideas are presented by courses based on these syllabuses? What do they teach about Third World countries and their peoples? About relationships between the Third World and the First World? About urbanization and migration? About the localization of disadvantage in the inner cities? How do they help pupils to understand the processes which shape their lives? How appropriate are they as the basis of geograpical education in a multicultural society?

THE RESOURCE SHEETS AND THE 'KEY IDEAS'

When a school decides to adopt GYSL, a set of pupil resource sheets are usually bought. These are used instead of textbooks. Although teachers may supplement the sheets with materials of their own choice – or reject them altogether – the materials reviewed here form part of the official GYSL Kit and are likely to be presented to children as learning-resources in most schools where the syllabus is used. There is no guarantee that all teachers will use the materials critically; some may be oblivious to their shortcomings. There is nothing presented with the GYSL Kit which would help teachers counter the assumptions on which the resources are based.

The syllabus is presented in terms of 'key ideas'; the learning-materials support them, and examinations test whether or not they have been learned. Some of the ideas are highly questionable, but the teachers' guide gives little indication of how they can be questioned critically. For example, the key ideas state that 'certain characteristics of cities appear to be universal', including 'competition for land at the centre, resulting in high rise development', and 'the problems of inadequate provision of housing and transport due to rapid growth'.[1] But the present state of affairs in Western industrial cities is the result of a specific course of historical development.

GYSL does not give adequate consideration to what this course of development may be, or investigate its inevitability. The city is a spatial form which reflects social processes. A city which has a relatively poor inner zone surrounded by relatively well-off suburbs is a concrete manifestation of social inequality. In order to understand the spatial form, it is necessary to comprehend the processes by which inequality came into being and by which it is perpetuated. GYSL presents 'the facts' with no indication of how they were produced or how they could be changed. 'The facts' are put forward as key ideas which are supported by learning-materials. Almost inevitably, the questioning of current reality will be discouraged through this approach to course design.

AN EXAMINATION OF SOME GYSL RESOURCES AND KEY IDEAS

GYSL presents a study of urban problems. One of these problems is considered to be immigration and several of the scheme's resource sheets either take it as their subject or refer to it. A look at one of the key ideas tells us about GYSL's perspective on the issue of immigration: 'Immigration can lead to severe pressure on resources. This may result in unemployment, homelessness, a breakdown of the transport system and a general deterioration of urban life'.[2] Thus an introduction to immigration connects the issue with unemployment and the idea of a deteriorating urban life.

Dallas USA (resource sheet 4.2, Cities and People unit)

Dallas is presented as a 'dream city' which has three problems:

* Dallas is a visual mess – fine new buildings jostle rundown shacks, unsightly parking areas blot the town, festoons of garish advertising defile the walls, and raw, unfinished or abandoned building sites proliferate.

** The crime rate is also a disgrace and has been growing at three times the rate of population increase.

*** Nineteen per cent of the population is negro and economically deprived – though by most American standards the 'deprived' negro is well off.

Dallas is a visual mess; the crime rate is a disgrace; and 19 per cent of the population is negro. These statements are juxtaposed on the resource sheet. Are criminal behaviour and skin colour necessarily related? If not, why the juxtaposition of these statements? Although economic conditions are mentioned, there is no attempt explicitly to link the incidence of crime with that of economic or social deprivation, with relative powerlessness or the acquisitiveness associated with low social status in a consumer-oriented society. In fact skin colour is presented as the only relevant factor, because, although the American negro is economically deprived, 'by most American standards, the deprived negro is well off'. What does this mean? One of the consequences of using this resource sheet in the classroom without questioning the underlying assumptions and the juxtaposition of these statements may be that racism is fostered unintentionally.

'Change within cities' (resource sheet 4.9, Cities and People unit)

This sheet looks at the role of estate agents in forcing up the price of houses in the inner city. But what may be the learning outcome of using the following information?

My mother had lived in that house for 45 years. It was a white neighbourhood but the black area was not far away and it was spreading out. Then four years ago our area underwent a drastic change ... a black family moved in and within six weeks it had all changed. We became the only white family left on the block. People just panicked and moved out ... Then last year came the last straw for us. Just opposite the church, a few doors from where we lived, two black teenagers grabbed my purse and knocked me down ... Then somebody threw a fire bomb through the window of the house next door ... The police said it could have been meant for us, the only whites left on the street.

The extract ends on the rather lame note: 'This city is an example of what happens when you try to keep people in ghettos.'

In terms of fostering racial harmony this resource sheet is likely to be less than helpful. The grave concern here is how the teacher uses the material. As an example of inflammatory reporting it could be useful; used simply to illustrate movement in cities it could reinforce racist attitudes. No help is provided on the issue of combating racism in the GYSL teachers' guide.

'Bantu Africans into the Republic of South Africa' (resource sheet 4.6, Cities and People unit)

The materials suggest that black Africans are immigrants. But black Africans would probably view the white minority as the immigrants, and may feel that it is only the imposed apartheid policy which creates the 'Bantustans' from which the black people 'emigrate'. In the hands of some teachers, perhaps this resource sheet could be used as an example of bias. But, used uncritically, it is likely to misinform and miseducate.

Besides presenting the notion that South Africa belongs unquestionably to the whites, this resource sheet promotes the idea that whites are doing the blacks a favour by giving them jobs. On mining the following information is given:

For almost 80 years Bantu recruits have been going to the Witwatersrand to work in the gold mines. About 222,000 of the 350,000 or so Bantu recruited each year are from adjacent foreign countries. Each year nearly 80% wil have returned for their second, third or fourth annual contract. The numbers of temporary immigrant workers are decided by agreement with each foreign country, and no foreign Bantu can be employed in the mines unless he has arrived in South Africa legally. When the miner has served his contract he returns to his home country. A large part of the earnings of the miners is sent back to their families – some two million Bantu outside South Africa are partly or wholly dependent on such income.

It seems that mining can't be too bad. They keep coming back for more. South Africa is just about supporting all the neighbouring countries as well as its own population. What would the blacks do for a job if they didn't work in the mines?

On mining-compounds the information is as follows:

Where the Bantus live – the mining compounds

The goldmining companies have built settlements within the mine areas for their immigrant workers. Accommodation is free. There are blocks of modern apartments for indunas (headmen) and hostels for other workers. Some of the hostels for single men are bright modern buildings furnished in modern style, with libraries, rest rooms and other amenities. There are sports facilities available and the miners can use some of the cinemas and shops in nearby towns. (Adapted from 'The Golden Magnet' South African Embassy, London)

There is no mention of the fact that African mineworkers earn £13.80 a week, on average, whereas white miners earn £112.24 per week.[3] Nor is there a hint of the dangers in mining, for blacks. Over the period 1936–66, 19,000 men, 93 per cent of them African, died as a result of accidents in gold mines, an average of three deaths per shift (International Defence and Aid Fund, 1978). No mention either of who gets the profits from gold-mining, or of British investment in the industry.

On Bantu townships:

In the last thirty or so years there has been an enormous growth of manufacturing industry of all kinds in South Africa. Most of the factories are in or very near the cities, and their growth has led to large scale immigration into the cities. Wages and working conditions are often better in the factories than in the mines – though average income for many is very low – and they have naturally attracted large numbers of Bantu workers. Unlike the mining companies, though, most industrial firms do not provide accommodation for their employees. The workers have to find somewhere to live in the Bantu sections of the towns. (The policy of the white minority who govern South Africa is to compel the separation of white and non-white people except where they have to work together.)

The old Native townships became overcrowded and shanty towns and squatters' camps grew in number and squalor. In Johannesburg the Native Affairs Department has planned to clear the slums, reduce the scatter of native locations and concentrate the Non-Europeans in a small number of settlements away from the European areas. There are now over three-quarters of a million people living in the town known as Soweto (South-western Township). The sprawling, barrack-like accommodation is often a long way from places of work, and means a difficult and expensive journey each day.

Immigrant Bantu workers and South African non-whites (Bantu, Asians and coloureds) then, are found concentrated either in the mining compounds or in the Government built urban townships. They are at the same time a part of the city, yet separate from it.

The Pass Laws are not mentioned, nor is 'Bantu education'. We are told that 'the Native Affairs Department has planned to clear the slums ... and concentrate the non-Europeans in a small number of settlements'. Slums are what the blacks create. Settlements are what the whites provide for them.

Non-whites 'are at the same time part of the city, yet separate from it'. GYSL fails to make clear the extent to which these people are separate; they have no legal right in the country; no vote; they can be shifted to the Bantustans when they are no longer useful, or if their behaviour is considered to be subversive; they can be arrested for being in a white area without a pass, and they are constantly harassed by the police. Perhaps the GYSL resource sheets should supply such information.

'Calcutta, India' (resource sheet 4.3, Cities and People unit)

I wish to look closely at the sheet on Calcutta because its perspective is one that is presented in most other school textbooks, as well as in the teaching-pack for GYSL.

The explanatory framework within which Calcutta's problems are analysed is one which helps foster the view that individuals are responsible for creating the poverty in which they live. Under the title 'A city under strain' is provided the following information:

Calcutta is not a wealthy city and it has proved impossible to house and provide amenities for this great inward surge of millions. More than three-quarters live in slums or in tenements with one family to a small room. The problem is complicated because almost a quarter of the city's population lives a single life and two-thirds are male.

It is well-known that millions have the pavement as their home. Streets are strewn with sleeping families at night. But the pavements also remain almost as littered during the day. It is evident that thousands of people either lack the energy or the need, being unemployed or unemployable, to move from their gutterside homes.

Many, clad in filthy rags or nearly naked, loll about obviously starving or half-dead. In the city centre scores of lepers and cruelly mutilated unfortunates beg unheeded.

Is there a Health Department? Yes, but roadside stalls sell food openly exposed to dust and flies which carry cholera germs. Huge garbage dumps remain uncleared and pavements are strewn with rotting trash. The gutters are the public lavatories. Dead and dying dogs as well as humans lie about the footway.

In the suburbs conditions are far worse, with hundreds of thousands crammed together in disease-breeding *bustees*, hutments built in fetid areas which lack sewerage or running water. Tap water is unsafe to drink and often runs black.

The city's water supply and sanitation were adjudged near breakdown as long ago as 1959 by a team from the World Health Organisation. Century-old sewage pipes, which leak, run alongside the water mains. Plans for improvement have been pigeon-holed for years.

Is there a Transport Department? Yes, but public transport is so inadequate that trams built for 75 people carry 200 and hundreds daily risk their lives by hanging on to the footboards of overloaded buses.

Is there a Highways Department? Yes, but roads and pavements everywhere are in appalling condition, unrepaired and crumbling.

The message: Calcutta is teeming with dirty, starving people who live in gutterside slums. The explanation: They are 'unemployed and unemployable'. 'Lack of jobs in rapidly growing third world cities has led to a great dependence on domestic work, self employment and scavenging.'[4]

The course fails to explain *why* there is a lack of jobs. The shortage of employment in many Third World countries is related to the policies of European- and American-owned companies which favour the processing and packaging of agricultural products in the First World. This policy, associated with tariff barriers imposed by Western governments, helps to ensure that processed and manufactured goods produced in the Third World occupy a poor competitive position in the world market. In effect, Western policies help to prevent the development of industry in countries such as India. So there may be another explanation for Calcutta's poverty. It is not that the people are unemployable; it is that they are denied jobs. Perhaps the resource sheet should present this explanation as well.

The idea that Third World peoples are involved in little more than scavenging is not likely to foster positive attitudes towards them. The individualization of failure implicit in the notion of scavenging legitimizes the current misconception that individuals are the architects of their own fate. Unless Calcutta's city-dwellers are seen as victims of an on-going process of underdevelopment in which capitalism plays an important role, they may be blamed for their own poverty.

In fact, GYSL suggests that the people create their own problems:

Who migrates and why

Less than half the population of Calcutta were born in the city. The enormous growth in population in recent times has been largely due to immigration. The immigrants are of two main sorts. There are the refugees from Bangla Desh (formerly East Pakistan), mostly Hindus, who left the Moslem state of Pakistan when it was formed in 1947.

The other immigrants have come to the city to seek work in the factories and docks. Large cities are always a magnet for people in the surrounding countryside, and Calcutta is no exception. It is the focus of an area in which live about 150 million people mostly villagers. It is usually the young men who leave the villages in order to send home a few rupees a month to help support their families.

What the immigrant finds

The young immigrant sees nothing of the gracious old suburbs of Alipore or Bal-lygunge or even their much grimmer successors of Howrah. He sees the nineteenth century sprawl of central Calcutta, the banks of the Hooghly, blanketed with jute-mills and the 'temporary' hutments which are the permanent homes of millions of Indians. Instead of the clear skies of home, a heavy industrial haze; instead of the green paddy fields of Bihar, a view of grimy old factories; instead of the clean cosiness of father's mud-walled cottage, a part-share of a room in a tumbledown tenement or a corner in a stinking shanty of reeds and palm-leaves.

These extracts suggest that the problem is immigration. The cause: people come to the city looking for work. The solution: to stick to the 'clean cosiness of father's mud-walled cottage'. The immigrants should have stayed at home. There would be no problem if they went away.

What is the framework within which problems and solutions are defined in the GYSL sheet on Calcutta? The reasoning goes something like this. Why do people come to the city? Because they have no jobs. Why haven't they got jobs? Because there are too many people. There should be fewer people. Perhaps they should stop having so many children. They should use contraception. The solution to the unemployment problem is in the hands of individuals. The unemployed are to blame for the fact that they have no jobs. Thus capitalist ideology may be fostered and school children may be encouraged to think of the Indians as incompetent.

First–Third World relationships

The GYSL course may lead to incomplete comprehension of patterns and processes in world cities. Another of the key ideas reads as follows: 'The very rapid growth of Third World cities has led to extreme overcrowding, inadequate provision of housing and extensive areas of squatter settlements on city margins.'[5]

Although this may be true, it is necessary to recognize the processes which have led to growth. One of the main reasons for the movement of people from the land into the cities was the introduction of plantation agriculture to supply European and North American markets with primary products. Multinational corporations continue the process of exploitation initiated in the time of colonial rule. Land once used in a labour-intensive way to produce food crops now grows tea, coffee, sisal, cocoa and rice for the world market. Capital-intensive production of cash crops has created food shortage and unemployment in 'developing countries'. In India, the 'green revolution' – an agricultural programme which involved the use of chemical fertilizer, pesticides, new strains of rice, irrigation and mechanization and which was financed partly by the Ford and Rockefeller Foundations – has been directly responsible for forcing the poorer farmers off the land while enabling the rich to get richer. Those farmers who couldn't afford the pesticides, fertilizer and new strains of rice, in competition with those who could, found that they were unable to sell their crops. Thousands of small farmers were put out of business and had to go to the city looking for work.

Immigration into Britain (resource sheet 4.7, Cities and People unit: 'Commonwealth citizens into Britain')

What of the section which deals with immigration into Britain? The framework is the same; individuals are responsible for racial tensions; an improvement in the behaviour of immigrants will solve the problems. On race relations we have the following:

Living together. An Indian family moves next door to a Jamaican family

We moved next door to people of a different race: a Jamaican family, people with a different religion, different customs and a different colour of skin.

Before my acquaintance with our new neighbours, I didn't feel too bad to have Jamaicans as our neighbours. I was disappointed, obviously, because every person who moves to a new house hopes to have the same people as themselves.

My immediate reaction when I found our neighbours hostile was that of dislike. It was not because of the colour of their skin; colour doesn't matter in the slightest to me. I don't differentiate between one colour and another. I believe that I am a person and everyone else is the same as me, every person to me is equal. You are born black, white, brown, yellow, et cetera, and it cannot be helped what colour you are born. I judge a person by what that person says, and by that person's actions.

It was not long when arguments began and they soon became common. Not a day passed without a row between the families. The language difficulty between my parents and our neighbours made it even worse as they could not talk things over in a respectable and civilized way.

When we did our cooking we opened the windows in the kitchen, if we didn't, steam from the pots collected in the kitchen. The neighbours complained how the horrible smell of our cooking came over their wall and into their garden. We would certainly have liked this not to have happened, but we had to keep the kitchen window open because it became sticky and humid if we didn't. This was an everyday thing. We had to cook and as long as we cooked they complained.

We didn't want all this to get serious and so we didn't complain about them but they certainly made things difficult for us. They had loud parties that went right the way up to one or two o'clock in the night, making it impossible for us to get a good comfortable sleep. At daytime when we had visitors they put the radio on so loud that it became difficult for us to keep our voices down to be clearly audible. In the end we had to tell them not to make too much noise when they had a party and to keep the radio low. This only infuriated them more and it became impossible for us to have any understanding at all with them. It was not long when it became so serious that the police was called in once.

The other people of the neighbourhood blamed us because all this started when we moved in. But the Jamaicans were disliked before as well and so the blame fell on both families.

Gradually we, as well as our neighbours, realized that we were giving ourselves a bad name and also our races. It was when they realised that that they began to cool down and for once think. We decided to forgive each other about the way we had acted. We decided to overcome the difficulties we had had and the only way we could do this, we found out, was to act in a friendly manner. We did not have to change our custom, religion, etc. but change our attitude and behaviour. (Written by a 16-year-old Indian boy in a Midlands school)

The Indians' food smells; the Jamaicans have noisy parties; the police have to be called in to settle arguments; after police intervention both families realize they are giving their races a bad name; they decide to change their attitudes and behaviours.

The resource sheet 'Commonwealth citizens into Britain' follows the one on Calcutta. Is the hidden message that British cities will soon be like those of India if we don't do something to stop immigration? The resource sheet links the term 'immigrant' with skin colour. What is the significance of this?

The message in the resource sheet is that coloured immigrants came to Britain for jobs and that some cities have more of them than others. What is likely to be the effect of using this information in geography lessons without putting it into historical perspective? Britain's colonial past is a relevant consideration. It is not mentioned. When the present is considered outside of its historical context, the result is often a biased view of the facts. But bias or a distorted understanding may have effects in terms of attitude or behaviour.

During the 1950s and the 1960s the government New Town policy was instrumental in the relocation of industry outside London. It became difficult to get licences to increase factory space in London, while grants and cheap industrial premises were made available to areas with Development Area status. Thus the decline of employment in the inner city is one of the unintended consequences of government economic strategy.

The decision of multinational corporations to move to more profitable locations has also had an effect on the availability of jobs in London. The research by R. Dennis (1978) into manufacturing decline in London and Manchester suggests that the largest single creator of unemployment in the previous decade was the complete closure of factories (as opposed to relocation). The Canning Town Community Development Report (1974) comments, 'Industry is collapsing with a dramatic loss of the traditional work in the area. The decisions controlling the exodus are taking place in the boardrooms of some of the country's most profitable companies.' The report argues for a measure of social control over industry.

The influx of immigrants from the West Indies during the 1950s was partly in response to a government-sponsored advertising-campaign for workers to run the transport system. At the time, wages were too low to attract British workers. Other groups of immigrants have come to England as a result of Britain's colonial past. Their concentration in poorer areas of the city, and their association with poverty and 'the deteriorating urban life', was partly determined by low wage levels in their work and partly the result of racism. Perhaps these are the ideas which GYSL should be putting forward if there is to be any real attempt to get pupils to understand immigration and inner-city impoverishment.

Employment and unemployment

The syllabus puts forward the idea that 'many work units are part of larger organizations, and depend on decisions made elsewhere'.[6] However, there is no questioning of whether this is a good thing, whether it is inevitable or whether it is changeable. The presentation of key ideas as facts excludes explanations, but, more importantly, asks no questions. Part of GYSL's summary of key ideas states that 'there is a tendency for the size of work units to increase to benefit from the advantages of large scale production'. Again, there is no explanation of who benefits, nor any mention of the disadvantages of large-scale production.

The syllabus also notes that 'there are many different reasons for the decline of jobs in an area. These include ... new techniques or equipment demanding fewer employees ... and ... high production costs due to high wages and difficult conditions of work.' Is the suggestion here that unemployment is inevitable, unquestionable and therefore acceptable? There is no hint of inefficient management, monopoly price-fixing amongst multinationals or high interest rates as contributory causes of high production costs.

Housing

It is important, in the context of countering attitudes which hold 'immigrants' to blame for inner-city problems, to examine issues such as housing. GYSL explains the problems of inadequate housing and transport in the city as the creations of 'rapid growth'.[7] But 'growth' is not explanation enough, nor is growth a natural evolution unaffected by political considerations. Growth alone does *not* produce inadequate housing. What about national income and its unequal distribution amongst families? What about a system where income, not need, determines the quality of a family's housing? Problems of mobility and car ownership are also clearly affected by personal income and the workings of a politically controlled public-transport system.

The syllabus recognizes that 'there are usually marked differences between residential areas within a city'; these are listed as 'differences in age, design, quality, cost and tenure of housing'.[8] If geography syllabuses seek to study different residential areas, they should also examine the social system under which such differences arise; opportunities are unequal and reinforced by institutions. Banks and building-societies operate to the disadvantage of poor areas within our cities (see Dennis, 1978). Activities and the built form are interrelated. Yet the built form and the social relationships within it can be changed. In putting forward the idea of the city as it is today, is it possible that an acceptance of the *status quo* is being fostered, and through it, political complacency? What are the implications of a *status quo* education? Who benefits from such an education? And, ultimately, who suffers?

CONCLUSION

GYSL has been by no means comprehensively criticized here, but a closer look at some 'key ideas' enables us to approach an examination of the political significance of the content. The course may foster an unquestioning acceptance of the *status quo*; it is suspect in terms of education in and for a multicultural society – it fails to counter misconceptions about the nature of the relationships between immigration and unemployment and it fosters misunderstandings of the processes which operate in Third World cities; it sees unemployment as inevitable; it cannot be described as education for participation in decision-making; it does not relate social inequality in urban areas to the class system, nor does it take responsibility for helping pupils to understand the mechanisms of the class system in perpetuating both social inequality and current spatial form.

NOTES

1 London Regional Examining Board CSE Syllabus document, p. 7.
2 Ibid., p. 9.
3 Department of Statistics, Government of South Africa, Pretoria, June 1977.
4 Syllabus document, p. 10.
5 Ibid., p. 7.
6 Ibid.
7 Ibid.
8 Ibid.

REFERENCES

Dennis, N. 1978: Housing policy areas: criteria and indicators in policy and practice. *Transactions of the Institute of British Geographers*, 3 (1), 2–22.
Dennis, R. 1978: The decline of manufacturing employment in Greater London, 1966–1974. *Urban Studies*, 15 (1), 63–73.
International Defence and Aid Fund 1978: *This is Apartheid*. London: IDAF.

Organizing for Responsive Schools

40

Did they all get into the Ark?
Blackshaw Nursery

Patricia Potts

The 1970s saw a boom in specialist pre-school services for children with disabilities, which developed in isolation from mainstream provision. In this chapter, Patricia Potts argues from a standpoint opposed to this expansion. She asks what kind of ordinary pre-school setting could accommodate not only all children, including those with disabilities, but also all the services they require, delivered to the children in their community. Blackshaw Nursery offers one such environment where some professionals are collaborating in a community setting. But its progress towards becoming a comprehensive provision has been limited by other professionals who prefer to work from their own centres of control.

Blackshaw Nursery in south London has places for forty pre-school children, is open from 7 a.m. to 10 p.m., and is mainly used by parents working shifts in the adjacent hospital. The building is imaginative, a children's ark, purpose-built but flexible, and it facilitates a combination of care and education. Parents are closely involved and are represented on the voluntary management committee. There are regular and increasing links with health, education and social services. The nursery is the only one of its kind in the country.

LOOKING FOR A CONTEXT FOR INTEGRATION

There is a dilemma for professionals who wish to see community-based provisions for pre-school children extended to cater for those with disabilities and other difficulties – first, because such provision is generally sparse. On the one hand, specialized provisions tend to be based in the premises of individual statutory authorities or single-client-group voluntary societies, and, on the other hand, non-parental childcare is still often seen as undesirable: 'I think the state, surely, has got much greater priorities at the moment than to fork out large sums of cash for groups of women, feminists largely, who want somebody else to look after their children. Far better they look after their own children' (Tony Marlowe, Conservative MP for Northampton North, 1983).[1]

Where childcare is not seen as something to be avoided, it may still be seen as 'compensatory', a service for particular groups of children rather than for all children. This is true of Strathclyde's recent report on under-fives (Strathclyde Regional Council, 1985), which otherwise contains many progressive recommendations. Pre-school provisions as a whole are described as 'compensatory services for the disadvantaged'.

So there is tailor-made provision for children classified into groups by disability, an increasing amount of it based on home-visiting schemes, and there's daycare for children classified into groups by degree of social or economic disadvantage. Most of the former are part-time and run by the health or education authorities, whereas many day nurseries, run by social services, provide full-time places. Specialist services such as speech therapy and physiotherapy are not routinely delivered to the non-specialized settings unless there is a special unit attached. 'Mainstream' pre-school provisions such as playgroups and nursery schools or classes are part-time and they tend to exclude both of the groups I have just mentioned. The present system for under-fives, therefore, is patchy, complicated, a mixture of statutory and non-statutory, for the providers, and largely voluntary for the consumers. And much of it is chronically insecure owing to a lack of guaranteed funding.

SEGREGATION IS EASIER

The effects of professional specialization can make co-operation and a sharing of roles with overlapping client groups difficult, particularly when roles have been carefully defined and the context for working is clearly marked as the territory of one, rather than another, profession. Purpose-built or specially adapted accommodation for children with physical, mental or sensory impairments can mean that they are hidden away on their own. It may be thought that appropriate help is more important than this isolation or than the issue of whether or not these children should have an opportunity to belong to ordinary groups – which, if they are pre-school groups, are often thought of as unnatural themselves:

The chairman of the [West Sussex] County Education Committee, Mr Kenneth Ball, said the best nursery education was provided in a good home by good parents. 'I am very much anti too much nursery school education', he declared, 'I do not want to see a professional hierarchy starting to teach young children away from their parents.'[2]

This line of argument implies that the 'natural' situation for young children is to be at home with their non-working mothers (not fathers). Home-visiting schemes for children with disabilities support this view and, although many families welcome the privacy, the gain in confidence and the often tremendous progress that their children make, these schemes do not provide the parents with a choice of setting, nor their children with the opportunity for social integration.

The pressure to categorize children into discrete groups is strong. Combining daycare, education and therapy, therefore, is extremely difficult, particularly in a setting which can also meet the needs of parents, whether working or not, by means of flexible hours, low cost or social contacts. Any provision which can be described as 'generic' tends to have a poor status and is associated with a lack of 'professionalism'.

There are many children with difficulties already placed in ordinary pre-school playgroups and nurseries. But this does not represent a process of integration nor a commitment to the implementation of a coherent policy, because these children are usually admitted on a priority ticket which is frequently seen as quite compatible with exclusion at five, as if the temporary placement were one of the 'special' features of the overall programme.

My aim here is therefore to identify a pre-school provision which aims to be inclusive both of children and of services, and to see how comprehensive it could be in practice.

WHO IS BLACKSHAW NURSERY FOR?

Blackshaw Nursery was opened in the autumn of 1981 and moved to its new building in April 1982. It was established primarily as a response to the childcare needs of parents working non-standard hours in the National Health Service, and to this extent its 'community' is clearly defined as the hospital next door, where 70 per cent of the employees are women. The local childcare campaign which initiated the project was particularly concerned to ensure equal opportunities for these women to pursue their careers by developing a childcare facility of very high quality. About a quarter of the places at Blackshaw go to families in the area, but the report on the first year of the nursery describes the demand as 'almost unlimited'. Because of this, there is a long waiting-list and an admissions policy, but selection criteria consist of such things as the family's need for a place, their time on the waiting-list and the age of the child, not the characteristics of individual children. There is no primary client group as far as the children are concerned, and a policy of equal opportunities is set out in the constitution of the nursery's association, which aims 'to provide day care for children of working parents ... with a proportion of day nursery places being reserved for the children of NHS staff, without distinction of sex, race, religious, political or other opinions'.

FUNDING

The nursery is funded by the Department of the Environment and the local borough council via an Urban Aid grant, which paid for the building and provided a subsidy for the first five years. It costs about £138,000 a year to run the nursery, about £57 per week per child. Most parents pay £27.50, the local childminding rate, although some pay less and some, whose children fill the small number of unsubsidized places, may pay up to £40 a week. Fees have to cover at least half the running costs, the balance being met, at the moment, by the Department of the Environment, the borough and the district health authority. Funding is uncertain and, because of this, the 'community' places will tend to be filled by families on fairly high incomes.

STAFFING

There are thirteen members of staff, including the officer-in-charge, a nursery teacher and two part-timers, funded from the Urban Aid grant. The Manpower Services Commission (MSC) pays for a bookkeeper, a clerk–typist, a gardener–handyman, two kitchen assistants and four temporary nursery workers. Along with their salaries comes £450 a year per employee which goes towards equipment and running-costs. The MSC contribution is now (1985) in its second year. The original management committee had rejected the idea of MSC involvement, but the present members argue that conditions for the workers concerned are the same as for the others and that the year's experience is valuable for the nursery workers' careers. But it does mean that four nursery workers will change each year.

GROUPING

At first, children in the nursery were grouped according to age, but in 1982 'family' groupings were adopted. Babies (there is space for up to five) are based in their own room up to the age of eighteen months with their own worker, but join the older children for meals and some activities. The older children are divided into two groups of around fifteen to twenty, each with their own group of staff and their own large playroom. Anxieties about this kind of 'vertical' grouping were expressed by parents through their representatives on the management committee, and as a result staff made greater efforts to inform them about the structuring of the daily activities and arranged smaller peer groups for short periods of teaching each day. The small group sessions (for younger, as well as older, children) are organized by staff with a teaching-background, but all staff may become involved. Apart from these sessions, children have time for free play, music and movement, stories, and outdoor play on the large equipment. So it has been possible for parents to exert an influence over the running of the nursery as well as enjoy the ease of access in a workplace nursery.

DAILY ROUTINE

A complicated staff-rota system operates so that the majority of workers are on duty when the largest number of children are in the nursery, with sufficient cover early and late, and bearing in mind a working-week of thirty-six hours. The staff–child ratio is 1 : 5 or 6, and 1 : 4 or 5 for babies.

Each playroom, or 'end', of the nursery (see figure 40.1 for symmetrical design) has its own routine of activities planned by each group of staff for their particular children. Planning is done informally, and formally at monthly meetings.

Breakfast is from 8 to 8.30 a.m.; there's a break for a drink at 10.30, followed by lunch at noon, tea at 3.30 p.m. and supper at 7 p.m. Activities planned for the sessions between breaks may alternate messy play with more constructional toys. Children have a good sleep after lunch in the smaller rooms off the central playrooms and they make regular trips out in the nursery's minibus.

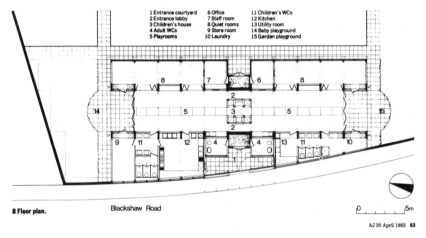

1 Entrance courtyard	6 Office	11 Children's WCs
2 Entrance lobby	7 Staff room	12 Kitchen
3 Children's house	8 Quiet rooms	13 Utility room
4 Adult WCs	9 Store room	14 Baby playground
5 Playrooms	10 Laundry	15 Garden playground

8 Floor plan.   Blackshaw Road   0 |____|____| 5m

AJ 20 April 1983 **63**

Figure 40.1   Plan of Blackshaw Nursery

ARCHITECTURE

The architects who designed Blackshaw Nursery, John Jenner and Nigel Greenhill, are responsive to changing social patterns within local communities, one of which is the growing need for childcare. 'We want to encourage self-help initiatives … to fashion new concepts for childcare, adapting the form to suit the group.' And they find it 'refreshing' to design for children: 'Children are natural consumers of raw architecture-space, acoustics, textures, colours, light. Children respond to them naturally.' Jenner and Greenhill work with their clients over a long period of time, providing the concrete support of their design and incorporating within it their clients' suggestions and ideas. It may be years before a community project receives funding, so the architects' plans can help to maintain the group's commitment and optimism. 'We don't seek as architects to impose our concepts of design. All sorts of people can make contributions to the design at a practical and a more conceptual level.'[3]

Plate 40.1 Blackshaw Nursery: exterior

Plate 40.2 Blackshaw Nursery: interior

The building is single-storeyed and symmetrical in layout, although the site is not rectangular, with a children's playhouse dividing the two playroom mirror-images (see the plan in figure 40.1 and the photographs in plates 40.1 and 40.2). At each far end there is a mural painting above the windows, one representing 'day' and the other 'night'. Children who do not walk, talk or use the lavatory are already included in the nursery as babies, and older children who cannot do these things could also use the building. Surfaces are safe, and many features, such as the porthole windows, are at child's-eye level. There are lips at the doorways, however. The architects argue that 'It's only prejudice that prevents childcare provision being combined with other provision. In other societies you can have "public" meeting spaces for everyone.'

SPECIAL SERVICES

The community physician and a health visitor are among the professionals who regularly visit the nursery, and many routine pre-school health checks are carried out in the nursery. A speech therapist has been to the nursery and organized the carrying-out of programmes in her absence. Children have also been able to visit the nearby child-development clinic while remaining on the nursery's roll. In this way, there is access to specialized services without the labelling attached to being a 'patient' or the later placement consequences of attending a special unit. Children do not have to relinquish their membership of the nursery, for they can attend both.

CHILDREN WITH DIFFICULTIES AT BLACKSHAW?

The sorts of difficulties faced by some of Blackshaw's children include speech and language problems, behavioural and emotional problems and mild hearing-losses. Most ordinary pre-school groups include children who experience such problems, though not, usually, where they have been severe enough to be identified formally. Health-service personnel do not see the nursery as the right place for children who have already been given a 'handicap' label and tend to use a multi-professional diagnostic unit for children about whom there are serious worries. Identification can therefore be a ticket to special resources, but it also restricts a child's choice of pre-school group. Professionals are aware, however, of the consequences of segregated placements and are keen to support children in the ordinary nursery if their difficulties are seen as temporary, not 'constitutional'.

For children with marked physical or mental impairments they express a protective attitude, arguing that a special unit helps families to come to terms with this situation and meet up with others whose experiences are similar, while at the same time providing a more appropriate social life for their children. Whether or not this division of services for children reflects a 'natural' state of affairs or not could be debated, of course, for the planning that results in different kinds of provision reveals the attitudes and priorities of the planners rather than different kinds of humanity among children. Many professionals believe that specialized training and the concentration of resources immediately to hand are essential and justify the segregation of their consumers.

Bhatia

Bhatia came to the nursery at eighteen months and she cried for a month. She never slept, did not eat solid food and made very few speech sounds. She could be violent, she screamed and she showed no warmth towards adults or children. The other children were frightened at first, but they came to tolerate her long before her behaviour changed. They would say, 'She's done it again!', as if it was just part of daily life. The professionals involved were undecided about the causes of Bhatia's problems but help was focused on speech therapy and toilet-training within the nursery. After a year, Bhatia did not scream any more, but the nursery workers still felt hopeless, ('It would have been so easy to reject her'), much as they remained committed to her.

The change in Bhatia came with the first signs of affection: 'If she'd hurt herself, she'd come to you to touch you or cuddle you.' Gradually she came to show affection to everyone, but particularly to her own nursery worker. A special day unit does exist, but the staff at Blackshaw say, 'it would not have been right'. When Bhatia was two and a half years old contact was made with the child-development clinic to help with toilet-training. This has amounted to a family therapy service, for the child psychiatrist who visits the nursery to see Bhatia there has proved to be a great support to the family. The speech therapist visits twice a year to give advice on programmes for the nursery staff to follow.

Bhatia has been attending a mainstream infants school since Easter 1985, and the nursery is in touch with her teachers. Although she is still a bit of a loner, Bhatia's speech has improved so that she can chat away, and she has made the transition very well.

Robert

Robert is now three, and when he started at the nursery at eighteen months his behaviour resembled Bhatia's. Developmental checks were carried out at the nursery and he was found to have a marked hearing-loss. He had an operation and grommets fitted. His hearing improved but his speech and behaviour did not, and he is still very restless. Like Bhatia, Robert attends a multi-professional clinic and he spends one day a week there with his mother, which she finds very helpful. In the last six months a 'quite dramatic' change has occurred; Robert is still very demanding but warm and 'trying hard' now with his speech. He is almost toilet-trained. Nursery staff do feel, however, that he will need extra help before he goes to infants school and he may attend a language unit. It is not yet agreed for how many hours or

364 Organizing for responsive schools

when exactly it will start. Blackshaw *could* provide what Robert needs, but at the moment lacks adequate space, staff and money.

One of the problems for children in a workplace nursery is that they may live out of the borough and so may be referred to a unit nearer their home, making it difficult for them to remain in the nursery because their own local authority will not pay for a placement outside the home borough.

MAKING THE MOST OF BLACKSHAW

Like any scarce resource, Blackshaw Nursery is hard-pressed to meet the needs of its community. It is under-resourced, as some jobs which turned out to be essential were not outlined in the original proposal, and, for example, there is a hectic period around 2 p.m. when, owing to overrunning and overlapping of their parents' shifts, all the children might be in the nursery together. There was pressure to fill the nursery very quickly, although the building was not ready, and there has always been too little time for the staff to meet together. There have been major disagreements about the running of the nursery, and the lack of opportunities for discussion between members of staff, who are often exhausted, has made resolving them hard, sometimes impossible. But the fundamental commitment is there, as is shown by the way in which the children flourish, and Blackshaw is potentially a comprehensive provision. As it does not provide daycare for non-working parents, however, its clientele is limited in practice.

Blackshaw is based in the community; it aims to combine care and education and it provides a range of services to families within the nursery itself. Blackshaw could meet the needs of a much wider group of children, but its funding is insecure and it is crowded. A planned extension to the building would include a new teaching-room, a staffroom and a larger babies' room.

The ordinary nursery workers have proved to be invaluable key workers, carrying out specialized programmes and providing the emotional support for the children that part-time clinics and units cannot.

Whether or not the number of full-time day nurseries can be expanded and their staffs supported in such a way as to make a process of integration possible and welcomed will depend on a revision of the value systems from which they represent a significant departure.

A COMPREHENSIVE SYSTEM FOR ALL CHILDREN UNDER FIVE?

Community-based provisions are contracting rather than the reverse, and the future for London groups looks very bleak now, after the demise of the Greater London Council. But, for it to be possible to include all local children in a pre-school group for as many hours a week as they wish, there needs to be a change in the pattern of provision, as well as more of it.

At a recent conference the participants in a working-group were discussing this issue and they came up with a number of concrete suggestions: for example, that there should be nursery centres combining care, health and educational provision, membership of which would depend upon catchment areas, not individual characteristics. There should be a core staff of teachers, nursery workers and therapists sharing the same conditions of service, and local multi-professional teams should visit regularly. In rural areas voluntary nurseries and playgroups might be necessary. To guarantee joint funding and a mechanism for planning, legislation is necessary. The local community health council could act as a reviewing- and evaluating-body.

Another idea was for 'family-support centres' which would be drop-in centres with play facilities and which could attract permanent funding if services such as paediatric out-patients' clinics shared the premises. Specialized training for staff was rejected in favour of awareness courses. In this way it would be possible to move away from the separation of children with and without 'special needs' and think of services for all families with children under five. One parent described a social-services playclub which was open all day, was *not* geared to 'assessment' and provided support for parents and children alike, as a place 'where we can just be ourselves'.

There are clear implications from these plans that non-parental childcare should be seen as potentially a positive experience for children, that a coherent policy needs to be developed for all under-fives and that this should be initiated and supported by legislation. Two recent documents have made recommendations which move in this direction. The Strathclyde *Under Fives* report (1985) recommends that

The Pre-Five Committee and the Pre-Five Unit should give priority to the matter of development of specialist services for children under five with special needs on a corporate basis as detailed in this report, including:

a   developing the provision of day services in collaboration with parents and voluntary groups;
b   following a pattern of integrating children with special needs into standard forms of Pre-Five provision whenever appropriate to their needs;
c   ensuring that information on the special needs of a child is shared between the services concerned to allow consistent advice and support to be provided;
d   providing small assessment units to be attached to and included in existing nurseries in Strathclyde.

Similarly, the Fish Report on special educational provision in the area of the Inner London Education Authority (1985) notes that:

The development of a range of provision and services for children below the age of five involves education, social and health services and voluntary agencies. A rationale for the placing within this range is also essential as are small panels or groups to make informed decisions. We recommend that the Authority, in cooperation with Health and Social Services and voluntary agencies, develop a plan for appropriate mechanisms, at a local level, for interprofessional cooperation.

Finally, parents who use Blackshaw Nursery have this to say (Russell, 1985):

Blackshaw has given me the confidence to continue in my career knowing the child is as happy as could be.

Play and stimulation at Blackshaw are good. I would not have left him there otherwise as these are very important to me. Blackshaw provides more opportunities than I could at home and his social development is also advanced for his age.

I like to feel I can come and see her if I want.

The staff are remarkable. They are warm and the atmosphere is nice, and this is even more important than the facilities, the building and so on.

I feel his physical confidence and the development of his motor skills are largely due to the nursery.

In choosing childcare, I look for staff who are fond of kids. Blackshaw is exactly what I wanted in terms of both people and resources.

NOTES

1 Quoted in National Childcare Campaign Programme *Who's Looking after the Children?*, BBC Open Space programme, September 1984.
2 *Bognor and Chichester Observer*, 21 March 1985.
3 First Words: *National Childcare Campaign Newsletter*, September–October 1983.

REFERENCES

Inner London Education Authority 1985: *Educational Opportunities for All: report of an independent review committee* (Fish Report). London: ILEA.
Russell, L. 1985: *Childcare at Work*. London: Blackshaw Nursery.
Strathclyde Regional Council 1985: *Under Fives: final report of the Member/Officer Group*. Glasgow: Strathclyde Regional Council.

41

The Topaz Rabbits know their yellow sounds

Annabelle Dixon

*What form of classroom organization is most conducive to the learning of all pupils?
The answer to this question must depend on one's view of how children should
learn. In many primary classrooms, children are grouped by ability, and tasks are
allocated to them by the teacher for an allotted period. Indeed the pupils' entire
school life is tightly regulated by the institution. Annabelle Dixon, a primary head
teacher, argues that such settings leave children little chance to contribute to their
own learning and develop a sense of independence; and they curtail individuality.
A more responsive environment, where children are given more control over their
own work and where there is space for all to develop their own interests and powers
is a lot more complex, but no less highly organized and planned.*

A few years ago a colleague remarked to me, in words fashionable at the
time, that there was both a surface and a deep structure to the infant school,
and that this went largely unacknowledged. Those who visit infant schools
occasionally, as opposed to working in them, will probably recall the experience as a sunny impression of groups of self-motivated children involved in
a variety of activities; how fortunate child and teacher were, to be as yet
removed from the pressures of the wider world.

So who decided that those three children should paint and who decided
what it was they were painting? Why is *that* group of children reading and
why are they reading *those* books in particular? What prompted five children
to sit around *that* table using *that* maths apparatus? Did they decide to? If they
decided for themselves, were they allowed to make other similar decisions? If
it was decided for them, what was the basis of that decision?

Given a group of very active young children and four walls within which
to contain them, certain decisions have to be made fairly rapidly: what
happens, where it happens and when it happens would seem to be the most
obviously pressing. The processes of differentiation, however, would only
appear to come into action when decisions about grouping the children have
to be made. Or do they? My contention is that such processes can and do
happen at every level in the infant and junior classroom. They range from
the permanent, explicitly and consciously undertaken – 'My better readers
sit at that table' (some infant and junior teachers being as adept at dissembling

about streaming as are their counterparts elsewhere in the education system)
– to the entirely temporary: 'Those who want to help with planting bulbs,
put your coats on.' In between lie an enormous number of decisions about
when, what and how the children learn, which, while not necessarily being
unconscious decisions as such, may very well reflect unconscious values and
most certainly reveal basic assumptions about the very nature of learning.

'The Robins have measured their handspans' ran a message across a
blackboard in an infant school recently. In other schools it is just as likely
that 'Squirrels', 'Daisies' and 'Lollipops' also managed this feat. In a mixed-
age class, such groupings may well reflect age, but for the present I shall
assume that the groupings are based on ability and/or stage in reading. It is
by no means an uncommon practice, and probably the only person who is
fairly certain that it is harder for parents and children to tell that a 'Rabbit'
is deemed superior to a 'Hamster' is the teacher herself; the children and
parents have no such illusions. So why should the teacher go to such lengths?
Partly, I would suggest, a residual conscience about grouping children by
ability and partly giving room for manoeuvre. While it is difficult to deny
that Group 1, by definition, is a certain distance from Group 5, the relative
seniority of a 'Daisy' to a 'Tulip' is thought to be difficult to establish.

While parents may anxiously watch for the metamorphosis of their 'Badger'
into a 'Hare', it will be as unlikely in school as it is in nature. However, the
power of the teacher is clearly perceived; it is seldom the children who elect
themselves into various groupings. Where they do, and it is usually on a
friendship basis, often the result is to group those of like intelligence together,
a fact not unknown to teachers. Letting children group themselves can often
mask the fact that they are reproducing subtle social groupings, in a way that
teachers often dare not do (but are grateful to the children for doing it for
them): those of like race and neighbourhood often band together, to say
nothing of like sex. Grouping by alphabetical order or age is not unusual
and at least carries the merit of selection on grounds that are not socially
divisive. All seven-year-olds were once five themselves, and five-year-olds
can look forward to being seven.

But the question still remains. Why group them at all? Most answers
appear to be based on logistics: that learning experiences can be better
organized, that one can timetable more effectively and that the children stand
a better chance of having equal access to resource materials. In practice,
from my observation, these claims are rarely met. For example, although
'Hamsters' may get more of the teacher's time, it is unusual for a teacher
who groups in this way not to withhold a share for them of, for instance,
beautiful collage materials such as velvet and lace, when she knows from
experience that 'Hamsters' will 'just smear glue over them and call it a
house'. Whatever the basis of the grouping, the fact remains that the teacher
exerts great control, both socially and intellectually, over the children's lives
in the classroom to an extent that can prove basically inimical to the way in

which young children learn. Fundamentally, I believe, it reflects how the teacher perceives learning, the child as a learner, and the child learning how to become a learner.

Looked at in this way, the many differentiation processes that can be observed in the infant classroom, from the self-evident to the subtle, are highly informative: many would see in them evidence of the need for social control by the teacher, and of bias towards features such as intelligence and towards certain races or social classes. While unfortunately there probably is such bias, I believe it is not the whole picture: to eliminate the worst of the differentiations it would be necessary for the teacher to see the children's learning in an entirely different light.

Teachers on the whole *are* interested in teaching and they are concerned about their children's progress in the acquisition of various skills and infor- mation, but the strong impression is that the process of children's learning is virtually irrelevant to a large majority. None the less, without such an interest in and knowledge of a coherent theoretical base, teachers will not feel confident in the children's own ability to become learners and the result will be that groupings, time, resources and children are highly organized. In other words, the surface structure will not only look pretty but also be systematic. In a managerial sense this will indeed be so, but at the same time it will probably militate against real pace and depth in the children's intel- lectual and social development. The organization of their real learning is in fact alarmingly superficial and disguises or positively conceals a deep inco- herence about the true nature and development of children's learning.

To take an example: which child is most likely to be learning about time? Paula is in a group that is 'doing' maths, probably from a wordcard or a book, and she will be so occupied from 9.30 to 10.10. Her subsequent record sheet will state that she has covered 'Time' because she has filled in the o'clocks and, if she's a 'Rabbit', probably the half-pasts and the quarter-tos. This is useful and necessary information but it could probably be covered fairly quickly with the whole class in a couple of sessions. Cliff, in another classroom setting, has become interested, at about the same time of day, in a seconds-timer, prompted in the first instance by the teacher, who, contrary to popular misconception, has a definite role to play in this kind of classroom organization. He tries to find out how long he can walk around the room balancing various articles on his head. This in turn requires him to think of a way to record his achievement. With breaks for sundry occasions such as dinner and assembly, he works at it for the rest of the day, totally involved.

It's not hard to see which child would fit the parents' image of 'work'. If the class-teacher doesn't really understand how children learn, she will certainly not be able to defend the practice of letting a child apparently wander round a classroom with a cushion on his head for a good part of the day, even though later tests may very well discover that Cliff has the better concept of time.

This might go some way towards explaining why numbers of infant teachers prefer not to know, or to forget what they know, about the nature of young children's learning; better an apparent and approved 'orderliness' than face the implications of structuring the children's environment to match their development. Added to which, it has to be said, establishing and running a non-differentiated classroom takes a great deal more organization, however unappreciated this might be at first glance. To borrow or extend a quotation, organizing time, resources and children into various groups is child's play in relation to organizing one's time and resources for real opportunities for 'child's play' – for which read opportunities for scientific and mathematical observation and discovery, opportunities for children to use their imagination in sand, puppets, dressing-up, and so on. And all without the constraints of the various imposed differentiation processes.

Differentiation in terms of time, then, confines certain learning experiences to specific times of day, one of the most obvious being 'work' in the morning and 'play' in the afternoon. The very division itself defines those learning experiences that are supposed to happen within it. Thus work and play become strongly differentiated, as do English, maths and 'topics', whatever the last may mean in the context of an infant child's ideas about the world. On record is the child who recently told a visitor that they did 'Fletchering' on Mondays, Wednesdays and Fridays, and Maths on Tuesdays and Thursdays. (For the uninitiated Fletcher is the author of a series of Mathematics work books through which countless pupils dutifully plod.)

Teachers themselves get caught up in their own parcelling of time, and when they would like to extend a particular activity they feel constrained by their schedule. Young children themselves can become quite anxious if their timetable is not adhered to. As a result, both get trapped inside the system; the teacher becomes less able to be flexible, or subtle in her response to the children, even when she would like to be. The needs of the system start to come first.

The effect of differentiation processes within the classroom upon resources has already been touched on; it is inevitable that, if children are grouped and time is divided, the children's access to resources will be affected. It's nice to think that all the groups will have a turn at using the Lego each week, for example; but knowing that your carefully constructed supertanker will be destroyed in minutes so that the 'Limpets' can have a go tomorrow somehow takes the edge off building it in the first place. The result is, understandably, children who don't put their inventiveness and imagination into such activities, and teachers who complain about mediocrity. Ruth may well use up all the Lego (and all of Wednesday) making an enormous airport and it will stay up until Friday. The non-differentiated classroom is essentially a well-furnished classroom and alternative activities are to be found. Meanwhile Ruth's skill and achievement are recognized. And, who knows? It might be John's or Susan's turn to think big next week. 'Taking turns' involves real compromise, not necessarily exact minutes.

Certainly, the resources are 'shared', but who decides on the sharing? If children are to learn about sharing, taking turns and the proper use of scarce resources, it is they who have to make the decisions for themselves and stand by their decisions. It should be said that opportunities for these kinds of decisions should be appropriate to their level of social and moral development: who isn't still haunted by *Lord of the Flies*? Non-differentiation is sometimes mistakenly thought to mean non-interference and non-structuring, when actually it contains a high percentage of both. It's just that it isn't done in the traditional, recognizable manner.

So what does a non-differentiated classroom look like? Much like the original visitor's impression of busy children involved in a variety of activities for most of the time; there are probably quieter times and class times during the day and time when some of the children are recording what they've done or are inventing new worlds to write about. Would children who were only used to writing about television topics or copying from cards come up with the wonderfully unexpected story title 'The bear who was allergic to fairies'? The children do not work in anything except self-chosen groups, which dissolve and take new forms according to a different activity. Physical constraints dictate the number of children at each activity: two clamps on the woodwork table mean a limit of two children. Although the children might have a certain minimum number of tasks to undertake during the week, mostly 3R skills, the content and duration is largely decided by the child, unless the teacher decides it is the moment to introduce a new process which might need some directed practice.

Some children, especially if they come from a background of very formal school experience, can feel rather threatened – a point to which I return further on. In this kind of classroom, though, a teacher really knows the children as individuals and such children are quickly noticed and are then given more initial support.

Learning to live and learning to learn in such classrooms are by no means automatic processes, and failure to recognize this may well have been partly responsible for the failure of progressive education to establish its credibility. There are no set rules in establishing such a classroom, but enthusiasm (permanent) has to be matched by caution (temporary). Not all children are initially able to take on the responsibility of making their own decisions. They may well have come from very directive, very formal classrooms or homes, where their security has been bound up in pleasing teacher or parents. Such children are often either very tentative or find it hard to concentrate on anything except tasks with a definable end.

In practical terms this means, in the early days of a new class, establishing a timetable that suits the experience of the majority of the pupils. It may be a very tedious stage for the teacher, but it has its undoubted benefits: the children get to know a new teacher and her idiosyncratic ways; they get to know the classroom, its resources, the necessary regulations that entail keeping it in some sort of order that the children can perceive. Paradoxically, a reception class may not necessarily have such needs and will accept life as it comes and feel a certain freedom to change it if it doesn't suit them. 11.15 a.m.: 'Why have you got your coat and bag, Paul?' 'Think it's time I was going home, I done school for today.' After a couple of years schooling, though, children are very aware indeed of the constraints imposed on them by teacher and routine. For instance, with a new class I had recently, the word got around like the proverbial wildfire that not only had I neglected to chide a child for writing 'wint' (rather than went) but that I didn't seem to *mind* it. Infant equivalent of shock–horror: last year's rules specifically denied the word's existence in written form. It is such examples, apparently trivial, that really tell you about children's expectations, needs and insecurities.

It may take nearly two terms to build up a readiness for a more open-ended timetable, sometimes only ten weeks or so; having the same class for two years pays impressive dividends. It may be necessary to make, though, a bold start at the beginning of the year to abandon grouping on anything other than a friendship basis or according to the task in hand. Dismantling grouping later in the year is particularly difficult for both children and parents.

Although it is a problem rarely acknowledged except amongst practitioners, trying to establish a non-differentiated learning environment in an open-plan setting can positively hinder progress in this direction. Colleagues' enthusiasm for it apart, the constraints of space and resources encourage a tendency towards differentiation. The timetable is a salutary example of what can happen when five teachers, four 'homebases', 129 infant children, one craft area, one Wendy house, 129 chairs and a fair number of tables have to be accommodated in one cavernous area. Although changed by the advent of a new head, it was a timetable that lasted for five or six years, the ultimate in differentiation. The 'home bays' to which an equal number of children were allotted were 'Jade', 'Sapphire', 'Topaz' and 'Amber'. The children were vertically grouped and the timetable reference to 'Rabbits', 'Dogs' and 'Budgies' indicates this grouping-technique. Thus a child might be an Amber Budgie, a Topaz Rabbit or a Jade Dog. (The less fortunate were referred to as 'remedial Rabbits/Dogs/Budgies'.)

As can be seen from figure 41.1, the nature and duration of every child's activity was detailed with a military precision which often took two or three days of each summer holiday to finalize.

The emotional effect on the children was to make them very dependent on the timetable. It also meant that children were infrequently addressed by their own personal names and more often by the group they were in. One wonders whether a child addressed as a friendly pet today might not be insidiously addressed as a number tomorrow. On record is the mother who rang up, not to find out if Johnny was swimming, but whether the Budgies were. A six-year-old Amber Budgie can be quite overcome when it realizes that it is doing combined sounds (six) with Sapphire Rabbits when it *ought*

	Monday	Tuesday	Wednesday	Thursday	Friday
A.M. 1	D Maths. Extra cards 10 a.m. PE B News R News (AS words in area)	Hymn practice—new rabbits with student (Mohammed to AS) D Movement B+R Group skills in Dining-Bay + reading (double sounds)	D Music B+R Peak maths 11.30–12 Recorders	4 Cooking with EP D Peak maths B Video–'Alive and kicking' R Movement	9.10 Recorders D Peak maths B Movement R Music Room
A.M. 2	Remedial Dogs– reading and words D News B Practical maths in Bay + reading R Craft D Dinner-time reading	D TV (4 readers to PS) MD Reading at 11.15 B Music R Maths + apparatus + reading + phonic sheet	D Measuring (AE half Dogs) B English–Rainbow reading R English–Rainbow TV Nature project every 2nd wk with half Dogs	D 4 every 2nd week to measure with student. Reading + English B Craft TV follow-up + colour cards with AS R English + reading	D English + reading- group skills in Dining-Bay Combined sounds B Peak maths + reading R Reading
P.M. 3	D Sapphire craft B TV R Sapphire craft 3.00 Tape story	D Craft + readers B Group time in Bay –practical maths R Maths skills	D Comprehension or Rainbow B Peak maths 2–2.30 PE R 1.30–2 PE Set English work with student	2 Clay. 4 Sewing at 2.00 D Imaginative writing + reading + phonics + handwriting B English–phonic books + handwriting R TV	John, Penny, Sukhvinder –phonics with AS D New maths + finish work + reading B Games + reading R Craft in Bay + reading

Figure 41.1

to be doing craft with what's left of the Topaz Budgies after the others have gone to do their nature project. In such a highly organized system, where is the opportunity, the time, the place for reflection, observation and exploration? These are vital mental activities if children are to make any kind of attempt at making their world a coherent place to live in.

Timetables such as these exist in all their dubious glory because of an unspoken need to impose order on life, especially life as presented by a large group of potentially anarchic thinkers with emotional responses lying only too close to the surface. Why are we as teachers afraid of the apparent chaos offered by alternative methods? Why are we afraid to let the children be learners in their own right? Perhaps because we in our turn were not allowed the time and chance to explore the outer world and our inner feelings. As teachers, though, we have one advantage – a certain courage: a courage to change things, even if gradually. By exploring the world alongside the children, we too learn what it is to be a learner and pass on our increasing confidence in ourselves by giving increasing opportunities to the children.

42

Setting out the store: Hillsview Infants School

Cilla Biles

In this chapter, Cilla Biles tells how she and her staff at a Newcastle infants school set about developing a curriculum for the school, based on children learning from first-hand experience. The pupils made many visits out of school; then the experience was preserved, extended and exploited by re-creating the visited environment in the classroom. This provided a continuous, rich resource for developing interests, for practical learning and for problem-solving.

INTRODUCTION

Hillsview Infants School is situated on the edge of a large council estate, North Kenton, on the north-west outskirts of the city of Newcastle upon Tyne.

The school caters for 130 infant children and has a nursery unit of forty places. Attached to the school, but serving the whole city, is a speech and language unit known within the school as Class 7.

The school is organized on a two-form entry basis. The staff consists of six infant-teachers, one non-class-based teacher and two auxiliaries. The nursery staff consists of two nursery teachers and two nursery nurses. Class 7 has its own class-teacher and a teacher–therapist who works between the infant and junior units. During the last three years we have shared an extra teacher appointment with the junior school to help us to develop our community and parental involvement.

The single-storey, flat-roofed building is positioned around an inner court-yard. We share a generous, though windswept, site of six acres with our junior school, which is adjacent.

The school and estate were built some twenty-five years ago during a major rehousing-scheme for tenants from the inner city. The area was later designated a 'social priority area'. North Kenton is a fairly well established community. Several second-generation families are now in school and quite a few pupils share family relationships.

In recent years the building of Kingston Park, a vast mixed housing-estate separated from the school by an industrial estate, has provided another catchment area. The ratio of pupils attending from each area is almost exactly equal. The school thus serves two geographically separate communities.

How could we meet the needs of all our children? How could we provide experiences which would extend the able children whilst providing incentives and interest for the less able; which would develop personal and social skills; which would enrich the children's experience?

The situation and the challenge will be a familiar one to many teachers. Our efforts to meet that challenge were to be the starting-points of several avenues of curriculum development.

Parental involvement in their children's learning was considered high on the priority list. Parents need assurance of their own importance in their children's lives and to understand that learning and attitudes to learning are not confined to school. Shared family experiences give opportunities for recall and discussion. Knowledge of what is happening in school means further plans can be made, to repeat, or add to, these experiences. Home and school complement each other.

Resources both in and about the school were to be extended and used to the full. A reading resource area was established containing reading-books and appropriate back-up materials which were graded by staff and colour-coded by parents. A reference library was established here too. A group of parents came regularly to play reading-games with the children. Library visits, story sessions and a home reading-scheme began. A reading-booklet was produced containing advice and suggestions on the ways parents can help their children using home- and family-based activities.

A comprehensive maths scheme was introduced giving continuity and allowing for individual progress.

Science, art, cookery and PE resources were also added to, so providing scope for a wider range of activities.

We looked outside our school and considered the playground resources. Parents painted games such as hopscotch and snakes-and-ladders on the yard surface. A garage and home corner appeared on the walls. More ambitious plans were made, and play dens, a vegetable garden, sandpit, lawns and flowerbeds were added to the nursery garden. Parents were invited to enter a competition to design a monster for the sandpit. Besides designs and drawings we received stories and poems.

We put another sandpit, a vegetable garden, a small pond, a mini-beast garden and an animal pen in the inner courtyard.

We looked at our resources in terms of teacher talents and we held a series of in-service courses for all the staff on class activities emphasizing progression. The first sessions were on claywork, next printing, sand and water and then play. We studied the nature of play, its social and emotional value and the contribution it could make to the children's learning. (Through play the children have the opportunity to relive and absorb, and re-enact their experiences.) Sensitive teacher intervention encourages involvement in the play situation and the use of real tools wherever possible adds a touch of realism.

The audio-visual resources available were considered. We opted for more cassette recorders and evaluated the use of television programmes. TV programmes were felt to be expensive, the stimulus limited and subjects often not suitable to a whole class's needs. They involved timetabling, and to an extent dictated the curriculum without always inspiring new developments. The camera chooses the view and the whole experience becomes second-hand. We agreed not to have a TV for one year. Each year since then staff have voted not to rent a TV. However we have, lately, conceded that a TV with video would be an asset. We could then show what is relevant, when and to whom we wished. This was confirmed recently in a top-infant class literature-based project on Robinson Crusoe. The children had tried several self-supporting activities such as making pots, grinding corn and making bread and butter. They had watched a goat being milked and had made cheese from its milk. A BBC series of programmes on the story of Robinson Crusoe was being broadcast at the same time. Discovering this the teacher borrowed a video recording of the same. She chose extracts to show the children which enabled them to identify with the characters and their problems. The level of excitement and interest was high. The class-teacher thought this was the best way to do such a project and would wish to organize future projects similarly.

Without TV, we concentrated on providing stimuli based on first-hand experience. Children have a natural spontaneous curiosity about the world around them. Watch a group of children walk past a puddle! We would build on that interest by introducng them to a wider world to investigate. The excitement of personal discovery would provide the starting-point for discussion, observation, recording and inquiry at all levels. Children with limited use of language would be given something to talk about. We would go out and about, make visits and welcome visitors.

We hired a minibus for one morning each week. We set up a rota for its use and timetabled the supernumerary to work with that class for the whole day. Parents accompanied us and a registered list of parent volunteers drove. With this arrangement we could make two trips so that a whole class could share the outing. Most outings were within a five-mile radius of school but the minibus considerably widened the range of experiences. Visits within the immediate environment could be made on foot.

These outings were carefully prepared. Teachers made preliminary visits if possible, to make personal contacts, note danger points, particular interests, length of time taken and limits of access and involvement offered. Children were included in planning so that they could look forward to their outing and join in the preparations. All accompanying adults were fully informed of progress and the purpose of the visit. The visits were immensely successful. Parents, staff and children said so. But, afterwards, 'Do we have to write about it!' and similar comments showed dwindling enthusiasm. How could we retain the excitement of the visit? How could we extend the interest to provide incentives for research, experimentation and problem-solving, for language enrichment and creativity?

The practice grew that following an outing the children would re-create, as realistically as possible, the visited environment.

THE CAFÉ: RECEPTION CLASS

Class 6 were making buns one morning. The conversation turned to cafés. They talked about buying cakes and orange juice when they went shopping with their parents. They said they would like to visit the café in Kingston Park when they went shopping for cookery ingredients.

Some children said they would like to make a café in the class. They were talking about what they would need when one child suggested going to a 'real one' and asking the ladies who work there.

The class went to visit in groups. They bought their own orange juices and enjoyed being customers. The ladies who worked there were very obliging and told the children about menus, and the various aspects of the job.

The children returned to school with words such as 'menu', 'uniform', 'crockery', 'cutlery', 'service', 'waitress', 'cook', 'manageress' and 'supplier'. They talked about how the food was prepared and linked this with cooking at school. They discussed what they would need in their café: a kitchen, sitting-area, counter, till, food, crockery and cutlery. They decided to make dough food: dinners, teas, puddings. We talked about meals, which brought in times of the day, breakfast, dinner, tea. Some children found twelve o'clock on the clock and four o'clock – teatime. They wrote about the meals they enjoyed and drew pictures of them. Menus were written and priced using 1 p coins, with a maximum price of 10 p. The children enjoyed role play and became waitresses, cooks, customers, dads and mums, salespeople. They became interested in types of food, what was good for you and what was bad for you. This led to work on care of the teeth. When the children's interests had begun to follow a different line of inquiry, the classroom project finished.

THE BUS: CLASS 7 (SPEECH–LANGUAGE UNIT)

Interest in the café project was generated from the children's own activity. Other starting-points may be teacher-inspired, suggested by parents, develop from other curriculum areas, from classroom chats or from reading-books.

Interest in the class bus grew initially through the children reading the early books of the Link Up reading-scheme, in which a bus and driver figure prominently, and through a tour of the city made by the class on the top deck of a bus.

On returning to school the children made a bus with cardboard. This involved estimating lengths, cutting and painting, and they discussed and made various destination signs, some of them referring to local destinations, some reinforcing vocabulary from the reading-scheme.

Play in the bus involved the children in a great deal of spoken language, creating situations where they were motivated to ask questions, (they find this very difficult) and providing a framework around which they could structure simple but spontaneous sentences. They also, some of them for the first time, used language to project into imaginary situations and roles and transcripts were made of their play. Three of the children in the group were still at the stage of counting and matching numbers below ten, and the bus tickets were all priced and colour-matched with real destinations, thus involving recognition of the appropriate numeral and counting of coins.

By watching the children play through the routine of catching the bus, the teacher noticed that they often fidgeted with things within their reach. She fastened a string, with beads and matching figure, by the bus stop. As she hoped, the children counted the beads whilst waiting for the bus.

This timely intervention by the teacher is important. She or he must be sensitive to the children's needs. Observation of the activity will help pinpoint the appropriate time and method: a bit of role play or providing the right props may help solve a problem.

THE NEWSAGENT'S: MIDDLE INFANTS

This class decided to have a newsagent's in the classroom in response to interest generated by play in the new home corner. They wanted to develop a shop to help with our number work and thought a newsagent's would be different and that it would also link well with the house, as we could have a delivery boy.

The teacher originally approached the local newsagent to see if he could let them have some out-of-date newspapers, comics and magazines. He was very generous. He gave shop overalls, dummy sweet boxes and stands and, most useful of all, his old order-book. The children gained a great deal from the shop, taking orders, paying bills and delivering to the house. The local newsagent visited the class shop when it was completed and was impressed by the interest and enthusiasm shown by the children.

The class went on to make their own newspaper; they sold sweets at the newsagent's and made a block graph of 'our favourite sweets'.

THE COMMUNITY AS A RESOURCE

In the classroom the standard home play corner disappeared, as classes used the space to re-create a range of different environments – in addition to those already mentioned, a hairdresser's, a bakery, a sweetshop, a butcher's shop, a library and a clinic. We found that through this creativity the children relived and absorbed their experience, extended their own play, and provided a learning-resource within the classroom which the teacher could use to her advantage.

The hairdresser's shop needed style books, appointment books, a telephone, price lists, a clock, hair-driers, rollers. The library contained reference and story books, children's own illustrations and writings, a ticket system and a date stamp. The children sorted books, filed tickets, became authors and illustrators.

Problem-solving situations arose naturally. A visit to a garage prompted, 'How can we make a car-washing machine with rollers that turn?', 'How does the air get in the wheels?'

The open-ended aspect of the activity means that children at all stages can be included in an appropriate way. The use of real tools wherever possible – bicycle pump, hammers, screwdrivers, and so on – adds authenticity. The children are able to experiment and find answers to their questions. Reference skills are practised, new skills discovered, basic skills reinforced.

The community and its environment become a curriculum resource.

HILLSVIEW SQUARE

As each project finished in the classroom and new interests started, the staff considered the prospect of sharing their classes' work to provide a resource for the whole school.

The front entrance area to the school is a large, little used space which had not proved suitable for other ideas – too dark for display, too barren for teaching purposes, too cold for a library – but was ideal for this scheme. So the idea was born to establish within this area a resource based on the children's first-hand experiences within the community to be shared by the whole school. Whatever local shopping, environmental or community topic classes were doing was to continue within each class until finished and would then, if suitable, be transferred to the entrance hall.

First shops were a hair salon, a sweetshop, a newsagent's, a bakery, a greengrocer's, a butcher's and a café. Some items needed modification or repair before they could be used. Quality was to be the keynote and as many real tools and situations as possible were to be introduced. £12.50 was spent on paint and some material for aprons and tablecloths. Much ingenuity was needed to create shopping-bays, screens, and so on.

Enthusiasm ran high and parents quickly became interested. 'Every school should have this', said one. Gifts began to arrive: a real coffee pot and cups and saucers for the café, clothes for the boutique (some refashioned by talented staff), curlers and curling-tongs, jewellery, and so on. Cardboard boxes were converted into a washing-machine, a tumble drier, and screens for changing-rooms.

The children started to use the area. They loved it and still do. Groups of children of different ages can work or play together with an auxiliary, a nursery nurse, a teacher or parent. Teachers can utilize the area for work purposes, and there are some wordbooks, wordcards and shopping-bills available. Others will be made as the need arises.

A fish-and-chip shop, clinic, dentist's, post office and library were soon added to the scene and the need for a name arose. 'Hillsview Square' was chosen by the children.

It soon became apparent that bringing these projects out of the classrooms and putting them together created further opportunities for extending them. The café, which had begun in the reception class, required more menus, which were very realistically priced by the older infants.

Visiting a hairdresser or dentist means that appointments must be made. A clock, an appointments book, a telephone and directory needed to be made. Everybody in school has a number and we have a 'Yellow Pages' for the shops.

One thing leads to another. Parents supervised sessions of baking and selling cakes in the bakery. With the money thus made the children contributed towards an incubator and were able to hatch their own duck eggs and give the ducks swimming-lessons in our pond. The children have gardens where they grow their own flowers and vegetables. We were able to sell them through the greengrocer's and use them for cookery. The boutique proved enormously popular and was extended to include a hat and shoe shop.

Hillsview Square itself provided incentives for further developments. A post office needed a sorting office; the café required an adjacent cake shop.

OLD-TIME SHOPPING: TOP INFANTS

After contributing to and experiencing other class projects in the Square one class decided to explore other shopping-areas. Four areas were chosen: a very modern shopping-precinct close to the school; the market in the new Eldon Square complex in Newcastle; and two areas where the influence of the Victorian era was much in evidence – the Central Arcade and the old covered market.

With the help of mothers, visits were made and worksheets, provided by the local Architecture Workshop, were enthusiastically completed by the children, who found many other things of interest whilst tracking down shapes, patterns, colours, and so forth. Discussions took place; rubbings, sketches, plasticine moulds and notes were avidly worked upon. In the Central Arcade the general public seemed intent on joining in our work and in this way opportunities were provided for the children to give explanations about their activities. Follow-up work was completed, and sheets from a Schools Council pack on shopping were incorporated at this time.

A Victorian general store was set up in the classroom, the children adapting a shopfront from those seen on their visits. Artefacts were borrowed from

Northern Counties College Museum. Other provisions were pens and ink, bill-headings, bills of 1900 showing prices, old money, costumes of the period. Children produced a stock-book. Staff and parents gave fantastic support, and the children saw objects which they found very exciting, such as an Edison phonograph. One mother provided plates which pictorially represented the trades of that period, but when it was discovered that they were Wedgwood they were admired, discussed and hastily sent home again.

After experience of this shop a member of Benwell Drama Centre came in, in the role of a university professor who had heard of the children's expertise on shops in the Victorian era and wanted them to help him set up a museum. This involved the children in discussion, using their library skills to research, designing Victorian shopfronts, deciding which shops to put in the museum (voting took place) and setting up the museum. The children chose a barber's shop, a toyshop, a dress shop and a hatter's.

Authenticity was aimed for both in objects and in experiences. For example, the barber's shop had its shaving-mug, brush and soap, but we did draw the line at actually using the real cut-throat razor. The dress shop had Victorian dresses in it as well as the children's reproductions. Much creative work was completed in the setting up of the museum and measurement was a predominant feature of both dress shop and hatter's. The children took the decision to write descriptions of articles in the museum, but, after a visit to a local museum, they decided to make a tape-recording describing objects in the shop.

Great interest was shown in the decorative Victorian books which various people had provided, and a parent brought to school a calligrapher who lived in our local community. He showed the children examples of his work and on several afternoons came into the classroom, where the children could watch him at work and experience his art themselves. The culmination of this work was a costume performance of old-time music hall, to which all parents and friends of the school were invited. The hats were made in the hatter's, of course.

INVOLVING THE NURSERY

The nursery, too, played an important part in all this development. The closest liaison possible is kept between school and nursery, and nursery staff are fully involved in policies regarding progression, continuity and development. Their long experience of visits and parental involvement was valuable to us in many ways.

The nursery children enjoy their explorations of the neighbourhood and have many local friends: the school gardeners, the dustbin men, the community policemen and the many residents who pass by our nursery garden.

A favourite place to visit is our city farm. We can borrow small animals to visit us for a day. This interest in animals is to be the starting-point of

'Hillsview pet-shop'. Models of animals will be made for the home corner and appropriate foods sold through the shop. A real guinea-pig for the nursery will add some authenticity.

In their vegetable garden the children have grown their own peas, beans, turnips and potatoes. They matched these with the pretend ones in the shop and then found pictures of them in their books. They harvested their crops and 'sold' them through the greengrocer's. Then they bought them back, made soup and shared it.

The home corner provides many opportunities for socializing, role play and communications. A further development was to set up specific rooms for a period of time. A dining-room, kitchen, bathroom, sitting-room and bedroom were each introduced in turn. A current project about water, washing and drying will eventually come into the Square and add interest to the launderette. The children always enjoy dressing up, and this has been furthered by the introduction of a jewellery shop: fantastic cardboard glasses with coloured lenses, necklaces of beads and pendants are now on sale.

Besides these contributions to the Square, the nursery children benefit from the wide range of activities and equipment available. They name, compare and match various items, discuss the provision made and may suggest ideas of their own. They meet older children and join in their play and activity. By sensitive intervention the adults concerned can extend and enrich the children's language and stimulate their interest in the world around them.

A great deal of liaison work between nursery and school takes place. Hillsview Square strengthens these links by providing a resource for play and learning to be shared by all. Children meet new members of staff, other parents and older children in a friendly situation. This integration is part of our policy of discovering the community in which we live.

CLASS 7

Class 7, the speech and language unit, was luckier than the rest of us. They had a minibus one morning every two weeks. A small group from other classes joined in each visit filling up the seats. They helped with the follow-up work in the afternoons.

These regular outings were of immense value to Class 7. The children in this group have a wide range of language handicaps. They all have, to some degree, problems of articulation which makes understanding of their conversation impossible at times. Their own comprehension of language may be extremely limited, so that they don't understand what others are telling them. They haven't assimilated basic language structures and need highly programmed teaching to do so. The children can rehearse their therapy in their play. This helps to bridge the gap between formal therapy and spontaneous language and builds towards greater language competence.

A visit by Class 7 to the fish quay resulted in a fish-and-chip feast in the staffroom. Then a pretend fish-and-chip shop was set up in the classroom. Mushy peas, chips and sausages were made from dough. Towelling was cut into fish shapes, sewn together, stuffed and painted yellow. The results looked exactly like breadcrumbed fish. Scoops were cut from plastic bottles and the friers were cardboard boxes from the local supermarket covered with sticky back silver paper! From this source we were also given a small mound of polystyrene trays.

CONCLUSIONS

We have realized, under our noses, a living resource for extending all branches of language work – something to talk about, record, create and discuss. There are endless opportunities for tackling problems: 'Now we've made a hamster cage with a door that opens, how do we keep it shut?' There are incentives too, for other areas of the curriculum. Maths, creative activities, technology, science can be presented realistically and purposefully.

Because of the open-ended aspect of the work, children can challenge themselves by tackling situations which extend their normal classroom activities, learning to cope with large amounts of money on price lists, to use an alphabetically listed directory, scale drawings, maps and plans. The children gain confidence and self assurance. They become more observant and outward-looking. They develop inquiring minds and can clearly express themselves and their experiences in a variety of ways. Through their ensuing activity and play the children relive and absorb their experiences so identify with and appreciate themselves, their neighbours and their surroundings. They develop a positive self-image. They can share in decision-making, make suggestions and help organize the work. They can accept responsibility with the encouragement of their teachers. There are opportunities for all children to participate and develop, and constructive co-operation between children is fostered.

The success of each stage of development encourages staff to undertake more ambitious projects. Their expectations of the children are heightened and they become experts at exploiting new situations. The parents can become more actively involved in their children's life at school by sharing their experiences or demonstrating their talents.

Putting the projects in a central place to be shared by all means further opportunities to draw on. Mixed-age groups of children can work and play together. Children can demonstrate their contributions, share new-found skills and learn from each other. It wides their experience.

Using the community as a curriculum resource has helped us to achieve our aims. We have found a source of inspiration on which to base a wide and balanced curriculum, full of first-hand experiences and popping with problem-solving situations.

43

Secondary schools as a resource for everyone's learning

John Sayer

John Sayer, formerly the head teacher of a large comprehensive school, sees two major interconnected impediments to progress in secondary education: the subject system with its associated timetable, which downgrades the status of so much educational activity deemed 'extra-curricular', and the sixteen-plus examination system, untouched in its essentials by GCSE reforms. John Sayer's proposals for reform are twofold. First, the secondary curriculum should go modular, with all relevant activity in or out of 'the school day' accounted for. Second, the class should be abandoned as the basic learning-group. Groups should be small, and formed and reformed as new tasks call for new groups.

INTRODUCTION

Schools are now forced to live an organizational lie. Their physical structure is determined by a nineteenth-century maximum-control unit called the classroom; their curricula, despite all the additions and modifications, are still largely determined by a public examination system established in 1917 to reflect the regulations of 1904; and their staffing is still essentially according to class size and subject specialism.

Meanwhile, their avowed aims have changed out of all recognition, and are in conflict with observable practice. Pupils and courses have been aggregated upon the existing physical and organizational structures, to the point at which these creak wretchedly. There is little correspondence between the staffing of schools and the expectations upon school staffs, and recent disputes have been directly caused by that mismatch. There is an even greater mismatch between the educational needs or interests of young people and the school qualifications they believe they require, which take over the overt organization of the school.

Much of the recent planning for the integration of children with needs deemed to be educationally 'special', into schools described as 'ordinary', has wrongly assumed that the latter should remain as they are, and support be provided to enable the new element to be yet another aggregate, or be absorbed into the system as it now exists. This chapter is written on the contrary assumption that secondary schools will have to change rapidly and radically anyway, with or without the integration of those previously sheltered from them in special schools. Some of the changes are readily identifiable; but the greatest change of all will have to be towards an organization which is capable of constant change, not only to respond to already known needs, but to be responsive to future demands which nobody can be sure of knowing many years in advance.

From inside and outside the system, fingers are pointed at known deficiencies and wrong priorities: too great an emphasis on subjects and on examinations which will lead to the academic success of a minority at the expense of relative or outright failure by a rejected majority; overemphasis on knowledge-building and regurgitation subject by subject, and too little regard for the whole learning process, for those skills not encapsulated in a subject curriculum or related to a qualifying examination; inability to recognize young people's contribution to each other, or to encourage them to manage their own learning; glaring irrelevancies, incoherence, omissions and outmoded habits; little sign of adaptation to the rapidly changing lifestyles and career opportunities or lack of them, for which school is a prelude and preparation; little-enough shift in the system to enable the school and the community to grow together and learn from each other. In many schools, the rhetoric of change is there; but most are trapped in an organization which conditions a largely unchanged reality.

PRESENT PRACTICE AND PRIORITIES

Teachers are recruited and trained by subject specialism. Whatever else they may be prepared for, the subject is the basis of their appointment and that to which most of their time is devoted. Other calls upon them are considered to be extras or interruptions. They are organized in subject departments, and only after the demands of the subject programme have been met are they made available for work which is not subject-specific.

Some subjects are more important than others, for future qualifications. So their demands for time are given priority, and their organizational requirements – frequency of impact, location, groupings – also come first, leaving the more flexible or less demanding subjects to squeeze into odd corners of the day and the building, if necessary with classes split between teachers. For similar reasons, the overall programme of those who are approaching public examination has priority over earlier years, and sometimes over those of the same age who are not served by public examinations anyway. These priorities become even more apparent during industrial disputes.

As falling rolls affect the school population above the age of fourteen, the priorities become sharpened to the point of taking out the 'less important' options, particularly the expressive arts, social- and life-skills groups, and extra-curricular activity. As teachers find themselves blocked in career aspirations and uncertain about the future, they are forced back into the apparent security of the subject they came to teach, and are more reluctant to explore the margins, in case they find themselves treated as marginal. There *is* a lot of good practice and development; but it is in spite of the basic organization of schools and not because of it. Governmental gadflies urge on the old horse-drawn carriage of the curriculum whilst at the same time overloading it, preventing its overhaul and replacement, and even tethering it permanently to the repainted post of a 1917 school certificate.

Because the school system is organized to give priority to subject-certificate qualification, all specialisms must be represented in the two-year array of options leading to certificates at sixteen. For them to be options, they must figure in the pre-fourteen timetable too, visibly and separately. So the fragmented single-subject overcrowding of the timetable in the early years of secondary schooling is caused and maintained by the examination system. Without future surrender value, no educational programme is taken seriously for its own sake.

Curriculum analysis has been largely reduced, therefore, to the formal subject programme. It does not include the extra-curricular activities which are declared as essential to the planned intentions of a school but left to happen by individual initiative, corporate ethos or magic, without time, training or resource. Nor does it include school visits, field studies, musical-instrument teaching and the many other accepted features of school life which are squeezed into the tolerance levels of the system, negotiated as concessions, felt as interruptions. There is an overlay, for about one third of the school year, of public and school examination timetables, which affect not only those being examined but also the specialist teaching-spaces where others would normally be learning. The in-service education and training of teachers does not figure on a timetable; it is resented by parents and other teachers because it is seen to result in the absence of the regular teacher and because other teachers have to be drafted in their 'free' time to replace such absentees. Nobody sees that it is the inadequate system which creates the problem, not the professional activity.

So teachers are organized as though most of their time, about four fifths, were spent in classroom subject-teaching, and everything else packed into the remaining one fifth of the school day; whereas the only sound research into their professional activity (Hilsum and Strong, 1978) shows exactly the opposite: the timetable of subject lessons is only one fifth of the whole of their professional activity, and the other four fifths goes uncharted, unrecognized and unrewarded. That is the organizational lie of my first sentence, and at the root of much present misunderstanding, conflict and dissatisfaction in secondary schools.

ORGANIZING FOR THE FUTURE

School organization has to become the instrument of change – not change to a different system, but constant change. Change will reflect the changing context of the school; the political will of the society it serves; the lives of those it helps to learn; the professional development of good practice. But change will also be generated by the climate and corporate will of the school community itself.

Planning context can mean one of two very different approaches: either a school is given a definite slice of the customer cake and is left to consume it; or it is identified as a contributor to the education of people who are also learning in other settings. Either could be described as the school's share; but they lead in opposite directions. The first works inwards; there are times of the day, week and year when customers are expected to come in and stay in, and the school curriculum is pursued at those times and in that place. When schools were established, they were the main sources of knowledge; and, when they were made compulsory for certain age-groups, that meant getting them in and not letting them out until they were a finished product. Times have changed: schools are now, to be sure, a significant part of young people's learning experience, but have to be related to other significant parts, latching on to learning through new media, acknowledging a linkage with lives lived at home, work and leisure. Schools are an early part of lifelong learning, and are becoming increasingly a continuing part of it, through community education. For that direction to be developed further, school organization requires a revolution towards responsiveness. Coherence has to be external as well as internal to the school programme. The whole curriculum is not just about school. The school day and the school timetable in isolation cease to have meaning.

This chapter will outline two radical practical changes in organization which could have a profound influence on the school's capacity to lead into future contexts. The first is already happening: a modular approach to school programmes. The second appears to have assent in principle rather than practice: an organization derived from learning-groups. Both are vital to those who have previously been considered to need attention beyond what an ordinary school could provide.

Modular approaches

Various experiments and proposals have emerged recently, to express the school programme in short sections or modules. One of the most accessible, though by no means the most radical, is the ILEA report *Improving Secondary Schools* (Inner London Education Authority, 1984). Instead of courses being described in one- or two-year sequences, they are built of complete elements, of perhaps forty to fifty hours, or across a number of weeks, perhaps half a term. Each element is assessed in its own right, and contributes to a record of achievement. The school organization is built like blocks. These may be confined to the formal subject curriculum, a painless transition from existing standard practice; or they may include the non-formal and extend beyond the compulsory school programme.

Even if a modular system is confined to the formal subject timetable, much can be done which has otherwise proved too difficult for most schools. It remains possible to build a long course studied in depth, across a whole year, two years or more; it will be a progression through perhaps six or twelve half-termly modules. But, because each module is discrete, it is also possible for a student to put together a batch of modules across subjects, and be accredited with as many as six in different subjects instead of six in the same subject through the year. Breadth and depth then become organizationally compatible. This is particularly important as schools try to manage whole package courses, such as some of the existing City and Guilds 365 or Foundation courses, or the new framework for the Certificate in Pre-Vocational Education, and make them compatible with single-subject curricula. If they are not compatible, the result is a separate group of lower achievers on package courses, with the single-subject courses targeted at an increasingly academic and prestigious subject examination, in the incoming General Certificate of Secondary Education. Modular programming could be both an antidote and a preparation for better things to come.

It becomes possible for groups of teachers to explore the interconnections of their work in a module of half a term, and combine to develop skills across or without subjects, in ways which are impossible if they are grappling with the whole of a year's course or even more. We shall see also that it becomes possible to release teachers for a module in the year, to have time to develop connecting work. So an organizational framework can be created which makes compatible the single-subject, interdisciplinary and skills-based programmes with all of which schools are now involved.

Moreover, it then becomes possible to meet the needs of individuals much more flexibly, through continuous counselling and review. It is no longer necessary for those pursuing single-subject courses to terminal qualification to be separated for all their activities from those committed to 'package' vocationally oriented courses, or indeed from those whose needs are not best met by long-term commitment of either kind. So this has particular interest to those of us who recognize the yawning gap between the processes of many special schools and units, and the ability to cope with the linear organization and demands of much that goes on in mainstream schools. Modular stages give all students an opportunity to see and understand what it is they are committing themselves to; to set targets within reach; to have credit for achievement in the short term, and the option of continuing if so motivated, or of achievement in a different short course if not. A modular approach also enables schools to offer 'balance' and 'breadth', however interpreted, not necessarily all at once in a weekly diet, but across a longer period, perhaps returning to a subject after a break. Finally, if there were a general practice across the country of modular programming, with credit for each module of half a term, this would ease the problems of removal from one school to another; and if the modular structure were standard in an area, it would help schools to co-operate and interchange teachers or pupils.

So far, we have considered only a modification in the way courses are expressed in the formal, compulsory part of secondary schooling. What of all those other activities which are associated with schools, and the many more which would be if school organization were more flexible? Planning access to the curriculum for all must, after all, include all activities planned and intended through the school, and access to the extensions curiously called extra-curricular can be most important and has been the most neglected in moves towards comprehensive integration.

There are, indeed, subjects in the formal curriculum which make no organizational sense without related opportunities beyond the timetable: notably music and physical education, but also, in their different ways, foreign languages, home economics, and indeed anything remotely 'relevant' to children's lives in any subject. Look at music: it is expressed in a school timetable as one hour each week in class; unmentioned in the formal curriculum are instrument-teaching, choral and orchestral practice, school performance, involvement in the community's music-making, visits to concerts or concerts brought into schools. All of these are actually happening already, but over and above school organization, often impeded by it and seen to interrupt it. In a modular record, credit would be given for forty hours building towards a musical performance, whenever the hours have been in the day and week; or for instrument-learning, which already lends itself to graded achievement by modular stages. Course modules could be offered to adults alongside children, and related to existing courses in adult education. Short programmes of this kind would lend themselves to linkage with distance learning, broadcast series, and contributions from visiting artists. If the music-making day were recognized to be across sixteen hours rather than five, it would be possible for those active musicians already constantly involved to be taking other classroom modules rather than the required minimum classroom ingredient, which can at present hold them back, disenchant them and in fact add to the imbalance of their curricular experience; or they would contribute to a performing-arts module, using their music activity to broaden their own work and others'. A quite different view of balance and breadth begins to emerge.

With this, there emerges a different role for teachers, too, requiring time, development and adjustment. A modular approach to school organization does, however, make it possible to include in programming precisely those training-activities which at present are seen as interruptions to the teaching-day, or which are taken outside working-hours in order to avoid interruption. A teacher or group of teachers can be timetabled into a training or curriculum-development module for half a term, without interrupting anyone or anything. Professional development and in-service education can be included in the planning of the school organization, and be a part of the staffing calculation. Short and long courses can be programmed in, the latter being interpreted as a sequence of modules. The distinctions between in-house training and external courses with secondment need not be so sharp.

Learning-groups

There is no reason to plan ahead on the assumption that the class of thirty will remain the basic unit of organization, or that learning-groups will continue to be formed from children of the same year of birth. Good classroom practice already works to learning-groups of five to eight, co-operating in experiment, in use of resources, and in programmes adapted to the group's needs. So why have the classroom? The answer is unlikely to be about learning. It may be about control; indeed, more time seems to be spent controlling a class than in teaching; and if HM Inspectors are correct in their observation that more than three quarters of the talk in classes is teacher talk, and are right in looking for that much pupil talk instead (Department of Education and Science, 1980), the reasons are not far to seek. If a teacher has at the same time to control thirty and teach, methods have to combine mass control and teaching. That means teacher-dominant modes for much of the time, with pupils following instructions, notes, and textbooks. Establish, instead of a class of thirty, five working-groups of six, with the teacher intervening for one fifth of the time instead of for four fifths, and it is more likely that learning situations will be created which at the same time bring out the individual and enable pupils to learn together as a team. It is also more likely that other adults will be involved with them, in each of the purpose groups or in any of them as required. We are pointing, then, towards the learning-network of small groups of children and helping adults, including members of their families, with teachers as organizers of group learning experiences. The question of 'withdrawing' pupils with special educational needs from the classroom ceases to have meaning if the classroom ceases to be the unit of organization. In any one learning-group, of the size which industry-trainers would stipulate for quality circles, we would expect provision to be made for one or two who might in other circumstances have been withdrawn; and the provision will include the resource of the other members of the group as well as adults and individually appropriate material resources.

The mixture of ages, not just in the obvious example of music, would also become more possible and would no longer be made artificially unnatural for those of school age. At present, many schools are limited to considering what is an appropriate programme for pupils of the same age, and are organized accordingly in one-year courses, one-year groups, and in tutorials with those whose date of birth falls in the same year. From this system and attitudes associated with it derive many of the artificial notions of special educational need: we have norms of expectation according to the chronological age, and those not within reach of the norm are deemed to require special and possibly separate attention. In a modular structure combined with small purpose groups as the learning-unit, it should become much easier to look at individual needs and responses across the board, and to have some courses in vertical groupings, making the decision according to individuals and small groups, and not because the organization is chronologically determined from the start. From the age of about fourteen, the organization can be developed to offer programmes of formal and informal education to all-age groups in a local community programme, of which the school is a central part and teachers a major resource.

CONCLUSION

What is briefly outlined here and developed in detail elsewhere (Sayer, 1985) is an approach to change towards a whole-school/whole-community resource for learning. It could be adopted without changing school courses at all, and perhaps that has to be a first stage; but it is conducive to change introduced in smaller units, without requiring the whole organization to be restructured again. In most schools, change towards a modular structure can be managed in stages, and the same applies to a transition to small-group work. At each stage, understanding, consent and commitment are as necessary for teachers as they are for pupils and parents. The likely outcomes, however, include a 'bottom-up' approach to the use of time, with or without school guidelines to ensure pursuance of such policies which have to be common; a change of the school day to encompass and reflect all the learning-activities for which the school can be a resource; a pupil-centred approach to appropriate course-building; a modification of school hierarchies; more emphasis on assessment and evaluation at points other than those at present monopolized by public examination; and more likelihood of recognized achievement at all levels, stages and ages. The greater the recognition given to the time and self-training needed by teachers to adapt to and develop these new approaches, the more likely are schools to be able to exploit them fully.

Many of the changes made possible by altering the organization of schools will be in keeping with the conditions required to make 'ordinary' schools into places responsive to a wider range of needs, including those described as 'special'. Needs are special only in so far as normal provision does not extend to them.

REFERENCES

Department of Education and Science 1980: *Aspects of Secondary Education.* London: HMSO.
Hilsum, S. and Strong, C. 1978: *The Secondary Teacher's Day.* Windsor: NFER.
Inner London Education Authority 1984: *Improving Secondary Schools* (Hargreaves Report). London: ILEA.
Sayer, J. 1985: *What Future for Secondary Schools?* London: Falmer Press.

44

Anti-sexism as good educational practice

Frankie Ord and Jane Quigley

Making a school more responsive to the needs, interests and aspirations of all its members involves changing the power relationships within it. The disparity in power between men and women is highly visible in many schools and may make a mockery of attempts by the school to represent girls or boys as equal in value. In this chapter Frankie Ord and Jane Quigley describe how the women in one school began to try to change the organization to produce a more even distribution of power and resources and to alter the devaluation of women within the school and its curriculum.

Implementing anti-sexist education involves change: a long and often painful process of changing people, changing ourselves and changing institutional procedures and structures. Change involves an uneasy balance between conflict and consensus – between moving too fast or too slow, between taking people with you or leaving them stranded and antagonistic. We recognize that power is not given up easily but is fought for both within the individual (raising consciousness) and then confronting institutional sexism. But we also recognize that we live in a deeply sexist society and what we can achieve within our schools is dependent to a large extent on how legitimate the issues are seen to be amongst colleagues, the education authority and the state.

This concept of change as balance is important in other ways too. Sexism must be confronted in both the hidden curriculum and in the actual organization and content of what is taught; we must work both at consciousness-raising and at changing educational practice; we must share our time between working with teachers and working with students. Do we concentrate on formulating whole-school policies or focus on small, sometimes trivial issues? When do we take on the more contentious issues (for example, sexual harassment, or male discipline procedures), and when do we opt for 'safer' issues (for example, register in alphabetical order or girls wearing trousers all year)? (Though having said this we are aware that in some schools all anti-sexist issues are 'hot'!) There is no one answer and each school will find its own 'balance for change'; but a recognition of the complexities of the struggle should guard against a rigid adherence to the notion of a *correct* formula.

Before considering in more detail how change has been effected in one London school, we want to make a few general comments that are applicable to our school and, we hope, more generally also.

It is very important that anti-sexism be seen as good educational practice rather than as an isolated or peripheral issue. It is too easy to dismiss gender as the concern of a few frustrated left-wing women and to see girls, along with blacks, as a problem to be placated with the odd concession. Eventually we do want to see gender and race as legitimate approaches to educational practice, so that in a consideration of, for example, option choice, mixed ability, the role of talk in the classroom, the perspective is anti-sexist and anti-racist. However, there is a long way to go before this situation can be realized.

In the meantime, one way we can avoid being marginalized is by operating through already-established school structures. If schools have, for instance, an academic board where curriculum decisions are made, then anti-sexist recommendations should be considered here and justified in terms of general educational principles. Similarly, tutor meetings, faculty meetings, staff-association meetings are the proper forums for anti-sexism to be raised. Gender must always be seen as a school issue, not a minority concern. After all, the under-achievement of half the school population – even if it is only the girls – can be emphasized as a legitimate area for teachers and educational institutions to consider. If the ultimate goal is real structural change in schools rather than cosmetic tinkering, then a first step is surely to avoid the 'working-party mentality' approach, where interested or partisan groups organize on the periphery of traditional school structures, able to make only the occasional foray into the real power base. Rather, we have a powerful case to put to schools and we must present it 'centre stage'. This, at least, has been our experience.

Stress is an increasingly recognized feature of teachers' lives and obviously taking on anti-sexism is not going to decrease it. As teachers, we face daily onslaughts on our egos and our confidence just from the nature of our job. We are also often tired and as a profession chronically short of time, resources and money. We need therefore to develop strategies to minimize the likely negative effects of attempting to implement anti-sexist practices. A working-party or support group is very important here, as is setting realistic, short-term goals and enlisting the support of 'popular' figures within the school.

First, the need for *a support group*. Without the active encouragement of other people, the familiar syndrome of failure, resentment, giving up is only too possible. It is frightening how quickly we run into hostility or dismissive amusement when quite small changes are suggested, and facing such reactions alone can be a daunting prospect. As we commented earlier, it is as well to be aware before beginning that power is not given away, that there will be conflict and that we need to be prepared for it. Opposition takes various forms: aggressive personal attacks, the raised eyebrows of 'Oh no, not this again', the stereotyping of one or two members of staff as 'the equal-opportunities people'. In this situation a support group is both a retreat and a base from which to launch further initiatives. It is also useful to remember that there are sources of support outside the school. Groups such as WedG (Women's Education Group), magazines such as *GEN* (the journal of WedG), and *CASSOE (Campaign Against Sexism and Sexual Oppression in Education*, a newsletter) provide a wider network and can prevent individual school groups from feeling isolated and insignificant. Equally important is that a support group can help us keep a sense of proportion. It should be a place where we can laugh at ourselves, at our mistakes and see that we don't take ourselves too seriously. It is essential to avoid the siege mentality, where school – and life – becomes a grim battle against a hostile world. One of the strengths of the Greenham Common women is that they come across as real people – warm, funny, human. And no one can doubt their effectiveness and commitment! We don't have to be martyrs or fanatics; in fact, the earnest crusader is often her own worst enemy as she wears herself out emotionally and physically while alienating even the potentially sympathetic. Developing anti-sexist strategies in schools is important, and we are committed to it. But it doesn't encompass the whole meaning of life, and our successes – and our failures – need to be kept in proportion.

Which brings us to the second strategy for success – *the setting of goals*. Nothing is more debilitating than constant failure, especially after an enormous amount of effort has been expended. We found that the sense of confidence gained from winning several small concessions was a source of strength and a basis for taking larger initiatives. Again, there is a temptation to minimize what we've achieved; it looks so paltry when compared with what has to be done. But we need to keep a sane awareness that institutional change is almost imperceptible and that hundreds of years of patriarchal dominance is not going to be overturned in our lifetime.

Lastly, if possible, it is very useful to have the support of one or two *key members* of staff. With depressing frequency, implementing anti-sexism in schools is still the prerogative of Scale 1 and Scale 2 teachers, who often lack experience and almost certainly lack power. Effecting change under these conditions is really an uphill battle. However, the situation is changing. Increasingly equal opportunities is becoming a legitimate educational interest and, although this has obvious dangers – you can kill an initiative or revolutionary movement as effectively by absorbing and neutralizing its energy as by opposing it – it also has possibilities which must be grasped. For instance, the appointment of equal-opportunities advisers in some boroughs and the establishment of equal-opportunities posts within schools means that equal opportunities is becoming a career possibility. This has two repercussions for feminists in schools. On the one hand, it means that head teachers, faculty and year heads, chairs of staff associations, and so on, can be more easily persuaded to see the expediency of anti-sexist issues. Secondly, it gives committed feminists an opportunity to get into positions of power themselves. There's a lot to be said for pulling from the front rather than pushing from behind: at least it makes a change!

We began this chapter talking about balance, and this concept applies also to relations between feminists working together in schools. We want to avoid the all too familiar spectacle of the Left tearing itself apart over internal differences. There is no one right way forward and we should adopt a flexible and conciliatory approach, accepting that there will be variations in style, beliefs and practices and allowing people the space to work in their particular way. What follows now is an account of how, from these general principles, one school has begun to develop anti-sexist practices amongst staff and students.

ONE SCHOOL'S EXPERIENCE

Brondesbury and Kilburn is a split-site London comprehensive in Brent. It is a social priority school of 800 pupils and sixty staff. It is largely a working-class school of girls and boys, and is racially mixed. For the last three years we have been battling against possible closure and falling rolls.

We began in 1977 with our own lives. A number of us became increasingly irritated with the school administration's persistent use of the 'Miss', 'Mrs' titles, despite our wishes. Irritation grew to anger, first from the liberal belief that our right to be referred to in the way we wanted was being ignored; then, as consciousness developed, we realized that these titles were symbols of a society which defined women according to their relationships with men (either you had one or you were still waiting!) and that this said something important about our position of power. The issue was raised at a staff meeting, when a popular and erudite deputy head linked the discussion to the wider oppression of women, to the lives of Jane Austen and Charlotte Brontë and to the educational experience of his daughter. The staff was gripped. Many women who at previous meetings had always remained silent gave their support by referring to their own lives. The vote was over-whelmingly in favour of the use of 'Ms' when a title was deemed necessary.

However, the vote was translated to mean that women staff-members had to inform the school secretary if they wished to transgress from the normal 'Miss'/'Mrs' position, hence labelling themselves extremists. Although a significant number of women did 'sign up', we were not organized enough, or indeed confident enough, to challenge the official interpretation.

Still, important change had occurred. People who trivialized the issue before the staff meeting certainly did not wish to, or dare to, afterwards. The intellectual tone of the discussion meant that, for as long as most of us stayed at the school, it would be difficult to sneer at feminism. Although we didn't all argue for the introduction of 'Ms' from the same viewpoint, for the first time we did experience some female solidarity.

In fact, it was not until 1982 that the school officially adopted 'Ms' as the norm for female teachers. However, exercise books, minutes, school brochures, even staff meetings reflected the acceptance of the new title well before this date.

By 1982 a number of significant changes were occurring both inside and outside our school. The growth of the women's movement, a much increased awareness about sexism in society generally and for us in Brent, the appointment of Hazel Taylor as equal-opportunities adviser all gave status and 'legitimacy' to our case. Inside our school, several feminists occupied powerful positions: a deputy in charge of the curriculum, a head of maths, head of fifth year. Most significant was the new chair of the staff association, a popular and strong feminist who was elected unopposed.

We took up the issue of sexism almost immediately. Several of us planned a 'mini' campaign both to increase staff awareness and also to bring about much-needed curricular change. Forever conscious of the danger of being dismissed as 'strident, male-hating and humourless', we produced a leaflet which included jokes and cartoons, as well as quotable quotes, relevant statistics, discussion questions and an invitation to attend a staff-association meeting where an articulate feminist was to speak, and wine and cheese would be served. We distributed the leaflet to all faculties and year groups, so discussion would take place before the meeting.

Our choice of speaker was good. She began with a series of factual and statistical slides which demonstrated that sexism in schools was not the product of over-heated feminist imagination. Her cool, reasoned delivery convinced those members of staff which a more impassioned polemic would have failed to reach.

A lively discussion was followed by the setting up of the inevitable equal-opportunities working-party, which represented all faculties. We reported back to the staff association two months later with a paper which argued for short-term practical changes: for instance that registers and class lists be alphabetical, that girls be permitted to wear trousers all year and that the option system be changed so that home economics and technology were not placed 'back-to-back'. Though well over half the staff voted in favour of these proposals, only the last one became official school policy at once, owing, in part at least, to the feminist deputy head in charge of curriculum. The other two met resistance of a kind which is both depressingly familiar and difficult for ordinary teachers to combat. We were told that school uniform is the responsibility of the governing body to legislate on; we had to wait for an agenda short enough to include our item. As for the registers, a Department of Education and Science ruling apparently made it impossible for us to reorganize them alphabetically. We pursued this ruling – the famous Form 7 – and as expected it proved easy to overcome. In September 1983 all registers were listed alphabetically.

Light-headed though these victories left us, no one would suggest that we were moving at a heady pace. Nor that our changes were radical. However, the organ of progress had been the staff association, and, as its aim was to be the voice of the ordinary teacher, we moved only as far as people were prepared to go. Meetings had to be well attended for decisions to be listened to by the hierarchy and – finally – implemented.

Our only real power lay in our collective voice. Therefore, though sexual harassment and the possibility of organizing single-sex groupings in certain subjects were raised in discussion, not enough powerful voices were prepared to be allies in taking these issues further.

Changed consciousness about language stemmed from this time. The 'Ms' debate had emphasized the symbolic power of words, and, in public meetings throughout the school, teachers made a concerted effort to use 'she' as well as, or instead of, 'he'. Terms such as 'headmaster' and 'chairman' became, apart from the occasional lapse, obsolete. What happened behind closed doors and cupped hands is difficult to say, but, broadly speaking, brochures, worksheets and internal exam scripts followed the language norm we had defined; and once more one of our strengths was the deputy head, who was in a position to keep a vigilant eye on all faculties' written work.

And so, despite huge compromises and a snail's pace, we finished 1982 feeling that progress had been made in small, immediate steps and that change was at least possible.

In June 1983 our school committed itself to anti-sexist and anti-racist practices during a day conference where we were formulating overall school aims and objectives.

Yet, despite the magnitude of these commitments, little was happening on the feminist front. The debate had been moved off centre stage to the wings of a working-party, where discussion continued, but out of sight and earshot of most of the staff. Perhaps some teachers assumed too that sexism as an issue had been dealt with and that it was time to move on to the next educational fad. Perhaps also some of us needed a rest. For a while, we closed our classroom doors and carried on work there, rather than in the more conflictual atmosphere of the staffroom.

Towards the end of 1983 we entered our present phase. We reconvened the working-party, encouraged more teachers to join from a wider faculty base and gave it the more combative title of 'the anti-sexist working-party'.

We wanted to use the network of meetings already set up rather than to create a whole new plethora of our own. We were also determined that, in a school which paid lip service to good education equalling anti-sexist education, there should be full staff involvement. Anti-sexism was not to be a hived-off issue for a few half-crazed enthusiasts to tackle; it was and is the responsibility of good educationalists.

With these aims in mind, we presented a report to our curriculum-planning body which recommended that anti-sexism be included on the agendas of all year and faculty meetings, and that each head write a report outlining what had been tried so far in her/his department and what was envisaged for the future. Their reports are now ready for circulation, and in a joint meeting between the planning body and the working-party early next term recommendations and priorities will be established.

We used the third-year consultative evening, an established and popular event, to begin a dialogue with parents. We worked with tutors and pupils to produce displays which put a strong feminist case. We used pictures and photographs, statistics, charts and quotable quotes which teachers and students alike thought appropriate. WedG, an organization based in inner London, helped us find suitable pamphlets to hand out to parents. Tutors, who had already established firm contact with the parents of the children for whom they were responsible, gave them out.

The evening was most successful; we had used a meeting already calendared and had worked with other members of the school.

Recently several of us attended a discussion on sexual harassment, organized by WedG. We were impressed by the short film *Give us a Smile* and thought its everyday pithiness, its cartoon form and its relevance to experiences of women would make it suitable material for sixth-form female students. Sixth-form tutors have agreed to work with us in running a half-day conference on anti-sexism for pupils. They have also agreed to single-sex groups for this occasion.

Currently in pairs we are investigating a particular area of concern in the school. Careers, sex education, PE, the language of reports, our ignorance of arranged marriages, examination results are all being considered from a gender point of view. Once reported on, findings will be taken to a staff-association meeting and recommendations placed in the hands of the decision-makers.

Simple practical strategies have included the setting-up of notice-boards in prominent positions and as part of the general area reserved for the staff association. We now have a reading-area for teachers to browse through the endless amounts of literature we have received. A member of the working-party is responsible for labelling the material and for sending reports of a specific nature to the appropriate department.

Our personal development and our own lives have been of considerable concern. We recognize the danger of committed teachers becoming burnt out, losing hope and energy, especially now when more demands than ever are being made of us. We try to keep ourselves afloat by celebrating any success, by inviting outside speakers to talk to us, by including reports from any courses or conferences attended (and by always making wine *et al.* available at our meetings). Articles of general feminist interest are circulated frequently, and our other female deputy head is remarkably efficient about informing us of relevant courses.

There is a different mood now; a united group meeting in formal and informal working situations is less apologetic in its approach; consequently the response is more antagonistic. The balance is tipped towards conflict rather than consensus.

Alongside work with teachers, we shall conclude with some examples of what has been tried with our students. We have taken the experience of two year groups and one faculty.

A year ago, first- and second-year tutors conducted an investigation into how students saw themselves and their futures. This was done through a diary entry set at a future date and a questionnaire. They also monitored teachers' classroom language, the oral participation and seating-arrangements within the classroom, the use of playground space, corridor behaviour and the number of female and male students involved in the compensatory department. The results were as expected and left little room for complacency. One of our brightest second-year students saw her future as 'waking up to the twins crying and yelling ... nagging to Fred as he runs to work in a hurry ... going to the shops'. She commented on her day, 'a normal day, nothing interesting happened'.

Boys were seen to demand and receive far more teacher time in the classroom in keeping with the findings of Dale Spender (1982) and many others.

As a result of these investigations, the tutor team made various suggestions about the best way of giving a fair deal in the classroom. They included cutting whole-class discussions to a minimum, breaking the class into small groups for talk and learning wherever possible; monitoring time spent with the students in the classroom; and being firm about spending equal amounts with all students.

Though fourteen teachers from a variety of departments agreed to these suggestions, they were never put before a meeting of all staff and therefore have not been widely implemented. It is interesting to note, though, that the English faculty has drawn similar conclusions.

First- and second-year tutors now use morning tutorial periods for single-sex discussions. The school's reserve-tutor system (teachers who cover for absent colleagues) is used for the remainder of the pupils. During these twenty-minute periods, much is discussed, not least sexuality and the way young females are taught to regard their bodies. The school's graffiti have provided a good starting-point.

One measure of change is the great increase of female students who now approach their tutors for informal chats about their bodily image. They are also much more likely to ask for help in removing offensive graffiti – feelings of shame have diminished.

The fifth-year pupils have been confronted with anti-sexism in a different way; a symposium was held where tutors invited various community-based organizations such as the National Abortion Campaign, Women Against Violence Against Women, the Brook Advice Bureau and the National Council for Civil Liberties to lead discussions. This was the first time that tutors and students had seen the value of single-sex groupings, especially for girls. It was a positive learning experience for many of us.

As an example of faculty initiatives, we include the report written by the English department for the curriculum-planning body mentioned earlier.

The English Department's strong commitment to anti-sexism and anti-racism is on the grounds that good educational practice necessarily involves providing all students with equal access to all knowledge that the school deems valuable. We recognize that anti-sexism must be confronted on two levels: the overt curriculum content and the hidden curriculum, for example, classroom organization.

Generally speaking, we think that making gender a 'topic' is a less useful method of approach than thinking of gender as a perspective on work in English. The former approach can too easily lead to the 'we've done women in the fourth year' mentality so that sexism is seen as a problem like capital punishment, abortion, the generation gap, etc. Approaching gender as a perspective on English teaching also means that we can use traditional classroom readers usefully. For example, we can ask such questions as:

– how many of these novels are written by women?

– how many have women or girls as their main characters?

– how many contain examples of positive, well-balanced relationships between boys and girls?

how are mothers and fathers portrayed in these books?

Examining the stock of class readers with these questions in mind might reveal distinct gaps and imbalances in the overall picture pupils are getting of femininity/masculinity from 'official' classroom reading. Again, looking at particular books in detail can provide instructive examples of how sexist stereotyping operates in books. Focusing on a book from the position of the female characters is another way of challenging or revealing the sexist assumptions implicit in many of our class readers.

Below are some suggestions for classroom practice which were adopted by the department:

Firstly, *seating arrangements*. It was felt that a variety of seating arrangements can be adopted to suit the tasks set in the lesson. Mixed groups and single-sex groups within the class can both have a positive function. Secondly, *teacher style*. Up front teaching militates against girls as boys demand and get more teacher time. Generally the faculty supports lessons which involve small group work. Thirdly, *role play with role reversal* can be of particular benefit to students. If the students really adopt the role they can cross sexual divides. This is also a useful technique for studying class readers. *101 Dalmatians* is a wonderfully different experience for students when Mrs Pongo becomes Pongo! Finally, teachers need to work hard at encouraging the assertiveness of girls, and ensuring that girls get a fair share of teacher time.

Other small but significant gains are: books are chosen with strong female characters; we've joined Letterbox Library;[1] drama lessons with role reversal often take place; classroom tasks are allocated equally to male/female students (i.e. girls operate video, help move furniture); individual teachers have worked on topics related to gender. For example, women's images in the media; workbooks, looking at class readers from an anti-sexist stance have been produced in collaboration with the Brent Curriculum Development Support Unit.

This initiative has enabled us to work with teachers from other schools and has also meant that technically the finished product is of a very high standard. The first of these booklets on 'Summer of my German Soldier' is currently being piloted in four Brent schools.

For the future we plan to extend and develop initiatives we've begun, in particular concentrating on finding more suitable literature for classroom use and making the presentation of women a central theme in our media studies programme.

CONCLUSION

It is obvious that considerable change has occurred at Brondesbury and Kilburn, but how to evaluate what we have achieved is a more complex problem. Psychologically there is a tendency to swing between euphoria and depression depending as much as anything else on the sort of day we've had! More importantly perhaps, our political perspective also determines criteria we use to evaluate the importance of the changes we've made. We think we have achieved some significant organizational and procedural changes: the anti-sexist working-party meetings appear on the official school calendar; home economics and technology are no longer back-to-back; non-sexist language is the norm in all school correspondence; we have begun to monitor our school-leavers to see if there are significant differences between girls and boys in what happens to them after school.

It is much more problematical assessing changes in attitudes, image and self-esteem. It is our impression that girls at Brondesbury and Kilburn are less invisible than they used to be. Tutors comment on girls' increasing assertiveness and expressed concern about sexist graffiti or verbal sexual abuse from the boys. Girls are more confident in English orals – they will more readily contradict the boys or assert their right to have single-sex groupings for discussions of 'sensitive' issues such as rape, arranged marriages, abortion. Although difficult to quantify, such changes are nevertheless of the utmost importance.

To end where we began: with ourselves. We know that, as people, as women and as feminists working at Brondesbury and Kilburn, we now have a more intelligent and profound awareness of the nature of patriarchy and how it oppresses all women. We know that this knowledge has increased our confidence and determination to confront and oppose the oppression. And of no less significance are the firm friendships we have formed amongst ourselves as we have struggled to effect change.

NOTE

1 Letterbox Library is a non-sexist children's bookclub. Its address is 1st Floor, 5 Bradbury Street, London N16 8JN.

REFERENCE

Spender, D. 1982: *Invisible Women: the schooling scandal*. London: Writers and Readers.

45

Comprehensive schools and TVEI: a threat or a challenge?

Alan McMurray

The simmering discontent with secondary education amongst politicians of all persuasions and the trend towards centralization set the stage for the coming of the Technical and Vocational Education Initiative (TVEI). It was financed from outside the Department of Education and Science by the Manpower Services Commission (MSC). This was a major intervention by central government aimed at forcing one section of the school population to be more responsive to the needs of industry and the economy. Alan McMurray believes both that TVEI will fail in its own terms, and that it undermines the comprehensive principle. He argues that it is better to leave vocational training to employers, who know what jobs are to be done. Schools should concentrate on enabling children to become effective citizens in a democracy, not merely compliant contributors to the economy.

INTRODUCTION: BEFORE THE FLOOD

Since the end of the Second World War the question of the nature of the secondary-school curriculum has generated more discussion, initiative, enterprise and endeavour than any other area of education – inevitably so, because it stands right at the centre of the educational process. Perhaps equally inevitably, we have failed to reach a consensus view in anything other than the broadest terms, because of the autonomy given to schools – some may say the autocracy permitted to head teachers – to determine their own philosophy, ethos and structure. Those teachers who entered the profession in the early 1950s have lived and worked in an era of continuous change, development and, until recently, expansion. After the development of the tripartite system initiated by the Butler Act of 1944,[1] the 1960s saw a number of significant developments: the Newsom Report, appropriately entitled *Half our Future* (Central Advisory Council for Education, 1963), looked closely and perceptively at the problems of educating those children broadly categorized as non-academic, while its counterpart the Crowther Report (Central Advisory Council for Education, 1959) made recommendations about the education of young people from 15 to 18 and the route to further and higher education for all. In 1960 the Beloe Committee (Secondary Schools Examination Council, 1960) reviewed the welter of alternative examinations, outside those provided by the GCE boards, that were finding increasing, if confusing, favour in the secondary-modern schools, and established the Certificate of Secondary Education as an alternative to GCE 'O'-level. Almost inevitably, with such a surge of concern for the nature of the secondary curriculum, the Schools Council was established to explore and encourage curriculum development in many fields.

The problem since 1944 has been a falling-away of consensus about the nature and content of the secondary curriculum. Before that it was relatively straightforward: the grammar schools had their syllabuses prescribed by the School Certificate and Higher School Certificate, and there was nothing to correspond to 'second-chance' 'O'-level courses, courses to upgrade CSE grades to 'O'-level grades, or the vocationally oriented courses offered by the City and Guilds Institute of London, the Royal Society of Arts and the Business and Technical Education Council; while the council schools, or 'senior schools', as they were known, concentrated on ensuring that the country's future 'hewers of wood and drawers of waters' were given as sound a grounding as possible in the three Rs, knew a number of dates of kings and queens of England, knew the rough position of the main capes and bays (the absence of which in today's curriculum has been lamented by the British Travel Agents' Association, a view which, laughable as it may appear at first, is none the less representative and indicative of a widely held view of the instrumental nature of education), could do a bit of painting and drawing and, if the child was male, could make a reasonably accurate mortise-and-tenon joint or, if female, could 'bake a fine cake and sew a straight seam'. And, if, as a new entrant to teaching, you were not exactly sure what you should be doing, then you could look it up in the *Handbook of Suggestions for Teachers* (Ministry of Education, 1937).

Those days are long gone. But it is worth pausing to reflect on them for a moment, because there exists, in the 1980s, a growing feeling in some sections of society that a return to such a state of grace would be no bad thing: this, after all, was the education system which allowed many of society's elected leaders to become the men and women they are, and some have perceived the decline in the country's prosperity and moral values as a result of the extent to which education has lost its way.

The only fixed points would appear to be at the beginning and at the end of the full-time educational process. There has not been a great deal of debate about the work of the infants' school: indeed, most infant teachers seem to have an enviably unswerving sense of purpose. There has been discussion about method – the Initial Teaching Alphabet (Pitman and Pitman, 1969) of the 1960s and 1970s, for example – but there always seems to have been general agreement about the ground to be covered. Similarly, whatever discussion there may have been about what is necessary to achieve a first in English at Oxford, or in mathematics at Cambridge, has not provoked widespread concern in educational circles. Within the provision of full-time education, it is the primary schools who appear to have had the best opportunity to develop their curriculum and ethos. They have always been shielded from the constraints imposed by examinations at sixteen-plus; and the removal, for the majority, of the pressures of the eleven-plus examination, and the development of a consensus view in the Plowden Report (Central Advisory Council for Education, 1967) have enabled them to explore freely ways of revitalizing their curriculum.

No. It is in the comprehensive schools that we have failed. It would be presumptuous to draw out the inadequacies and irrelevancies of the average comprehensive-school curriculum for the majority of our students when David Hargreaves (1982)[2] has done so to such telling effect. He has struck at the root of the problem: that the intellectual–cognitive curriculum which forms the broad base of the curriculum of the majority of our comprehensive schools is no longer relevant, if indeed it ever was, for 80 per cent of the young people who populate those schools. It is rooted in the traditional grammar-school curriculum, which itself has been the implementation of an ethos and philosophy which holds, for example, that a grade C in French or history is of greater significance and value than a grade A in art or woodwork.

THE FAILURE OF PAST SOLUTIONS

Such sentiments are, of course, nothing new. But it would appear that the teaching-profession has done precious little about them to any good purpose. Take, for example, the debate on the sixth-form curriculum and examinations, which has been permeated with acronyms and abbreviations, such as the ABC (the Agreement to Broaden the Curriculum), GSA (General Studies Association), CEE (Certificate of Extended Education), let alone the cryptically simple expression of alternative proposals for 'A'-level, such as N and F, I and Q. That debate has been going on for twenty years, yet, apart from the relatively recent and entirely welcome movement to provide breadth in the form of Business and Technical Education Council and City and Guilds courses, which begs a lot of questions about the relationships between schools and colleges of further education, basically nothing has changed. This is perhaps the classic example of our failure to determine our curriculum; others come readily enough to mind. The recommendations of the Newsom Report, referred to earlier, were enthusiastically taken up by many schools who had already begun to see the irrelevance of a watered-down 'academic' curriculum for the majority of children, although the identification of the group of children who benefited from this enthusiasm as 'Newsom children' ran counter to the growing ethic of the emergent comprehensive schools with their emphasis on non-differentiation. The Humanities Curriculum Project (Schools Council/Nuffield Foundation, 1970), developed by the late Lawrence Stenhouse at the University of East Anglia, placed a heavy emphasis on participative learning, but failed to find general acceptance because there was no publicly supported machinery to enable teachers to acquire the skills necessary to implement the approach. Design education, with a similar emphasis, in the traditionally 'practical' areas of the curriculum, on participative learning and problem-solving, was widely and enthusiastically embraced in Leicestershire, the county of its origin, but by and large elsewhere the concept was adopted only where Leicestershire missionaries had obtained influential posts. But throughout the 1960s and the 1970s such developments as these were greeted with a guarded, and sometimes cynical, scepticism, and they failed to become widely adopted.

The reason for this must surely lie in the exceptional autonomy allowed to schools in the English school system, an autonomy which is the wonder of the rest of Europe. Such a system has tremendous strengths, not the least of which is the flexibility it gives to schools to respond to the needs of the communities they serve. But there is little doubt that society and government are coming to see education as a scapegoat for our social, moral and economic ills: radical changes are felt to be necessary in the education system if such ills are to be eradicated. Schools, however, appear to be unable, or unwilling, to recognize and correct their weaknesses; and the situation is ripe for an outside agency to force an entry into the 'secret garden' of the curriculum and say, 'This is what you will do'. And that is precisely what David (later Lord) Young and the MSC did in November 1982.

The 'watchers' in the education business saw it coming; indeed, since James Callaghan's speech at Ruskin College in 1976, the move towards greater central direction and control of the curriculum has become increasingly evident. Callaghan instituted what became known as 'The Great Debate', initially a concern about standards but rapidly and inevitably a debate about content. There followed a volume of conferences and reports. One of the most significant pointers appeared in the preliminary pages of *The School Curriculum* (Department of Education and Science, 1981), a document which repays close study for an understanding of the growing trend towards centralization of curriculum control. The first hints of what is to come are to be found in the Foreword by the Secretaries of State. After a somewhat cursory reference to the Department's publication *A Framework for the Curriculum*, and an even more cursory one to the Inspectorate's discussion document *A View of the Curriculum* (Department of Education and Science, 1980a, 1980b), the message is quickly and clearly spelled out: 'The present paper offers guidance to the local education authorities and schools in England and Wales on how the curriculum can be further improved.' And in case anyone fails to appreciate the subtleties of meaning of 'guidance': 'We shall shortly issue a Circular to the authorities and the schools calling the paper formally to their attention.'

From there on the tone and style of the paper are generally prescriptive, and often directive. We are reminded in the Introduction (para. 2) of the legal basis of the Secretary of State's concern: 'This aim [that education should serve the individual needs of every pupil and student] ... is embodied in the 1944 Education Act's reference to the duty to secure education suited to each pupil's age, aptitude and ability.' Subsequently (para. 7) we are reminded that this same Act obliges the Secretaries of State 'to promote the education of the people of England and Wales', a duty which is subsequently described as 'inescapable'. Other examples leap from the page: under the heading 'Educational aims', the broad aims stated in the earlier *Framework for the Curriculum* are repeated, and, although there is a brief acknowledgement that the original statement provoked some comment, 'The Secretaries of State commend it, without further refinements, as a checklist against which schools and authorities can test their curricular policies.' This view is underlined in the section entitled 'The recommended approach' (para. 18) with three clear and unequivocal propositions for local education authorities and schools to note. Finally, to show they mean business, the Secretaries of State inform us that they 'will themselves be responsible for taking further the work which is now required on science and modern languages'. The messages are plain for all to see.

Since then these messages have come thick and fast, whether the replacement of the developmental Schools Council with the more instrumental Curriculum and Examinations Councils, or the proposals for the reorganization of teacher-training, based on a clear but limited concept of the nature of the secondary curriculum. It is easy to assume that these developments are exclusively the outcome of some all-embracing Conservative Party plot. It is perhaps salutary to recall a story, recorded in *Education*, that at the begining of November 1982, just before the announcement of TVEI, the National Economic and Development Council met to consider a paper on education presented by Sir Keith Joseph. This was apparently quickly dismissed as trivial and irrelevant by those present. 'What education needs,' said Norman Tebbitt, 'is a short, sharp shock', using a phrase beloved of Tory politicians. 'No,' replied the General Secretary of the Trades Union Congress, Len Murray, 'what education needs is a pneumatic drill.'

THE COMING OF TVEI

And so, appropriately enough at the beginning of Advent 1982, David Young, Chairman of the MSC, appeared as a messianic Action Man to present education with the medium of its redemption, the New Technical and Vocational Education Initiative, or NTVEI, from which the 'N' rapidly disappeared and from which the 'E' has gradually been elided, although whether this is a result of philology or philosophy it is difficult to say.

The TVEI was more than a set of proposals for discussion. The initial proposal, in November 1982, was to set up a pilot scheme, initially for ten projects but subsequently expanded to fourteen, each project to provide a four-year course, commencing at fourteen years, of full-time general, technical and vocational education, including appropriate work experience. Both the criteria for the pilot schemes and the outline of the contents of the courses were set out in such detail that there was little room for negotiation or manoeuvre. Local education authorities were invited to make submissions, and the tempting, indeed irresistible, bait which accompanied the proposals was funding by MSC to the tune of £7 million (see Manpower Services Commission, 1984, the first official report on the first and second stages of the scheme).

A number of things characterized this initiative. First, it came from the MSC and not from the Department of Education and Science: a clear indication that it was directly sponsored by government. Secondly, it was totally directive: indeed, it was initially accompanied by vague threats from David Young that, if local education authorities did not co-operate, sterner measures would result, although in fact these threats were subsequently acknowledged by their author to be meaningless. Thirdly, the timing for setting up the project – submissions had to be made by March 1983, for courses to begin the following September – was of an accelerated scale the like of which the education service had never before witnessed. Fourthly, of course, there were the sums of money involved, presenting wealth undreamed-of in the service since the balmy days of the 1960s. It came at a time when reduction in public expenditure had resulted in the education service in most authorities being cut back to the bare bones, leaving nothing for any kind of development. It is worth noting that by the middle of 1984 the picture was considerably less rosy: although the initial promise by MSC was to finance TVEI courses for five years, the funding for these courses from 1986 will have to be taken on board by local education authorities themselves, a funding which they will be obliged to make if they are to keep faith with the students who have already embarked on the courses, and one which, in the vast majority of cases, will only be found at the expense of other areas of the service.

The offer was Mafia-like to both schools and local authorities: by the time the second round of submissions was sought early in 1984, no more than half-a-dozen authorities had declined to take part, for reasons of either principles or politics. Not only was there to be more of everything – teachers, micro-computers, typewriters, lathes, and so on – but there was also a ready-made opportunity to provide a meaningful curriculum to the growing number of students repelled by the traditional curricular diet, and to counter the growing pressure from parents and governors to ensure that education equals qualifications equals jobs.

Any initiative that endeavours seriously to break the deadlock of the fossilized and antediluvian curriculum which has for too long been inflicted on too many generally acquiescent young people is to be welcomed. But there are reservations and apprehensions about TVEI, arising partly from the nature of its introduction, partly from the content of the courses, and partly from the manner in which it is to be implemented, that need to be explored further.

THE RESERVATIONS ABOUT TVEI

First, it seems to have been conveniently forgotten that the initiative has come from a body, the MSC, whose educational credentials are not strong. The TVEI Steering Committee is not overloaded with accredited educationalists, and it is significant that the Director of TVEI, John Woolhouse, is a man whose experience is largely in the field of industrial training.

A second reservation must surely concern the timing of the introduction of the TVEI, at a time when unemployment is at its worst for fifty years. As with the Youth Training Scheme, another MSC initiative, there is an unverbalized but implicit assumption that TVEI courses can provide passports for jobs. This is not, one hopes, what we are intended to assume; if it is, then it is a grossly immoral piece of hoodwinking.

But these two reservations are relatively insignificant when compared with the third, which is the possible effect TVEI may have – may even be intended to have – on the organization of schools and so on the comprehensive system. TVEI is intended for only 60 per cent of the population of each age cohort. It appears to be a 60 per cent that is designated by subtraction: it is what is left after the 25 per cent of slow learners at one end of the ability spectrum and the 15 per cent of above average students at the other end have been subtracted. What sort of structures can be expected as a result? Quite probably there will be a large number of schools with three bands in them, and not just in the fourth and fifth years, because preparation for the TVEI band is bound to seep down into the curricula of the third and second years. Such schools are multilateral, not comprehensive, schools. The majority of secondary schools in England are schools for eleven- to eighteen-year-olds with about 800 students on roll. What will happen to these? Each year group in such a school contains only about five forms of entry, i.e. about 150 students. The demands on the resources of such schools to organize viable courses for ninety students per year group will be considerable; even more considerable will be the problem of organizing viable courses for the twenty to twenty-five students requiring a wide range of choice of academic subjects. What may well be possible in a typical large upper school (for ages fourteen to nineteen) with 500 or more students per year group, such as those to be found in Leicestershire, will be out of the question in 'average' schools. The temptation will be for local education authorities not to spread the jam thinly over a number of schools but to concentrate it – if, indeed, jam can be concentrated – in one or two specially designated schools. Possibly they would become known as technical schools. It would be a short and logical step to concentrate the academically able students in other schools, and the slow learners in yet others. But the development of comprehensive schools in the 1960s and early 1970s, which was achieved in many authorities by combining existing schools and making two sets of buildings into one, has reduced the number of separate schools available; and this situation has been exacerbated by further closures of school buildings as a result of falling rolls in the late 1970s and early 1980s. Small schools of slow learners would not be viable, and local education authorities would be obliged to resort to housing these students in their technically oriented schools. All of a sudden the shades of the 1944 Act would become the dark night of the bipartite system, in which the comprehensive school would disappear without trace.

By the beginning of the 1984–5 academic year, the machinery for evaluating the first year of TVEI schemes had begun to swing into motion: it will be some time before any comprehensive and authentic picture is available of how the initiative is being implemented. Clwyd, in North Wales, has put much of its TVEI money into a technology centre. Emrys ap Iwan school, at Abergele, in the same authority, has used its allocation to revitalize its curriculum with the introduction for all students of short modular courses, of nine weeks duration, in the fourth and fifth (and eventually the sixth) years, breaking the restrictive and demotivating lock-step of traditional two-year courses to 'O'-level and CSE. In Herefordshire, a TVEI centre operating in conjunction with fourteen schools and colleges within a twenty-five-mile radius has been established. In Bedfordshire, buses and coaches fitted out as mobile technology laboratories have been set up, able to augment the needs of any of the authority's schools at a moment's notice. Such initiatives are to be applauded; but in other areas there already appear to be numbers of schools who have forsaken their comprehensive principles and identified groups of TVEI students – shades of 'Newsom students' and 'ROSLA students' before them – who follow discrete courses parallel to 'academic' and 'slow-learner' courses in other parts of the school.

There appears to be evidence enough that concern for the future of comprehensive schools is neither fanciful nor alarmist. In an interview reported in the *Times Educational Supplement* on 15 July 1983, the Secretary of State was asked, 'Do you accept the doubts of those who say that TVEI, far from encouraging all pupils to do some vocational work, will create a divide similar to the old grammar/secondary modern divide?' He replied,

I think it will be much more untidy than that. I hope it will be much more untidy. There will certainly be some who tend to concentrate on academic work and we need them. But I hope for the good of them too, we can gradually coax the curriculum setters to introduce a shade more practical work for all. Then there will be those whose potential is very definitely technical and then there will be those whose potential is both.

Further evidence that the comprehensive system is under threat is to be found in the events of the winter of 1983. In the preceding autumn, three education authorities seemed to be getting the message that the Secretary of

State was giving out, both in his own words and in his support for TVEI and its possible implications. The education committees of Solihull, Redbridge and Richmond sought to reintroduce bipartite systems, thinking, presumably, that this was the way that the tide was running. But, if they were in touch with the views of the Secretary of State, they were sadly out of touch with the views of their electorates, and all three proposals were defeated as a result of organized and orchestrated parental opposition.

But perhaps the most disturbing evidence of all is quoted by Professor Brian Simon, of the University of Leicester, in an article entitled 'To whom do schools belong?' (Simon, 1984). Writing about the concern of Department officials with the question of social control, he quotes a remark attributed to an anonymous official: 'People must be educated once more to know their place.' The horrendous implications of such a statement are surely entirely self-evident. Remembering that when W. E. Forster introduced compulsory education for all in the first Education Act in 1870 he said, 'We must educate our masters', the wheel appears to have turned full circle.

In an article entitled 'Vocationalism: the new threat to universal education' (Holt, 1983), Maurice Holt looks more closely at the proposed content of TVEI courses. He underlines quite clearly the fallacy of the assumption that developed during the second half of the 1970s that the school curriculum should develop 'the personal skills and qualities as well as the knowledge needed for working life', a quotation from the 1981 government publication *A New Training Initiative* (DES, 1981). Holt points to evidence from America: a study undertaken in 1981 concluded that 'There was substantial evidence that trade and industrial training had no economic pay-off .... Training programmes unco-ordinated with specific and permanent jobs may be no more relevant to jobs than school-based programmes.' When the earliest comprehensive schools were established in the mid-1950s by the Inner London Education Authority, schools of considerable reputations, such as Kidbrooke, Crown Woods, Tulse Hill and Wandsworth, developed strongly vocational courses in their curricula, in trades as diverse as millinery and bricklaying, since they felt that such specifically vocational courses would meet the needs of non-academic students. But not everyone wanted to make hats or lay bricks and it was found impossible to cater for all the needs of all the students. The idea was gradually abandoned and the schools reverted to what they knew at heart they could, and should, do best – to provide a broadly based liberal education and leave the specialized processes of vocational training to those with the resources and the expertise to do so: the colleges of further education and the many industrial training-schemes.

This, as Maurice Holt also points out, is a lesson that has been learnt in Japan, whose status in industrial and technological development is undisputed, where all children follow a broad, general course, and where, incidentally, computers are unknown in the classroom; and in Sweden, where the law forbids direct vocational training in comprehensive schools for under-sixteens. Even the very title 'Technical and Vocational Education Initiative' would appear to be inappropriate. A technical education? The youngsters for whom it is intended will be society's young men and women at the turn of this century; but who, in the light of the rapid developments in technology over the last fifteen years, would be fool enough to predict the technology of fifteen years hence, and for which presumably this technical education is a preparation? And vocational? What sort of vocation? Unemployment does not appear to be among the options for which this vocational education is a preparation, nor do job-sharing, half weeks or voluntary work. Certainly it cannot, or at least it should not, be for the same vocation throughout life.

In short, TVEI would appear to be an educational equivalent of convenience food: it is prepackaged and is accompanied by a tempting aroma, but ultimately it distorts your growth.

THE ALTERNATIVES

What, then, are the alternatives? TVEI is but one element of an overall strategic plan for technical and vocational training known as the New Training Initiative (NTI). Another such element is the Youth Training Scheme (YTS), which aims to provide on-the-job training, along with a period of extended education, for school-leavers over a period of one year. The two schemes appear to be strangely unco-ordinated, for in essence the one would appear to be a duplication of the other. There is little doubt that, although the YTS is intended to be regarded as an attempt to provide wider opportunities for vocational training, it is none the less a political response to growing unemployment. But, whatever the political connotation of YTS, the concept of on-the-job training linked to actual employment is a laudable one, and has been so since the apprenticeship system was first developed in the Middle Ages. It is also laudable in that it is encouraging many employers to realize that there is more to employee-training than saying, 'That's where you clock on, and there's the toilet.' The YTS links skills to the work situation, a far stronger motivation for young people than learning necessarily abstract 'families of transferable skills' in a school, which is a major element of TVEI courses. If we regard vocational training as an important part of the education of any young person, and few would deny that it is important, then it would appear that the YTS, after leaving school, is far preferable to TVEI, in school, as a preparation for work.

Secondly, schools must now concentrate on the job that they are best equipped, through their tradition, their expertise and their resources, to do: to provide an education for young people that is broad and liberal in concept, that gives as great a recognition to the importance of the expressive, artistic and creative skills as it does to the intellectual skills of knowing and reasoning. Not simply to provide them with 'coping skills', because that has a defensive ring to it, but to make them able to find and establish for themselves a place in society as caring, committed and compassionate members of it. The Inspectorate document *Curriculum 11–16* (Department of Education and Science, 1977) recognized that education was about personal development and autonomy: 'Pupils are members of a complicated civilisation and culture, and ... have nothing less than a right to be introduced to a selection of its essential elements.' There speak educationalists as distinct from trainers. The elements that have always made up our curricula are as important today as they have ever been: the skills of verbal and numerical communication; an awareness of the influence of science, technology, heritage and environment on our lives today and in making our society what it is; an appreciation of how our lives are enriched by the visual and aural arts. To these traditional elements we are at last beginning to add the development of individual and interpersonal skills and qualities in an environment that offers understanding and guidance, rather than assuming that such things develop by chance, as a result of the the ethos and atmosphere, the hidden curriculum, of the school. These are things we must embrace, not in a separate and discrete department, with its head of personal education, or as a separate subject that is added to the examination menu so that a student may get a CSE grade 1 in 'life skills' – the implications of getting 'ungraded' would be unthinkable! – but as part of the development of young people to which all teachers can contribute, whether or not through the medium of their specific teaching-role.

Thirdly, educationalists must seek to break the tyranny of the lock-step of the 'fourth- and fifth-year course', if our paramount concern is the needs of individual students. Some will protest that many courses are linear; but we should ask ourselves how many courses are governed by Parkinson's Law, filling much of the time available by going over ground that was already thoroughly covered in the first three years, and possibly in the primary schools before that. 'O'-level and CSE syllabuses, for those who seek such qualifications, impose their own constraints. But such courses can still be available, and indeed made more appropriate to the needs of students: why should not the able student sidestep the hurdle of 'O'-level English literature, for example, and spend four years studying 'A'-level English, which would then be possible to a depth and richness which in the present pattern of five terms is completely unachievable? Developments such as the Oxfordshire Certificate of Educational Achievement, with its emphases on graded assessment and continuous profiling, present a golden opportunity for such a change in practice. But, if we are to meet the needs of the majority of young adolescents in the mid–1980s, we must seriously question the concept of the unbroken two-year course lasting through the fourth and fifth years. As an adult, you have to be singularly committed to the learning process to undertake a course of study of two years or more duration; and it is a remarkably small proportion of the population which is of that cast of mind. Yet we expect young people, whose minds and spirits are more free and undisciplined than our own, to do just that. Educationalists speak increasingly of the importance of a 'negotiated curriculum', by which they mean ensuring that students should determine for themselves, with whatever guidance they may require, the course and subjects they wish to study. But in practice, faced with no alternative but to choose a course of two years duration at an age when the vast majority have only a hazy idea of what they wish to do at the age of sixteen, let alone eighteen, twenty-one or twenty-six, they settle for what they regard as the easy way out, and take the opportunity to say goodbye to those subjects which they find intolerably boring and continue to work at those they find rather less so. Why not, then, a continuing choice, which can be continuously renegotiated? Modular courses whose duration is no more than a week, a month, a term, a year. Having learnt as much as you wish, or can, about photography why can you not do an intensive course in computer-programming?

The corollary to this must be that it should be possible to do this at any time in your life. At the moment, the age of sixteen represents a tremendous hurdle for young people. Some clear it easily; many catch their toe on the bar and stumble on landing, but are lucky enough to regain their balance; far too many crash into it, and collapse on the other side, perhaps never to rise again. How many young people feel when they leave school at sixteen that they cannot return? Our interests, our needs, cannot possibly all be fulfilled by the age of sixteen, seventeen, eighteen or twenty-two. Life's formative moments do not suddenly cease to happen once we have left the classroom. Many people do not take up a hobby, or pursue a new-found interest, until well on into their lives. For many years now we have been expressing our realization of the need to educate young people to be able to handle all the various pressures and changes of a complex and sophisticated society, and prepare them for a world of work where they may undertake a number of different careers during their lifetimes. The rapidly growing development of personal- and social-education courses, with their emphasis on life skills, is undoubtedly a step in the right direction. But there are still too many schools who say to their departing students, as they usher them out through the front door for the last time, 'Nice to have had you here. Don't forget your survival kit', and slam the door behind them. The door should always remain open for them to return and return again throughout their lives so that they can be helped as grown men and women to make whatever fresh adjustment is necessary. If we mean what we say when we talk about a flexible educational response to a continually and rapidly changing society, where our aim is to help people of all ages to respond to the many different situations with which they will find themselves faced during their lifetimes, then we must cease to regard our schools as institutions solely for the education of young people – although that will undoubtedly long remain their prime purpose – and see them as educational resources for the whole community. In short, the community school. Or perhaps not the community school, or even the comprehensive school, but the continuing school.

We have a responsibility to make the culture of our society accessible to everyone, regardless of age, sex, colour, creed, ability and all the other characteristics that divide us today, in an ethos and environment that promotes social harmony and common purpose. To achieve this, fundamental changes will be necessary to the structure and organization of our schools. But TVEI is a misguided and transient response to superficial perceptions of the state of our society, and it will create, if we are not sensitive to its potential implications, division and even intolerance.

NOTES

1 Education Act 1944. 7 & 8 Geo. 6. This Act was the foundation stone of the post-war educational system.
2 David Hargreaves subsequently became Senior Inspector for the Inner London Education Authority and led the committee which undertook a major inquiry into secondary education in ILEA.

REFERENCES

Central Advisory Council for Education (England) 1959: *15 to 18* (Crowther Report). London: HMSO.
—— 1963: *Half our Future* (Newsom Report). London: HMSO.
—— 1967: *Children and their Primary Schools* (Plowden Report). London: HMSO.
Department of Education and Science 1977: *Curriculum 11–16*. Working papers by HM Inspectorate: a contribution to current debate. London: HMSO.
—— 1980a: *A Framework for the School Curriculum: proposals for consultation by the Secretaries of State for Education and Science and for Wales*. London: HMSO.
—— 1980b: *A View of the Curriculum*. HM Inspectorate series 'Matters for Discussion', 11. London: HMSO.
—— 1981: *The School Curriculum*. London: HMSO.
—— 1981: A New Training Initiative. London: HMSO and Cmnd 8455.
Hargreaves, D. 1982: *The Challenge for the Comprehensive School*. London: Routledge and Kegan Paul.
Holt, M. 1983: Vocationalism: the new threat to universal education. *Forum*. 25 (3), 84–6.
Manpower Services Commission 1984: *TVEI Review 1984*. London: MSC.
Ministry of Education 1937: *Handbook of Suggestions (for the consideration of teachers and others concerned in the work of public elementary schools)*, rev. edn.
Pitman, Sir J. and Pitman, J. 1969: *Alphabets and Reading: the Initial Teaching Alphabet*. London: Pitman.
Schools Council/Nuffield Foundation 1970: *The Humanities Project: an introduction*. London: Heinemann.
Secondary Schools Examination Council 1960: *Secondary School Examinations other than the GCE*. (Beloe Report). London: HMSO.
Simon, B. 1984: To whom do schools belong? *Forum*, 27 (1), 4–5.

Contributors

Muriel Adams is a Remedial Teacher in Grampian.

Glenys Andrews is Co-ordinator of Brent Learning Resources Service. She was formerly Primary Co-ordinator for the Education of Pupils with Learning Difficulties, Fife.

Valerie Antopolski teaches at Bourne Primary School, Cambridge.

Gerry Bailey is Head Teacher of Edgewick Community Primary School, Coventry.

Cilla Biles is Head Teacher of Lemington First School, Newcastle-upon-Tyne. She was formerly Head Teacher of Hillsview Infants School, Newcastle-upon-Tyne.

Gill Blake is Deputy Head Teacher at St Michael's Middle School, Bowthorpe, Norwich. She formerly taught at Mulbarton Middle School, Norwich.

David Boalch is Deputy Head Teacher of Galleywall Primary School, ILEA.

Tony Booth is a Lecturer in Education at the Open University.

Terri Carey is a Head of Year at Lilian Bayliss School, ILEA.

Mary Caven teaches at Prior Weston Primary School, ILEA.

Jenny Corbett is Senior Lecturer in Special Education at North-East London Polytechnic. She was formerly Liaison Lecturer for Students with Special Needs at a college of technology in a London borough.

Mike Cowie is Assistant Head Teacher (Curriculum) at Linksfield Academy, Aberdeen.

Annabelle Dixon is Head Teacher of Holdbrook Primary School, Waltham Cross, Hertfordshire.

Elyse Dodgson is Director of the Royal Court Young People's Theatre Scheme. She was formerly Head of Drama at Vauxhall Manor School, ILEA.

Patrick Easen is a Lecturer in Primary Education (In-service Training) at the School of Education, University of Newcastle-upon-Tyne.

William Fordyce is Depute Director of Grampian Education Authority.

Martin Francis teaches infants in Normand Park School.

Christine Gilbert is Head Teacher of Whitmore High School, Harrow.

Dawn Gill is a member of the Anti-Racist Strategies Team at the ILEA Centre for Anti-Racist Education. She was formerly Head of Geography at Quinton Kynaston School, ILEA.

Susan Hart works as a Support Teacher in an outer London borough. She was formerly Head of Special Needs in an ILEA comprehensive school.

Robert Hull is Head of English at Windlesham House School, West Sussex.

Anne Jones is Deputy Head of Springfield Junior School, South Derbyshire.

Stephen Jones is a Division Head at Bosworth College, Leicestershire.

Peter Kyne is Principal Learning-Support Teacher at Auchterderran Junior High School, Fife.

Eileen Lorimer is Principal Teacher, Special Educational Needs, at Linksfield Academy, Aberdeen.

Hellen Matthews is Principal Teacher, Department of Learning Support, at Dyce Academy, Aberdeen.

Alan McMurray is Head Teacher of Hind Leys College, Leicestershire.

Annabel Mercer is a Learning-Support Teacher at Craigmuir School, Edinburgh, Lothian.

Andrew Meredith is Head of Music at Westfield School, Sheffield.

Jan Moore is Head of Special Needs at Chesterton Community College, Cambridge.

Frankie Ord is Head of English at Brondesbury and Kilburn School, Brent.

Ross Phillips is Head of Humanities at Bosworth College, Leicestershire.

Gervase Phinn is Adviser for Language Development for Rotherham.

Patricia Potts is a Lecturer in Education at the Open University.

Jim Presly is Principal Teacher, Biology, at Dyce Academy, Aberdeen.

Sallie Purkis is Senior Lecturer in History at Homerton College, Cambridge.

Jane Quigley is Deputy Head of English and Deputy Head of First and Second Years at Brondesbury and Kilburn School, Brent.

Stewart Reid is Principal Teacher, Modern Languages, at Linksfield Academy, Aberdeen.

Carmen Renwick is Assistant Head Teacher at the Lady Adrian School, Cambridge.

Stephen Rowland is a Lecturer in Education in the Division of Education, University of Sheffield.

Helen Savva is an Advisory Teacher with the ILEA multiethnic inspectorate.

John Sayer is a Visiting Fellow at the London University Institute of Education.

Stuart Scott is the Deputy Warden of Hackney Teachers' Centre, ILEA. He was formerly Director of the ILEA Collaborative Learning Project.

Karen Skoro is a member of the Curriculum Support Team of the Minority Group Support Service, Coventry.

Will Swann is a Lecturer in Education at the Open University.

Alan Ward is a freelance lecturer, writer and presenter of 'science happenings' for primary-school children and teachers. He was formerly a Senior Lecturer in Science Education at the College of St Paul and St Mary, Cheltenham.

Charles Weedon is Principal Learning-Support Teacher, Ballingry Junior High School, Fife.

Jane Woodall is an Advisory Teacher for History in the ILEA. She formerly taught history at Vauxhall Manor School, ILEA.

Index

Index by Gill Riordan